On Your Own

On Your Own

A Widow's Passage

to Emotional & Financial

Well-Being

Alexandra Armstrong, CFP®
Mary R. Donahue, Ph.D.

Earlier editions of this book were published in 1993, 1995 and 2000 by Dearborn, a Kaplan Professional Company.

This book is available at special quantity discounts to use as premiums and sales
promotions, or for use in corporate training programs. For more information,
please contact Dorothy McGee, Armstrong, Fleming & Moore, 1850 M Street
NW, Suite 250, Washington DC 20036-5813, dmcgee@afmfa.com

**This publication is designed to provide accurate and authoritative
information in regard to the subject matter covered. It is sold with the
understanding that the Authors are not engaged in rendering legal,
accounting, or other professional services by publishing this book. As
each individual situation is unique, questions relevant to personal
finances and specific to the individual should be addressed to an
appropriate professional to ensure that the situation has been evaluated
carefully and appropriately. The Authors specifically disclaim any liability,
loss or risk which is incurred as a consequence, directly or indirectly, of
the use and application of any of the contents of this book.**

Cover Design by Jessica "JD" Smith – Creative Director of Perception, Inc

PRINTED IN THE UNITED STATES OF AMERICA

00 01 02 10 9 8 7 6 5 4 3 2 1

Library of Congress Cataloging-in-Publication Data

Armstrong, Alexandra.
    On your own : a widow's passage to emotional and financial well-being
    / Alexandra Armstrong, Mary R. Donahue.— 4th ed.
        p. cm.
    Includes bibliographical references and index.
      ISBN 0-7931-3727-6
      1. Widows—Finance, Personal. 2. Financial security. I. Donahue,
    Mary R. II. Title.
      HG179.A724 2000
        332.024'0654—dc21
    00-009303

DEDICATIONS

This book is dedicated to my mother, who taught me how to be a survivor by her example; to the Religious of Sacred Heart at Stone Ridge, who gave me the education so that I could write this book; and to my husband, whose encouragement, patience, and advice helped me complete this book.

—Alexandra Armstrong

This book is dedicated to my parents, who, in an age when it was not the norm, established for me the concept that it was a woman's right to reach her potential, whatever it might be. To my late husband, George, whose unconditional love and support enabled me to expand my horizons and better define my personal goals, and to my daughters, Laurie and Rachel, with whom I mourned, grew, and thrived.

—Mary R. Donahue

Acknowledgements

We would like to thank the following people for their assistance in making this book a reality: Beverly A. Anderson; Douglas A. Critchell; Laurie Donahue; Jennifer Engels; Betsy Fleming; Ryan Fleming CFP®; Maureen Geimer; Connie Golleher; Roberta Gosier; Louise Gussin; Rhoda E. A. Hackler; Amiri Joseph; Virginia McArthur, Esquire; Jerry J. McCoy, Esquire; J. Riley McDonald; Mary Moore, CFP®; Thom Norris; Ethel Rosenberg; Adele Winters; Emily H. Womach.

Special thanks to Karen Preysnar, CFP®, who provided technical assistance, to Dorothy McGee, who typed the manuscript, to Carrie McClurkin, who did research as well as Matthew Thompson who assisted with the publication.

Contents

Preface

Preface

TERROR, FEAR, PAIN, loneliness, paralysis, anger, numbness, sadness, panic, weakness, helplessness—these are some of the all-too-familiar emotions that crash and swirl around the fragile ego of a woman who has just become a widow.

The loss of your husband is likely to be the most traumatic event of your life. You did not choose to be a widow, you don't like being a widow, and you are overwhelmed by the enormity of the issues you are required to handle as a result of the changes in your personal circumstances.

We first wrote *On Your Own* in 1993 to help widows cope better with the dramatic alteration that occurs in their lives following the loss of their husbands. A second edition followed in 1996 and a third in 2000, primarily incorporating changes in tax law and investment climates.

Then came the terrorist attacks of 9/11 and the Iraq war, which created more widows who were reacting to the sudden and unexpected death of their husbands. Because of these events, we decided it was time to update our advice once again. Recent statistics indicate that most women will find themselves alone at some time, whether by choice or as a result of divorce or widowhood. To ignore the possibility of bereavement or estrangement and the emotional and financial consequences is to deceive yourself. Not planning for this event does not prevent its occurrence. The reality is that you can reduce the trauma resulting from your loss if you know what to do in your time of crisis.

In this book we view the widow's recovery as a series of building blocks. We start the book with the widow's initial grief response, then move through the recovery process to an ultimate state of emotional and financial well-being. Our book reflects our strong belief that there is a connection between your financial recovery and your psychological recovery.

It has been said that grief coupled with lack of financial knowledge is crippling. We believe that the better you as a widow are able to come to terms with your loss emotionally, the better able you will be to address the financial consequences. Similarly, the more you understand about your financial situation, the less anxious you will be, which in turn will contribute to your emotional healing.

As we traveled around the country talking about our book, we were surprised and pleased to find that the book had a broader audience than we had originally envisioned. Women told us *On Your Own* was of interest not only to widows but also to adult women of all ages. It provided an opportunity for many mothers and daughters to discuss an important subject previously ignored. Divorcés too, found that although they were experiencing a different kind of loss, many of the coping devices and financial information provided were helpful to them.

In this latest edition of *On Your Own*, we have updated the content once again, including Web site information as well as current financial and psychological trends. Our goal in this latest edition is to provide you with additional information that will enable you to cope better, not only during this critical time but also in the years ahead. We hope our book will help you deal with the enormity of your loss and also guide you along the path to emotional and financial health. We have purposely provided this information in a basic yet comprehensive format. We have presented the material so that you can read from cover to cover or select individual chapters for specific information. Our ultimate goal is to enable you to be emotionally and financially self-reliant.

In discussing what we thought should be included in this updated version, we reiterated the fact that you cannot put all widows (or widowers, for that matter) in one category. There are young widows and old widows. There are those with dependent children, those with older children, and those without children. Some husbands died after a long illness, and others died suddenly. Some widows had been very dependent on their husbands, others more independent. The marriage might have been happy or happy only when viewed in retrospect.

We also think that the healing process cannot be put into specific time frames. Widows require varying periods of time to heal, depending on a variety of factors, such as the circumstances of the husband's death, the widow's preexisting mental health, her religious orientation, the available emotional support from friends and family, and her financial background and knowledge. Progress is not linear. Just when a widow thinks she has it all together, she may have a relapse.

It is difficult to recover from the loss of anyone close to you. However, no death has so many psychological and financial implications and leaves the survivor feeling so helpless and alone as the death of a spouse.

Our personal experiences contributed to our decision to write this book. Each of us was forced to cope with the major consequences of death in our families. Here are our stories.

ALEXANDRA ARMSTRONG'S STORY

Although I am not a widow myself, my mother was widowed when she was 48 years old and I was 8. Dad had been ill for some time, and taking care of him had depleted the family's resources. In order to make ends meet, Mother went to work for the first time as a clerk in a dress store two years before he died.

By the time Dad died, there was very little money left, but there was a small life insurance policy ($10,000). Mother used this money as a down payment on a small house in Georgetown, Washington, D.C., that cost $18,000. My older sister and brother, who were just starting to work, assumed responsibility for the mortgage. Although I took their generosity for granted at the time, in retrospect I realize how tough that must have been for them on their own limited budgets.

My mother and I lived principally on the income that came from Veterans Administration benefits, Social Security, and her salary. My grandfather had set up a small trust fund that provided some extra income from time to time. The checks from this fund often made it possible for us to get through the end of the month. After a while, Mom noticed that the checks were smaller, and their payment was sporadic. Because she was not knowledgeable about financial matters, she asked Dad's brother to help her investigate what was happening to this important source of income. After he looked into it, he brought her the bad news that she had been the victim of white-collar crime. The person who managed the trust fund for her had "borrowed" the money to cover his own expenses. He intended to pay it back to the fund but was never able to do so. By the time my uncle had taken an inventory of what was in the trust fund, very little money was left.

Although I was young when it happened, I understood the ramifications of this discovery—we didn't have this much-needed income. When I was older, I realized that if Mother had known more about investments, she might have been aware of the problem earlier and might have been able to avert or at least minimize the disaster. This event had a profound impact on my life. I resolved I would learn as much as I could about how money worked so I would have financial control of my own life.

We might not have had much money left after Dad died, but Mom certainly made up for any loss of income by the abundant love and care she gave me when I was growing up. She talked the nuns at the convent school I was attending into giving me a scholarship, because she believed a good education was essential to my future and it seemed clear that I would have to support myself.

In school I discovered that I actually liked and had an aptitude for mathematics. After completing college in 1960, I found a job as a secretary in the research department of a regional New York Stock Exchange firm located in Washington, D.C.

In 1965 I became the personal assistant to a woman partner in the firm, Julia Montgomery Walsh. When I started working for Julia, she was a young widow supporting four sons. It seemed that I was destined to be involved with widows, whatever I did!

In 1966, I passed the test to become a stockbroker and worked with Julia's clients until we started our own firm in 1977. By that time I had completed the courses to be a Certified Financial Planner practitioner(CFP®), a program that taught me about various aspects of financial planning, not just investments. At the time, financial planning was a relatively new concept but one that seemed logical to me. Looking at all aspects of a person's financial situation before giving investment advice made more sense to me than giving investment advice in a vacuum. At the new firm I established the financial planning department.

In 1983 I left that firm and opened an independent financial planning firm in downtown Washington, D.C. Today we have 15 employees who provide individuals with financial planning and investment advice. Although our firm has never focused exclusively on single women as clients, many have gravitated to our firm. We have enjoyed working with women who want to be in control of their financial futures.

Today about 50 percent of my clients are women. In view of my experience with my mother and others like her, I have enjoyed helping women learn more about investments. I find raising the level of my clients' financial consciousness to be personally satisfying. As I tell them: Don't confuse a lack of knowledge with a lack of ability to learn. I believe that this knowledge will enable them to better control their financial future. The more women know about finances, the less apt they are to make mistakes. The old adage "Money can't buy happiness" might be true, but I have found that it sure can make life more comfortable.

MARY DONAHUE'S STORY

I was a professional and supposedly enlightened woman when my ostensibly healthy husband, almost 22 years my senior, collapsed and died on January 21, 1980. Until his death, I had never been an active participant in our family's financial decision making, nor did I believe I needed to be.

My childhood and teenage years were relatively uneventful and monetarily trouble free. I attended a private school through eighth grade and a public school through high school in the New York City area. My father, a physician, provided a comfortable lifestyle for us, although we were never indulged. I never gave much thought to money. It was there if

I needed something, but it was not limitless. College was a given and not a privilege.

As I reflect on the expansion of women's roles and choices, I often ponder how it was that my traditional dad imbued in me the sense that I could accomplish whatever I chose to accomplish while simultaneously telling me that my professional choices were nursing or teaching. I chose the latter as a springboard to my present career in psychology.

Professionally, my young adult years were spent attending graduate school, working first towards a master's degree and subsequently a doctoral degree in psychology. During this time, I was employed initially as an elementary school teacher and then as a school psychologist. This latter position led to a special assignment on a project funded by the National Institute of Mental Health. The project focused on establishing educational programs for seriously disturbed and learning-disabled children utilizing the skills of supervised paraprofessionals. My husband-to-be was one of the project coordinators.

Before our marriage, we had many in-depth conversations about the implications of the disparity in our ages and its potential impact on our intention to have a family. Because we were in allied professions that focused on the well-being of the individual, we were sensitized to this area in our personal lives, in contrast to financial matters. This sensitivity was reflected in our lengthy, probing conversations. Conversely, we spent hardly any time discussing financial matters and did not have a financial philosophy.

My husband's personal background included working from the age of 11 through the Great Depression years to earn money to obtain a higher education, including graduate degrees. There was no family money. Whatever he accrued was the result of his own earning power. Clearly, he could be described as conservative.

As time went on and we had two daughters, we discussed how to divide our available time to maximize their time with both of us. We made a conscious decision to shift our workloads. At this point in our lives, I had begun to develop a private psychology practice. By mutual agreement, my husband took a consulting job that provided him with considerable flexibility in terms of committed time, and I gradually increased my private patient hours from a few hours a week to two-and-a-half days a week. We shared equally in the raising of our daughters. However, again by mutual agreement, he managed matters pertaining to the maintenance of our home and our finances, while I basically organized the children's lives and the internal care of the house—fairly typical and definitely traditional.

The following conversational exchange took place with some degree of regularity and predictability. He would say, "Mary, we really need to find time to review our financial situation, because you need to be more familiar with this area of our lives." I would predictably reply, "Yes, you are absolutely correct" and, equally predictably, never made the time to do so.

Therefore, I was totally unprepared to steer our financial ship following my husband's sudden death. I had no idea where and how to begin to undertake all of the tasks before me and deal with our financial needs as well. My husband had had no life insurance, and there were no provisions for our minor children other than Social Security. So there I was left without warning: a single parent with total responsibility for my daughters. It appeared that I would have to assume their financial support in full, run our house, and expand my part-time practice if we were to survive financially. I was emotionally in shock and financially overwhelmed! Where to start? Where to turn? I was most familiar with parenting, somewhat familiar with running the house, but not at all familiar with finances.

I chose to start in the area in which I had the least knowledge: finances. There were several reasons. First, at some point my husband and I had decided to consult a financial planner to help us look at this area of our life. We had been recommended to Alex Armstrong, met with her, liked her philosophy, and felt she could be of assistance to us. It should not come as any surprise to the reader that the work with Alex was almost exclusively handled by my husband. Second, Alex knew more about my finances than I did. Third, and perhaps of greatest importance, she had the comprehensive financial knowledge I knew I needed. In the process of sorting out where I stood, she was invaluable. This financial planner is now the valued friend with whom I have collaborated in writing this book.

It is my opinion that whether financial news is good or bad, some knowledge is better than no knowledge. I found that my lack of financial information intensified my fears and anxieties and contributed to my remaining in a state of paralysis. This lack of financial information also may intensify a widow's grieving response.

I often remind Alex of the time when, discussing some point with me over which I was equivocating (as usual, trying to determine what George—my husband—would have wanted me to do), she turned to me and in a somewhat stern, frustrated, teacher-to-pupil manner said, "For heaven's sake, Mary, you make decisions every day in your work. What prevents you from making them in this area?" In a sense, at that moment I grew up monetarily. Although I have regressed on occasion, I have for the most part forged ahead, rightly or wrongly, as a responsible adult, not second-guessing myself or trying to do what I thought my husband or parents would have wanted me to do.

Realizing in retrospect the mistakes I had made in resisting financial knowledge and understanding some of the psychological factors responsible for my resistance, I wanted to join Alex in providing to widows—at a time when they are most vulnerable—some sort of guidance that could integrate the emotional and financial aspects of this painful period.

THE STORY OF FOUR WIDOWS—
DIANE, SUSAN, AUDREY, ELIZABETH

Alex and I have each practiced our chosen profession for over 30 years. This book is based on personal and professional experiences we have had with numerous widows during this period of time. From these experiences, we created the stories of four widows. The hypothetical composite profiles that follow were created to illustrate various personality traits, financial situations, financial philosophies, ages, and family circumstances. We hope these composites help you identify factors in your own life that are likely to play a role as you move through the various stages of grief.

If your personal financial circumstances are different from those of our hypothetical women, do not feel this book has no relevance for you. We have attempted to present those financial issues that confront most widows. Your personal finances may be different, but your needs are the same.

You may identify with the reactions of one or two or possibly all four of these widows. The purpose of the profiles is to make this book not just a textbook or a helpful handbook but one to which a new widow can relate in terms of her own experiences. As you read the ensuing chapters, you will follow the progress of these four widows as they mourn and subsequently rebuild their lives. In the process, you will be rebuilding your own life. We wish you the best on your personal journey to emotional and financial well-being on your own.

PART ONE

Picking Up
the Pieces

1
Reacting to Your Loss

And a woman spoke, saying, Tell us of Pain.
And he said:
Your pain is the breaking of the shell
that encloses your understanding.
—Kahlil Gibran

ACCORDING TO THE CENSUS BUREAU, in 2004 the adult female population in the United States numbered 117,295,000. Of these women, 11,146,000 were widows. In contrast, the same census indicated that the adult male population numbered 110,048,000, and of these men 2,648,000 were widowers. In other words, widows outnumbered widowers by a ratio of four to one.

A woman can become a widow and a man a widower at any age. The 2004 census data indicates the ages at which this life change occurred and the numbers within each age range:

	Widows	Widowers
Under 25	18,000	7,000
25–29	42,000	8,000
30–34	67,000	20,000
35–39	135,000	30,000
40–44	162,000	54,000
45–54	633,000	203,000
55–64	1,458,000	293,000
65–74	2,768,000	626,000
75–84	4,042,000	984,000
85+	1,823,000	421,000

Source: U.S. Census Bureau, *2004 Annual Social & Economic Supplement*

Contemplating these national statistics is sobering. Regardless of the reason, men do not experience the loss of a spouse to the extent that women do. The need for women to live, survive, and thrive in a widowed state is considerably greater than that for her male counterpart.

Most married women and men consciously avoid thinking about the possible death of their mates. Being widowed is a state or stage of life that any woman might be forced to assume without warning, whether or not we are ready to do so. The individual circumstances surrounding the death of your husband, your relationship as a couple, and your individual personality characteristics will have an impact on your response to your loss. Both common denominators and individual circumstances affect anyone experiencing grief.

For example, universally experienced emotions may be manifested in different ways, depending on a woman's personality. In this book, we will discuss two widely accepted theories of the grief process: the "stage" theory and the "tasks of mourning" theory. The bibliography lists several books that elaborate on these theories and the grief experience.

Before we discuss the "stage" theory of mourning, it is important to keep in mind that although we refer to the emotions about to be described as "stages," you may not experience these emotions as a smooth progression from one step to another with no overlaps or regressions. Some women experience the grieving process as waves cresting and pounding against the shore, while others experience it as climbing an endless, steep staircase to an imperceptible top.

The stages referred to are not defined by days, weeks, or even years. Most widows go through these stages in sequence, although the time required to move from one stage to the next varies according to the individual. The amount of time you require to go through the various stages is the right amount for you.

THE STAGE THEORY

Stage One: Shock

The initial response to the death of one's husband, regardless of the circumstances, is usually shock, disbelief, denial, and a kind of numbness. Most widows are aware of having experienced these emotions on learning of the death of their spouse; however, the manner in which they display these emotions varies considerably. For example, one woman may go through the time leading up to and through the funeral in what superficially appears to be an unemotional manner, responding calmly to questions and making decisions. Another woman may be incapable of making any decisions, leaving the arrangements to others while being unable to stop weeping. Surprising as it may be, both women may be experiencing the same emotion.

This emotional similarity may be unexpectedly revealed months or years later when a friend or relative comments on some incident that occurred during the days immediately following a spouse's death. The widow may have no recollection of the incident even though she thought she had been in control and was functioning rationally. Often, she is surprised by this personal revelation.

The numbness or state of shock a woman experiences in the generally brief initial stage of grief is the body's way of protecting itself. It is as if your body's emotional immune system kicks in in an attempt to protect you from a major emotional or physical illness. Unfortunately, the emotional trauma you experience in response to your husband's death lowers your total resistance both physically and emotionally. Following the initial grief phase of the mourning process, it is not at all uncommon for widows to experience a recurrence of symptoms related to a previously diagnosed physical or emotional problem of their own or to develop signs of a new physical or emotional problem. These may include sleep disturbances, excessive fatigue, visual difficulties, eating difficulties, irritability, drastic mood swings, and changes in bowel and bladder functioning. Some women even feel that they are developing some of the same symptoms their spouse experienced in the early part of his illness (if an illness was the cause of death).

Stage Two: Sorting Out

When a widow emerges from the initial stage of grief, many conflicting and rapidly changing emotions are frequently experienced. In this second phase of grief, she is beset by a myriad of emotional responses, including but not limited to guilt, anger, frustration, yearning, betrayal, bitterness, and sadness. Sometimes it is difficult for a widow to sort out just what she is feeling. If she is unable to locate an item for which her deceased spouse had primary responsibility, she may experience anger or frustration. These feelings may be directed toward her deceased spouse or turned inward toward herself. If the former, she may feel guilty for having such a response; if the latter, she may become increasingly depressed. Some women find themselves carrying on conversations with their deceased spouse in an attempt to deal with a given problem and remain connected to their loved one. Another way of remaining connected is to keep an object of clothing or other item that represents their spouse close at hand. This is a common practice and one that need not be of concern.

Sometimes during this second stage, widows find themselves forgetting (albeit for brief periods of time) that their spouse is gone. As a result, they may begin to question their sanity. Surprising as it may seem, this too is a normal grief reaction during this second stage of the mourning process.

Still other widows may become unreasonably irritated with a family member and then berate themselves for being irritated. One widow described herself as often feeling like an emotional yo-yo during this second stage of the grieving process. What is perhaps most difficult about this stage is its unpredictability in terms of time and content. The emotions experienced are usually intense and varied, leaving the widow in a chronic state of upheaval. When she emerges from this stage, a widow may feel as if she has been in a fog or an extended state of confusion.

Stage Three: Rebuilding

You enter the last stage of the mourning process when you accept the absence of your loved one from your daily life. It is only at this point in the mourning process that you can look at yourself in a new way. It is a rebuilding process that allows you to redefine yourself in terms of both personal and financial goals, needs, and objectives.

A woman brings to marriage her background as a child, an adolescent, a daughter, or a granddaughter. Then she develops her identity as a wife and perhaps a mother. So, too, to this new stage of growth—widowhood—she will bring the totality of the past. Her previous self-image is maintained but is reshaped by this present stage of life. It is a time in life when thought processes need to be modified to one in which the primary focus is *I* as opposed to *we*. Now there is a need to contemplate a life in which personal desires are more important than shared desires. She should be able to do so without a sense of guilt or feeling disloyal to the memory of her loved one.

A caution with regard to this third stage of mourning: Do not attempt to move forward in your life by duplicating the past. Trying to find another man to replace your husband is not a healthy way to approach this third stage. You may or may not develop a significant relationship with another man. The important consideration is not to attempt to repeat the past. Find yourself and what is right for you as an individual in this new stage of life before you attempt to reattach, if that is your preference. Remember that at this point in your life you are not the same person you were when you married your husband. Life experiences have undoubtedly left their mark on you, as should be the case. The same is true for any man with whom you might become involved. It takes time to rebuild your life. Don't shortchange yourself.

THE TASKS OF MOURNINGTHEORY

A recently proposed explanation of what takes place following the death of a loved one defines the grieving process as a series of tasks. J. William Worden, author of *Grief Counseling and Grief Therapy,* and other researchers suggest that there are four tasks of mourning. "Tasks" are thought of by some as more in keeping with the mourning process because by definition the word "task" suggests something to be accomplished without implying a given time frame.

The first task of mourning is the acceptance of the loss. This task is affected by a number of factors. If one's husband dies from a lingering illness in which he experienced identifiable pain and a gradual decline in the ability to enjoy life, acceptance of his death often takes less time. If his death was sudden or occurred under questionable circumstances—such as an accident, homicide, or suicide—this first task may take longer to accomplish. In our current world situation, there is a greater incidence of sudden unexpected loss as the result of military or terrorist activities and natural disasters.

Geographic distance from one's husband at the time of death adds yet another complicating factor to the mourning process. The age of the deceased and other significant losses endured within the recent past will likewise affect the first task. For some widows, the quality of the marriage may be a factor. If your spouse never fulfilled your expectations, you may feel tremendous emptiness when he dies. It may be exceptionally difficult to accept that he is gone and the hope of someday realizing certain dreams with him is no more.

The second task of mourning occurs after a widow accepts the reality of her husband's death. For most women, acceptance of the loss— the first task of mourning—occurs within two or three months. For others, this process takes longer. The acceptance of the death of a spouse opens the door to responding to the pain of grief. This is similar to the second (sorting out) stage of the stage theory.

Many strong emotions are experienced by widows when responding to the pain of grief, including anger, rage, guilt, depression, withdrawal, and feelings of isolation. Some widows report being overwhelmed by one emotion, while others report having some or all of these feelings to different degrees. Rapidly changing emotions often leave a widow feeling frustrated and out of control. It is common to hear a widow express her concern about what she is now experiencing. This is often in contrast to what was previously experienced in the mourning process, which may have been much less emotional and tumultuous.

If a widow feels she is recovering because she is experiencing minimal pain and begins the second task of mourning, in which pain is truly realized, she may feel she is regressing. This is not the case. Rather, it is a component of a process. If you are unable to complete any task, there is reason for concern. If this is not the case, recognize that the pain you are currently experiencing is a healthy part of the grief process.

Sometimes well-meaning family members or friends encourage you to keep occupied and to become involved in a number of activities to prevent you from feeling pain. Although well intentioned, this is not good advice. It is very important and necessary to allow yourself to express your loneliness, your pain, and your rage as well as to be provided with an opportunity to talk about your loved one. You need to be able to express your feelings for as long as necessary in order to move on to the third task of mourning. Sometimes your friends and family may appear to be unwilling to listen to you, an attitude that usually reflects their own discomfort. If this is the case, you should seek help from a professional counselor or a group with whom to share your feelings (see chapter 3).

The third task of mourning, as described by Worden, is "adjusting to an environment in which the deceased is missing." Basically, this translates to how well you are functioning as an individual without your husband. Are you appropriately handling the demands of daily life? While working on this task, you need to address many details related to your husband's estate. These details may include such financial items as your budget and his investments as well as the more mundane aspects of daily life, such as walking the dog or caring for the lawn. This is the time to begin to think about yourself as an individual woman rather than a wife. The fourth task of mourning is acknowledging that you are in a different place while realizing the role your deceased spouse played in your life. Although this person is no longer physically present in your life, he has become an integral part of the present you. You would not be the person you are today if you had not been his wife. In dealing with this task, you should realize that you are alive and continue to have human needs, wants, and desires that now have to be met in a different way than they were in the past.

When you reach this task, you need to evaluate such things as what you need to do, what you would like to do, and how you would like to spend your time. You may have to acquire new skills or adjust to a different quality and style of life. It is a time when you emotionally withdraw from the deceased and focus on the living. Some widows feel renewed guilt when contemplating moving on or experiencing new things because their husbands are not there to share them. This is a feeling you need to overcome.

It is hard to suggest time frames in which these tasks of mourning are accomplished. However, it is unlikely that they will be completed in less than four seasons because you tend to reflect on aspects of your life with your spouse in every new season of the year. You usually need to review both special and ordinary events that occurred each season. As a result, the fourth task may not be completed until the end of the second year or the beginning of the third year of mourning. Widows experience many emotions while completing this fourth task. Sometimes you may feel so uncertain about what you would like to do or think you could do that you become frustrated with yourself. It would be inappropriate to leave this chapter without briefly focusing on the impact of the death of a parent on children. Like the widow, children respond to death in a variety of ways. They too must accustom themselves to their loss. Rarely do young children envision life without a parent as a caretaker. They experience loss in stages, as do their mothers, and may manifest their feelings in behavior or in words. Some children work at denying what has happened to so drastically change their life. They may become withdrawn, avoiding people and activities that had previously provided them with pleasure; on the other hand, they may attempt to function as though nothing has happened to alter their life. One needs to be sensitive to these issues in the various phases of mourning. If a child appears to exhibit a given type of behavior in the extreme, seek professional help (see chapter 3).

It is not uncommon for a child to feel in some way responsible for the loss of a parent. Like the surviving parent, a child usually goes through a phase in which he or she feels abandoned by the absent loved one. The child's response to loss may also be reflected in academics, grades, or school behavior in general. If the child is a teenager, he or she may attempt to be even more connected to his or her peer group than is the norm for the age. Be aware of the teenagers' potential for "acting out" behaviors, such as alcohol or drug use, to dull the pain and allow them to avoid dealing with what has happened in their lives. In some ways, the child's loss is twofold; the deceased parent is unavailable but often so too is the surviving parent. Caught in her own response to grief, a widow may be unable to respond to her child's needs.

SUMMARY AND CONCLUSION

To summarize, try to remember that you are engaged in a process—a painful process that must be experienced from beginning to end in order to reach a healthy new place. Many, many factors impact your recovery.

Death has been described by several philosophers as man's final stage of growth. As a widow, you too are in a growth phase, one not of your own choosing but one that is yours to mold following the healthy process of grieving.

We now introduce you to our four hypothetical widows as they go through the various stages of recovery.

DIANE

Suddenly Widowed with Dependent Children

Diane, age 42, looked at her hand, which was holding the cordless phone receiver. Had she heard right? She had just received a call from Larry, a personal friend and a partner in her husband's law firm, who informed her that in the middle of a partnership meeting her husband had slumped forward in his seat and lost consciousness. When efforts to revive him failed, the rescue squad was called, and he was rushed from his downtown Washington, D.C., office to George Washington University Hospital. Larry said he would pick her up and take her to the hospital.

In a fraction of a second, Diane's world turned black. She felt paralyzed, rooted to where she stood in the familiarity of her cheerful kitchen with her hand on the phone. She didn't know what she had said to Larry. Her three children—Erin (age 15), Jeremy (age 11), and Alice (age 7) — were due home from school in an hour, and Jeremy had soccer practice. How long had she been standing there? The next thing she knew Larry was at the door.

Her next awareness was of being at the hospital in a small room, where a somber doctor stood before her. She really didn't know what he said other than that Mark, her husband of 20 years, had had a massive heart attack and was dead. But she was uncertain about even that. Larry was there beside her, talking in a rational manner to the doctor. Both Larry and the doctor pressed tissues into her hand to stem what she later realized was a flood of tears.

A nurse led her to the room where Mark lay with medical paraphernalia still attached to him. She supposed she should do or say something, but she felt numb, as she dabbed hopelessly at the tears that kept pouring from her eyes. Without warning, Diane's world had changed forever. Somehow, some way, she had signed some papers, and then Larry took her home. The children were huddled together in the family room, looking toward her for something. In her current state, she was unable to comprehend what.

Friends and family seemed to materialize out of nowhere and began to take over. In her current state of numbness, Diane let them. Mark had always handled everything. She had felt so protected and cared for by him. Gradually, over the next several days, she comprehended that people expected her to make certain decisions and provide certain information. In her present emotional state, however, she was not capable of making decisions, nor did she have the information she was expected to have.

Before she married Mark, Diane had always been taken care of by her dad. She had never lived alone. After her marriage she had moved from her parents' home to an apartment with Mark. At some point in the days after Mark's death, Diane realized that her dad had resumed his parental role with her. It allowed her to feel somewhat safe yet at the same time somewhat uncomfortable. Somehow she got the message that Mark had not written a will. Apparently this was a serious problem. Her dad was particularly critical of Mark for not having attended to this matter. Diane was hurt and angered that her dad could think poorly of him at this moment.

Before her marriage, Diane had been a paralegal (she had prepared herself for this job in a college program). In fact, she and Mark had met while working for the same law firm, the very one he was working for at the time of his death. Mark had risen to partner status in seven years, and the firm had grown from 10 people when they met to more than 100 currently.

Over the years, with Mark's approval, Diane had spent increasing amounts of money on the household and the children. They lived in a $900,000 home, and she learned for the first time that she was responsible for a mortgage of about $500,000. She felt overwhelmed on all levels. She had always been supported by Mark, and now she didn't know where to turn. She was willing to accept help, advice, or kindness from anyone who offered it.

In her initial response to the loss of her husband, Diane was incapable of comprehending the implications of her new state. She felt as if she were in some timeless place surrounded by fog and mist, disconnected to life. Sometimes she was aware of saying something to her mom, dad, the children, or Larry, but she felt detached from the woman who walked through the rooms of her home and responded to questions or comments.

Many people attended the funeral, but Diane wasn't even certain who was responsible for the funeral arrangements. She knew she had been asked a great many questions, but other than selecting the clothes Mark was to be buried in, all the while crying hysterically, she couldn't remember her answers to any of the questions.

Friends and relatives commented on what a beautiful funeral it was and how well liked Mark had been. Diane restrained herself from beating on them with her fists for their well-meaning but, for her, empty comments. She felt numb and alone—lost in her own disconnected world.

Diane's Profile

Personal Profile When Widowed

Age: 42
Occupation: Homemaker (paralegal before marriage)
Husband: Mark
His age at time of death: 45
Cause of death: Heart attack
His occupation: Attorney (partner in a large firm)
Years married: 20
Place of residence: Bethesda, Maryland
Children: Erin (15), Jeremy (11), Alice (7)
Parents: Father (68), mother (65)
Will: None

Personal and Professional Support People at the Time of Death

Stockbroker: Scott Truitt
Life insurance agent: Jack Blafford
Estate planning attorney: Mary Sue Ryan
Mark's friend at the firm: Larry Larry's wife: Gail

New Personal and Professional Support People

Financial planner: Dorothy Trumbull
Firm benefits representative: Karen Hutchinson
Erin's friend's widowed mother: Jennifer Greenberg
Jeremy's friend's divorced mother: Nancy Martin
Support group friends: Lisa, Robyn, Marcy

SUSAN

Suddenly Widowed with Elderly Mother

Susan, a 50-year-old executive with a nonprofit association based in Seattle, Washington, could not believe she was once again single. She had just about given up the idea of marriage when she met Lance 13 years ago. They had been married for 12 years now and, despite their individual family demands, had been happy. She hasn't been able to process the events that led to his death. It didn't seem possible that it was only two weeks ago that she had been informed of his accident. A teenager had run a red light and plowed into Lance's car. Lance had been taken to the hospital, where doctors had identified internal bleeding as well as several broken bones. Complications stemming from the internal bleeding subsequently led to his death in the early hours of the morning.

Susan was not feeling up to dealing with Lance's two children from his first marriage. They had never really accepted the fact that their father had married her. Adam, age 25, had recently begun to talk with his father about going to graduate school. Leslie, age 21, was a senior in college.

Lance, with his accounting background, had managed their finances. He always told Susan what he was doing, but she tuned out his lengthy explanations as to why he selected one investment over another. Because of her work experience, she considered herself a woman with a fundamental understanding of money matters, even if she did not know the specifics of their current financial situation. Although she was dreading it, she knew she had the ability to take charge of her financial life.

In light of their individual financial responsibilities prior to their marriage, Susan and Lance had worked out a premarital agreement that left their respective assets to their dependents—in Lance's case, his children; in Susan's case, her mother—but they had recently amended this agreement. Lance had decided to leave his $500,000 insurance policy in trust for his children. If Lance died, Susan would receive the interest income from this insurance trust until she died, and then the children would receive the principal. Lance's will stipulated his children would receive $25,000 each when he died. The rest of his assets were left to Susan. She anticipated that once Adam and Leslie were apprised of these financial facts, they would be upset and threaten to contest the will.

On this chilly morning, Susan's thoughts turned to the impact of Lance's death on her 80-year-old mother, whom they helped support. A couple of years ago, with the help of a geriatric care manager, she and Lance had selected and moved her mother into a nearby Continuing Care Retirement Community (CCRC). She had been relatively happy there, but Susan had noticed recently that her short-term memory had started to deteriorate. She did not know if her mother's current residence would be adequate to meet her needs if she needed more care. She was certainly glad that she and Lance had decided against bringing her mother to live with them. There was no way she could personally care for her mother given all of her new responsibilities.

On learning of Lance's death, Ron, Susan's 55-year-old brother, offered to help in any way possible. Susan had her doubts about how much help he could really be. Although he and Lance were the same age, she didn't think of them as contemporaries. Lance had been so much more knowledgeable when it came to financial matters and had accomplished so much more, both personally and professionally, in his lifetime.

Susan needed to do something to remind herself that Lance was really gone. The last time she spoke to him was just before he left work on the day of his death. They had talked on the phone in the late afternoon, as they usually did, to discuss their plans for dinner and the evening. Lance had volunteered to pick up the milk and bread they needed on his way home from the office. Susan said she would start dinner, and they ended the conversation with their usual "I'll see you in a bit." Little did she know these would be the last words he would say to her. Nothing profound or unusual—just normal and comfortable. Now everything was abnormal, uncomfortable, and unreal.

Although others had offered, Susan had insisted on making all the funeral arrangements herself. Ron had accompanied her, but she needed to make all of the decisions, down to the most minute details. This process helped her realize Lance would not be walking through the door at any minute. Ron had said at some point that he didn't know how she could deal with so many things and remain so calm. He said, although he had never been married, he didn't think he could have handled such a traumatic event as well as Susan was handling Lance's death.

"If he only knew—I'm probably not handling it at all. I can't even believe it's real. I need to remind myself that all of these arrangements are for my husband. It's just something to occupy my time that feels familiar." Susan felt Lance would have been pleased with the funeral. "How macabre," she thought.

Lance had wanted to be cremated, so at least Susan didn't have to deal with selecting a coffin. She kept feeling her reactions were strange, but she was not prepared for such an event. Her husband had been a healthy man—why should she have given any thought to the likelihood of his death? Susan didn't like the lack of control she was experiencing over her thoughts and feelings.

Susan knew she had much to do in the days ahead, but she wasn't ready to face it. She kept telling herself she needed to focus on one day at a time and get through it. She just hoped and prayed she would find the internal strength to meet the demands about to be made of her. She had no professional advisors of her own. She thought this was something she needed to correct in the ensuing weeks.

Susan's Profile

Personal Profile When Widowed

Age: 50
Occupation: Executive, nonprofit association
Husband: Lance
His age at time of death: 55
His cause of death: Car accident
His occupation: CPA (partner in a large firm)
Years married: 12
Place of residence: Seattle, Washington
Stepchildren: Adam (25), Leslie (21)
Parents: Mother (80), father (deceased)
Sibling: Ron (55)
Will: Yes, plus premarital agreement

Personal and Professional Support People at the Time of Death

Lance's partner: Harry
Harry's wife: Emily
Attorney: Tim Longwood
Stockbroker: Bob O'Brien
Lance's assistant: Sarah Stone

New Personal and Professional Support People

Bank trust officer: John Stepstone
Assistant trust officer: Ellen Peabody
Psychologist: Dr. Catherine Coleman

AUDREY

Corporate Widow with Adult Children and Grandchildren

Audrey, age 62, had spent the past year, as she had in previous years: trying to meet her husband's needs. John was 66 when he died following a protracted struggle with lung cancer. He had spent the majority of the last year of his life in the hospital, and Audrey had not missed a day visiting him in the three months before his death. A part of her was relieved that the agony was over; another part looked with apprehension at the tasks ahead.

John had been an executive with a major corporation in St. Louis and had taken early retirement at age 62 because of his poor health. The couple had health insurance through his company. John had managed their personal finances, and Audrey had managed their home, particularly the entertaining, at which she was a master. She sometimes wondered how far John would have gone in the company if she hadn't been the excellent hostess she knew she was. As she and her daughter left the hospital this last day, the doctor commented on what a support Audrey had been to John, and she realized just how draining the last few weeks had been. She was exhausted. She was confident that John Jr., age 40, would arrive shortly to give advice and take over any task requested of him and even some that were not.

Audrey had been married to John for 42 years. Where had the years gone? She and John had never really been happy. She had stayed with him because life never seemed that bad, there were children to consider, and you just didn't divorce a man who had always provided for you!

Audrey knew that John had a will. She remembered they had once met with an attorney to review it. Other than that, she knew practically nothing about their finances. John managed that aspect of their lives and told her what specific items she could and couldn't spend money on. She thought about the day, 22 years ago, when they purchased their home for $50,000. What a major financial outlay it had seemed at the time! Now it was worth about $400,000. Audrey was glad that they had so little left to pay on the mortgage ($20,000). Audrey's thoughts moved to her daughter, who drove her home on the memorable day of John's death. Joanne, at age 35, had three young children, and she and her husband, Keith, never seemed to be able to make ends meet financially.

How different her children were, much like the difference between John and herself. She wasn't looking forward to dealing with John Jr. in the days ahead. She knew he wanted to help, but she resented his patronizing manner. At one time, they had been really close, but since he had become a successful physician, their relationship seemed to be different.

What would she do with her life? She had never worked. There were many unanswered questions that made her somewhat anxious, but at the same time she was experiencing something else—a new sense of being on her own for perhaps the first time in her life. In a way, it was appealing. At the same time, she didn't think this was what she was supposed to be feeling, and she felt guilty about this recognition of what her past life had lacked. She thought she would understand it all much better in the days ahead.

One thing that surprised Audrey was her inability to realize that the long ordeal was over. John had actually died. He had been ill for such a long time that the finality of his death seemed somewhat unbelievable. She was having more difficulty accepting his death than she had thought she would. She couldn't get in touch with what she was feeling. Sometimes she thought she felt loss, yet at other times she just felt numb. "How odd," she mused.

Audrey, Joanne, and John Jr., worked out the funeral arrangements. Both children were willing to do anything their mother felt unable to do. Audrey didn't find the details of the funeral too taxing. The staff of the funeral home was helpful, which made the process less painful. In addition, the family's minister knew them very well, so discussing the eulogy and service was relatively easy.

Actually, what she found most difficult was talking to their many friends and John's former coworkers, an unfamiliar feeling for Audrey. She was such a social person, yet she did not quite know what to say to these people. On the one hand, she was sorry John had died, but, on the other hand, she was relieved that the agony of his long, drawn-out illness was over. Somehow it didn't feel quite right to express these feelings, even though they were very real to Audrey. She found she left most of the initial conversations with other people to the children.

Audrey selected what she would wear to the funeral without weighing one outfit over another. It was almost as if she had previously made this decision, although she was not conscious of having done so. What an unfamiliar experience, thought Audrey. It was very different from her feelings when her mother and father had died. She didn't feel it necessary to sort it all out in the present, but she knew she would spend many hours reliving and reviewing her reactions.

Audrey's Profile

Personal Profile When Widowed

Age: 62
Occupation: Homemaker
Husband: John
His age at time of death: 66
His cause of death: Lung cancer
His occupation: Corporate executive (retired)
Years married: 42
Place of residence: St. Louis, Missouri
Children: John Jr. (40), Joanne (35)
Grandchildren:
John Jr.'s children: Casey (14), J.T. (12)
Joanne's children: Jamie (6), Heidi (4), Noah (2)
Parents: Deceased
Will: Yes

Personal and Professional Support People at the Time of Death

Attorney: Albert Humphrey
Mr. Humphrey's assistant: Sally
Accountant: Gary Lewis
Physician: Dr. Peter PaPadisio

New Personal and Professional Support People

Financial planner: Ken Silver
Cold-call broker: Walter Postman
Real estate agent: Georgia Brown
Friends: Lionel Dawson, Janet Pine

ELIZABETH

Older Widow with No Children

Elizabeth and Ben had been married for 55 years. In fact, Elizabeth could barely remember a time when she hadn't been married. Now she was 75, and Ben had just died, at age 83. Eighteen years had gone by since Ben had sold his small business in the Boston suburbs. His health had been deteriorating over the past several years, and Elizabeth had become frustrated by his memory lapses and confusion. He had always been somewhat of a hypochondriac, but she thought it was his way of guaranteeing him of getting her attention. She wondered whether he would still be alive if she had taken his physical complaints more seriously. Yesterday morning she had been unable to wake him. It had been only 24 hours since he had died, yet it felt like so much longer.

At 75, Elizabeth had her own problems. She didn't know how she would manage alone. She had been depressed periodically over the last 15 years and had some heart problems, although "nothing terribly serious," according to her doctor.

Elizabeth and Ben had no children. They had lived a simple life—a few friends, some entertaining, and church suppers. Their comfortable home was worth approximately $300,000 now. It didn't seem possible it was worth so much. They had paid off the mortgage years ago, so they owned it free and clear. Ben had always said he didn't want her to have any financial worries when he "kicked the bucket."

Elizabeth knew Ben had some financial advisors, although she had never met them. She wondered how he came to select them, who they were, and how they would deal with her. She had no knowledge whatsoever of their financial situation. She thought Ben had a will. At some point she remembered his telling her that their investments were worth half a million dollars, but she wasn't sure if she had understood him correctly. She wondered where the investments were held and what they would mean for her.

Elizabeth knew she had to make arrangements for Ben's funeral. She had called her older sister, Abigail, as soon as the rescue squad told her they couldn't revive Ben, who had passed away peacefully during the night. She had also called her pastor, who appeared almost immediately after her call.

Pastor Appletorn had been so considerate. He had contacted the funeral home and spoken to the director, who arranged to have

Ben's body removed from the home. He told her which papers she had to sign and why they were necessary. He also insisted on contacting her closest friend, Mabel, and making sure she would be able to spend the night so Elizabeth wouldn't be alone. The pastor promised to return when Abigail arrived to finalize plans for the funeral. Elizabeth was grateful that Mabel had agreed to stay until Abigail arrived. She had always thought Mabel was good at managing things. She would be a big help, and it would be good to have her around

Elizabeth was frightened. She didn't know what she was supposed to feel. She had never been alone. She had always had a role: daughter, sister, and then wife. What was she supposed to do in this new role of widow? Who would take care of her? She had always clung to the thought that Ben would be there to take care of her if anything happened to her, even when she knew he really couldn't do that any more. Now she could no longer even pretend he would be there. She had been so involved in caring for him that she had never given any thought to the fact that he might die. "Why hadn't I?" she mused. "There must be something wrong with me."

Elizabeth was very nervous. She couldn't eat or sit still or think about anything for more than a few minutes. She cried a lot, but she wasn't sure she knew why she was crying; she was just scared. She felt a little better after Abigail arrived because Abigail had always looked out for her when they were young. She recalled how Abigail used to tease her about being "afraid of her own shadow."

Elizabeth let Abigail participate in making all the arrangements for Ben's small church funeral. In fact, if she were really honest with herself, Abigail had managed it all because Elizabeth couldn't even decide what to wear. Abigail patiently looked through Elizabeth's closet and selected something dark and conservative. In the evenings, Abigail tried to console Elizabeth, sometimes patting her hand and encouraging her to relax a bit. Part of Elizabeth felt as if she were lost someplace. It reminded her of the way she had felt following some minor surgery years ago when she was regaining consciousness—there but not there. She hoped she would feel better soon.

ELIZABETH'S PROFILE

Personal Profile When Widowed

Age: 75
Occupation: Homemaker
Husband: Ben
His age at time of death: 83
His cause of death: Age-related deteriorating health
His occupation: Small business owner (retired)
Years married: 55
Place of residence: Boston, Massachusetts
Children: None
Parents: Deceased
Siblings: Abigail (77)
Will: Yes

Personal and Professional Support People at the Time of Death

Pastor: Pastor Appletorn
Friend: Mabel
Attorney: Francis X. Carroll

New Personal and Professional Support People

New attorney: Frederick Grossfeldt
Church friends: Sam and Sarah Weatherly
Trust officer: John Samuels
Assistant bank manager: Suzy Riley
Accountant: Deborah Greenfield
Friends: Lucy Thornton, Abe Stein
Real estate agent: Jerry Winthrop

2

Identifying Your
Personal Characteristics

This above all: To thine own self be true,
And it must follow, as the night the day,
Thou canst not then be false to any man.
—*William Shakespeare*

IN ADDITION TO THOSE EMOTIONS experienced by all widows, there are individual differences that are the result of many factors. These may include your individual personality, your personal health, economic factors, your age, the ages of your children, the circumstances surrounding the death of your husband, and whether you considered yourself happily married. The manner in which you cope with this new stage of widowhood depends on your individual personality characteristics as well as the role money or finances have played throughout your life. Just as your parents made clear how they viewed the importance of schoolwork and other activities, they also made you aware of how they felt about money. Few of us pay attention to how or where or why we have formed our financial identity, yet it plays an important role in our lives. You are more likely to be aware of your personality traits than your attitude towards money, so we will review them first.

In your current state, for example, you are most likely feeling emotionally fragile. If so, is this feeling unfamiliar, or is it compatible with your psychological functioning before your loss? Based on your knowledge of yourself, is this feeling likely to be short lived or long-standing? Knowing yourself has an effect on how you will proceed. If you are someone who tends to have very strong emotional reactions to life events but is able to regroup in a relatively short period of time, you may feel comfortable contemplating meeting with a lawyer, an accountant, or a financial advisor within the first few months of your loss. If, however, you are someone who has always had a difficult time coping with major emotional upheaval and has needed support from your husband or other family members, the passage of time is not likely to make a major difference in your ability to deal with this aspect of your life by yourself. What is critical here is for you to use your knowledge of yourself as a guide to assist you in the process of addressing the emotional and financial challenges you'll face.

It is desirable for each widow to develop an awareness of the personality characteristics that will impact her ability to deal with this new phase in her life. You need to be aware of how you respond to stress, make decisions, and feel about risk as well as how able you are to function independently. In assessing yourself, take into consideration your basic personality traits and previous as well as present functioning. In addition, you need to review the meaning of money in your life and how you arrived at your beliefs in this area. These individual personality differences and your financial philosophy will affect to a large extent your ability to steer your personal ship to psychological and financial independence.

It is important at this point in responding to your loss to identify those personal qualities that have played a dominant role in your life to date. The way in which you have interacted with others and solved problems is determined in part by your personality characteristics. Perhaps you never gave this much thought and are unfamiliar with the qualities that dominate your decision-making processes. To help you in your self-analysis, we are providing you with three aspects of personality that are common to everyone and to which all widows will be able to relate. These individual factors are significant and will help you understand your reactions as you go through the experience of loss.

YOUR PERSONALITY CHARACTERISTICS

Are You Primarily a Thinking or a Feeling Person?

Do you respond to your world primarily on an intellectual basis? In other words, before making a decision, do you gather as much information as you are able to obtain, do research, weigh the alternatives, speak with a variety of people, and develop flow charts or whatever else will allow you to make an informed decision? If so, you use primarily thinking or cognitive processes to reach conclusions.

Other individuals are more spontaneous in their decision making. They may wake up in the morning and decide on a given course of action based on such factors as the temperature, the sun, a feeling, or a mood. The differences between these two types of personalities may be illustrated by the way they would place bets at a track. One person studies the conditions of the track, the odds, and the past performance of the horse, the jockey, and the trainer, while the other places a bet based on the horse's name, the colors of the jockey's shirt, the color of the horse, or something else that evokes a personal response. This is not meant to suggest you never have any emotional responses if you describe yourself as using primarily thought processes, or vice versa. We have provided you with the extremes of these qualities but recognize that most people do not function in a way that incorporates 100 percent of one approach over the other. All of us have both components within us. What makes us different is the degree to which we use one characteristic or the other.

Are You Primarily Extroverted or Introverted?

It is also important to understand yourself in the areas of extroversion and introversion. For example, if you are a woman who is outgoing, enjoys socializing with others, seeks the company of others, and is frequently described as very friendly, companionable, and active in any number of areas, you would be described as extroverted. If you are extroverted, you are more likely to seek out others for advice, support, information, and even direction. You may look toward social activities as a reason for not addressing what needs to be addressed.

An introverted woman is one who tends to engage in more individual pursuits, such as reading, crafts, music, or any activity you can do by yourself. If you are introverted, you are likely to look within yourself, obtain printed matter, check out the Internet, or consult one trusted friend or spiritual leader in formulating a course of action or direction. Again, few of us fall exclusively in one category or the other. However, on reflection you will be able to identify which behavior pattern you lean toward.

Are You Primarily Dependent or Independent?

Another important characteristic the widow needs to be aware of is her need to be dependent or independent. Some women have been conditioned or have allowed themselves to believe that it was preferable to leave major decisions to their spouses. They were pleased to be taken care of by their husbands, protected and treated as though there was no need for them to be involved in any decision making outside the home. Perhaps to the widow, being sheltered from such decision making was a statement of her husband's love.

Others, regardless of their involvement with financial decision making, have carved out an area of independent functioning for themselves. Women may involve themselves in all sorts of activities—a profession, a job, volunteer activities, artistic pursuits, various courses of study, and so on. Such women may have wanted to be involved with the financial aspects of their married life but felt it would have been hurtful to the spouse or the marriage to challenge an economic decision or request inclusion when investments were made.

Research indicates that the loss of a spouse is the single most emotionally stressful event in an individual's life. For most women, the task of managing our finances by ourselves follows close behind this event. This is basically true, regardless of one's personal circumstances at the time of a spouse's death. For those widows who have paid the monthly household bills during the course of the marriage, the statement about the stress of managing finances is somewhat less applicable. When interviewed, however, this group of women reported that their ability to function effectively in this familiar area was somewhat diminished immediately following their loss. Obviously, the more familiar you are with your family's finances, the better able you will be to take charge of your situation following your initial adjustment to your loss. Many women, we have found, pay the monthly household bills but are not that familiar with the investments their husbands have made on behalf of the family.

Understanding which of these personality characteristics have been dominant throughout your life will assist you in determining the most helpful approach to your new personal situation. However, understanding the significance of money in your life will also help you address the critical issues before you.

HOW YOU FEEL ABOUT MONEY

Perhaps more than to any other area of your life, you give little thought to your views on money. Whereas you are bombarded by a variety of questionnaires and articles in magazines and on television about how to find and maintain a compatible long-term relationship with the significant other in your life, rarely if ever is your attention turned toward the importance of your personal financial views, how you obtained them, and their impact on the selection of your significant other.

Your attitudes about money, as well as the development of most of your other characteristics, go back to childhood. What were your parents' attitudes toward money? What role did money play in your childhood? Along life's journey you internalize financial beliefs. For example, were most of your parents' arguments focused on money issues? Did you as a child dread those times when your parents had financial discussions? Was it your perception that money matters were an area in which your father felt your mother had no place? Did you internalize the belief that women and girls were not competent to have valid opinions or that it wasn't feminine to understand math? Messages with regard to money are incorporated over a lifetime and are a part of your belief system, whether or not you are aware of it. Erroneous financial beliefs may complicate your life at this time of loss.

Studies indicate that through grade 6 and possibly through grade 8, girls and boys tend to exhibit equal achievement in math. Beginning with middle school, gender issues surface. Girls do not do as well as boys in math. As a group, they consistently obtain lower math scores. This pattern continues through high school. Several theories have been proposed by way of explanation, but to date there is no generally accepted hypothesis as to why this is the case.

During childhood, you received financial messages from other sources in addition to your family or school. For instance, you may have attended a particular church that presented a person's financial position in terms of good or evil. In some cases, accumulated money was viewed as a good thing, and in others it might have been associated with the work of the devil. How you responded to these types of money messages is rarely part of your conscious recall.

Another common source of money messages is from the media. In the 1950s and early 1960s, a variety of television series presented stereotypic male-female roles. People raised primarily during those years have a very different image of a woman's role with regard to money than people raised in the 1980s and 1990s. Women whose parents' lives were affected by the Great Depression of the late 1920s and early 1930s are likely to have a very different attitude toward taking risks than women raised in the past 20 to 30 years.

Thus we see that a variety of factors as well as the society at large contributes to our financial beliefs. It is still likely that the majority of widows today were raised in an era when male-female roles were clearly defined; namely, the man was the head of the household and the breadwinner, while the woman was the child-care provider and the homemaker.

You should not overlook the role money played in your childhood. Was it a given and not often discussed? Was it a means of receiving recognition and approval? Was it attached to the receiving of love? If you did something deserving of reward, was it usually in the form of something monetary? Did you get a coveted doll or a special book or did you receive a dollar award? Whether all of this was formally articulated or merely understood, it should not surprise you to learn that you have a financial history that has resulted in the shaping of your own philosophy about money. It should also not surprise you to learn that, in general, women place a higher value on the quality of their relationships than on obtaining financial success. What are the implications of these differences for a widow?

Of immediate concern to most widows is the issue of having sufficient funds to survive. Regardless of the widow's financial situation, most women are worried about making ends meet. There are a few women at the other end of the spectrum who will enjoy the opportunity to spend money as they want without feeling the need to justify their spending to their spouses. In most cases, however, making ends meet is the primary concern.

This concern is closely related to one's usually deeply embedded feelings about risk. Perhaps because women are so often stereotypically portrayed as being irresponsible about money, they tend to be more conservative than their male counterparts when it comes to making financial decisions. In the early stages of your widowhood, you will find yourself trying to make decisions in line with what you believe was the decision-making practice of your husband, father, or other significant financial figure in your life.

You have now arrived at a point in your life when it is important for you to review and assess both your individual personality characteristics and your financial perspective. It is time to come to terms with how best to deal with who you are in relation to the decisions you will now have to make. For example, you may be a woman who is unable to mobilize yourself from your emotional paralysis following your loss. If you are such a woman, you may feel the need to turn to a loved one or friend for assistance. Allow yourself to do whatever you feel is best to help you cope with the issues before you.

On the other hand, you may need to respond to your grief by occupying your time with making lists or itemizing things in order to regain a sense of control over your life. If you are such a woman, is this a pattern with which you are comfortable and familiar? Are concrete tasks helpful to you in meeting your emotional needs?

SUMMARY AND CONCLUSION

Only you will be able to determine what is right for you. Whatever your personality characteristics, finding yourself in a position where you are required to take control of your money is likely to be unfamiliar and uncomfortable. Keep in mind that change is a part of life and you are not sentenced to maintaining the beliefs or misconceptions of the past. As you gain knowledge, you may find yourself modifying your previous concepts about money in a healthy way. It is now your choice to move forward with new knowledge or remain where you have been.

Diane

Diane's Personal Characteristics and Financial Attitudes

Diane, our youngest widow, is primarily an extroverted, feeling woman who tends to be more dependent than independent. As you progress through her story, you will note that family issues will motivate Diane to function more independently than at any previous time in her life.

Up until this point in her life, Diane had responded to life events primarily on an intuitive level. She has always been extroverted, likes people, has many friends, and tends to rely on her instincts or feelings when formulating opinions. If she perceives something to be a particular way, she accepts her perception and rarely seeks objective information to corroborate her impression. She would often tell Mark her feelings about an individual, an event, or even a movie, leading him to affectionately describe her as "wearing her heart on her sleeve."

Diane had always been treated as a child with regard to money. In her parents' home, her dad made all the financial decisions for the family. Her mother would ask her father for money for food, clothing, and other household expenses. As Diane matured, it was understood that if she wanted money for a prom dress or a special activity, she would have to ask her father for the money. For the most part, Diane's financial requests were honored. She was never expected to have a part-time job during high school, and she accepted her father's attitude about money as a given.

It was not surprising then that when Diane married, Mark assumed the role her father had played in her life. Diane never questioned whether this was good or bad; rather, it was the way life was with regard to money. Diane's childlike attitude to money continued into her marriage, and children do not have to be financially responsible. This immature outlook about money placed an added burden on Diane following Mark's sudden death.

Significant personal characteristics: Extroverted, feeling, dependent
Significant financial attitudes: Childlike, dependent, helpless

Susan

Susan's Personal Characteristics and Financial Attitudes

Susan is relatively independent. She has both extroverted and introverted qualities but leans toward the latter. She has always been an excellent organizer. Sometimes she doesn't pay sufficient attention to the feelings and ideas of others in her desire to get a task completed in the most efficient fashion. Effective and relentless in her ability to accomplish a stated goal, she has always been viewed as an excellent executive in her organization. Within her company she is known to have both innovative ideas and the skills to implement them. Her need to get the job done and look at the facts concerning a given issue is one of the qualities with which her stepchildren had always had difficulty. Nothing she had done had endeared her to them.

As far back as she could remember, Susan had been aware of the significance of money. Plainly and simply put, there was never enough of it to make ends meet. The lack of money created constant tension between her parents. She knew her father tried hard, but he never made that much money. He would periodically attempt to get her mother to look seriously with him at their financial problems but to no avail. Susan had always been very conscious of not making unnecessary financial requests of her parents. She expected her mother, who had worked part time at a local dress store, to have a better understanding of money matters than she did.

At some point in her teenage years, Susan realized that, contrary to what she thought was supposed to be the case, her older brother had as little comprehension of money matters as did her mother. It was understood that Susan was the one who could be counted on to be supportive of her father and do without during her growing-up years. As soon as she was old enough to do so, she obtained a part-time job and tried to stretch her money to pay for extras she might need, such as a class trip or a special dress.

Given her past, Susan had little tolerance for risk. Following her marriage to Lance, she had allowed herself to relax and rely on him when it came to financial investments. In some ways, perhaps, she had welcomed the opportunity for the first time in her life to be less consumed with finances and making ends meet. In some strange way it allowed her to experience the childhood and adolescence she had never had. Although she did not feel confident about her knowledge of their total financial picture, Susan knew that she had the ability to manage her checkbook and seek out financial information on the Internet and from other sources. She was concerned about whether or not she could maintain the same standard of living she had had with Lance now that she was alone.

Significant personal characteristics: Mixed features of extroversion/introversion, thinking/feeling, dependence/independence
Significant financial attitudes: Lack of confidence/self-confidence, low risk tolerance, some knowledge

Audrey

Audrey's Personal Characteristics and Financial Attitudes

Audrey has always been somewhat outgoing. She has also been realistic about her life. Those who know her think of her as practical and as having a great deal of common sense. Family and friends often look to her for assistance when dealing with personal issues because of her calm, matter-of-fact approach to their problems. She has made it a practice to obtain information about various matters before making a decision; in fact, a part of her analyzes facts without even realizing she is doing so. She possesses the capacity to look at herself realistically, is open to new ideas, and has the ability to change her views.

Audrey had grown up in the Midwest. Her father and mother had traditional family roles. Her father went to work and supported his family on his salary. Her mother stayed at home and was clearly responsible for the nurture and care of the children. Dinner was on the table every night at precisely 6:00 P.M., when her father walked in the door with his newspaper rolled tightly under one arm and a slim briefcase in his other hand.

As with so many things in her life, Audrey had pragmatically accepted whatever was done in her parents' household. She never questioned whether or not it was right or wrong, good or bad; it was just the way life was during her years of growing up and reaching adulthood. After marrying John, she had followed his lead in financial matters. Audrey had no complaints, although if she had thought about it, there was no real reason why they did the things they did financially as a family. She accepted what life had to offer, including John's financial decisions, and dealt with it. There was always enough money to support a comfortable lifestyle. The corporate life, although sometimes dull, was stable, and she felt financially secure. In retrospect, Audrey believed she made major decisions affecting her life for primarily pragmatic reasons.

Significant personal characteristics: Mixed features of extroversion/introversion, thinking/feeling, dependence/independence
Significant financial attitudes: Confidence in her ability to learn, open to learning, questionable risk tolerance

---

Elizabeth

Elizabeth's Personal Characteristics and Financial Attitudes

Elizabeth has always been a dependent person in need of a great deal of support. She is usually more content when by herself or in a small group. Throughout her life she has placed a high priority on loyalty and consideration for the welfare of those closest to her, particularly her husband, Ben. She always worked to make their home a comfortable place and one that Ben would be proud of. The activities she enjoyed the most were her various arts and crafts projects and her involvement in her church's programs. She was particularly proud of her needlepoint and quilting. Elizabeth always cared deeply about the misfortunes of others, whether it was someone she saw on television or a personal friend or acquaintance. She has always related simplistically to her world, relying on her emotions and feelings when assessing a situation or an individual. She has tried to follow the Golden Rule: "Do unto others as you would have them do unto you."

Elizabeth had absolutely no financial knowledge nor did she have any interest in acquiring any. She had internalized from childhood the concept that it was her husband's responsibility to take care of her, just as it had been understood that her father was financially responsible for her when she was a child. In reality, Elizabeth was very childlike, expecting to be taken care of by someone.

As a child, Elizabeth looked to her sister to solve her problems. If she had any question and was uncertain as to whether or not to mention it to her parents, she would consult with her big sister. She had never had a bank account of any sort before her marriage to Ben. Until his health deteriorated, she had never written a check on their joint account without first discussing it with Ben. Being financially knowledgeable was a concept beyond Elizabeth's comprehension. It was plainly and simply something she had never had any interest in, whether as a child, a teenager, or an adult. If Elizabeth were honest with herself, she had to admit that she always enjoyed being taken care of by someone in her life. Somehow being taken care of said to her that she was loved and deserved to be looked after.

Significant personal characteristics: Introverted, emotional, dependent
Significant financial attitudes: Childlike, dependent, vulnerable

3

Dealing with Your Emotional Needs

Mourning is essentially a process of unlearning
the expected presence of the deceased.
—Elisabeth Kubler-Ross

AT SOME POINT, the finality of your loss becomes real. It might be in a matter of days, weeks, or even a month or more. It is at this moment that you realize your husband is no longer there to protect you or to rely on for emotional or financial support. When this awareness occurs, you are in the second stage of mourning or facing the second task of responding to grief, depending on your orientation. Acknowledging that your husband is no longer there is a painful awareness, one often accompanied by an emotional response. Remember that during this phase of the mourning process you are likely to experience a variety of strong emotions. In order to move forward you must assess the degree to which your emotional state is affecting your actions and judgments.

Among the factors impacting your passage through this part of the mourning process are your specific personality characteristics and the financial circumstances in which you find yourself. In addition, the nature of your marital relationship appears to play a role in your responses. The important thing for any widow is to assess her personal reactions and gauge how close they are to her normal emotional responses to stress. Is what you are experiencing now fairly typical of what you are accustomed to experiencing, or do you feel at odds with yourself? You need to make this determination in order to know how to proceed.

FAMILY AND FRIENDS

If you are surrounded by family members and close friends when your husband dies, they will undoubtedly make every effort to be there for you in whatever way they can in an effort to be helpful. This may include preparing food, assisting with the funeral arrangements, contacting out-of-town relatives and friends, or doing anything else you may request of them. You are fortunate if you have your loved ones around you during this painful period, but keep in mind that they may not continue to be available to you in this way for any extended time.

In our highly mobile society, at the time of loss you may find yourself in a city in which you have no close family members or friends. Being surrounded by loved ones at a time of personal loss is both emotionally supportive and helpful. For most people it feels easier and safer to express their feelings within their family or to long-standing friends than to others. Some people, however, are more comfortable expressing their emotions to strangers because strangers have no prior knowledge of how they function and therefore they are under no pressure to maintain an image.

Thus, when you are alone or isolated from your family at the time of loss, it is important to find a substitute for what your family would have provided in a different era. Don't feel embarrassed because you are feeling weak and need the support of others. It's normal! Simply allow yourself to act on your realization of this need.

If you are uncomfortable displaying emotion, it may be difficult for you to allow your friends to know you need support. Perhaps you do not know how to ask for help. Sometimes, although willing to help, friends don't know what to do or how to approach you. If your support group consists primarily of friends, allow them to be there for you. Don't think you are imposing on them. Friends, by definition, are there for both the good and bad times. Allowing yourself to depend on existing friends does not preclude the advisability of seeking out new people in your life. You may even feel more comfortable sharing your feelings of loss with a relative stranger in similar circumstances than with those with whom you have previously been close.

Following loss, many widows find themselves in need of some special assistance beyond that available from family and friends. Those first contacted for additional help or support are usually one's personal physician or spiritual counselor. Keep in mind, however, that the roles of a physician, spiritual advisor, and mental health professional are different and unique.

If you find that your behavior, for what appears to be an excessive period of time, is uncharacteristic of you and simultaneously you do not feel connected to your life, seek some help. Sometimes it is difficult for you to determine whether what you are experiencing is within the norm or beyond it. If that is the case, it is advisable to seek the services of someone more knowledgeable about these matters in general. It can be more harmful to remain miserable and uncertain.

PHYSICIAN

Your physician is an excellent individual with whom to discuss whether what you are experiencing is normal for the grief process. He or she is aware of what you have recently gone through and is in a good position to help you understand what you are experiencing. A physician can prescribe medications if needed or make referrals to others who can help. Your physician will also work with you to identify the type of help likely to be most beneficial to you and refer you to the appropriate individual or facility to provide this support.

SPIRITUAL ADVISORS

Some widows feel unable to move forward without coming to personal terms with the death of their husband. If religion has played a major role in your life, you may feel the need for some private talks with a spiritual advisor—a minister, priest, rabbi, or another designated person. Spiritual advisors have considerable experience counseling people who have suffered a loss and should be consulted if their input will in any way be helpful.

In addition to the physician and spiritual advisor, there are other professionals available to provide more specialized assistance in the areas of grief and loss. Included in this group are widow support groups and mental health practitioners familiar with the specifics of loss and grief.

WIDOW SUPPORT GROUPS

Some women find more comfort in the companionship of others who have gone through a similar experience rather than seeking the support of a spiritual advisor or physician. If, for example, before your loss you were essentially a gregarious person who enjoyed the company of others, you might benefit most from a widow support group. Having an opportunity to share your feelings with other widows is often very reassuring.

You may find that your existing friends, although wanting to help, may be unfamiliar with what you are going through. You and your husband probably socialized primarily with other couples. Now, as a widow, you may feel less comfortable with your coupled friends. When they invite you to join them in an activity, you may feel they do so not because they truly enjoy your company but because they feel it is the right thing to do. For example, if they invite you to join them for a dinner, there is often discomfort about what to do when the bill is presented to the table. The husbands might insist on paying your portion of the bill, which may make you feel awkward and unwilling to join them on future occasions. Do not hesitate to clarify your feelings about this before sharing social occasions with existing friends.

Joining a widow support group will provide you with an opportunity to share your feelings with others in similar circumstances. You will hear how other widows have responded to these social situations and how they solved the problem for themselves. Here, too, you will be in a position to develop new social contacts without the awkward aspects of associating with couples.

Widow support groups vary in format from place to place and within areas, but they are basically widow-to-widow, woman-to-woman, or widow-to-widower group situations. Some groups have a professional leader or leaders, while others do not. Some have a defined number of sessions, while others are more open and ongoing. The cost varies, with some basing their fees on a predetermined number of sessions and others allowing one to pay a nominal fee per session attended. Some groups focus on the widow with minor children at home, others on the older widow, and still others on widows in a broad age range. Some groups are designed for the newly widowed, whether male or female. Consider the type of group that will best meet your needs. There are no rights or wrongs!

Customarily, the groups are small, providing an opportunity for the widows to get to know one another well. In fact, many women extend these contacts beyond the group, and it is not uncommon for strong bonds to develop among the widows. These friendships often long outlast one's active participation in the widow support group. Some women have told us they don't know how they would have made it through the first months of widowhood without the support of the women in their group. No one agency or facility sponsors such groups. For the most part, you can find out about them from a friend, physician, or spiritual counselor.

Sometimes churches and synagogues offer groups for the recently bereaved. You might prefer such a group instead of a widow support group. For information regarding such groups, it is best to contact someone at your own church or synagogue. If they do not have any groups of this nature, someone should be able to direct you to a facility that does.

THE INTERNET—FRIEND OR FOE?

If you have a computer with Internet access, you have an invaluable source of information at your fingertips. Log on to one of the many Web sites available for the bereaved. (We have listed several of these resources for you at the end of this section.) It is always a good idea to have your personal professional advisors review the information you receive online; they can help you decide what applies to your particular circumstances.

Among the variety of services the Internet provides are chat rooms, where you are able to talk via computer with others who, much like yourself, are attempting to deal with feelings of loss or grief. However, a word of caution with regard to this complex means of communication: Some people use the chat rooms to present an image of themselves that is inaccurate and misleading. A chat room provides an opportunity (sometimes to ease the pain of grief) for creating a make-believe person, perhaps someone they wish they were, in contrast to the person they are in reality. This may be harmless, but it also provides an opportunity for unscrupulous individuals to abuse the chat room concept for personal gain.

On the other hand, some widows with whom we have spoken report having established both meaningful and significant relationships by entering chat rooms. In some cases, this has resulted in deep friendships and even new expansive experiences that otherwise might not have been available to them.

MENTAL HEALTH PROFESSIONALS

If you are not inclined to consult your primary care physician or a spiritual advisor about what you are experiencing but feel or fear you are in a dysfunctional state, here are some guidelines to assist you in determining whether or not you could benefit from professional help.

If, for example, you don't understand much of what you are experiencing, feel emotionally out of control a great deal of the time, have rapid and extreme mood swings, or find yourself having difficulty organizing and sustaining a thought pattern, you may want to consider consulting a mental health professional or grief counselor. Don't feel embarrassed or crazy if you decide to seek the services of a mental health professional. Like your physician, this professional will help you determine if what you are experiencing falls within the usual range of emotions experienced following a loss or if there are more serious issues that need to be addressed.

Many types of counselors are available to help widows through this difficult period: psychiatrists, psychologists, social workers, and counselors specializing in issues of loss or grief. We present here an overview of the background and training of these specialists to help you understand the differences among them.

Psychiatrists

A psychiatrist is a doctor who has gone to medical school, completed a medical internship, and then completed a psychiatric residency, frequently at a hospital specializing in the care of the mentally ill. He or she may have obtained additional training in a given treatment technique. Psychiatrists for the most part are the mental health practitioners currently allowed to prescribe medication to alleviate the debilitating feelings associated with depression and other mental or emotional disorders. In a few states, psychologists are also able to prescribe medication after following a specified course of study.

Psychiatrists may also provide psychotherapy on an individual or a group basis. They bill you for their professional time on a fee-per-session basis; the fees for individual sessions are somewhat higher than those for group sessions. Make sure you understand the fee structure and office policies of the individual practitioner you select. This information should be readily available to you. Some psychiatrists even provide the information in writing so you can review it at home. (Health insurance coverage for these sessions is discussed later in the chapter.)

Qualified psychiatrists must be licensed in the state in which they practice. Sometimes they are licensed in more than one state. They will have met the requirements to practice medicine with a specialty in psychiatry. As with other physicians, psychiatrists will probably display their licenses and training certificates in their office; if that is not the case, inquire about their qualifications. Psychiatrists, like other physicians, are required to obtain a specified number of continuing education credits each year. The number of credits required is set by the state that issues the license. This means that psychiatrists must attend classes, meetings, or workshops or complete online training that pertains to their practice. Continuing education ensures that they remain current in their field of expertise.

Psychologists

In order to practice as a psychologist, an individual must have completed a four-year college program followed by a four-year or five-year doctoral program designed to prepare him or her for the practice of psychology. The study of normal and abnormal behavior is required and is a component of any such program. After completing this part of the training, those who decide they want to work with people on a therapeutic level move on to an appropriate internship program in an approved treatment facility. Here, psychotherapy training under supervision is provided. Many undergo additional training in a particular therapeutic approach.

In terms of providing therapy to clients, there is considerable similarity between the treatment provided by a psychiatrist and the treatment provided by a psychologist, although most psychologists are presently unable to prescribe medication for their clients. However several states are moving toward licensing psychologists for prescribing medication. Psychologists, however, are the only mental health professionals trained to administer and interpret psychological tests. Any mental health professional who feels it would be helpful to his or her work with a particular client to obtain the information provided as a result of psychological testing must seek the services of a psychologist. Fees depend on the tests to be administered and the time required to administer, score, and interpret the material.

Psychologists' fees are charged on a per-session basis. Psychologists will clarify the fee structure and office practices either before or at the time of the first session. Many give their clients a written statement of policies and practices as well as answer any questions.

Psychologists must be licensed to practice in the state in which they work. They have been qualified to perform the service they provide by satisfactorily completing a licensing exam following their formal academic and internship programs. Evidence of training and licensure is usually visible in the psychologist's office, but never hesitate to ask if you are uncertain. Psychologists are also required to earn a stated number of continuing education credits on an annual basis. The number of credits is determined by the licensing board of the state in which the psychologist practices. Such requirements assure the client that the psychologist has maintained his or her competence in a given field.

If you do not know anyone in a position to provide you with a referral, contact the psychological association in your state (e.g., Maryland Psychological Association).

Social Workers

Licensed social workers are also required to complete a specific training program. Following the completion of a college course of study, these individuals frequently proceed to a master's-level and sometimes a doctoral-level program with an emphasis on individual and community services. Social workers also complete an internship in their particular area of interest. Here, too, many licensed social workers find themselves working with individuals or groups in a manner similar to psychologists and psychiatrists, but social workers are not required to complete a doctoral program to treat individuals with emotional problems.

Social workers bill their clients for professional time in the same way that psychiatrists and psychologists do. Social workers' fees are based on their background and training and are usually somewhat lower than those charged by psychiatrists and psychologists. There are always individual differences, but in general a psychiatrist will charge more than a psychologist and a psychologist will charge more than a social worker. Social workers also have a continuing education requirement set by the state in which they practice.

Professional Counselors

There are other counselors who have not completed a required course of study to become a psychiatrist, psychologist, or social worker. These people have a master's-level education in a given area, such as grief counseling. They are recognized as certified professional counselors if they have completed the course of study and internship required by the jurisdiction in which they work to practice in a given area of expertise. They are licensed by the state in which they practice and display their license in their office. These counselors will charge a fee for their services usually comparable to those charged by social workers.

Licensing for mental health professionals as well as for physicians and dentists is handled by the department of health and mental hygiene in the state in which they practice. All of the continuing education credits earned by these professionals must be submitted to the designated review board on an annual or biannual basis in order to maintain a license to practice. Again, continuing education requirements are determined by both one's profession and the state in which one practices.

MEDICAL INSURANCE

Many health insurance policies include coverage for mental health services. In general, psychiatrists and psychologists are recognized mental health providers, although there is considerable variation in the coverage for the services provided by social workers and counselors. If you have any questions about your insurance plan, contact your carrier to clarify your coverage. If you are unable to deal with this yourself, ask a family member or close friend to obtain the information for you. If your health insurance plan provides coverage for such consultations, the mental health provider will assist you in obtaining the appropriate reimbursement for the services rendered. If you have a managed care plan, contact the group for information about obtaining coverage for mental health treatment as well as referrals.

SUMMARY AND CONCLUSION

Regardless of how you have viewed yourself in the past, this may be a time to seek out the services of a professional with experience helping people cope with grief and loss. Or perhaps you need the support of others who are experiencing what you are experiencing. Regardless of what you are feeling, make an effort to identify what you need and try to locate the appropriate individual, group, or agency for help. Whatever you seek, keep in mind that the choice is yours and the purpose is to help you through the time of maximum stress in your life.

In large measure, your personality type and the way you have dealt with emotional issues in the past will determine the approach that best meets your needs. Some widows need time alone to work through what they are feeling. Concentrate on what you are experiencing and determine whether or not you need some sort of intervention. Exercise has also been determined to be a helpful to those in the mourning process. Give yourself time to explore this area in your life as well.

We cannot stress sufficiently the point that there in no one right or wrong approach for all widows, this is the time for you to identify what you need and find the necessary assistance to meet that need. In making this decision, consider your basic personality traits and present emotional state. Whatever you do, make yourself and your needs the priority. Even if you feel others need you, keep in mind that your ability to help anyone depends on your ability to help yourself.

Following are some suggested organizations that may be able to assist you:

American Association of Retired Persons
Grief and Loss Programs
601 E Street, NW
Washington, DC 20049
888-687-2277
www.aarp.org/families/grief loss

American Psychiatric Association
1000 Wilson Boulevard, Suite 1825
Arlington, VA 22209
703-907-7300
www.psych.org

American Psychological Association
750 First Street, NE
Washington, DC 20002
202-336-5500
www.apa.org

National Association of Social Workers
750 First Street, NE, Suite 700
Washington, DC 20002
800-638-8799
www.socialworkers.org

National Self-Help Clearinghouse
Graduate School and University Center
City University of New York
365 Fifth Avenue, Suite 3300
New York, NY 10016
212-817-1822

Bereavement and Loss Center of New York
170 East 83rd Street
New York, NY 10028
212-879-5655

In subsequent chapters, you will follow the choices our hypothetical women made in obtaining the help they needed in dealing with the loss of their husbands.

Diane

Reactions to Dealing with Her Initial Emotional Needs

Diane had a hard time focusing on anything in the initial stage of grief. She was so disoriented and upset by her husband's sudden death that she could not think clearly. She was using all of her energy just to stop crying. Several weeks after Mark's death, however, she awakened one morning, and, after what had now become her familiar feelings of terror and vulnerability had subsided, she thought for the first time about what her children must be going through.

Until this point, Diane had functioned in an almost automatic manner, going through the motions of daily responsibilities and signing papers that her dad and Larry, one of Mark's law firm colleagues, said needed to be signed. On this particular morning, she thought about the children. She really had not had the emotional strength to address their needs at all. She contemplated what they must have been going through without their father, even though they never really had much of an opportunity to spend daily time with him, and a nonfunctional mother. In a sense, following Mark's sudden death, the children had been forced to manage without either parent. For a moment she contemplated with sadness the fact that the children would never have the opportunity to know their father as she had known him.

Diane needed to move beyond these thoughts and become more functional. What could she do? If only she knew someone who had had a similar experience. She and Mark did not know anyone among their couple friends whose spouse had died. Clearly, their friends would be unable to relate to her present situation. Then she remembered Erin, her older daughter, mentioning that her friend Nicole's dad had been killed in a boating accident a few years ago. She didn't even know Nicole's mother's name. Diane felt somewhat ashamed of herself when she recalled her casual, matter-of-fact response—"Oh, that's too bad"—when Erin told her about Nicole's dad. Now here she was, some years later, in the same situation.

Diane determined to ask Erin for the name of Nicole's mother. She wanted to talk with her and find out how she had dealt with these unbearably painful feelings. When Erin returned from school that day, she gave Diane the name of Nicole's mother, Jennifer Greenberg, and her phone number. Diane wasted no time contacting her and even surprised herself by not being concerned about how her call might appear to Nicole's mom. Jennifer turned out to be very understanding and helpful and spent almost an hour talking to Diane.

For the first time since Mark had disappeared from her life, Diane felt there was someone who understood what she was feeling. Perhaps it was just that she didn't feel quite so alone in the world. Jennifer had many helpful suggestions. She told Diane she didn't know how she would have survived without the help of the women in her widow support group. Diane shivered at the mere use of the word *widow*. That's what she was, though, a widow, so she had better try to accept it.

A widow support group—Diane had never heard of such a thing. Jennifer explained how such a group worked: The one she went to met once a week for eight weeks in nearby Chevy Chase. Jennifer knew that the coordinator, Lisa, would be able to provide a great deal of support to Diane. Jennifer went on to say she had become very close to two of the women in her group—they had even gone on a vacation together this past summer. She said she was working now but would be available to Diane to provide support and information. Diane thanked her profusely. "What a warm, caring person she is," Diane thought. She called Lisa immediately upon hanging up the phone and left a message on her answering machine. Diane felt calmer, but she wasn't sure why.

As we have noted earlier, Diane is primarily a feeling, extroverted, and relatively dependent woman. Therefore, it is consistent with her previous behavioral patterns for her to turn to others for advice.

Diane and Mark had decided to place the children in private schools, which they believed provided a better educational environment. Would they be able to continue at these schools? Diane had no idea. With her feeling approach to life, she was able to get in touch with what the children themselves were likely to be feeling. Emotionally, they had been left to fend for themselves. She felt the need to apologize to them for not having been there for them and promised herself that she would be more sensitive to their needs in the future. She resolved to listen to what they were expressing on an emotional level.

Diane wasn't quite sure how she was going to accomplish all that needed to be accomplished. She felt like a child herself because someone had always taken care of her financially. Now, she knew, she was supposed to act like a grown-up, but she didn't really know what that meant. She guessed she would be expected to make decisions about money. A part of her was angry at herself as well as both Mark and her dad for allowing her to remain financially immature, while another part of her sought ways to remain a child. Her thoughts moved to the helpless glances the children had furtively turned in her direction when apprised of their father's death and how she had been unable to respond to them. She realized she had to be more responsive to them and for their benefit attempt to deal with her financial situation. She needed to pay attention to what she was being told about her economic situation because it would have an impact on all of them. If at all possible, she wanted to keep the children in their present schools, even if it meant making some sacrifices.

Although a logical and pragmatic approach to life was not part of Diane's personality structure, her strong feelings about what she wanted for her children would, in the weeks ahead, help mobilize her. These feelings would also enable her to comprehend what steps she needed to take in order for her to assess her total financial situation and eventually make a decision, which she believed would have a major impact on the development of her children. At this moment, they were the most important consideration in Diane's life.

She resolved to ask her friends how to go about assessing the viability of the private schools for the children. Although tempting, on both an emotional and financial level, she knew she didn't want to get into this issue with her dad or Larry. Surely her friends would be helpful in this area.

As indicated in chapter 2, Diane was primarily an extroverted, dependent, feeling woman. Therefore, it is not surprising that she would turn to her friends for assistance when faced with a task with which she had little familiarity. It is common for extroverted individuals to be comfortable seeking the help of others when it's needed. Diane's intuitive characteristics and reliance on her instincts can be seen in her decision not to involve Larry or her father in her review and assessment of the children's school placement.

Susan
Reactions to Dealing with Her Initial Emotional Needs

Susan had a hard time accepting that Lance was dead. The fact that he had died suddenly complicated her situation. This is not surprising because dealing with sudden death, particularly of a healthy person, compounds the early phases of the mourning process. Techniques Susan had used in the past to deal with difficult times were not working for her, but then she had never had to deal with something so traumatic. She thought she could have handled Lance's death better if he had been older or had had a long-term illness. In fact, he had always been healthy, so his death was totally unexpected. The only way she could move from her current state of disbelief and shock to some semblance of functioning was by resuming patterns of behavior she had previously found helpful. She had always had a pragmatic approach to life and been attentive to details. In her work experience, she had found it helpful to make lists of matters needing her attention and possible ways to approach issues.

Shortly after the funeral, Susan began to compile lists of matters she needed to deal with that were related to Lance's death and the order in which they needed to be addressed. It was helpful to do something that felt familiar, something beyond her emotional paralysis. This activity enabled her to feel more in touch with the world and daily events. It was as if her emotional life existed in its own orbit, separate from the requirements of daily life.

While making lists allowed Susan to feel more in touch with life, it also made her realize she was spending her time writing and rewriting her lists, prioritizing and reprioritizing, yet she was unable to get started on anything. She was becoming frightened. This was not characteristic of her. She had always been able to act on what needed to be done in a timely manner—in fact, it was one of the qualities Lance appreciated most in her. She wondered how long she would be in this state of inactivity, unable to move.

Susan had to do something to come to grips with what was happening to her, but what? She recalled a TV talk show she had once seen that focused on various mental health professionals dealing with different aspects of grieving. At the time she had commented to Lance, "I wonder why anyone would want to spend every day dealing with death." Now she thought this very type of person might be able to help her better understand what was happening to her. Was what she was experiencing normal for women in her circumstances, or was something more serious happening to her?

Susan reflected on the time 14 years ago when she had considered seeing a mental health professional to better understand her feelings about never having married. Actually, it was shortly before she had met Lance. She wondered if she still had the name and address of the woman doctor to whom she had been referred by one of her co-workers. At the time, her co-worker had indicated that the doctor was a therapist interested in dealing with women and women's issues. Susan wasn't sure her present situation as a widow was one that would be within this therapist's area of interest or expertise. On the other hand, Susan was a woman, and women's issues were ostensibly one of this therapist's areas of expertise. She guessed this doctor would tell her whether she had the skills to work with her or not. Susan thought she'd feel better if she could talk to someone other than a friend or relative about what was happening to her, someone familiar with what she was experiencing.

Although she hadn't wanted to admit it to herself, Susan had begun to feel symptoms of menopause before Lance's death. She based this conclusion on her realizing she had been feeling hot or cold for no apparent external reason and was more irritable, which was out of character for her. She was also experiencing other signs, including unfamiliar mood swings, increased fatigue, changes in her sleep patterns, and, what she was most afraid to acknowledge, memory lapses. She knew she needed to discuss her fears about her total functioning with a professional. Was what she was experiencing her response to Lance's death, was it menopause, or did the two impact on each other? Susan knew she could not explore this concern with a man, even though she accepted that there were competent male doctors. How she hated feeling this way!

Since Lance's death, she had had considerable difficulty sleeping through the night. It had been helpful to have her trusty note pad at her bedside to jot down her thoughts and feelings. From reviewing these notes it was clear to her that she needed some professional help. She thought she still had the doctor's name and phone number in her address files at her office. She'd look it up when she got to work and see if the doctor was still in practice. If she couldn't locate the doctor's name and number, Susan thought she would ask another woman in her office for the name of the person she'd taken her daughter to see when her daughter had a miscarriage.

Susan knew she needed to get beyond her present state. There was too much to do, and she didn't have the luxury of remaining immobilized. She acted on these feelings that very day. She located the doctor's name, and, as she stared at the phone number, she realized her palms were sweating. Slowly, she tapped the numbers on her phone and heard the phone ringing. A woman answered, "Dr. Coleman's office." Susan was pleasantly surprised—this was like calling any other doctor's office. She wondered why she had expected this phone call would be answered differently from phone calls at any other doctor's office. She was taken so off guard the woman had to repeat, "Dr. Coleman's office." Susan asked if Dr. Coleman dealt with grief issues. The woman told her Dr. Coleman was a psychologist familiar with grief counseling but that her practice was not limited to this area. She suggested Susan make an appointment to meet with Dr. Coleman and discuss her specific needs. The receptionist gave Susan the address and a lunchtime appointment for the following Thursday.

Susan was glad she finally had found the strength to see Dr. Coleman. The doctor's office wasn't at all intimidating. It was in an office building not far from where Susan worked. Dr. Coleman was very reassuring and comforting without making Susan feel there was something wrong with her for seeking professional help in dealing with Lance's sudden death. She explained to Susan she could help her address what she was experiencing emotionally. She confirmed that Susan's emotional responses were indeed intensified because she had begun to experience normal physical and emotional changes related to menopause.

Dr. Coleman said she had worked with other widows in Susan's situation and appreciated how difficult it was for anyone in such a vulnerable state to begin to deal with all the necessary paperwork and financial issues. They would, therefore, also focus on the demands of daily life. When Dr. Coleman used the word *widow,* Susan was taken aback. Her image of a widow was someone her mother's age. She'd have to look at why she had such a negative response to this word. She should probably discuss it with Dr. Coleman, but there was not time for that today because her session was just about over. She thought it would be important to start with these feelings at her next session.

When Susan left Dr. Coleman's office, after having scheduled her next appointment, she felt not quite so alone for the first time since Lance had died. She knew this was an important step for her.

The varied aspects of Susan's personality are seen in her ambivalence about seeing Dr. Coleman. Before making the appointment, she recognized that she needed professional help, but she was reluctant to act on this realization because her private, introverted side resisted this recognition. In a way, she felt that she should be able to handle matters by herself. Her independent, thinking side also resisted, but her dependent side allowed her to accept her present limitations and make an appointment to see Dr. Coleman. Once there, her logical, pragmatic qualities allowed her to take advantage of what Dr. Coleman had to offer her.

Audrey

Reactions to Dealing with Her Initial Emotional Needs

It was about three weeks after John's death, but to Audrey it felt like the first morning after the funeral. She sat at the scarred, wooden breakfast table and had her morning coffee by herself while allowing herself to think about her future. She had come to appreciate such private moments during the particularly demanding last months of John's life.

Audrey reflected back on the last days of John's life. She wondered if she had made the right decision when she determined to leave John in the hospital and not use hospice help at home. Everything she had read and heard about hospice care suggested that these people did really good work and were very helpful to both the patient and the family. The number and Web site were still on the kitchen bulletin board. In the end, she thought she had made the right decision because she felt John was too sick to be moved.

Audrey, without realizing it, had given a good bit of thought to her needs following John's death. She had accepted life without John as something more than an existence to be endured. Her new status would allow her to explore as yet unidentified avenues she would not have had the courage to investigate while John was alive. She didn't know why that was so, but she was sure that it had been the case. She was determined to take personal charge of her situation and not allow her son to assume the role of primary advisor and financial decision maker, which, knowing him, she felt confident he intended to do.

Audrey had not met with John's attorney in years but knew that he would handle John's will. She determined to make an appointment to see him by herself. If she found herself able to relate to him and understand what he told her, she would move ahead on her own. If she didn't feel ready to move forward on her own, she would ask her daughter, Joanne, to accompany her and later John Jr. She wanted him to know that she appreciated his caring and concern but that she was not a feeble old woman unable to think or act on her own.

Audrey's pragmatic yet thought-oriented approach to life enabled her to think reasonably well in her adjustment to her new circumstances. Perhaps more so than in the situations of our other hypothetical widows, John's lingering illness had gradually accustomed her to her new state.

Audrey stretched and moved to the sink to place her coffee mug in the dishwasher. In doing so, she caught a glimpse of herself in the large hall mirror and was startled to see how much thinner she appeared. She went upstairs to her colorful yellow-and-blue bedroom and took a good look at herself in the bedroom mirror. She certainly had lost weight. She hadn't even realized it. She wasn't really feeling sick. She was more tired than usual, but she had attributed her fatigue to the toll John's illness had taken on her. What about her weight? It was clear her clothes didn't fit right anymore. She wondered when all this had happened. The green plaid skirt she removed from her closet this morning was at least an inch too big around the waist. Why hadn't she realized this before? It certainly didn't just happen. She couldn't remember when she had last prepared a meal for herself. She usually grabbed some crackers and cheese or other snack with a cup of tea in the evening.

Audrey didn't want to overreact or underreact. Certainly, weight loss was one of the first symptoms of what was subsequently diagnosed as John's lung cancer. She had a positive attitude about life and the future but didn't feel comfortable ignoring health concerns. Better to be safe than sorry. She didn't even need to look up Dr. PaPadisio's phone number; it was engraved in her mind. She dialed the all-too-familiar number, identified herself to the receptionist, who expressed her sympathy about John's death, and asked for an appointment for an annual physical. As she did so, she recalled she hadn't had a physical since John's cancer had been diagnosed two years ago.

Audrey's childhood had led her to accept much of what life presented without much question. She possessed characteristics of extroversion/introversion, thinking/feeling, and dependence/independence. Her balanced personality allowed her to acknowledge as she looked in the mirror that she had indeed lost weight. On a feeling level, she did not want to think about what might have caused her weight loss. However, ignoring weight loss was not acceptable to her because her pragmatic, thinking qualities recognized the need to explore the situation further before jumping to any conclusions. She lost no time in contacting Dr. PaPadisio's office to schedule an appointment.

Elizabeth

Reactions to Dealing with Her Initial Emotional Needs

Elizabeth, at age 75 with few outside interests or support people, was emotionally very needy. She had really never been on her own before. Her older sister, Abigail, had come from Florida to be with her for the funeral. Elizabeth felt safer having Abigail in the home but was embarrassed by her dependency on her older sister for support. She wondered if Abigail was more confident and worldly when it came to money matters because she had never married and had been forced to make so many decisions for herself. Elizabeth was dreading Abigail's departure and begged her to extend her stay. Abigail did stay for a few more days than she had planned but finally had to return to her retirement home in Florida. She encouraged Elizabeth to give serious thought to moving to Florida to be closer to her, and Elizabeth promised to consider the idea.

After Abigail left, Elizabeth felt alone. She was terrified, panicked, and didn't know where to turn. Who would take care of her? How would she survive? Her thoughts raced in all directions. Her friend Mabel had been so kind and had already given so generously of her time. Besides she didn't know how to go about talking to Mabel about some of these very personal matters. She also felt as though she would be disloyal to Ben if she talked to Mabel about their financial situation. Suddenly, she remembered that her minister, Pastor Appletorn, had made a home visit shortly after Ben's funeral. It had felt good to see his familiar, friendly face. He had encouraged her to come see him at the church. She felt safe with him, too, and in her loneliness determined to accept what she viewed as his ministerial but kind offer to make an appointment to see him. She hoped that he would be able to provide her with some guidance regarding the steps she needed to take in her newly widowed state.

Elizabeth's personality characteristics as well as the way she had lived her life made it difficult for her to cope with her newly widowed state. She was emotional, dependent, and introverted, a combination that did not provide her with good coping skills. She had no financial knowledge and, if the truth be known, she didn't want to deal with financial matters or make decisions about money. Ben had always said, "There, there, now, no need to worry your pretty little head about silly numbers." Elizabeth had a considerable need to decrease the anxiety and stress of finally having to deal with her finances.

She also knew she would be required to deal with lawyers or other business advisors about Ben's will and estate, but she had no idea how this process began. Did someone contact you, or were you supposed to know you had to contact the lawyer? Perhaps Pastor Appletorn would know someone who could accompany her on this dreaded trip—she felt so stupid about financial matters!

Elizabeth was desperate for support and help. To obtain it, she was willing to risk initiating the contact with her minister. Her timidity would have prevented her from taking such a step in the past, but she did feel comfortable with him, and he was the only person she could think of who might be able to help her with what lay ahead. Her inability to function independently overcame her need to keep to herself. Elizabeth allowed her pattern of turning to others for advice to move her to seek the assistance of someone she viewed as more knowledgeable than herself. She recognized that she did feel comfortable with Pastor Appletorn and that he was the only person she could think of who might be appropriate to talk to and help her with what lay ahead.

Elizabeth looked at the clock and realized it was too early to call Pastor Appletorn. She suddenly thought about the morning paper. She didn't recall bringing it into the home since Ben had died. She guessed Abigail or Mabel had done that for her. Well, today she would do it herself. She thought she would try to read it while she had her coffee. When she opened the door, she was surprised to see, in addition to the paper, a small, bedraggled, forlorn-looking gray-and-white cat peering up at her. It looked lost and confused. She and Ben had never had pets because he was allergic to both cat and dog hairs. She remembered that some neighbors at the very end of her street had moved away about four days ago. She wondered if the cat had belonged to them.

Elizabeth didn't know what to do. Should she feed the cat and take it in, or should she call the humane society? The cat looked helpless and pathetic, kind of the way she felt and as if it wanted her to do something. She wondered if she and the cat weren't in the same boat—alone and frightened. She didn't think it would hurt to give the cat some milk, although she really didn't know what cats ate or drank. Maybe if she brought it into the home it would provide her with some companionship. She decided to be daring and feed it. She found herself smiling. The cat seemed so pleased to be allowed into the home. It had a really cute face.

PART TWO

Getting Organized

4
Organizing Your Finances

You've got to be careful if you don't know where
you're going, because you might not get there.
—*Yogi Berra*

YOU MAY NOT HAVE BEEN INVOLVED in the financial process at all during your marriage. On the other hand, you may have handled everything financial, including investments. Perhaps you were somewhere in between—you paid the household bills and balanced the checkbook for the household but weren't involved in the investment selection process.

Many people have the misconception that if a woman has worked outside the home for pay, she is familiar with family finances as well. Often the opposite is true: Working wives are often less involved in finances than nonworking wives because they may feel they have no time to spare after coping with their job, household, children, and husband. Remaining uninvolved in finances works relatively well until a working wife's husband dies and she finds herself with insufficient financial experience and knowledge.

Money has traditionally been considered the male province. However, many men know little about money management or investing. Further—and this is much more dangerous—they may think they know more than they do. This problem is compounded if the husband dies prematurely. He may have thought he had plenty of time to accumulate money for a comfortable retirement, and therefore he may have invested in some riskier ventures with the idea that he had plenty of time to shift to more conservative investments later.

Regardless of how financially knowledgeable you are, the numerous tasks you are currently facing can be overwhelming. How do you start to make order out of chaos? In the next few chapters, we discuss the basics of determining where you are financially. This chapter covers how to organize the information you currently have available. In chapter 5 we discuss how to work with your three key advisors: your lawyer, your accountant, and your financial planner. Chapter 6 lists other people and agencies providing additional information you will need to construct an accurate picture of your situation. In chapter 7 you develop a budget, and in chapter 8 you calculate your net worth.

If you are unable to handle any or all of these jobs, ask someone to help you—but at least review these chapters so you have an idea of what has to be done. The sooner you understand your financial picture, the sooner you will be able to move toward recovery. The anxiety caused by uncertainty will be removed. Some widows find getting their financial papers in order therapeutic, whereas others find it overwhelming, particularly initially.

A word of caution: In this initial stage, a widow may feel compelled to take some kind of action—any kind of action—to demonstrate to herself and others that she is in control of her life. If this is what you feel, resist the impulse. Take no drastic action, such as selling your home, quitting your job, moving in with or closer to your family, buying insurance, loaning money to a family member or friend, or making a major investment. There is no need to make major decisions immediately. In fact, there are compelling reasons not to make any decisions that are not absolutely necessary at this time. Now is not the time for irrevocable action. Having said this, however, we also advise that you not carry inaction to an extreme. A time will come when action is wise and necessary. Then, if you take no action, you are in fact making a decision not to take responsibility for your financial life, whereas now is the time to determine what your situation is so that you can intelligently plan your future.

The following tasks need to be accomplished in the first few months after your husband's death. Do not let the list overwhelm you. Assign yourself one job at a time, and don't get discouraged if each task takes longer than you anticipated.

LOCATE YOUR IMPORTANT PAPERS

Hopefully, you and your husband had a file cabinet in which all important records were kept. We say "hopefully" because this is the sort of thing that everyone means to do and never gets around to—or your husband may have set up an elaborate system and never explained it to you or you didn't pay attention when he did. The records might also be in a computer, a safe-deposit box, or an old shoe box. In some states, a jointly held safe-deposit box is sealed as soon as a spouse dies and cannot be opened without a court order.

Regardless of where your important papers are located, you need to look for a copy of your husband's will, his and your Social Security cards, your marriage certificate, his military discharge papers (if applicable), his insurance policies, his birth certificate, and birth certificates of your minor children. These papers will be needed to establish claims for Social Security income, life insurance proceeds, and veterans benefits.

Don't panic if you can't find your husband's will. Your lawyer may have a copy. If there is no will, then the estate will be settled by the laws of the state in which you live. Contact the probate clerk in your county (see your yellow pages under local government listings) to find out what action to take. We recommend that you use a lawyer to help you with this task because it is easy to unintentionally omit something that could cause subsequent problems. (See chapter 5 for more on this topic.)

SET UP A WORK AREA

Designate a special area—preferably a desk—devoted specifically to your financial affairs. If you have a file cabinet, fine. If not, go out and buy a basic two-drawer fireproof file cabinet and file folders. Some people prefer to use accordion files, which enable them to carry multiple files with them when they meet with advisors; others use both kinds of files. Do whatever works best for you.

SET UP FILES

Label the files. If you are in doubt about combining two topics, make two files. If you can't locate a document, make a file folder for it anyway in anticipation of eventually filling the file. If you use a file cabinet, one drawer can be devoted to papers you need to settle the estate and another drawer for more current financial papers. Eventually, some of these estate files will be moved to your personal files, but while you are settling the estate, these should be kept separate.

The *estate drawer* would include files for the following:

- Safe-deposit box location and key
- Your husband's will
- Copies of your husband's death certificate[1]
- Social Security records for every member of the family
- Your husband's life insurance policies
- Last year's tax return
- Your marriage certificate
- Your husband's military discharge papers (if applicable)
- Naturalization papers (if applicable)
- Divorce agreement (if applicable)
- Trust agreements for any trusts your husband may have set up or been the beneficiary of
- Most recent statements for checking, savings, and money market accounts in his name or joint names
- A list of credit cards in his name or joint names
- A list of certificates of deposit in his name or joint names
- Stock brokerage statements in his name or joint names
- His retirement asset statements (IRA, Keogh, company pension plan, etc.)
- Real estate titles and deeds for property owned
- Most recent mortgage statement
- Prenuptial or postnuptial agreement (if applicable)
- Title insurance
- Car registration or lease agreements
- Recent statement of managed portfolio (if applicable)
- Recent statements from mutual fund companies in your husband's name or joint names

---

1. You may need copies of your husband's death certificate several years hence, so make sure that you request several more copies than you think you need for present use. We suggest a minimum of 20 death certificates.

- Stock option plans
- Health insurance policy (or policies)
- Partnership agreements

Hopefully, most of the information you need for these files is someplace in your home. Your job is to get the files into one central location so they are easily accessed during the next year. Once you no longer need them to settle the estate, some of them will become part of your personal files, but for now it is a good idea to separate the estate files and the personal files.

The *personal drawer* would have the following files:

- Current bank statements
- Stock brokerage statements
- Retirement asset statements (IRAs, etc.)
- Children's accounts
- List of credit card numbers
- Credit card account bills (one for each creditor)
- Mortgage statement
- Other liabilities (college loans, car loans, personal loans)
- Life insurance policies (list of insurance companies, policy number, and coverage)
- Health insurance policies
- Disability insurance (if applicable)
- Long-term-care insurance
- Car insurance policy
- Homeowners insurance policy
- Personal liability insurance policy
- Home title
- Household inventory
- Receipts for major purchases
- Warranties and instructions
- Medical records

- Will with your lawyer's business card attached
- Living will
- Powers of attorney
- Trusts
- Burial instructions
- Naturalization papers (if applicable)
- Social Security card and recent benefits statement
- Cemetery deed
- Safe combination
- Safe-deposit box location and key
- Birth certificates for each member of the family
- Divorce agreement (if applicable)
- Military discharge papers (if applicable)
- Information related to current year's tax return
- Current bills
- List of current advisors (see chapters 5 and 6)

We realize these are a lot of files and may appear to be an overwhelming amount of paperwork. If you feel unable to cope with all of this, ask a family member or friend for help. Use setting up the files as an opportunity to socialize with a relative or friend. The most common complaint we hear from widows is the amount of paperwork involved in settling an estate. This is a legitimate complaint, but the paperwork has to be dealt with in order to figure out where you are financially.

If you are reluctant to ask a friend to help, in most metropolitan areas you can find individuals who will help organize an estate's paperwork. Typically, these "daily money managers" as they are called, will charge an hourly fee depending on the complexity of the work. Some charge an hourly fee; or if the work is ongoing, they will charge a monthly fee. At this time, there are no federal licensing requirements for daily money managers, so you'll have to rely on referrals, references, and periodic reviews. For further information, contact the American Association of Daily Money Managers (703-492-2913) or visit its Web site www.aadmm.com.

ORGANIZE AND PAY APPROPRIATE BILLS

Gather all your bills in one place and then divide them into three groups—your bills, your late husband's bills, and joint debts. You are responsible for paying both your own and joint debts. Your husband's debts should be paid from the estate account which you will set up.

If a bill you receive addressed to your husband is not a familiar one, do not pay it. A stranger (or a friend) may tell you that your husband owed him or her money. If this happens, make sure you have written proof that your husband's debt is legitimate. Have your lawyer check its accuracy before agreeing to pay it. (If you don't have a lawyer, you may need to consult one.) We recommend this precaution because there are unscrupulous people who take advantage of widows by sending them bills demanding payment for items or services they claim the husband ordered.

Itemize the current bills, making clear whose debt it is. If you have a high cash reserve, you may have no trouble paying them all. If your reserve is not high, you will have to decide which bills must be paid and which can be delayed. Mortgage payments, utilities, health and property insurance premiums, and car-related expenses should be paid first. If you don't think you have enough money to pay all your bills, it is best to write the creditors explaining your situation—that you know you owe them money and plan to pay it but you will have to pay a lesser amount until you have a better picture of your total financial situation. If you have difficulty doing this, ask someone to help you with this task.

Here again, if you feel overwhelmed by all this and can afford to do so, hiring a daily money manager (see the previous section) can help you get organized, particularly in this initial stage.

SET UP A BOOK TO RECORD ESTATE INCOME AND EXPENSES

We discuss putting together a budget in greater detail later (see chapter 7), but at this point any income you receive that was due your husband before his death (such as dividend checks) should be kept in an estate account separate from the rest of your money. When you visit your local bank, discuss the mechanics of setting up the estate account. Meanwhile, write down any checks you receive, the date received, the amount of the check, and the payor. Similarly, ask for receipts and keep a record of any expenses incurred while settling the estate.

SET UP A FINANCIAL DIARY AND A MONTHLY CALENDAR

Buy a five-by-seven-inch spiral notebook and a month-at-a-glance calendar. The notebook will serve as a financial diary for you to list what you need to do and to record what you have done and when. Don't buy a larger-size notebook because it will be cumbersome to carry with you. On the other hand, a very small size that would fit in your purse is too small to hold all the information you need. Your financial diary will be a helpful reference book should you want to recall a conversation you had with one of your advisors or anyone else. Most recent widows think they are operating perfectly rationally at the time of a meeting, but, as we mentioned earlier, a month later they may have no memory of what happened at that meeting.

On the first page of your financial diary, make a list of projects you want to or must accomplish. Then look at your month-at-a-glance calendar and decide when you are going to do each task.

In your financial diary, keep a daily account of whom you see and what was accomplished. In this book, record all conversations (phone calls or in person) that relate to your financial affairs. When your advisors see you keeping notes, they know you are serious! A phone call from you that starts, "On June 6th, we agreed that you would do such and such. It is now July 15th. How are things progressing?" puts your advisor on notice that you expect results in a timely fashion.

A typical to-do list for the first few months would read as follows:

- Get 20 certified copies of the death certificate
- Make appointments to see my lawyer and accountant (if you don't have either one, see chapter 5)
- Open a new bank account in my name (if you don't already have one)
- Open a bank account in the name of the estate
- Notify all insurance companies involved and file claims

- Report death to Social Security (and Veterans Administration, if applicable) and apply for benefits
- Notify husband's employer(s) to file for benefits
- Transfer jointly held securities to my name
- Notify custodians of IRA, Keogh accounts, and any other retirement plans of my husband's death

BUY A THREE-RING BINDER FOR FINANCIAL STATEMENTS

When you buy the spiral notebook, the month-at-a-glance calendar, and the file cabinet, also buy a three-ring binder, a three-ring punch, and a set of dividers. In this binder, make a divider for each of the financial statements you receive. For instance, make a divider for each bank and savings account you have, putting the most recent statement behind each divider. The purpose of this binder is to create a record of all financial transactions that take place during the year, a record that will be helpful when you work on your taxes.

After you have set up your home office and financial records, you need to contact your key professional advisors. In chapter 5 we review the role of each of your primary advisors and what you need to accomplish at the first meeting with each. We also discuss how to select these advisors if that is necessary.

USING A COMPUTER TO HELP YOU

If you currently use a personal computer, you may want to keep many of these estate and personal records on it. For instance, if you have been paying the household bills, you may have been using an income and expense system such as Quicken, which could be adapted to divide income and expense items for your husband's estate and yourself. You can also keep a running to-do list and record your progress as the weeks go by.

On the other hand, if you have not been using a computer, we wouldn't recommend now as a time to start learning. As helpful as the computer is, learning how to use one can be very frustrating, and you don't need to add stress to your life at this point. Six months or more after your husband's death, you may want to explore using a computer. You could buy a computer book, ask a child or grandchild for help, and/or take a computer class to learn the basics. After becoming more familiar with the computer, you may want to purchase one suitable for your needs and use it to maintain your financial records. However, we recommend you wait to tackle this new learning experience until you have finished getting organized and are well into your second stage of mourning.

BUY A FAX MACHINE/COPIER

Even if you don't use a computer, a combination fax/scanner/copier can be invaluable. This machine is relatively inexpensive and very simple to operate. By being able to copy correspondence and records before sending them, you can facilitate your communication with your advisors. Try to avoid sending original copies of anything; send copies instead. If your advisors require an original document, ask them to return it to you after they are finished with it.

SUMMARY AND CONCLUSION

Although these tasks of organizing your financial records may seem tedious and unnecessarily time consuming, they are essential to determine what your financial situation actually is. In fact some widows have told us organizing this information has helped them feel better as they gain more control of their situation.

Diane

Reactions to Getting Organized

Diane had a very difficult time dealing with the initial financial requirement of getting organized. She had never been asked to do anything that involved money. The only request Mark had ever made of her in this respect was to write on a piece of paper the amount of the checks she wrote and place it on his dresser so he could enter these amounts in the check register and balance the checkbook. When she lived at home, before marrying Mark, her dad just gave her an allowance, and in her early working days she spent her paychecks on whatever she chose. Dad had never asked her to contribute to the household expenses.

The idea of setting up files did not appeal to Diane. Here she was with her world turned upside down, and she was being asked to expend her energies on paperwork! Despite her basic resistance, however, she realized that getting her paperwork in order could help her figure out how she was going to keep the children in private school, and that was a motivating factor. Also, setting up files would give her something to do with herself other than walking aimlessly around the home, crying and feeling that her life was over. She realized how difficult it was for her to do anything these days, even something as simple as grocery shopping.

Diane was looking forward to meeting the women in the widow support group that Lisa, the coordinator, had discussed with her. She was pleased the group consisted of women at various stages of dealing with their loss; maybe one of them could relate to what she was feeling. Lisa had said there was at least one woman in the group close to Diane's age. Diane wondered how the other women dealt with all this paperwork. On the other hand, maybe she should again call Jennifer Greenberg, the widow whose daughter, Nicole, was still a classmate of Erin's. Obviously Jennifer had managed to pay Nicole's tuition.

Diane knew she could no longer ignore what had been requested of her: she must set up financial records. Maybe if she were better organized, she could begin to look at whether or not she could afford the children's tuition. Perhaps she could get Erin to show her how to use the computer. There was probably a way to utilize it for this paperwork, but just thinking about it was exhausting. Learning something new would have to wait.

Diane vaguely remembered that Mark had told her that their important papers were in his desk. It was difficult for her even to go over to the desk and open the drawers—it brought back so many memories of Mark sitting at the desk working. She wished that she had paid more attention to what he had said about their papers.

She knew Mark had some insurance in addition to what the firm provided. Maybe there was something in his file drawer. Diane pulled the drawer open and found herself crying again as she recognized Mark's neat handwriting on the labels. Not only was there a file for life insurance, but also there were files for car, household, and health insurance. When she pulled out the life insurance file, she found four policies—each from a different company. It appeared that she would receive a total of $200,000 from these policies, but she didn't know what she had to do to receive the benefits.

Diane found another file marked "Estate Planning." Maybe this was where the will was. Unfortunately, it contained only some handwritten notes Mark had made on the subject. She knew that lawyers always joked about the fact that they were the last people to have wills, even though they insisted their clients have them. She wished she understood better the implications of his not having a will.

It was becoming obvious to Diane that she needed someone to help her sort all this out. Perhaps someone in the widow support group could be of help.

Diane's To-Do List

- Call Jennifer regarding tuition options
- Go to widow support group meeting
- Find out about life insurance policies
- Attempt to set up files

Susan

Reactions to Getting Organized

Before marrying Lance, Susan had handled her own financial affairs. However, since they had been married, Lance had managed all the family's finances because he was an accountant and he enjoyed doing it. This had been a relief to Susan because she had her hands full working full-time, taking care of the home, worrying about her mother, and dealing with her stepchildren.

In her initial session with Dr. Coleman, her psychologist, Susan related her anxieties about her inability to act on any of the items she currently had on her many lists in the way she would have in the past. Dr. Coleman had suggested that Susan select the most important item from each list and place it on a single piece of paper. In this way, each sheet of paper would be devoted to the most important item from each list. When she completed acting on that item, she could cross it off and add another. Dr. Coleman suggested that for Susan this approach would be similar to the way she had functioned in the past and would minimize her present sense of being overwhelmed. If this approach didn't help, they would discuss other approaches in their subsequent meetings.

Susan was relieved to find that Dr. Coleman was addressing her practical concerns as well as trying to learn about her background. In their first meeting, Dr. Coleman had explained that her therapeutic approach could best be described as eclectic, meaning that she utilized aspects of various schools of psychological thought, rather than only one, in her approach to her clients. Dr. Coleman told Susan she felt it was essential to know something of a client's personal history in order to better understand the basis for what he or she was feeling or why he or she might be reacting in a particular way. However, she stressed that with Susan this would not preclude their focusing on her immediate needs, and she wanted Susan to make her aware of these concerns as they arose.

After her visit with Dr. Coleman, Susan decided her initial task was to set up a work area at home in her spare bedroom. She stopped at an office supply store to buy a two-drawer file cabinet and arrange for its delivery. Although she intended to set up computer records herself eventually, she thought she had better start by organizing the papers in the file cabinet. She also picked up a note pad and a calendar because she thought these would help her move ahead in the manner Dr. Coleman had suggested.

Susan's next task was to visit Lance's office and talk to Lance's partner, Harry, about Lance's personal computer records. As an accountant, Lance had set up an elaborate computer program for their personal finances. Susan had no idea how to access this information, although she did know how to use a computer. She would need some help. She planned to ask Harry about the various computer programs on the market so that she could choose one to use at home. She was sure that Lance's program would be too complex, but she liked the idea of having all the financial information she needed in one place on the computer. Susan hoped that someone at the firm could show her how to get started. Given her personality type, she was sure she could manage it on her own after some instruction if she was able to focus on it.

Meanwhile, Susan made a list of their bills and divided them into those she knew she had to pay—like the mortgage and condo fee—and those she was not so clear about—such as the VISA bill, which included client dinners Lance had hosted before his death. She made a note to discuss this with Harry because she knew Lance was usually reimbursed for client expenses. Harry had given her Lance's month-end paycheck, but because she wasn't sure what to do with it, she had not yet cashed it.

Susan realized she had a lot of accounts to keep track of and she needed to devise a system to keep track of all the statements. She had Lance's pension plan, her 401(k) plan, Lance's stock account, and the new trust account being established for Lance's children. The idea of putting the statements chronologically in a three-ring binder appealed to her organized style.

Susan needed to pull herself together and get on with the tasks ahead of her. Dr. Coleman's approach seemed to be working pretty well. Getting the files in order and making progress on the list of tasks she needed to accomplish made her feel a lot better.

Susan's To-Do List

- Set up and organize files at home
- Visit Harry regarding Lance's personal computer records
- Ask Harry about possible computer programs for her financial records
- Discuss with Harry business expenses incurred by Lance as well as his final paycheck

Audrey

Reactions to Getting Organized

Audrey had spent most of the past year visiting John in the hospital and had barely had time to keep their bills paid. However, the idea of creating order out of the current chaos appealed to her. It was something concrete she could do to demonstrate to herself she was in control.

John had already set up an adequate file system for all their important papers in his big desk in the den. While John had been sick over the past two years, Audrey had used his desk to pay the bills, so she had a pretty good idea of what their expenses had been. She decided to start keeping a notebook of her current expenses as well as people she needed to see. She realized that knowing the expenses of the past two years wouldn't be very helpful to her in estimating future expenses; however, it would be a place to start. She had been so wrapped up in taking care of John that she had had no time to spend money on anything except the basic necessities and medical bills. Fortunately, John's health insurance had been wonderful. They had had to pay very little out of pocket, but filing those insurance forms was so time consuming and tedious! She thought she might like to buy a basic fax machine—the kind that enabled her to make copies of correspondence as well. Then she could keep a record of bills she had submitted for reimbursement.

Audrey was glad she had decided to have a physical, which had been first on her list of things to do. Dr. PaPadisio's staff had always been helpful and considerate of her as well as attentive to John during the ordeal of his illness. It felt odd to Audrey to be focusing on herself in Dr. PaPadisio's all-too-familiar consultation room—the same room in which he had informed them of John's prognosis. Dr. PaPadisio had her sit down and tell him how she was doing both emotionally and physically. He listened carefully to what she reported and asked questions about her weight loss. He was pleased with her mental attitude and said they'd talk further after he completed his physical examination. Audrey thought Dr. PaPadisio was unusually thorough in his exam and wasn't sure whether he suspected something or was just being careful.

While getting dressed to return to his office, Audrey found that she was quite nervous, dreading what Dr. PaPadisio might say. When she sat down to talk with him, he seemed to sense her anxiety and quickly reassured her. He went on to say that in his initial exam he hadn't found anything that concerned him, but he would wait until he received the results of the blood work and other tests he had ordered before finalizing his medical report. He did tell her, however, that on the basis of what she had told him and his knowledge of the demands made on her time and energy in the last months of John's illness, he wanted to review her eating and exercise habit patterns with her.

Dr. PaPadisio gently admonished Audrey about the way she was eating and made several specific recommendations. He told her he wanted her to make a practice of eating regularly and offered suggestions about which foods to consider for breakfast to help her gain weight without increasing her cholesterol level. He suggested she have lunch with a friend or her daughter, Joanne, whenever possible—he thought it would force her to take the time to sit and eat in a more leisurely fashion and concentrate on what she was eating. He advised her to think about making the midday meal her largest meal of the day for the present. He knew from other patients how difficult it is to make the effort to cook only for oneself, but he wanted her to make herself something to eat in the evening, even if it was a frozen, microwavable, all-in-one meal.

Next, Dr. PaPadisio asked Audrey if she was exercising regularly. She admitted she wasn't. He asked if she still had her German shepherd; she assured him she did, adding that poor Achilles still looked for John and then looked at her as though he were awaiting his return. Saying that made Audrey realize how comforting it was to have had Achilles in the home with her all this time. She had really been neglecting him, she thought, by leaving him in the backyard. She or John used to walk him at least twice a day, but now she couldn't remember when he'd last been walked.

Dr. PaPadisio wanted Audrey to make it a practice of walking the dog once a day if the weather was suitable, gradually increasing the length of time she spent walking. He wanted to wait for the lab reports before discussing a more total fitness program with her. He commented that he understood she probably had neglected her own health because of the demands of caring for John and told her he'd have his receptionist contact her to schedule a follow-up visit after he received the lab reports. When Audrey left Dr. PaPadisio's office, she felt she had taken an important step in caring for herself. During John's illness she really had given up all of the things she enjoyed and felt were important to maintaining her health. She vowed to make an effort to focus on her physical health again, beginning with walking Achilles and eating more nutritiously and regularly.

Audrey decided she was ready to put together an agenda of what to accomplish in the next month. She needed to meet with the lawyer and the banker, check with John's company about his pension, find out about the insurance, and find someone to tell her what to do about his stock. When she drew up the list, it seemed like a lot to do, but she had learned a long time ago that if you tackle a big task a piece at a time, you can get through it all. She was determined to start her new life as soon as possible! The sooner she got started, the sooner she would be able to have an intelligent conversation with her son about where matters stood. She was sure he would want to have a serious financial discussion with her in the near future.

Audrey's To-Do List

- Call Joanne to make a date for lunch
- Eat regularly
- Walk Achilles daily
- Try to gain weight
- See lawyer
- See banker
- Call John's company about his pension
- Call about insurance
- Buy a fax/scanner/copier machine

Elizabeth

Reactions to Getting Organized

At Ben's request, over the past few years Elizabeth had gradually assumed more responsibility for paying their bills. This was due to the fact that Ben's increasing loss of memory had caused some problems, although she was finding her own memory wasn't what it used to be. If she didn't write down an appointment in a book, she was inclined to forget it, and sometimes she didn't remember everything that was said to her. In fact, it seemed that recently everyone was speaking in lower voices. She was having difficulty hearing what they were saying, and she felt awkward asking them to repeat themselves.

Although their checkbook was in pretty good order, the same could not be said of Ben's papers. The file cabinet she opened appeared to be crammed with old, out-of-date records. Elizabeth wasn't sure what to keep and what to throw out. She needed someone to help her figure out which papers were important and what to do with the rest of the stuff in Ben's file.

Elizabeth had never been asked to keep any records. Ben had taught her to enter the amount of each check she wrote in the check register as well as their deposits. Beyond that she didn't do anything, nor did she know whether Ben balanced the bank account, although she doubted it. She realized she had never given much thought to this aspect of their life.

Elizabeth did find a file labeled "Safe-Deposit Box," in which were an envelope and a key from their local bank; the key was clearly marked "Safe-Deposit Box." Elizabeth had intended to visit their bank anyway to talk with the manager about their accounts, and when she went she could also ask about opening the safe-deposit box because she had no recollection of Ben telling her about the contents.

Mabel, her close friend, had given Elizabeth a spiral notebook, telling her it had been a lifesaver to her in the early months after her own husband's death. Elizabeth stared at the clean, white pages in front of her and felt overwhelmed with all that was ahead of her. What should she put on the pages? How would she ever handle complex financial issues when she had never even balanced the checkbook? Women of her generation were not taught much about money; in fact, it had not been considered ladylike for women to talk about money. Elizabeth was really lost, but she knew she had to start the process so she would have some idea of her financial situation.

She knew she should make an appointment to see Ben's lawyer, but she really didn't know him very well. She decided to turn once again to Pastor Appletorn. She would ask him if he knew someone who could go with her to the lawyer's office. When Elizabeth met with Pastor Appletorn, he seemed to know what her worries were even before she explained them. He told her he had taken the liberty of speaking to a couple in the congregation about her. Sam Weatherly, an attorney, had recently retired, and both he and his wife, Sarah, gave a great deal of time to church activities. In fact, he had joined the church's finance committee. If Elizabeth was willing, Pastor Appletorn wanted to ask the Weatherlys to join them for tea. He thought Sam might be able to help Elizabeth deal with her financial questions.

Elizabeth was so grateful she began to cry. Just knowing someone was there was a big comfort. She was sure Ben would not have wanted strangers to know anything about their finances, but she determined to meet this couple and draw her own conclusions. She really wanted help in dealing with Ben's attorney. It felt good to have made even this small decision.

Pastor Appletorn arranged the tea for the following Sunday afternoon. Elizabeth felt guilty because she was looking forward to it. She didn't think she was supposed to look forward to anything at this point in her adjustment to her new state of widowhood. She even thought about what she might wear. She and Ben had practically stopped seeing people during the last year of his life because it was so difficult to predict when Ben would be coherent.

Elizabeth dressed very carefully and was ready considerably earlier than necessary. She wanted to make a good impression, and doing anything in a hurry tended to fluster her. She was somewhat amused when she realized that she had asked Mittens (the stray cat she had adopted) which of two outfits he thought she should wear. She had named him Mittens because his white paws reminded her of mittens.

Elizabeth arrived at the rectory punctually at 4:00 P.M. The Weatherlys arrived shortly after she did, and she liked them at once. They made her feel comfortable and talked about many things she could relate to before they began discussing her financial affairs. Sam Weatherly seemed very knowledgeable, and she thought she could trust him, so she gratefully accepted his offer to accompany her when she was ready to meet with Ben's attorney.

Elizabeth's To-Do List

- Visit bank about safe-deposit box and bank accounts
- Make appointment to see Ben's lawyer when convenient for Sam Weatherly
- Try to straighten out Ben's file of financial papers
- Force myself to begin using the spiral notebook Mabel gave me

5

Working with Key Financial Advisors

You gain strength, courage and confidence by
every experience
in which you really stop to look fear in the face. . . .
You must do the thing which you think you cannot
do.
—*Eleanor Roosevelt*

SETTLING AN ESTATE is not an easy task regardless of the size of the estate. Even if you or your husband never used professional advisors before, this is a time you should seriously consider using their services. We have observed that widows who seek professional help with various aspects of their emotional and financial situations progress more quickly to a state of well-being than those who try to do it all themselves.

Many widows initially rely on advisors their husbands had in place prior to their deaths. After your husband's estate is settled, you may want to find your own advisors, but at this stage it is easiest to work with those people familiar with your situation. However, if you find them unresponsive to your requests, replace them. The advisors' job is to help you, and if you are not being helped, they are not doing their job. At the end of this chapter, we have included guidelines for selecting advisors.

Well-meaning family members and friends may offer legal or financial advice. Keep in mind they don't know the specifics of your situation, and, as successful as they might be at managing their own affairs, their strategies may not be appropriate for you. So listen to them, but wait until you meet with your professional advisors before taking action.

Most advisors have no objection if you want to have a family member or friend with you at your initial meeting. This person may help you by asking questions you might not think to ask. Be sure to ask questions and write down the answers. There is no such thing as a stupid question—only a lack of knowledge in a particular field—and the advisor should welcome your questions. We realize having another person present when you talk to your attorney might jeopardize the attorney-client privilege, but we think the benefits of having a friend with you will often outweigh this drawback. Check with your attorney as to his or her preference in this regard.

REVIEWING THE WILL

If you are able to locate your husband's will, read it. The will names a person to settle the estate, commonly called an *executor,* or *personal representative (PR).*[1] The first thing you or the PR or the lawyer who is representing you must do is file the original will with the probate court. Most states require you to file a will within a certain period of time after the person's death. Your lawyer can tell you how soon it must be filed, or you can call the probate court and find out for yourself.

If there is no will, the probate court will appoint an *administrator* for the estates, also known as the PR. This may be a person such as yourself, your lawyer, a member of the family, or someone else. The PR, if not experienced in settling estates, should contact someone who is. Settling estates is not for amateurs unless your situation is very simple, and even then the rules and regulations are confusing.

Here are some questions you need to answer: Which creditors must be paid? Which expenses are deductible? How much can the PR be paid? Who receives the notices of probate? Through ignorance, you could easily make an incorrect distribution or miss a deadline, both of which could cost you money.

ADMINISTRATION OF THE ESTATE

Many people don't understand what the term *probate* means. It is simply the legal process whereby a court assures itself that a will is valid (or that there is no will), authorizes someone to wind up a descendant's affairs, and oversees the distribution of property to creditors and legal beneficiaries.

---

1. Some of the technical and legal terms we refer to in this chapter will vary from one state to another. In the interests of readability, we use generally accepted terminology.

Not all of your husband's property will have to pass through probate. For instance, property owned in joint tenancy with right of survivorship (both real estate and other assets such as a joint bank account) will not be probated but will go directly to the survivor. U.S. savings bonds that are co-owned or payable to a beneficiary are not included in the probate estate. Life insurance policies, deferred annuities, and IRA and other retirement plan benefits (unless the proceeds are payable to your husband's estate or the beneficiary has died) will be paid to the named beneficiary. Assets held in a living trust also escape the probate process. A lawyer or other professional advisor can help you sort through all the assets owned or partially owned by your husband.

The probate court will issue *letters of appointment* certifying the authority of the personal representative, which you will be required to supply in order to transfer assets. The various banks, brokerage firms, and other entities you contact usually require a recently dated letter of appointment (within the last 60 days). Therefore, you may have to go back to the probate court for more copies later.

We recommend you request 20 copies of the death certificate initially. These are usually supplied by the funeral director. When in doubt, *provide the parties requesting the death certificate with a copy.* If they need an original, they will tell you.

The personal representative's responsibilities may include the following:

- Send legally required notices to family and beneficiaries.

- File an inventory with the court of all money and property owned on the date of death

- Open a bank account in the name of the estate

- File periodic reports with the court and beneficiaries showing property received and amounts spent or distributed from the estate

- Obtain court permission to sell, lease, or invest property of the estate

- Have the value of the property of the estate appraised

- Deal with the creditors (determine validity of claims, reject improper claims, etc.)

- Communicate regularly with the estate beneficiaries

- Invest the estate assets until they are distributed

- File any necessary income (personal and fiduciary), estate, or inheritance tax returns. File employee tax forms, business tax forms, etc., as needed.

- Account fully for all assets collected and expenditures made from the estate

- Distribute the estate assets

As you can see, this is no easy task and one that is often best delegated to the professionals in the lawyer's office. They know what to do and can do it faster than you can. If you are anxious to reduce the costs of settling the estate, ask what you can do to help. But unless you are skilled in this type of activity, you may be more hindrance than help.

THE LAWYER'S ROLE

Your lawyer's function is to make sure that you are legally protected. Your lawyer should review the terms of the will with you and explain its implications. Unless your husband's lawyer was named as PR, you are not required to use him or her to settle the estate.

Your First Meeting

The lawyer is usually the first advisor you see. We recommend that at the conclusion of this meeting you ask the lawyer to send you a letter summarizing this meeting, reviewing what was covered and noting what action you need to take.

At this first meeting, ask how long he or she estimates it will take to settle the estate and when you can expect distributions to begin. If you are the PR, you can determine when these distributions will be made. Request a written estimate of what it will cost to take you through the estate settlement process. Many state bar associations require your lawyer to send you a *letter of engagement,* which includes this information. The fee is usually an hourly rate or a percentage of the assets involved and is paid from the estate assets. Also request periodic itemized bills so you can question any fee that appears to be out of line. This step prevents your being shocked by a huge bill at the time the estate is finally settled.

Find out whom you should call if you have a question. Most probate lawyers have very knowledgeable assistants and paralegals who are more readily available than the lawyer and can answer most questions you might have at lower hourly rates.

You should also establish what records you should keep and what the lawyer will keep. When in doubt, ask—and *don't throw anything away.* If you are inexperienced in dealing with financial matters, the lawyer can arrange to have a staff member come to your home and sort through things with you, or you can gather it all up and bring it to the lawyer's office. Of course, you will be charged for this service, but it will probably be worth the cost to make sure everything is covered. Information improperly discarded may have to be obtained or recreated at great expense. If your lawyer is unable to provide this service, you might consider using the service of a daily money manager to obtain some help with this task. (See chapter 4 for more details on AADMM).

Comment

Some widows—particularly older widows—tend to view the lawyer as a surrogate husband. Resist this impulse. Most estate planning lawyers have chosen this area of specialization because they care about people. As much as they would like to drop everything to talk with you every time you call, recognize the fact that they do have other clients who also need their attention.

THE ACCOUNTANT'S ROLE

You and your husband may have used an accountant in the past to prepare your income tax returns. If so, we recommend that you continue to use this same accountant to prepare your income tax return at least for this first, very important year. After the first year, you can assess the work done and the accountant's attitude toward you and responsiveness to your concerns. Then, when life is less stressful, you can decide whether you want to keep working with this accountant with future income tax returns.

There are several tax returns to be prepared: federal estate tax returns, state inheritance tax returns, federal and state estate income tax returns, and your personal federal and state income tax returns. Many lawyers prefer to file your estate tax returns rather than delegating that to your accountant. Make sure your accountant knows who your lawyer is so they can work cooperatively. Also make sure your lawyer and accountant know who is going to do which tax returns so there is no needless duplication or misunderstanding.

A federal estate tax return will have to be filed if the value of your husband's gross estate (including both probate and nonprobate assets) plus the amount of taxable gifts made by your husband exceeds $2,000,000.[2] The estate tax return is due nine months after your husband's death. Even if no estate taxes are due, a return should be filed so that the Internal Revenue Service (IRS) won't come back to you later with a claim. The values on this return also establish a cost basis for assets you may sell in the future. In addition, even if you don't owe a federal estate tax, you may owe an estate tax to your state of residence.

Federal and state income tax returns will have to be filed not only for the year your husband died, but also for the prior year if he died before filing a return for that year. For example, if your husband died in March, you will have to file income tax returns for the year he died and for the previous year (assuming he had not done that before his death).

In the calendar year your husband dies, you are required to file a joint personal return as long as you have not remarried by the end of the year. Thereafter, you will file as a single person unless you have dependent children. If you have dependents, then you file as "qualifying widow with dependent children" for the first two years after your husband dies and then as "head of household."

---

2. Two million dollars is the current "federal estate tax exclusion amount" for the years 2006, 2007, and 2008. The federal estate tax exclusion amount is the dollar amount of a taxable estate on which the federal estate tax is forgiven. This exclusion amount increases to $3.5 million in 2009. Then the federal estate tax disappears in 2010, and the exclusion amount reverts back to $1 million in 2011 and thereafter. **Be aware that these exclusions may change in the future.**

You and your husband might have put most of your assets in joint name. This means that, although your husband might have had a will, those assets go to you automatically as the survivor. If this is so, you will probably be using the accountant's services more than the lawyer's to compile a list of your assets and determine their current market value.

Your First Meeting

Your accountant will help determine what records are needed to prepare your tax returns and in what time sequence. Ask the accountant for an estimate of fees and what a reasonable time frame might be for this aspect of your affairs to be settled. Obviously, these will be only estimates, but note them in your financial diary. Also put down the name of the accountant's key assistant who will be available to answer your questions.

Some widows fail to have their major assets appraised because the total value of the estate is under the exclusion amount and, thus, no federal estate tax is due. You still should have all assets valued because this information helps determine the amount of taxable gain or loss when or if you sell an estate asset. In addition, in some states, you may be required to pay estate taxes to the state even though you don't owe federal estate taxes because of differences in state and federal estate tax laws.

In the case of your home, we recommend using an independent appraiser rather than a real estate agent. Such an appraisal costs more but will be more reliable. You can find the name of a certified appraiser in your yellow pages.

Comment

What if you don't have an accountant or really don't like your husband's accountant? If you don't have one, ask your lawyer or other advisors for a recommendation. If you don't like the accountant your husband used, we recommend you try to work with him or her until your income tax has been filed. Once this has been filed, you can look for a replacement.

Ask your accountant to give you an estimate of the income taxes you will owe so that you can make sure you have sufficient cash to pay them. In addition, ask the accountant for an estimate of what your income taxes will be next year. The accountant will help you determine how much should be withheld from pension payments or how much you should pay on a quarterly basis in the future. Having a good idea of what you will owe each year in taxes will be an important component of your future financial planning.

THE FINANCIAL PLANNER'S ROLE

In this initial stage, your financial planner will help you determine what your financial condition is. Your financial planner will help you put together a list of your assets and liabilities as well as your current income and expenses. If you do not have a financial planner, your accountant or lawyer can help you figure out your current situation.

Once these numbers are put together, your financial planner will help you determine what action to take now and in the future to help you become financially secure. However, it is important first to figure out exactly where you are before making any radical changes in your investments. Right now, your major concern is to determine whether you have sufficient income to pay your current expenses. Later, when you are better able emotionally to concentrate on financial matters, your planner will help you look at your longer-term goals, such as college education (for a child, grandchild, or yourself), aid for your elderly parents, and your own retirement.

Your First Meeting

In order to provide you with appropriate advice, financial planners need to have an understanding of your total financial situation. Before or at the initial meeting, the financial planner will ask you to complete a financial questionnaire, even if you are a current client. On this form, you would list your assets and liabilities and also indicate your estimated income and expenses now that you are a widow. With this information, your planner can help you put together a preliminary budget and help you make some initial investment decisions.

At this initial meeting, ask about the financial planner's fee for this current financial evaluation. Usually, you will be charged an hourly fee for this advice. If you and your husband worked with this planner before his death, this process is a lot easier because your planner will have all of your financial information.

Ask your financial planner to provide this analysis to you in writing. That way you will have something to refer back to in the future.

Comment

In the old days, the solution to a widow's need for more income was to find a rich man to marry. Today, statistics indicate that the chances for remarriage are slim. Therefore, finding a man is not a plan! Even if you do remarry, it may not be to a wealthy man—or you may choose to keep your finances separate. Some choose to live together without getting married, usually for financial reasons. (Your Social Security benefits may be reduced if you remarry.) Regardless, it is important to plan for your own financial security.

HOW TO SELECT THESE ADVISORS

Each of these key advisors must be knowledgeable, ethical, empathetic, and experienced in working with widows. Following are seven guidelines for selecting these professionals.

1. Ask your other professional advisors (accountant, financial advisor, banker) to recommend someone. Your widowed friends might also suggest someone they have worked with effectively.

2. Call the office of at least two individuals in each profession and ask for an appointment. Explain that you are looking for someone to help you and you want to meet for an initial consultation before making a decision. There should be no charge for this informational meeting. Ask what information you should bring to this meeting to make it most productive.

3. When you meet, ask the advisor if he or she will be handling your case personally or delegating it to an assistant or another person in the office. It is not unusual for an advisor to delegate part of the work, which often means that some of the work will be charged at lower rates. What is of importance is that your advisor take primary responsibility for supervising your situation. If he or she will not be doing all the work, ask to meet the person who will be assisting your advisor.

4. Ask what the advisor's hourly rate will be and how much he or she estimates the total bill will be. The more information you give your advisor in an organized fashion, the fewer hours he or she will have to spend finding the information and the lower the fee will be. However, you should not necessarily pick the person who gives you the lowest rate. The person who quotes a higher hourly rate may be more efficient or experienced and may take fewer hours to settle the estate.

5. Tell your advisor you expect to receive itemized bills on a regular basis so that you can question any bills that you don't understand or that might seem excessive.

6. Tell the advisor that you will have questions to ask occasionally. Although it is not your intent to call frequently, you do expect someone knowledgeable to respond to your phone calls in a timely fashion (within 24 hours).

7. Make it clear that you want the work prepared without unnecessary delays.

CREDENTIALS

Each profession has its own credentials. Familiarize yourself with the various professional credentials before selecting your advisors.

Selecting Your Lawyer

Your lawyer should be an estate and trust specialist. Check the *Martindale-Hubbell Law Directory*® to see if the lawyer you select is described as having had experience working with estates and trusts. If you are unable to obtain personal referrals, call your local bar association.

For complex situations you may need a more experienced lawyer. If so, there is a professional organization called the American College of Trust and Estate Counsel (ACTEC) composed of lawyers who concentrate on complex cases. The members must have a minimum of ten years' experience. However, there may not be a member in your town, or you may not need such a high level of expertise. In any case, make sure the lawyer you select has had considerable experience settling estates. Drafting a will is easier than settling an estate.

Selecting Your Accountant

The principal credential in the field of accounting is the Certified Public Accountant (CPA). However, some accountants are not CPAs but are *enrolled agents,* who specialize in preparing individual returns and can represent you with the IRS if necessary.

Your primary concern is that the accountant you select is experienced in preparing individual and estate tax returns (rather than corporate returns). If yours is a very simple situation, a tax preparer at a mass-market national firm might be helpful. However, you need to recognize that the first year you file a tax return after your husband's death everything is more complicated, so be careful in your selection.

Selecting Your Financial Planner

The best-known credential in the financial planning profession is the Certified Financial Planner practitioner (CFP®). To qualify as a CFP® practitioner, the planner must successfully complete a course of study in all aspects of financial planning and pass a comprehensive written exam. In addition, the practitioner must also have at least three years of experience counseling clients on financial planning matters. To retain certification, the planner must complete a minimum of 30 hours of continuing education credits every two years and agree to abide by a professional code of ethics.

The insurance profession has a designation for financial planners called Chartered Financial Consultants (ChFC). To earn this designation, the planner is required to pass a series of courses on financial planning (which are the same courses in the College's CFP® Educational Curriculum), meet experience requirements, maintain ethical standards, agree to take continuing education courses, and abide by a professional code of ethics.

There is also a group of CPAs who specialize in providing financial planning advice. They have their own designation— Personal Financial Specialists (PFS).

We realize this alphabet soup of designations is confusing. If the financial planner is charging a fee for giving financial planning advice and manages over $25 million, the planner should be a Registered Investment Advisor (RIA) with the Securities and

Exchange Commission (SEC) [3]. As an RIA, the planner must provide you with a FORM ADV, Part II. Ask to see this form as well as Part I; both will provide you with a lot of valuable information about the advisor's background and investment philosophy. Make sure you ask to receive this form and read it before you agree to be a client of the planner.

As with the other professional advisors you work with, it is important to ask what fees the planner will charge for providing financial planning advice. Today, most financial planners will ask you to sign a letter of agreement before doing any work for you. This agreement will outline what issues they will cover and will also include an estimated fee for this advice.

Financial planners are compensated in one of three ways: commission only, fee only, or fee and commission. Commission-only planners charge no fee or a nominal fee and are compensated primarily by the commissions generated by the products you buy through them. Fee-only planners charge an hourly fee or flat fee to provide financial planning advice. If you subsequently invest through them, they usually charge a percentage of assets managed. Fee-plus-commission planners (or fee-based planners, as they often are called) also charge hourly rates to provide financial planning advice. If you subsequently invest with them, they may charge you a percentage of the assets managed and/or they may receive commissions on investments you make.

For the initial financial planning services you require at this stage, we recommend you select a fee-only or fee-based planner who charges an hourly fee, just like your other professional advisors do. Make sure you ask for a written estimate of the fee you will be charged before agreeing to work with the planner.

HOW TO FIND YOUR ADVISORS

Estate Planning Councils

As you interview these three key advisors, ask if they belong to an Estate Planning Council. Members of this organization come from the legal, accounting, insurance, banking, and financial planning professions. Membership is a good indicator of whether your advisor is interested in working with widows. There are many good advisors

---

3. If the planner manages less than $25 million, the planner is regulated by the state in which he or she practices.

who might not belong to this organization, but members will be experienced in this field and have a strong interest in it. Be aware that such councils may not exist in smaller communities.

To locate an estate planning lawyer in your area, contact:

The **state bar association** located in your state capital (ask for a list of estate planning lawyers)

American College of Trust and Estate Counsel (ACTEC)
3415 South Sepulveda Blvd.
Suite 330
Los Angeles, CA 90034
310-398-1888
www.actec.org

To locate a tax advisor in your area, contact:

American Institute of Certified Public Accountants
1211 Avenue of the Americas
New York, NY 10036-8755
888-777-7077
www.aicpa.org/states/info/index.htm

National Association of Enrolled Agents
1120 Connecticut Avenue, NW
Suite 460
Washington, DC 20036
202-822-6232
www.naea.org

To locate a financial planner in your area, contact:

The Financial Planning Association
4100 East Mississippi Avenue, Suite 400
Denver, Colorado 80246-3053
800-322-4237
www.fpanet.org

Society of Financial Service Professionals
17 Campus Boulevard
Suite 201
Newtown Square, PA 19073
610-526-2500
www.financialpro.org

AICPA Personal Financial Planning Center
Harborside Financial Center
201 Plaza Three
Jersey City, NJ 07311-3881
888-777-7077
www.cpapfs.org

SUMMARY AND CONCLUSION

These three advisors—your attorney, your accountant, and your financial planner—are your primary helpers in the first stage of dealing with your finances after your husband's death. By this time, you should have a sheet in your financial diary that lists the name, address, phone number, and e-mail address of each of these advisors as well as their assistants' names. In the next chapter, we discuss other professionals whom you need to contact to organize your financial affairs.

DIANE

Reactions to Meeting with Key Advisors

In her feeling way, Diane knew what she wanted for her children. She anticipated that her family and close friends would try to talk her out of her desire to keep the children in their private schools. They would encourage her instead to be realistic, practical, and financially responsible, which might mean transferring them to public schools.

Upon reflection, Diane realized that Larry and the others at Mark's law firm were doing what they could to be helpful, but they had really only succeeded in confusing her. She decided she needed her own objective advisor—not a family member or friend—to help her reach the right decision about the children's schools. If at all possible, she wanted to keep them in their current schools. Mark had signed contracts with the schools before he died, and the first payments were due soon, so she had better get organized and find a way to figure this out.

Again, she decided to call Jennifer Greenberg and see if she had used someone in this capacity. She was pleased to learn from

Jennifer that in fact she had and enthusiastically recommended her financial planner, Dorothy Trumbull. Jennifer explained what role a financial planner or advisor could play and encouraged Diane to make an appointment to see Dorothy. Diane was so appreciative of how willing Jennifer was to provide her with helpful information that she asked Jennifer if they could get together some time for lunch or dinner. She knew Jennifer worked but hoped they could find a way to do so. Jennifer was receptive, which pleased Diane. She realized just how detached she had been from the lives of those less fortunate than herself before Mark's death.

Before she lost her nerve or changed her mind, Diane called Dorothy's office and made an appointment to meet with her. She asked what kind of information Dorothy needed to help her make the right decisions. She was tired of hearing from everyone what she should and should not do. In her present state she wasn't up to dealing with this issue with her father, her brother, or even Larry and his wife, Gail, as well meaning as they all were.

Diane was frightened at the thought of meeting Dorothy. This was the first time she had ever initiated anything related to finances. She knew she wanted and needed the help of an independent person, but she was afraid of the consequences of revealing her financial ignorance to this expert. She assumed Dorothy would ask her a great many questions she would be unable to answer. Diane wasn't sure she would even understand what this financial planner was talking about. She begged one of her closest friends to accompany her to this initial meeting because she didn't want to involve her family. Diane was greatly relieved when her friend agreed to join her. It hadn't been that long since Mark had died, and she was having a hard time facing the reality of his death.

The meeting turned out to be much less difficult and painful than Diane imagined it would be. Although she didn't have a lot of information, Dorothy didn't laugh at her or tell her she was foolish to even consider continuing her children in their private schools. Dorothy did tell her that she would need more information in order to help her make this decision.

When Dorothy discovered Mark had no will, she had difficulty concealing her dismay. She explained that, without a will, one-half of the assets would go to Diane and the balance to the three children. Diane would be appointed by the court to manage the assets for the children, but one-half of the assets actually belonged to them! Diane now understood why her father had been so upset. Dorothy went on to explain that if most of the assets were jointly held, the assets would go to her and would not be taxed until she died. Diane knew that the home and their checking account were in both of their names, but she wasn't sure what other assets they had or whether they were jointly owned. Obviously, she needed to do some homework.

Dorothy's questions caused Diane to realize that she knew nothing about Mark's life insurance. She remembered that the firm had provided Mark with life insurance coverage. Her dad had told her what she needed to do about the four insurance policies she had found in Mark's files, but, like everything else, she had ignored his instructions, incapable of action. Now that she realized that obtaining the information about the insurance might impact her ability to keep the children in their schools, she was motivated to learn more. It now felt right and necessary to explore this further.

Dorothy discussed the family's health insurance. She told Diane that the firm's insurance would cover them for 36 months after Mark's death, but she would have to pay the premiums that were formerly paid by the firm. Diane wondered if she was supposed to have done something about this sooner. She would have to ask Larry, although she was beginning to feel he was tiring of her constant need for his assistance.

Dorothy gave Diane a questionnaire to complete and made an appointment for her to come back and review it all with her. She explained that she would charge Diane an hourly fee for her advice. The more information Diane put together herself, the less Dorothy would charge her. Diane found the questionnaire to be a little intimidating because she was not used to financial matters. However, Dorothy reassured her about her ability to provide her with the information she needed. She checked the items she particularly needed to know to help Diane decide what to do about the children's education. She explained that the most important information she needed was what the family's assets, liabilities, and estimated sources of income were. Knowing that she had a professional advisor who was nonjudgmental about her ignorance or Mark's failure to prepare a will made her feel better.

These thoughts were unfamiliar ones for Diane. Just contemplating gathering all the necessary information was overwhelming. However, her desire to reach a particular goal— keeping the children in private schools—propelled her to overcome her resistance to addressing financial matters. The time had come for her to stop feeling sorry for herself and start doing something for the children.

SUSAN

Reactions to Meeting with Key Advisors

At this point, Susan found functioning at work and dealing with the many aspects of her mother's health needs almost more than she could handle. However, she knew she had to come to grips with her own financial status, particularly in view of her responsibilities for her mother.

The first step was to see Harry, Lance's partner and friend. He was very supportive when she met with him, telling her again how shocked and saddened everyone at the office was about Lance's sudden death. He introduced her to Sarah Stone, Lance's assistant, who was familiar with Lance's personal finance computer program. At the same time, Harry gave her information about a basic record-keeping software program as she had requested.

Sarah would help her with the estate and income tax returns. In fact, she had already applied for the estate tax identification number. Harry told Susan a return had to be filed for the estate within nine months of Lance's death. Sarah would prepare these returns, and the firm would bear the expense for this work.

Harry was aware of the $500,000 insurance trust Lance had created, which would provide Susan with lifetime income. When she died, the principal would go to Lance's children. They discussed the fact that her stepchildren would not be happy that they were not receiving more money now, but she wasn't ready to deal with them yet.

Harry recommended that Susan call the trust department of the bank Lance had named to act as the trustee for the insurance trust and ask for an appointment to go over the details. He volunteered to accompany her to the bank if she would like him to do so. Susan thanked him but said she thought she could handle that meeting by herself, although she recognized she could use some help with the stepchildren. She felt the news about their small, immediate inheritance might be better received from someone other than herself. Also the fact that the income generated by the children's trust would go to her was sure to be a problem for them. Harry agreed to help. Lance had discussed with him the reasons he had created the trust, and he thought that he could explain it to Lance's children. They might not like the terms of the trust, but he was sure it was a valid document.

Harry also told Susan that his wife, Emily, wanted to have her over for dinner and would be in touch with her shortly. Susan, usually a social person, hoped she would be able to deal with this kind gesture. Everything seemed to take so much effort these days, and she wasn't sure she was up to making dinner conversation. At the conclusion of her meeting with Harry, she felt somewhat relieved because at least she had put things in motion and was ready for the next round of appointments—with her banker, Lance's stockbroker, and the firm's benefits person.

The following week, Harry and Susan met with Tim Longwood, Lance's attorney. He went over the terms of the will and the trust with them. He assured Susan that there was nothing the stepchildren could do to get additional money. The two homes were in her and Lance's names and thus went directly to Susan. The insurance policy proceeds were payable to the trust at the bank. Lance had his pension fund, and Susan was clearly the beneficiary there. The only assets registered in his name exclusively were his stocks.

It did appear that Susan was going to have to sell some of these stocks to raise the $50,000 due her stepchildren. Tim advised her to do this as soon as possible to reduce family tension. He would be glad to talk with Adam and Leslie about their inheritance if that would be helpful.

AUDREY

Reactions to Meeting with Key Advisors

Audrey made an appointment to meet with Mr. Humphrey, the attorney. She anticipated that he would provide the guidance she needed in the near future. Undoubtedly, he would also want her to meet with John's accountant, Mr. Lewis. Following her initial meeting with Mr. Humphrey, she would involve her daughter, Joanne. She wanted to make sure she had more information before discussing anything with John Jr.

She was enjoying getting her facts together and keeping her notebook. It allowed her to feel she was not only useful but had the right to begin to make financial decisions for herself. She wondered whether she would have been able to get in touch with these emotions as quickly if John had not been ill for such an extended period of time.

Audrey felt good about her first meeting with Mr. Humphrey. He encouraged her to ask questions and acknowledged that this was a painful and difficult process. He emphasized that he didn't want her to feel foolish about posing any question any number of times. He introduced her to Sally, his assistant, and told her she would be working with him to settle John's estate. Sally was very familiar with the process of settling estates, and if he wasn't available to answer any questions, Sally would be. If for any reason Audrey wanted to speak to him personally, she needed to make that clear to the receptionist or Sally. He would contact her as soon as possible even if he couldn't do so the day she called.

To make sure Audrey was setting up the estate files correctly, Mr. Humphrey recommended that she make an appointment to meet separately with Sally. He was pleased to learn she was already well organized in this area. He also told her how to contact the Social Security Administration to determine what income she would receive in the future.

Mr. Humphrey asked her if she had a financial advisor. She said no but remembered attending a series of retirement lectures sponsored by her husband's corporation. She had been impressed with one of the speakers, a financial planner, and felt she would be comfortable calling him. Mr. Humphrey encouraged her to do so as he felt she needed someone to help her evaluate her total financial picture.

Audrey left Mr. Humphrey's office feeling better about the future. At least she had a list of instructions to follow and felt Mr. Humphrey would be helpful to her as she moved through the process of settling John's estate. She would ask Joanne to join her when she met with the financial planner.

When she got home, there was a message on her answering machine to call Dr. PaPadisio's office but that it was not an emergency. She appreciated his sensitivity to her built-in anxieties regarding calls from his office. When she returned the call, his pleasant receptionist told her Dr. PaPadisio wanted her to set up a follow-up appointment to go over her lab work and review the progress she was making with her exercise and eating programs. Audrey made an appointment for the following week. She had tried to do better with her eating but really hadn't focused on it. She hadn't yet made any arrangements to meet friends or Joanne for lunch on a regular basis and was hoping Dr. PaPadisio wouldn't ask her about it. The appointment with Dr. PaPadisio would force her to look at this aspect of her life in much the same way she was looking at the financial aspects of her life.

Dr. PaPadisio actually wanted only a consultation with her. He had his nurse weigh her, but, other than that, he just wanted to talk. He shared the lab work results with her, insisting that basically she was in good health but had neglected herself while caring for John. As he had previously indicated, he wanted her to seriously focus on nutrition and exercise. He encouraged her to take a class in nutrition or cooking that focused on cooking for oneself. Other patients had told him about courses they had taken through the local community college. If she wasn't interested in such a class, he would refer her to a nutritionist with whom he had a working relationship. Some of his patients had found this nutritionist both informative and constructive. He said he thought a class might be a better approach for Audrey because she would be with people in a similar situation. This often led to new contacts, which he thought might be enjoyable for her. She promised him she would investigate a class and get back to him about it as he had requested.

Dr. PaPadisio surprised Audrey by next inquiring about her golf game, asking if she was still playing. She hadn't thought about golf in a long time. She and John had been avid golfers, but both had given it up when John became ill. She realized she did miss it. She had played regularly with some women friends on Tuesday and Thursday mornings, and she and John had played a couples game on the weekends. At this point, she knew, her women friends had replaced her in the foursome, and, even if her game wasn't so rusty, she would be uncomfortable asking them if she could rejoin the group. However, she thought it might be a good idea to schedule some lessons with the golf pro. Although she hadn't given it any consideration before Dr. PaPadisio began asking her about her exercise program, she decided to take up golf again. At least she was able to tell him that she had taken his advice and had begun to take Achilles on a daily walk. She thought she was up to about three-quarters of a mile a day but wasn't sure. He was pleased with that and encouraged her to investigate other fitness activities.

Before Audrey left the office, Dr. PaPadisio asked her to schedule another appointment for the following month. He wanted to check her weight and possibly repeat some of the blood work. He emphasized that a preventive health plan was often the best medicine he could provide.

ELIZABETH

Reactions to Meeting with Key Advisors

When Elizabeth received the letter from the law firm with whom Ben dealt asking her to make an appointment with a Mr. Carroll as soon as she felt up to it, she panicked. Even his name—Francis Carroll—was unfamiliar. She knew she couldn't face any of this alone. She wished the idea of meeting with Ben's attorney and matters of this type didn't intimidate her so.

Elizabeth didn't agonize for any length of time about whether or not she should call the Weatherlys. She located the phone number and dialed quickly before she allowed herself to have second thoughts. Sam answered the phone, and, after some pleasantries, she read him the letter she had received from Ben's attorney. He reassured her that he had been sincere about his willingness to accompany her when she went for her initial meeting with Ben's attorney. He was somewhat surprised she had no recollection of Ben mentioning Mr. Carroll's name to her but said it would be best to go ahead and schedule an appointment. He gave her some dates when he would be available and asked her to call after she had made the appointment.

Elizabeth scheduled the appointment with the attorney for Wednesday of the same week. Sam and Sarah Weatherly picked her up. All three drove to the attorney's office, but Sarah left them to do some shopping while they had their meeting.

The law firm's reception area was very formal and intimidating to Elizabeth. When Mr. Carroll came out to meet her in the reception area, she was shocked—Mr. Carroll could not have been more than 28 years old! Ben couldn't possibly have worked with this young man! Mr. Carroll introduced himself and quickly explained that Ben's attorney had died about six months earlier and he had been given Ben's file. So that explained her lack of familiarity with the name!

Mr. Carroll perfunctorily expressed regret about her husband's death and started to usher her into his office. Sam slowed him down by introducing himself and stressing that all of this was new to Elizabeth. Sam understood that Mr. Carroll wanted to meet with Elizabeth alone but assured her he would wait until she had finished her meeting and not to worry about how long it took.

Immediately after Elizabeth sat down in his office, Mr. Carroll starting chiding her because she had not contacted the Social Security Administration, which reinforced her initial negative feelings towards this brash young lawyer. Sam had provided her with a list of questions to ask Mr. Carroll. As a result, Elizabeth learned for the first time that Ben had $500,000 in an account that was being managed by an investment advisor. Mr. Carroll seemed to indicate she would also need to meet with the investment advisor.

Elizabeth did not like Mr. Carroll at all. He was patronizing toward her and made her feel stupid. She didn't know how she was going to work with this ill-mannered man. Tears came to her eyes, but she worked at not letting him know how distressed she was. Now that she had met Mr. Carroll, she was especially pleased that such a kind man as Sam had brought her to the meeting. She would speak with him on the way home about whether she was required to work with this lawyer to settle Ben's estate. If she had a choice, she wanted another lawyer.

As soon as Elizabeth was back in the car, she asked Sam if she had to work with that arrogant Mr. Carroll. He told her she didn't. Before he could elaborate on what she could do, Elizabeth asked him if he would take her on as a client. Sam, in his considerate manner, told her he would be more than willing to do so if he were still in practice, but he wouldn't feel comfortable assuming so much responsibility for her knowing that he no longer kept up with the latest information on estate planning law. The way he said it made Elizabeth feel he was sincere and she wasn't a burden for whom he didn't want to assume any responsibility. Elizabeth apologized for asking him, but he assured her no apology was necessary.

Sam was quick to offer further help in the selection of a more appropriate lawyer, one with whom he thought Elizabeth would feel comfortable. He even offered to go with her to meet the various advisors she would need to contact to sort out her financial affairs. They agreed to start with the new attorney, whom Sam would contact on her behalf.

When Sam and Sarah Weatherly reached Elizabeth's home, they asked her if she felt up to joining them at their home for lunch after Sunday services that week. She said yes without even thinking. When she was changing her clothes, she wondered if she had agreed too quickly. Ben hadn't been dead that long, and here she was accepting social invitations. Ben would say she was "out gallivanting." She felt guilty, but she was also looking forward to spending some time with this friendly, thoughtful couple. She decided to bake her special angel food cake for the occasion. Mittens seemed to know something good was going on in the kitchen because he followed her every step while she put the ingredients together. He seemed to look at her with approval. She wasn't sure why, but she felt better having him in the home.

Sunday lunch was nice, and to Elizabeth's surprise, when they were ready for dessert, Sam told her he had asked one of the partners in his former law firm, Mr. Grossfeldt, to stop by to informally meet Elizabeth. If she felt comfortable with him, she could make an appointment to see him on a professional basis the following week. While they had coffee and cake, Elizabeth realized how easy Mr. Grossfeldt was to relate to; she knew she could talk to him about her financial affairs.

Sam and Sarah had another pleasant surprise for Elizabeth. They had also invited Pastor Appletorn to stop over for coffee and dessert. She was pleased when he appeared. It made her realize how supportive the pastor and other members of the church had been to her. She decided she would like to give something to the church. Maybe she could give them Ben's car. It was almost brand new and certainly had not been driven much. She did not feel comfortable driving anymore—it was easier to take cabs. She would ask Mr. Grossfeldt if this was a good idea when she met with him in his office.

6

Contacting Agencies and Resource People

Unanswered whys are a part of life.
—Earl A. Grollman

NOW THAT YOU HAVE MET with your primary advisors, there are other people and agencies you need to notify of your husband's death almost immediately. They will give you a better idea of what your assets are and what sources of income you can expect to receive. These other agencies include your bank and your insurance and mortgage companies. You also need to talk with the Social Security Administration, the Department of Veterans Affairs (if applicable), and your husband's employer. If you have an account with a stockbroker or an investment advisor, they need to be consulted as well.

BANK

You may be familiar with your bank accounts or not. In any event, call your bank and ask for an appointment to talk with the manager. Explain your situation and ask the manager to help you make any necessary changes to your accounts. If your husband had an account in his name, this should be changed to an account reading "Estate of." If you had a joint account, it will eventually be moved to an account in your name. If you have no account in your own name, you should establish one.

To transfer the bank accounts, you will need the recently dated Certificates of Qualification as proof that you are the personal representative and a certified copy of the death certificate. You will receive Certificates of Qualification when you appear before the clerk of the court in the county/city in which you live to qualify as the executrix. As for any outstanding checks on the existing accounts, you can arrange to have these honored or not as you wish. The bank should not automatically make payments out of your husband's account. However, if the personnel don't know of your husband's death, they will honor any checks presented and continue any automatic payments from his account.

In any event, open a bank account in the name of the estate. To establish this account, you would initially use your spouse's Social Security number and then substitute the estate's tax ID number when it is received from the Internal Revenue Service. Any income received from assets listed in your spouse's name should be deposited in this account.

All expenses associated with the administration of the estate—these include all expenses related to the funeral as well as medical bills—should be paid from the estate account. If you have already advanced payments from your own funds to cover these expenses, you should keep the receipts and reimburse yourself from the estate account once there are sufficient funds in it to do so. The receipts will be needed if a court accounting is required.

Ask to see a list of all accounts, both individual and joint, you and your husband have at the bank. These may include retirement assets (such as IRA accounts) as well as your checking accounts, savings accounts, and certificates of deposit. You may also have an investment account with your bank. If you have any loans with the bank, they may have to be renegotiated.

You may also have a safe-deposit box. The regulations that determine whether you have access to this box vary from state to state. In some states, you must have a tax assessor and a state registrar accompany you to the box to make sure you don't remove something before the estate assets are valued.

The manager should explain what services the bank offers, just as he or she would to any new depositor. You may need different services than your husband did. Keep in mind that the banker wants to retain your account. Just as you did with your other advisors, ask for a contact person to call with questions about your account.

You and your husband may have had accounts in more than one bank, which complicates the situation. You should notify each bank of your husband's death. Then follow up your inquiry with a letter instructing the bank to establish a new account.

You need to include in your letter a certified death certificate and a Certificate of Qualification.

Comment

Bankers are accustomed to helping widows, but be cautious about initially investing your money at the bank. Certainly, putting money in savings or money market accounts is fine because you can withdraw it at any time, but at this time don't make any longer-term investments. The manager may discuss with you the services offered by their bank's investment department and trust department. You may want to learn more about these options later, but right now your goal is to gather information about the assets available to you. *Don't make any long-term commitments until you have had time to look at your total picture.*

MORTGAGE HOLDER

If you had mortgage insurance, the insurance company will pay off the mortgage on your home on notification of your husband's death. If your husband had life insurance, you could use the proceeds to pay off the mortgage, although in most instances this might not be the best use for that money. Wait until you can ask your financial planner about this. In any case, you should advise your mortgage company that you will be the person responsible for making the payments henceforth. If you want these payments to be paid automatically from *your* checking account, make sure that the mortgage company has the bank account number of your new account.

REAL ESTATE TITLE

As part of settling the estate, you will want your joint properties retitled, which involves preparing a new deed and submitting it to the recorder of deeds in your jurisdiction. This should be done now to facilitate a sale at a later date. Your lawyer can take care of this for you.

CREDIT CARDS

Many of the credit cards in your husband's name were issued because of his earning ability and credit. If you don't have the same earning power, the credit card companies may be reluctant to provide you with the same lines of credit until you demonstrate your credit worthiness. Some widows solve this by neglecting to notify the credit card companies of their husband's death, but then, if you do this, it will delay your establishing your own credit history. Eventually, you should notify all credit card companies of your husband's death, although there is no urgency to do so.

Most investment firms offer credit cards connected to your investment account. This may be an easy way to start establishing your own credit.

LIFE INSURANCE AGENT

If your husband had an insurance agent, this individual will have information on all the life insurance policies in force and will provide you with the necessary claim forms and instructions to obtain the proceeds of these policies. If your husband bought from various agents over the years, you need to notify each insurance company of his death. A brief letter such as the one shown in figure 6.1 will suffice. The company will require a certified copy of the death certificate and a completed statement of claim. Some companies also require that the policy be submitted.

FIGURE 6.1 Sample Letter to Insurance Company

Your name and home address

Date

Dear Sir or Madam:

This letter is to advise you that my husband (*full name*) died on (*date*). His policy number was _____ . Please send me whatever documents I need to claim the proceeds. Would you search your files to determine if he had any other coverage with your company?

Sincerely yours,

Your signature

If you can't find the actual policy, you need to ask for a lost policy form. If you don't know the address of the insurance company, look in your phone book for a local office and call it to find out where to write to get a lost policy form.

If you are not sure whether your spouse owned life insurance and you can't find the policy or remember the name of any life insurance agent he might have been working with, look through your spouse's checkbook and canceled checks for payments made to an insurance company.

If your husband made the insurance proceeds payable to a trust, then the trustee is the person to complete the claimant's statement and submit the documents to the insurance company.

As the beneficiary of life insurance policies, you will be asked how you want to receive the proceeds. You can choose to receive this money in a lump sum, in installments over your lifetime or for a fixed number of years, or in installments of a specified amount until the proceeds run out. This is another decision you should defer until your advisor has looked at your total picture. In the meantime, you can leave the money with the insurance company and have it accumulate interest on the principal for you.

The insurance agent may have some suggestions as to how you should invest the money. Once again, at this point, even if the recommendations sound wonderful, don't make an investment you can't change later. Ask the agent to put these recommendations in writing so that you can consider these ideas seriously when you are ready to make your investment decisions. Also ask for a review of your own life insurance policies. If your husband was the beneficiary, you will have to change this designation.

MEDICAL INSURANCE

If your husband had been ill, you may be faced with a confusing array of insurance bills. One of your financial advisors can help you sort through the medical bills, review the claims for accuracy, and appeal denied ones. An organization called Alliance of Claims Assistance Professionals (ACAP) can be of help for a fee. For a referral to a member of this organization in your area, visit the internet site www.claims.org. Before hiring a claims assistant, who charges an hourly fee, make sure the ACAP member is licensed, bonded, and insured. Also check his or her references.

If you are covered under your husband's group health insurance plan through his employer or former employer, you should contact the employer to determine whether your current coverage will be affected.

HEALTH INSURANCE

We find widows are most concerned about health insurance coverage, particularly if they have witnessed the major expenses incurred by their husband's illness. If your husband had health insurance through his employer and the firm had at least 20 employees, the so-called COBRA regulations issued by the Department of Labor require his firm to continue to offer insurance coverage to you and your family for 36 months. It is likely that while your husband was employed, the firm contributed to or paid for this coverage. If so, your cost for this coverage will be higher than your husband paid. You will pay the group rate for yourself and your dependent children. However, after 36 months, you must find your own insurance, and this can be very expensive.

In some cases, particularly if you are concerned about your own health condition, you might want to go ahead and apply for your own insurance so that you are not in the position of coming to the end of the COBRA protection and find your health will not permit your being insured privately—or at prohibitive rates. If your husband was retired, health insurance may have been one of his retirement benefits. If he was over the age of 65, Medicare may have been covering him. He also may have had some kind of supplemental (Medigap) coverage.

SOCIAL SECURITY ADMINISTRATION

The toll-free number for the Social Security Administration is 800-772-1213, and you can call this number weekdays 7:00 A.M. to 7:00 P.M. The Web site is www.ssa.gov. Someone in this government organization will be able to answer most of your questions and can refer you to your local office if you want to make an appointment to see a representative. You can apply in person or by phone; we recommend that you make an appointment to meet with someone at the Social Security Administration office. Claims may be expedited if you go in person to the nearest office to sign a claim for survivor benefits. To file your claim, you will need the following:
- your husband's Social Security number and birth certificate
- your Social Security number and birth certificate
- your husband's death certificate
- your marriage certificate
- the birth certificates and Social Security numbers of your dependent children (if any)
- documentation of your husband's earnings the year he died (if he was still working) as well as the W-2 for the previous year. If your husband was self-employed, there will be no W-2 form available, so bring a copy of last year's tax return instead.

These documents (or certified copies of these documents) will have to be mailed if you apply by phone.

If your husband was receiving Social Security benefits at the time of his death, do not cash the check paid to him the month after his death. No benefit is payable for the month of death. If benefits were paid by direct deposit, contact the bank or other financial institution to request that any funds received for the month of death or later be returned to Social Security. If both of you were previously receiving Social Security payments, then you as the survivor may be entitled to receive a higher monthly benefit. This would be true if previously you had been receiving one-half of your husband's benefit. At his death you are eligible for 100 percent of his benefits (less if you are between age 62 and your full retirement age). You are not eligible to collect both your benefits and his benefits. To make this change, notify the Social Security office.

Under present regulations, if you are at least 60 years old, you may claim survivor benefits. However, the amount you receive will be significantly lower than what you would receive if the payments start after you reach your full retirement age. This ranges from age 65 to age 67, depending on the year in which you were born (see figure 6.2). The Social Security office will explain this to you in greater detail. If you are under age 60 and have dependent children who are under the age of 16 or are disabled, you are eligible for a mother's benefit. Your unmarried children will receive benefits if they are under age 18 or up to age 19 if they attend secondary school full-time or at any age if they are disabled.

If you are under age 60 and have no dependent children, you are not eligible for any payments, but you should still register your husband's death with the Social Security Administration and apply for the death benefit payment (currently $255). To receive this benefit you need to apply within two years of his death. If your
husband was previously married for longer than ten years, his former wife (if she is unmarried) is able to collect Social Security benefits as well. In other words, you will share his benefits with her, but this will not affect the amount of your benefits.

You can work while receiving Social Security benefits, and doing so could mean a higher benefit for you in the future. However, if you work and have not yet reached your full retirement age, your current Social Security benefits will be reduced if you earn more than the annual limit. In 2006 the limit was $12,480 (this figure is increased annually for inflation). If your earnings exceed the annual limit, your Social Security benefits will be reduced by one dollar for every two dollars your earnings exceed the limit. If you plan to work, you should take this annual earnings limit into consideration. You can read more about Social Security benefits on the Internet www.ssa.gov.

FIGURE 6.2 Full Retirement Ages for Social Security Survivor Benefits

Full retirement age has been 65 for many years. However, this is no longer true. For widows born in 1940 or later,see the chart below.

Year of Birth	Full Retirement Age
1939 or earlier	65
1940	65 and 2 months
1941	65 and 4 months
1942	65 and 6 months
1943	65 and 8 months
1944	65 and 10 months
1945-56	66
1957	66 and 2 months
1958	66 and 4 months
1959	66 and 6 months
1960	66 and 8 months
1961	66 and 10 months
1962 or later	67

Note: If you were born on January 1 of any year, you should refer to the previous year.

MEDICARE

You are eligible for Medicare if you are age 65 or older, or if you have received Social Security disability benefits for at least 24 months. Medicare has traditionally had two parts: hospital insurance and medical insurance. Hospital insurance (Part A) helps pay for inpatient hospital care and certain follow-up care. Medical insurance (Part B) pays for physicians' services and some other services not covered by hospital insurance. Starting in 2006, Medicare offers a third type of coverage (Part D) which provides prescription drug coverage.

In most cases you should opt for Medicare coverage if you are eligible. There is no cost for Part A coverage, but you are charged a monthly premium for Part B and Part D. In some cases it makes sense to defer enrollment in Part B and Part D, but it is important to understand the implications of doing so before you take any action. (See chapter 12 for more details.)

The Social Security Administration handles Medicare eligiblity and enrollment. If you are eligible for Medicare but have not yet enrolled, we suggest you call this agency for assistance in deciding whether you should enroll in any of the benefits available to you at this time (800-772-1213) www.ssa.gov.

VETERANS ADMINISTRATION

If your husband was a veteran, contact the Department of Veterans Affairs. A toll-free telephone service is available in all states. Most states also provide their own veterans benefits. Both the federal government and the state government will want the same information you furnished the Social Security Administration. If you are eligible for benefits, they will reimburse you for some of the burial and funeral expenses as long as you file a claim within two years after your husband's burial or cremation. You may also be eligible for a pension for yourself or your children. For further information, call 800-827-1000 or visit www.va.gov.

YOUR HUSBAND'S PENSION BENEFITS

Whether your husband was still working or was retired when he died, you need to contact the company benefits person at the last place he worked to determine what benefits you should be receiving in the form of pension income, life insurance proceeds, or health insurance coverage (see figure 6.3). If your husband was still employed when he died, you are entitled to receive group health insurance rates for yourself and your family for up to 36 months after his death.

You may have to decide how you will receive pension benefits from your husband's employer. Usually, you can choose to receive the full amount in either a lump sum or lifetime payments. If you do have a choice, ask for time to consult your financial planner before making this important decision. Usually your money will earn interest until you make the decision.

Your husband may have worked for more than one company and qualified for more than one retirement plan, so it is important to contact all previous employers just in case you might be eligible for pension benefits from more than one company.

FIGURE 6.3 Sample Letter to Employee Benefits Department

Your name and home address brackets (or italics) will help differentiate actual text of letter from specific information to be provided

Date

Dear Sir or Madam:

My husband *give full name and Social Security number* died on *date*. Please provide me with information about any employee benefits for which I am eligible as his widow. Please let me know if I have a choice of settlement options. I can be reached at *phone number*. I look forward to hearing from you soon.

Sincerely yours,

Your signature

OTHER RETIREMENT PLANS

Your husband may have had his own IRA and Keogh plans invested at his bank or with his stockbroker, financial planner, or insurance agent. Try to locate these accounts. Last year's tax return may be helpful in locating this information. Each plan is held by a custodian trust company. When the plans were established, the custodian for the retirement account should have required a beneficiary to be named. You need to notify the custodian of your husband's death. The custodian will notify the beneficiary.

Assuming you are named the beneficiary, these assets can be invested in your own IRA account, but you need to consult with your financial advisor to make sure this is a good decision. What you are trying to establish now is which retirement accounts your husband had and who is the beneficiary of each account. It is a good idea to determine this information as soon as possible even if you don't plan to withdraw any money from these accounts immediately. At the same time, if you have IRAs, Keoghs, or any other retirement plans in your own name, you will want to change the beneficiary on these as well (assuming your husband was the named beneficiary).

DEFERRED ANNUITIES

A *deferred annuity* is an investment made with an insurance company where your money earns interest sheltered from current taxation. Your husband may have purchased a deferred annuity through his stockbroker, financial planner, insurance agent, or bank. This investment is usually intended as a supplementary retirement investment because in most cases there are penalties for withdrawing the money before age 59 1/2. When the annuity was purchased, someone was named as beneficiary.

You need to inform the annuity company of your husband's death. The company will require you to send it the death certificate and will notify the beneficiary what options are available. Even if you are not the beneficiary, the proceeds of this annuity are still part of your husband's taxable estate if your husband was the owner of the annuity. See chapter 8 for more information about deferred annuities.

STOCKBROKER

Before your husband's death, you or your husband may have worked with a stockbroker. If so, you should inform the stockbroker of your husband's death and ask what paperwork is required to change the name on the account either to an estate account (if it was your husband's account) or to your name (if it was a joint account).

If the assets were in your husband's name alone, then they will go into an estate account and eventually to the heirs once the estate is settled. You or the personal representative can transact business in this account before the estate is settled, but you need the estate tax ID number to do so. The account will be retitled "Estate of John Doe; Mary Doe, Personal Representative."

FIGURE 6.4   Sample Letter of Instruction for Assets Held in Your Husband's Name

---

Your name and home address

Date

Dear Sir or Madam:

This letter is to notify you that *full name of your spouse* died on *date*, and I have been appointed as his personal representative.

Please change your records of ownership to "Estate of *name of your spouse, name of personal representative*, Personal Representative." Please report to the IRS all dividends and interest received after that date under the estate tax ID number *insert number here*.

Enclosed is a court-certified copy of the death certificate, an affidavit of domicile, and my recently dated appointment as personal representative.

Add the following paragraph if applicable

In addition, my husband was listed as custodian for accounts held in the names of *child(ren's names*. Please change the custodian to my name. The child(ren)'s Social Security number(s) will remain the same.

Sincerely yours,

Signature of personal representative

To transfer your husband's stock and bond positions, you need a court certified death certificate, notarized affidavit of domicile (provided by the stockbroker), the court appointment of the personal representative (dated within the last 90 days), the tax ID number for the estate, and a letter of instruction signed by the personal representative. A sample letter of instruction is provided in figure 6.5. For some assets, you may need a bank or a stock brokerage firm to guarantee the signature of the personal representative. In addition, some may require a new account application. Whatever is needed, your stockbroker or his or her assistant will help you with the process.

FIGURE 6.5   Letter of Instruction If the Stocks Were Held in Your Husband's Revocable Trust and You Are the Successor Trustee

---

Your name and address

Dear Sir or Madam:

This letter is to notify you that *name of your spouse* died on *date* and I have been appointed as his personal representative. Please change the title of this trust to *insert new name of trust*. The successor trustee is *insert name of successor trustees*. Please report to the IRS all dividends and interest received after the date of death under the new trust tax ID number *insert number here*.

Enclosed is a court-certified copy of the death certificate, an affidavit of domicile, and my recently dated appointment as personal representative. Also enclosed is a copy of the trust document showing the named successor trustees.

Sincerely yours,

Signature of personal representative

Transferring joint assets is usually easier. To transfer these, you need a certified copy of the death certificate, an affidavit of domicile, and a letter requesting transfer to your name (see figure 6.6). The letter of request should include your Social Security number. If you hold the stock certificates yourself, you need one set of papers for each company, and the stockbroker can help you process the transfer.

FIGURE 6.6 Letter of Instruction If the Stocks Were Held Jointly

---

Date

Dear Sir or Madam:

This letter is to notify you that *name of your spouse* died on *date*, and I was the joint tenant of this account *specify account number.*

Enclosed is a court-certified copy of the death certificate as well as an affidavit of domicile. Please transfer the assets in this account to my name.

Thank you for taking care of this matter for me.

Sincerely yours,

Your signature Your Social Security number

Ask the stockbroker to value the assets in any accounts you have (your husband's account and joint accounts) as of the date of death. The estate valuation for stocks and bonds will be based on the average of the high and low prices on the date of death. If he died on the weekend, you average the high and low prices for Friday and Monday and then average those two prices.

Do this right away while the information is easy to obtain. As we mentioned before, this information is important because the tax on the estate assets is based on this value or the value of the estate assets six months later. Further, the value of the assets in the estate used to determine the estate tax bill becomes your cost basis should you sell anything at a later date.

Your husband may have bought limited partnerships or non traded real estate investment trusts from your stockbroker or financial planner. If so, you need to notify him or her in writing of your husband's death, ask for an estate valuation as of the date of your husband's death, and request that the units be transferred to the estate name if they were owned by your husband. If the units were in joint name, they can be transferred to your name by the broker or planner, who will advise you as to the information required to effect the transfer. This process varies from company to company, and there may be a charge for the transfer.

Tell the stockbroker you don't want to make any radical moves before you and your financial advisors have looked at the total picture.

However, if the stockbroker recommends that you sell a particular security sooner rather than later because of negative news about the company, follow that advice. Request that the proceeds be put in a money market fund[1] to earn interest for the time being until you finish assessing your financial situation.

INVESTMENT ADVISORS/MONEY MANAGERS

The terms *investment advisor* and *money manager* are used interchangeably. Investment advisors are paid a fee based on a percentage of money managed. Your husband may have had a professional investment advisor manage his or your personal portfolios or his retirement assets.

You need to notify that investment advisor of your husband's death and ask for an evaluation of the account as of the date of death. In view of your new circumstances, also request written recommendations for any changes in the portfolio that was being managed. Again, this account (if in your husband's name) should be retitled to read "estate of" and should show the new tax ID number for the estate.

Ask for a copy of the contract your husband signed with this money manager. Most money manager contracts have a 30-day notification-of-termination clause. Have your lawyer review the document. Because the contract was with your husband and he is no longer alive, you don't have a current contract. Nevertheless, you will probably want to maintain this relationship until you have had time to look at your total picture.

TRUST OFFICER

Your husband may have been the beneficiary of a trust created by his family. Now that he is deceased, the assets of that trust will go to the specified heirs, which may be his children. The trust document will spell out what is to happen as a result of his death. It is important that you notify the trust officer of your husband's death and ask for a copy of the trust agreement if you are not familiar with its terms.

Your husband may have set up a trust for your benefit and named a bank as trustee. If so, make an appointment to meet with the trust officer so that you can discuss your situation. You will want to know what

---

[1] An investment in a money market fund is not insured or guaranteed by the Federal Deposit Insurance Corporation or any other government agency. Although the Funds seeks to preserve the value of your investment at $1.00 per share, it is possible to lose money by investing in the fund.

investment options are available to you, how often you will receive reports, and what the bank's management fees will be. Usually, the bank charges a percentage of the assets to manage the trust and also takes a percentage of the income generated. There is usually a minimum annual fee. Ask for a written schedule of fees for your files.

Unless the trust is worth over $500,000, most banks will invest the trust assets in their own managed account funds. You should ask them to give you a written record of how these investments have performed over the past year as well as the past five and ten years. You should have your financial advisor review this information for you to assess how well the trust department has managed assets in the past.

Have the trust officer explain how much annual income you might expect to receive from the trust account and how frequently it will be paid. Also ask if the trust document gives you the right to withdraw principal. In most cases, trusts provide the surviving spouse the right to receive the net income (after fees are deducted) earned by the trust as well as the right to access principal under certain conditions. Make sure you understand the terms of the trust.

MOTOR VEHICLES

If any of the cars you have were registered in your husband's name, you need to notify the local office of your state Department of Motor Vehicles so that the title or registration can be changed. Registration should be in your name when you sell, trade in, or give away the car. If you plan to keep the car and there is an outstanding loan against it, you may choose to keep making payments and delay correcting the registration until you sell the car. These are decisions that should be made with your financial advisor.

If your husband's car was leased in his name, you can turn in the car to the car dealership where the car was originally leased. You can terminate the lease, or, if you want to keep the car, the dealership will help you obtain a new lease.

PROPERTY AND CAR
INSURANCE COMPANIES

The insurance on your home, car, and valuables is often with a different insurance company than the one that provided your husband's life insurance coverage. In addition, you may have your home insurance with a different company than your car insurance. At a future date, you may want to make some changes here, using one company for both types of coverage, but now you need to change the existing policies to delete your husband as an insured party. Presumably, you will need the same level of coverage on your home, but it may be necessary to adjust your car coverage.

UTILITY AND TELEPHONE BILLS

Eventually you will want to change these accounts to your name, but this isn't an urgent matter. You may want to change your listing in the telephone book as well. Many widows choose to keep the listing under their husband's name to avoid annoying calls. Others opt for an unlisted number.

YOUR CHILDREN'S SCHOOLS

From an emotional as well as a financial point of view, you need to notify the principal of your children's schools of your husband's death. If your children attend a private school, you may not be able to afford to keep them there. After the principal knows your circumstances, then you can have a frank and realistic discussion about your financial options. The principal should also keep you informed of any behavioral or academic changes the children may display after your husband's death.

Following the death of a parent, a child (or children) may display changes in academic achievement and behavior. Some children continue to do well because the school represents the stability that no longer exists at home. Others deteriorate because their emotional upset prevents them from functioning as they have in the past. Some children are no longer able to participate in sports or other extracurricular activities as they had in the past. It is important for the widow to be aware of her children's needs in order to provide them with any assistance in the form of counseling they might need.

Many schools have guidance counselors who meet with small groups of children to deal with issues related to separation and divorce. Some schools might include in these groups children experiencing loss from death.

CLUBS, FRATERNAL ORGANIZATIONS, AND COLLEGES

You should notify all social and business clubs, fraternal organizations, and alumni groups of your husband's death. You may want to remain as a member of the social clubs. Some offer reduced dues for widows.

TELEMARKETERS

We realize that this last category of people doesn't quite fit in this chapter. However we didn't want to ignore this topic. There are too many stories about widows being victimized by strangers calling them on the phone and trying to sell them something.

If you are receiving unwanted calls from telemarketers, there is action you can take to prevent these calls. The National Do Not Call Registry is managed by the Federal Trade Commission (FTC). You can register up to three personal telephone numbers, including your cell phone. Once you register, telemarketers have 31 days to stop calling you. It does not cost anything, and your registration will remain in effect for five years.

You can register by phone (888-382-1222) or online www.donotcall.gov. If you receive unwanted telemarketer calls more than 31 days after you have registered, you can file a complaint. Note that charities and political organizations are allowed to continue calling you even if you register. If you make a purchase from a company, a representative from that company is also allowed to call you unless you ask the company not to.

SUMMARY AND CONCLUSION

By this time, you have set up a work area with a file cabinet. You have a financial diary partially filled with notes and a monthly calendar of tasks partially completed. You have contacted those people who need to know about your husband's death. Now it is time to organize the information you have gathered so far in order to plan your financial future.

Begin by making a list of people and organizations to notify:

- Banker
- Mortgage holder
- Recorder of deeds
- Credit card companies
- Life insurance agent
- Social Security Administration
- Your husband's former employer
- Other retirement plans
- Insurance company that issued your husband's deferred annuities
- Stockbroker
- Investment advisor
- Trust officer
- State Department of Motor Vehicles
- Property and car insurance companies
- Utility and telephone companies
- Personnel at children's schools
- Clubs, fraternal organizations, colleges

Now that you have identified your key advisors, make a list of important names and numbers (see figure 6.7). Put a copy of this list in your file labeled "Professional Contacts" and make sure a responsible person knows where this list is located.

FIGURE 6.7   List of Key Advisors (continued)

Employer:_____

Address: _____

_____

Phone:_____

Fax:_____

E-mail address:_____

Contact name:_____

Attorney:_____

Firm name: _____

Address: _____

_____

Assistant's name: _____

Phone:_____

Fax:_____

E-mail address:_____

Accountant: _____

Company name: _____

Address: _____

_____

Phone:_____

Fax:_____

Assistant's name: _____

E-mail address:_____

Financial planner: _____

Company name: _____

Address: _____

_____

Phone:_____

Fax:_____

Assistant's name: _____

E-mail address:_____

Mortgage company: _____

Phone:_____

Fax:_____

Contact name:_____

E-mail address:_____

Insurance agent (life):_____

Company name: _____

Address: _____

_____

Phone:_____

Fax:_____

Assistant's name: _____

E-mail address:_____

Insurance agent (homeowners): _____

Company name: _____

Address: _____

_____

Phone:_____

Fax:_____

Assistant's name: _____

E-mail address:_____

Insurance agent (car):_____

Company name: _____

Address: _____

_____

Phone:_____

Fax:_____

Assistant's name: _____

E-mail address:_____

Stockbroker: _____

Company name: _____

Address: _____

_____

Phone:_____

Fax:_____

Assistant's name: _____

E-mail address:_____

Trust officer: _____

Company name: _____

Address: _____

_____

Phone:_____

Fax:_____

Assistant's name: _____

E-mail address:_____

Investment advisor:_____

Company name: _____

Address: _____

_____

Phone:_____

Fax:_____

Assistant's name: _____

E-mail address:_____

Physician: _____

Address: _____

_____

Phone:_____

Fax:_____

Assistant's name: _____

Emergency phone: _____

Mental Health Professional: _____

Address: _____

_____

Phone:_____

Fax: _____

Assistant's name: _____

Emergency phone: _____

Name of school:_____

Contact name:_____

Address: _____

_____

Phone:_____

Fax: _____

Note: Make sure the school knows how to reach you in an emergency

Diane

Reactions to Contacting Agencies and Resource People

When Diane returned from her meeting with Dorothy Trumbull, her new financial planner, she called Mark's office and asked for the person who handled the firm's insurance plans. She was advised that Karen Hutchinson handled these matters, so she made an appointment to meet with her toward the end of the week.

It took a great deal of determination and courage for Diane to cross the threshold of Mark's office. It held so many memories for her. She didn't think she could bear to hear the expressions of condolence and concern from Mark's partners and the murmuring of the secretaries and other support staff to one another, which she was sure identified her as Mark's widow. She was sure they would also be commenting among themselves about her appearance and demeanor.

Diane was relieved that few people she knew were around when she arrived for her meeting with Karen Hutchinson. Karen was ready for her, and, after appropriate but brief condolences, she was all business. She explained that Mark had a life insurance policy with the firm that was worth $800,000. Diane had some options as to how she could receive this money, which the insurance agent handling the firm's account would explain to her. Karen gave Diane the agent's name and phone number. She confirmed that Diane would be able to maintain health insurance for herself and her children through the firm at their group rates for 36 months. Thereafter, she would have to make other arrangements.

In addition, Mark had a retirement account worth about $300,000, which he had managed himself and which was invested in stocks. Karen gave Diane the name and phone number of the stockbroker with whom Mark had worked. Finally, Mark had something called a capital account, which represented his investment in the firm. This account was worth $100,000 and would be available to her in the near future on a tax-free basis.

As Diane sat there and listened to Karen speaking in her dry, matter-of-fact voice, she allowed herself to be encouraged despite her lack of knowledge. By her rough calculations, it appeared that she had $1,200,000 coming to her from the firm. In addition it appeared she would receive $200,000 from Mark's other insurance policies. Surely this would be enough to allow her to keep the children in their present schools. She thanked Karen for her time and the information and prepared to contact both the firm's insurance person, Jack Blafford, and Mark's stockbroker, Scott Truitt.

As she left Mark's office, Diane made a mental note to share her feelings about going into Mark's office at her next widow support group meeting. As she walked toward her car in the parking lot—a familiar route for Diane in the past—she found herself thinking that the woman now crossing the street to the parking lot was not quite the same woman who had been married to Mark, the successful lawyer. Tears welled up in her eyes and rolled slowly down her cheeks. Mark didn't even know the women in the widow support group with whom she now shared her feelings and anxieties. Robyn, the schoolteacher, somewhat older than herself, had discovered that her financial situation was abysmal following her husband's illness and death. However, she was ever ready with a warm smile and words of encouragement for Diane. Marcy, in her late fifties, was eager to do whatever small thing she could to help Diane. Diane had come to rely on these new friends because they understood what she was experiencing. In some ways, she mourned the loss of the old Diane, yet she was finding strengths she never dreamed she had.

In her determination to move ahead in acquiring the financial information necessary to decide about the children's schools, Diane called both the firm's life insurance agent and Mark's stockbroker as soon as she got home. She reached Jack Blafford first and scheduled an appointment with him for the early part of the next week. Then she set an appointment to meet with Scott Truitt for the Friday of the same week.

Although she had considerable anxiety about going by herself to discuss money matters, Diane decided to believe what the women in her support group said about her strengths—they saw her as bright and outgoing. She would "bite the bullet" and try to see the insurance agent by herself. Jack turned out to be a very pleasant, well-dressed man about her age. He explained that she had some choices to make about the insurance money due her. She could receive it in a lump sum and invest it, or she could buy an annuity that would provide her with $3,454 in monthly income for the rest of her life. In fact, he told her that she had several choices as to how to receive the income. Until she decided what she wanted to do with this money, it would be earning interest at the insurance company.

Diane's initial reaction was one of relief. This nice man could handle the insurance for her, and she would not have to worry about managing such a large sum of money herself. She thought investing in the annuity was a good solution, but, to appear more adult, she told him she wanted to think about it for a few days. However, what he had told her made a lot of sense. He was so sympathetic to her situation. After she left, she reminded herself that she had promised Dorothy she wouldn't do anything without at least discussing it with her first. Diane was sure Dorothy would agree with the idea of receiving monthly income from the fixed annuity, but she would run it by her anyway.

Diane felt less secure about dealing with a stockbroker than an insurance agent. She considered asking one of the members of her support group to accompany her on this visit but decided instead to ask the mother of one of Jeremy's friends, Nancy Martin. Nancy was divorced, and Diane knew Nancy was more knowledgeable than she when it came to finances. (Almost anyone would be more knowledgeable than she was, she thought to herself wryly!)

Her appointment with the stockbroker, Scott, to discuss Mark's Keogh plan was not as successful as her meeting with Jack. Scott was a man in his midthirties who spoke very rapidly about the investments Mark had made. As nearly as she could determine, Mark had invested in stocks that didn't produce any income. Diane was sure Mark had some reason for doing this but had no idea what it might have been. She did know she needed more information before making any decision.

As she looked at the list of stocks Scott gave her, the page blurred before her. She had expected to see familiar company names. About 40 different companies were listed, but she had never heard of any of them.

Scott told her this retirement account should be rolled over into an IRA account—whatever that meant—and that she could not start receiving income from this account without paying penalties until she was age 59 1/2. He explained that if she did take money out of this account before that age, then she would be taxed on the income received, and there would be an additional surtax charged on any money she received. **(Technical note:** If Diane leaves this retirement account in Mark's name, she will not have to pay the 10 percent surtax on her withdrawals, but then she would not be able to name her own beneficiary. There are other exceptions that would allow her to withdraw from her IRA account in her own name before age 59 1/2.)

Diane's spirits sank. If she couldn't access the $300,000 in Mark's retirement account, the $1,400,000 she thought she had available earlier in the week to provide her with income had been reduced to $1,100,000. However, this still seemed like a lot of money. Instinctively, she didn't think Mark's retirement plan was invested as safely as it should have been for her and the children. Also, she didn't feel that Scott and she could work together effectively. She needed someone who would take the time to explain things to her, and Scott did not seem to be that person. She took the papers he gave her to complete and decided that she had better see Dorothy sooner rather than later about what action she should take next. As she drove to pick up her children's car pool and drop Nancy off at her office, Diane thought about how much more complicated her life was these days.

SUSAN

Reactions to Contacting Agencies and Resource People

As promised, Harry's wife, Emily, invited Susan to dinner. She accepted because intellectually she knew she should begin to force herself to socialize with others.Dinner was an emotional struggle for Susan, but she was pleased with herself for having made the effort, and the food was delicious. Susan realized this was the first time since Lance had died that she was aware of what she was eating and how it tasted. During dinner, Susan told Harry and Emily she had set up an appointment with the trust officer at the bank to discuss the $500,000 insurance trust.

Susan asked Harry if he had had a chance to discuss this trust with her two stepchildren—she was very anxious about their reactions. Susan knew that Lance's daughter, Leslie, would be particularly upset because she was entering her senior year of college. The $25,000 in cash left to Leslie would just about cover her college costs for the year. Eventually, Leslie would receive the money from the insurance trust but not until Susan died.

Harry had met with the two stepchildren, and, as Susan had anticipated, they were not pleased with the small amount of money they were to receive in the foreseeable future. They couldn't believe that their father had not left them more! Harry told them that Lance had discussed this with him before making these arrangements. Lance had felt very strongly that it was not good for children to have too much money at an early age. He believed they should make their own way in the world, as he had done. Lance thought that by the time the children received money from the trust they would be mature enough to handle it. Unfortunately, he had not had the chance to tell them this himself.

Susan decided to ask Harry about her mother's situation. Susan was concerned about her mother and felt it was her responsibility to take care of her, even if it meant that she had to personally contribute more to her financial support. It was at times like these that she felt overwhelmed by the tasks ahead of her. She was glad she had Dr. Coleman with whom to discuss these feelings.

Susan hoped that talking to the bank's trust officer would help her understand more about the $500,000 insurance trust Lance had established. She was anxious to know the terms of the trust and what the income from it would be. When she met with Mr. Stepstone, the trust officer, he explained that she would receive income from the trust for life. At her death, her stepchildren would receive whatever principal remained.

Mr. Stepstone said that the trust department would manage the portfolio so that Susan would receive a reasonable amount of income—4 percent annually—from the money in the trust. He explained that the trust could pay her more income, but in view of her relatively young age, he advised investing it so that the trust would grow in value over the years. Susan wasn't sure she wanted the trust to grow—after all, it only meant her stepchildren would inherit more money after she died. Mr. Stepstone explained that in order to increase the annual income, he needed to invest so that the principal also would grow. If the assets in the trust paid a higher income, then the growth potential would be limited. If, on the other hand, the principal increased in value and continued to pay 4 percent, then he expected that the income she would receive would increase over the years.

In his proposed plan, the $500,000 would provide her with about a $20,000 annual income. The management fees for this service would be deducted—50 percent from the income generated by the trust account and 50 percent from the principal. When he had estimated the 4 percent return to her, Mr. Stepstone had already deducted these fees.

This approach was reassuring to Susan because she was concerned about meeting her mother's costs in the retirement community, which she knew would increase annually. With the proposed level of income from the trust, it looked as if she could use part of that money to help cover her mother's expenses.

Mr. Stepstone explained that she would receive quarterly statements from the trust department. He would arrange to have the monthly trust income direct deposited into her checking account at the bank. Mr. Stepstone introduced Susan to Ellen Peabody, who would be assigned to manage her account. He told her that he was the head of the trust department and supervised all the accounts, but Ellen would be her personal trust officer and that Susan could call her with any questions she might have.

Next Susan contacted Lance's stockbroker, Bob O'Brien. Following Harry's instructions, she asked Bob to supply her with a current list of Lance's stocks. She also asked him to value the portfolio as of the date of Lance's death. Harry had previously explained to her that because the assets were in Lance's name, these stocks would be valued in the estate as of the date of death or six months later, whichever date Susan and her lawyer selected as most desirable to her from an estate tax point of view. Harry had told her that the date they chose for valuing the estate assets had to be the same for all estate assets.

During their conversation, Susan asked Bob which stocks he would recommend she sell to raise the $50,000 for her stepchildren. She intended to go over the portfolio in greater detail with him at a later date, but she wanted to make these sales now so she could resolve the situation with them as soon as possible. Bob said he would get back to her with his recommendations as soon as possible.

Susan felt she was making some progress. She had a lot of issues to sort through all at once, and she had to be careful not to neglect her job—after all, she couldn't afford to lose that income. Dr. Coleman had impressed on her that her primary responsibility was to herself, and maintaining her mental health was an important part of that.

AUDREY

Reactions to Contacting Agencies and Resource People

John Jr. had asked his mother when she would be ready to sit down with him to review her financial situation, and so far she had been able to postpone this meeting. She found it odd that it never occurred to him that she was capable of dealing with financial matters on her own. Fortunately, he hadn't pushed her about it. She realized that he was only trying to help and she shouldn't be so reluctant to accept his assistance. On the other hand, he was inclined to be domineering, and she wanted to sort things out for herself.

Audrey called the Social Security Administration, as Mr. Humphrey, her attorney, had told her to and found that as John's widow she would start receiving $1,167, a month, which worked out to about $14,000 this year. The nice person she spoke to told her she could instruct Social Security to direct deposit the money into her bank account, which she decided to do.

Mr. Humphrey told her to call the bank where the home mortgage was held. The lady at the bank informed her that the current amount due the bank was $20,000 and that she had eight years left to pay on their 30-year mortgage. The interest rate was 8.5 percent, and the monthly payments were $263. Audrey thought the interest rate seemed awfully high. She and John had discussed refinancing the mortgage or paying it off, but with John's illness they never got around to making a final decision. She hoped that when she understood her money situation better, she would be in a position to pay it off.

Mr. Humphrey had told Audrey that she should have the home appraised for the estate valuation. If she decided to sell the home, for tax purposes one-half of the cost of the home would be based on this appraisal and one-half would be based on its original cost plus improvements. Because its original cost was $50,000 and the home was now worth $400,000, her cost basis would be $225,000 (half the original cost [$50,000] plus half the current appraised market value [$400,000]).

This would mean there would be a $175,000 gain if she sold her home. Mr. Humphrey also explained that because the home had been their primary residence for two of the past five years and the gain did not exceed $250,000, she would owe no capital gains tax if she sold the home.[2] He emphasized that it was important to get an independent appraisal to establish the home's current market value.

It didn't take Audrey long to locate her file with her notes from the retirement lectures given by Mr. Silver, the financial planner. When she called his office and told the receptionist she wanted to meet with him, the receptionist said it might be helpful for Audrey to complete a financial questionnaire before their meeting. Audrey asked if it were mandatory for her to do this before seeing Mr. Silver. The woman assured her that it was not a requirement, but it would make their first meeting more productive. Audrey explained that she recently had been widowed and at this point just wanted to have an initial interview. The receptionist said there would be no problem with that and made an appointment for the following week.

Before Audrey had an opportunity to meet with Mr. Silver, she was contacted by a Mr. Postman, who called her on the phone and said that he worked for a local stock brokerage firm and was sorry to learn of her husband's death. Audrey found this comment a little odd as she had never heard of this man—perhaps he was one of John's friends from Rotary Club. However, she soon realized that

Mr. Postman did not know her or John; he just read the obituary notices as a way to identify potential clients. She told him firmly but politely that she did not intend to deal with a stranger. She was grateful for the support of the professionals with whom she was working. She was also very pleased with her decision to add what she hoped would be an additional support person by making an appointment to meet with Mr. Silver, the financial planner. She wondered what other widows did who didn't have anyone to trust.

Audrey liked Mr. Silver's initial greeting. His first question was, "How can I help you?" She told him about John's pension income and her Social Security income. She mentioned the stock in the company John used to work for as well as the $40,000 insurance money she had received. She told him of her concerns about Joanne and her anticipation that John Jr. would try to tell her what to do. She wondered if she should sell her home or keep it. Audrey was amazed at all the questions she asked this man whom she had just met, but somehow she really felt at ease with him.

Mr. Silver suggested that she take no immediate action. He told her

---

[2] Please note if Audrey had sold her house in the calendar year her husband had died, she would have had the full $500,000 exclusion ($250,000 of hers and $250,000 of John's).

that in order for him to advise her competently, she needed to fill out a financial questionnaire that would give him a better idea of what her income and expenses might be. At that point, they could determine if she had sufficient income and, ultimately, how best to invest her money. He asked her to fill in as much of the form as she could. If she had trouble, he or his assistant would be glad to help her.

When Mr. Silver asked Audrey how much investment experience she had, she confessed that she had very little. He said that he wanted her to understand what she was doing and assured her that there was no rush to do anything. He recommended that she leave the insurance money with the insurance company, where it would continue to earn interest. Because the company John used to work for was such a good one, he encouraged her to hold that stock for the time being.

Mr. Silver said that with the information she provided he could estimate what her taxable income and cash flow would be this year and next. He would also prepare a balance sheet listing her assets and liabilities. In order to do this, he also needed to see their last year's federal and state income tax returns. Audrey gave him the name and phone number of their accountant, Gary Lewis. She said she would call Mr. Lewis and tell him to send copies of the tax returns to Mr. Silver for his review. Mr. Silver told her that after he reviewed the figures, they could decide together what action to take to ensure that she had adequate income. To prepare these computations and make recommendations, he would charge her a fee based on the hours needed to prepare her financial plan. He would ask her to pay one-third of the fee up front and the balance on completion of the work.

Mr. Silver told Audrey that he would send her a letter of agreement that would outline exactly what services he would provide as well as an estimate of what the final fee would be. This estimate would be a quote of the approximate amount of time he thought it would take to prepare the plan. If he underestimated the time required, she would not have to pay more than the fee quoted to her in his letter. If he overestimated, then she would pay only for the actual hours expended. If the terms in his letter met with her approval, she would sign and return the letter to him, and they could start working on her plan. Audrey liked this approach because it would give her time to discuss the letter of agreement with Mr. Humphrey before she took any final action.

It was just about noon when Audrey left Mr. Silver's office. Dr. Pa-Padisio's words echoed in her mind, and she thought she should do something about lunch. But what? Should she call Joanne? It was too late to call one of her friends with whom she used to have lunch on a regular basis. She stood on the corner watching people hurry by as the lunch hour began. Rousing herself from her reverie, she decided to call Joanne to ask if she and the younger two children had eaten yet. If not, she thought she'd treat them to a picnic at home. She really hadn't had an opportunity to spend much time with her grandchildren this past year, and it would be fun to see them and have some time to talk to Joanne. Joanne was more than pleased with her mother's suggestion because she was just about to make the children their usual peanut-butter-and-jelly sandwiches for lunch which was their current favorite food. It would be great to have lunch taken care of by her mother. It had been so long since they had done something like that.

Audrey retrieved her car from the parking lot and drove to her favorite delicatessen en route to Joanne's home. She bought more than they could ever eat and toted the bags to her car in anticipation of surprising the children and her daughter. She felt somewhat lighthearted and allowed herself to enjoy the feeling.

The children were so excited to see her. They jumped up and down and tugged at her skirt. Joanne had to peel them off her legs so she could deposit the bags of food in the kitchen. Little Noah had changed so much since she had really looked at him—he seemed to have jumped from an infant to a toddler. Heidi, at almost four, looked different too. Both of them wanted to drag her off to look at some treasure in their rooms. Joanne allowed "Gran Gran" to be monopolized by the children for a short while before insisting that they all come to the kitchen to eat. The deli sandwiches smelled delicious, and clearly Joanne appreciated the change in daily routine. It turned out to be quite a festive occasion. The children were thrilled with the giant cookies Gran Gran had brought for them.

After lunch, Audrey agreed to read them a story before they lay down for their naps. She told them how much she had missed them and promised to visit again very soon. She thought she would not be there when they awakened from their naps and didn't want them to be disappointed.

Joanne settled the children in their beds for their naps and returned to the kitchen to have tea with her mother. Audrey seemed to be noticing things with new eyes. She had been so preoccupied with John's care, then the funeral, and the sorting out of her financial situation that she had been oblivious to everything else. Joanne looked a little weary, and Audrey felt badly she hadn't noticed earlier. When she asked Joanne if she was all right, her daughter burst into tears and said she was fine, but it was so difficult caring for the three children and simultaneously worrying about how they would manage on Keith's current salary. Also, she had apparently had more of a problem dealing with her father's death than Audrey had realized. They had always been so close.

Audrey put her arms around her daughter and shed some tears of her own. She hadn't thought sufficiently about what Joanne might be going through. As they wiped the tears from their eyes, Audrey shared with Joanne an idea she had just formulated. She told her about Dr. PaPadisio's recommendations about her nutrition. She thought it would be good for them to spend one day a week enjoying lunch and some shopping or whatever. She wanted Joanne to find a baby-sitter one day a week for about five hours, and Audrey would pay her. An outing like this would be good for both of them. They really hadn't had time for much mother-daughter togetherness since Joanne had married seven years ago.

Audrey also wanted to have the opportunity to get to know her grandchildren better and proposed to Joanne that she spend half a day a week with the grandchildren. She had always enjoyed participating with her children in their various activities and projects when they were growing up and thought it would be very rewarding to do some of the same things with her grandchildren. If Audrey did this, Joanne could have some time for herself, and Audrey would have an opportunity to do some of the things she had missed doing since her own children were young.

Joanne was taken aback by her mother's generosity, and thought she couldn't allow her mother to do so much for her at this time of stress in her life. Audrey overcame Joanne's reluctance by pointing out that what she was proposing would be beneficial to both of them. This persuaded Joanne to agree. She said she would try to find a sitter so they could get started on their "women's day out" as soon as possible. They hugged each other extra hard when Audrey left to return home and walk her dog. While en route, Audrey considered some of the other things she had been neglecting and determined to make more of an effort to contact some of the women with whom she had formerly been friendly. She knew they had tried to stay in touch, but she just hadn't been ready.

Elizabeth

Reactions to Contacting Agencies and Resource People

Elizabeth wanted to do something for her church because it had meant so much to her to have had Pastor Appletorn's assistance on both a personal and a spiritual level. He had found the time to meet with her and helped her get in touch with her faith. He reminded her of God's plan for all mankind. They talked about how important the church had been to both Ben and herself and that this was a time to lean on both the teachings of the church and members of the congregation. He emphasized that Ben was at peace now. Pastor Appleton had even had one of the members, Lucy Thornton, contact her to spend some time with her and discuss her own personal grief experience since she had lost her husband four years ago. Lucy was so open about her experience. She was able to speak about so many of the feelings Elizabeth had that it made her feel a little less alone. Talking with Lucy made Elizabeth feel somewhat better about facing her financial situation.

Sam Weatherly accompanied Elizabeth the following Tuesday for her appointment with Mr. Grossfeldt. The atmosphere of the office was leathery but warm. Mr. Grossfeldt explained to her that Ben's account was currently being managed by an investment advisor but in the future she should consider using the services of a bank trust department. He said that banks tend to be conservative, and their approach might be more appropriate at this stage of her life, especially because she had no dependents. He would be glad to introduce her to a trust officer at the bank he had recommended to many of his clients.

Elizabeth told him about her idea of giving Ben's car to the church, and he thought this might be a good idea. He suggested she talk it over with Pastor Appletorn. He might want to sell it and use the proceeds for current church projects. However, before she could do anything, she would have to change the car registration from Ben's name to her name. Elizabeth had a moment of panic—where did Ben keep the registration?

Mr. Grossfeldt also suggested that she consider doing some estate planning of her own. Before they did any of that, however, he thought she should put together the necessary information about her expenses, her income, and her current net worth. In a kindly, nonpatronizing manner he explained to her what each of these terms meant and what she had to do to provide him with the figures. He also made sure she knew where to find the information.

Elizabeth left Mr. Grossfeldt's office greatly relieved and thanked Sam profusely for introducing her to him. She thought that having a bank handle her money might be a good idea—she certainly didn't know anything about investments. She would follow Mr. Grossfeldt's suggestion and meet with the bank trust officer he recommended. Elizabeth needed to get better organized herself before changing advisors. She was most grateful to Sam. What would she have done without his help? Elizabeth told Sam that she thought she could get together the figures Mr. Grossfeldt requested, but that if she had any difficulties, she would like to be able to talk with him. He said in his considerate way that he would be pleased to help her if she needed assistance.

Before going any further, Elizabeth decided to visit her bank and check the contents of the safe-deposit box. Fortunately, before his death, Ben had moved everything into a safe-deposit box in her name. She had no trouble gaining access to it, but the assistant manager at the bank, Ms. Riley, said that in some states the safe-deposit box would have been sealed if it had been held in joint name with Ben. Elizabeth found little in the box when she opened it other than a few pieces of Ben's mother's jewelry.

With Ms. Riley's help, she set up an account for the income from Ben's estate assets and changed their joint checking account to her name, as Mr. Grossfeldt had told her to do. Ms. Riley was very helpful and urged her to call if she had any questions. Elizabeth was pretty tired by now. She had spent more time with other people than she had in quite some time and had a lot of information to digest. She thought she needed to go home and rest.

7

Developing a
Meaningful Budget

We couldn't possibly know where it would lead,
but we knew it had to be done.
—*Betty Friedan*

BY NOW WE ASSUME you have accumulated information about your financial situation. Now use this information to estimate what income you can expect to receive and what you think your expenses will be. Once you have these figures, then you will know if you have sufficient income on which to live comfortably.

To put together a meaningful budget, you need to do two things. First, you need to list your projected income sources. Then review your checkbook for the past year to determine what your expenses have been. With this information, you should be able to project future income and expense items.

In the next chapter, we review your assets and liabilities to determine if any of them could or should be repositioned to provide you with additional income should you discover you need more income than you are currently receiving.

PROJECTED INCOME SOURCES

We suggest that you start a new notebook for this purpose so the new information does not get mixed in with the estate settlement issues.[1]

When you contacted Social Security, the Veterans Administration (if applicable), and your husband's former employer(s), they told you how much income you could expect from

---

1. In this chapter and the next, we provide sample forms to enable you to put together the information you will need to make present and future financial decisions.

each source and when payments would start. List these sources and the amount and frequency of the payments in a notebook (see figure 7.1).

Under this income category, list everything you are sure you will receive. If you work, include your employment income. If you are self-employed, list your net income (the gross amount earned less expenses). If you have other sources of income, list them as well. Also list how often the income is paid: monthly (M), quarterly (Q), semiannually (SA), or annually (A).

There may be a time lag before the income from your husband's assets and pension plans starts coming in, so for a short period you may have to live on cash reserves. Be very careful to keep a record of any cash you receive during this period and its source. With money coming in from various places, you may inadvertently spend principal, which you may need later.[2]

It is a good idea to establish a separate bank or money market account for any payments you receive as the result of your husband's death, such as insurance proceeds, to make sure the money is segregated for investment purposes.

FIGURE 7.1 Sources of Income

	Amount	When Paid (M) (Q) (SA) (A)
Salary	$_____	_____
Net self-employed income	_____	_____
Social Security	_____	_____
Pension	_____	_____
Stocks	_____	_____
Bonds	_____	_____
Mutual funds	_____	_____
Other	_____	_____
Total	$_____	_____

---

2. If you are concerned about whether you will have enough money to pay all your bills, ask your attorney what to do. Paying the wrong bills may be a problem later.

CURRENT BILLS

Before estimating what your current expenses are, you need to list your current outstanding bills. As we discussed before, divide them into your bills, your husband's bills, and joint bills. If your husband had outstanding medical and hospital bills, they should be paid from the estate asset account.

If you are uncertain which bills need to be paid now and which later, ask your primary financial advisor for help. Keep records of which ones you paid and when. In order to estimate your future expenses, you first need to list your past fixed expenses and then your discretionary expenses.

CURRENT EXPENSES

Fixed Expenses

In order to project future expenses, first you need to review what your current expenses are. The easiest place to start is with your fixed expenses—those you are committed to pay at regular intervals. Some of them are due monthly; others, such as household and car insurance payments, are due annually or quarterly. Keep in mind that your future expenses may differ from your current expenses, but this is a good place to start.

Typical monthly bills include the mortgage or rent, car payments, and utilities. These expenses are fixed because you must pay them each month, but the amount may vary each month. If you want to regularize some of these payments, call the utility companies and ask if they have a monthly payment schedule. They will review your past bills and put together for you a monthly payment schedule that will require equal monthly payments. In this way, you can avoid receiving an unanticipated very high bill in any month.

You may also need to make quarterly federal and state tax payments, which your accountant will estimate for you. (If you don't have an accountant, you may want to consult with one at this time.) Mark in your notebook and on your monthly calendar when these bills should be paid. Later, when you pay them, mark the amount paid and the date.

Use a notebook to set up an inventory of your fixed expenses, as shown in figure 7.2.

FIGURE 7.2 Inventory of Fixed Expenses

	Amount Due	Date Next Due	How Often Due (M) (Q) (SA) (A)
Mortgage	$_____	_____	_____
Home equity loan	_____	_____	_____
Co-op/Condominium fee	_____	_____	_____
Rent	_____	_____	_____
Utilities	_____	_____	_____
Gas	_____	_____	_____
Electric	_____	_____	_____
Water	_____	_____	_____
Telephone	_____	_____	_____
Cable	_____	_____	_____
Internet service	_____	_____	_____
Loan payments	_____	_____	_____
Car payments	_____	_____	_____
Others	_____	_____	_____
Insurance premiums	_____	_____	_____
Medical/dental/vision	_____	_____	_____
Life	_____	_____	_____
Disability	_____	_____	_____
Long-term care	_____	_____	_____
Homeowners	_____	_____	_____
Car	_____	_____	_____
Personal Liability	_____	_____	_____
Other (flood, wind/hail, valuables floater, etc.)	_____	_____	_____
Taxes	_____	_____	_____
Real estate	_____	_____	_____
Personal property	_____	_____	_____
Federal	_____	_____	_____
State	_____	_____	_____
Other _____	_____	_____	_____

Discretionary Expenses

Discretionary expenses vary from month to month. These would include groceries, meals eaten out, clothing, dry cleaning, entertainment, vacations, personal care (health club, hairdresser, and drugstore), dues and subscriptions, cleaning people, gifts, and credit card debt, if any. Look at your checkbook to see what these have been in the past, and list them in your notebook. You may want to use one page in your notebook for each category. These expenses will probably change in your current situation, but to estimate future expenses, it is helpful to look at past expenses first (see figure 7.3).

FIGURE 7.3 Inventory of Discretionary Expenses

	Total Last 12 Months	Monthly Average
Groceries	$_____	$_____
Clothing	_____	_____
Home maintenance	_____	_____
Home improvements	_____	_____
Car maintenance	_____	_____
Entertainment	_____	_____
Dues (club, professional)	_____	_____
Subscriptions, books	_____	_____
Vacation trips	_____	_____
Domestic help	_____	_____
Household purchases	_____	_____
Gifts, birthdays	_____	_____
Dry cleaning	_____	_____
Drugstore	_____	_____
Hairdresser, nail care	_____	_____
Transportation	_____	_____
Yard maintenance	_____	_____
Education	_____	_____
Health Club	_____	_____
Unreimbursed medical expenses	_____	_____
Child care	_____	_____
Charitable contributions (cash)	_____	_____
Tax preparation fee	_____	_____
Unreimbursed business expenses	_____	_____
Legal fees	_____	_____
Accounting fees	_____	_____
Financial planning fees	_____	_____
Finance charges (credit cards)	_____	_____
Child-related activity expenses	_____	_____
Other: _____	_____	_____

PROJECTED FIXED EXPENSES

Now that you have an idea of what your previous expenses were, it should be easier to estimate what your expenses will be in the future, starting with the fixed expenses.

Mortgage Payments and Real Estate Taxes

If you own your own home, when you notify your mortgage holder of your husband's death, ask for an explanation of what your current payment includes. Real estate taxes and homeowners insurance are often included in the payment. Clarify whether your mortgage holder is paying the real estate tax or if you are expected to pay it. If the mortgage holder is paying, the lender estimates what your real estate taxes will be and incorporates them into your monthly mortgage payments. Once a year the lender looks at the actual real estate taxes you owed versus the estimated amount. If taxes due were in excess of the amount paid, then your monthly mortgage payment will increase. Real estate taxes are usually due annually or semiannually, and some people prefer to pay them on this basis. If your husband chose this method of payment, you need to be aware of it in order to avoid the shock of receiving an unexpectedly large tax bill.

You need to know the terms of your mortgage loan. On your monthly statement, or at least annually with your year-end statement, your mortgage holder sends you a statement of how much principal you still owe, how many years are left on the mortgage note, and what your current interest rate is.

Interest rates on some mortgage loans change periodically. These are known as adjustable rate mortgages (ARMs). You need to know if this might happen to you and, if so, when. You might even have an interest-only mortgage where you are paying interest but no principal. If you don't understand the terms of the mortgage (nowadays they are not always easy to figure out), have your accountant or financial planner interpret them for you and explain them in writing.

To develop a meaningful budget for the future, you need to know if your mortgage payment might increase or decrease. Many widows panic over the size of the payments. If they have the money available, they may want to pay the mortgage off right away. This is not usually a good idea. These payments provide you with tax deductions that you may well need. This is another major decision that should be made only after looking at the total picture. Right now you're trying to determine what bills you must pay on a monthly basis.

Home Equity Loans

Home equity loans (HELs) have become very popular in recent years. However, these loans are difficult to understand. Basically, a home equity loan is a line of credit against your home. Often, monthly payments are for the interest on the loan only and no principal is being repaid. For some HELs, the payment is fixed and will include both interest and principal. This loan is usually from a bank other than the one that holds your mortgage.

Typically the interest rate on HELs is not fixed and will increase or decrease according to what is happening to interest rates generally. The rate is usually higher than the one you are paying for your primary mortgage.

If you have a home equity loan, ask the lender to spell out its terms and conditions. Have your financial advisor look at the terms of this loan right away; because the interest rate is not fixed, this loan might be one you want to pay off or change.

Reverse Mortgages

A reverse mortgage is a special type of loan against your home that is available to homeowners age 62 or older. A lender pays you either a lump sum or a monthly income based on the value of your home. The money you receive is tax free and you do not have to pay it back as long as you live in your home. When you die or no longer live in your home, all of the money you borrowed, plus interest, must be repaid. The interest you are charged is variable (the interest rate can go up or down), and this may result in a much higher loan balance than you might anticipate.

If you had a reverse mortgage when your husband died, you do not have to pay off the loan while you are still living in your home as long as you keep it in good condition, keep it insured, and pay your property taxes.

If you move and sell your home, you will repay the lender out of the sale proceeds. However, if you have to go into a nursing home or if you move but you continue to own your home, the lender will require you to pay off the loan once 12 months has passed. This means that unless you have other money available to pay off the loan, you may be forced to sell your home.

At your death, the loan has to be paid off. This reduces the amount of money you can leave to your heirs. It also means they may have to sell your home in order to repay the loan.

PROJECTED DISCRETIONARY EXPENSES

Look at the expenses that seem necessary now but may not be in the future. For instance, it may not be essential to maintain two cars, keep a second home, or remain a member of a club. Again, these are decisions to make after you have gathered all the facts.

Spending money on groceries is not discretionary, but the amount you spend is. Your costs should be lower now because you are feeding one less person. On the other hand, other expenses may increase. For example, if you owned your own home and your husband was an avid gardener but you don't know the difference between a rake and a trowel, you may have to hire someone to help you take care of the garden, which will be an increased expense.

A word of caution: We strongly recommend that you postpone major purchases until you know your total financial picture. The money you spend now on luxuries might be needed later for necessities.

When you estimate your future discretionary expenses, we suggest you put down two budget figures: (column 1) the minimum amount you could live on and (column 2) the amount you would like to spend (including things you can do without if necessary) (see figure 7.4). For instance, you might have been accustomed to going to the hairdresser once a week, but perhaps you might decide to go once a month instead. On the other hand, belonging to a health club may appear to be a luxury, but it might be a necessity at this time to maintain your physical and mental health! After looking at your total budget, however, you may decide that going to the hairdresser once a week is more essential for your physical and mental health than the health club. Each widow needs to make the decision that is right for her.

FIGURE 7.4 Estimated Monthly Discretionary Expenses

	Minimum	Preferred	Actual
Groceries	$_____	$_____	$_____
Clothing	_____	_____	_____
Home maintenance	_____	_____	_____
Home improvements	_____	_____	_____
Car maintenance	_____	_____	_____
Entertainment	_____	_____	_____
Dues (club, professional)	_____	_____	_____
Subscriptions, books	_____	_____	_____
Vacation trips	_____	_____	_____
Domestic help	_____	_____	_____
Household purchases	_____	_____	_____
Gifts, birthdays	_____	_____	_____
Dry cleaning	_____	_____	_____
Drugstore	_____	_____	_____
Hairdresser, nail care	_____	_____	_____
Transportation	_____	_____	_____
Yard maintenance	_____	_____	_____
Education	_____	_____	_____
Health club			
Unreimbursed medical expenses	_____	_____	_____
Child care	_____	_____	_____
Charitable contributions (cash)	_____	_____	_____
Tax preparation fee	_____	_____	_____
Unreimbursed business expenses	_____	_____	_____
Legal fees	_____	_____	_____
Accounting fees	_____	_____	_____
Financial planning fees	_____	_____	_____
Finance charges (credit cards)	_____	_____	_____
Child-related activity expenses	_____	_____	_____
Other: _____	_____	_____	_____

COMPARING YOUR ESTIMATED
AND ACTUAL EXPENSES

It is important for you to keep a record of how you actually spend your money for the first few months and then compare it with your estimated expenses. You may be surprised at some of the differences between the two sets of figures. We suggest you make a page in your notebook for each expense category and then, as you pay each bill or spend cash, record it in your notebook. To make this record keeping easier, ask for receipts for everything. Mark an envelope for each expense category, and put the receipts in these envelopes.

Once a month total each expense category in column 3 of figure 7.4 and see how close you came to your initial estimate. There is no right or wrong here. Most widows find they have overestimated in some categories and underestimated in others. Initially, your grocery bills may be low because friends bring you food or invite you for dinner or you don't feel like cooking. After a while, this expense will return to something more typical for your new circumstances.

At the end of six months, review your initial estimates, compare them with the actual expenditures and develop a new budget, which should be more accurate. Then check this new budget every six months. After a while, you won't need to keep such close tabs on your expenditures. However, don't lose sight of the fact that it is essential to your financial security to know how you spend your money.

CASH FLOW STATEMENT

Now that you have calculated your income and expenses, you want to total both categories and find out if you have more than enough income (positive cash flow) or insufficient income (negative cash flow) (see figure 7.5).

This initial estimate of income and expenses will give you a better idea of your current financial situation. However, don't panic if you have a negative cash flow. Your advisor can help rectify this situation. You are still in the fact-gathering stage.

FIGURE 7.5 Cash Flow Statement

CASH FLOW STATEMENT AS OF _____

FOR:

_____

Estimated Income:

Salary	$ _____	
Net self-employed income	_____	
Social Security	_____	
Pension	_____	
Investments	_____	
Other	_____	
Total		$ _____

Estimated Expenses:

Fixed expenses	$ _____	
Discretionary expenses	_____	
Total		$ _____
Excess income/(Excess expense)		$ _____

Conversely, after putting this statement together, you may find that you have sufficient income to cover your current expenses. Although this information is comforting, you must keep your long-term situation in mind. Typically, expenses increase each year. What is sufficient income today may not be ten years from now. Furthermore, there are always unplanned expenses for which you have not budgeted but that must be covered.

When planning, make sure your income keeps pace with increasing expenses. If your cost of living increases at a modest 3 percent annually, you will need 50 percent more after-tax income 14 years from now just to buy the same things you are buying now. In other words, if $50,000 is sufficient annual after-tax income today, you will need $75,000 14 years from now and $100,000 24 years hence. In addition, periodically taxes (federal and state income, property, and sales) increase, and you need to budget for these as well.

SUMMARY AND CONCLUSION

In this chapter, you first itemized your current outstanding bills and determined which ones to pay and which ones to defer. Then you estimated what your future monthly income will be. Finally, you determined what your monthly expenses have been and what you estimate they will be in the future. These estimates will indicate if you have sufficient income to maintain your current lifestyle or if you have to make some adjustments.

Diane

Reactions to the Budgeting Process

Diane had a difficult time with her budget. She had never had to keep track of expenses. She just spent money on items needed for the home and the children, and Mark paid the bills. There always seemed to be enough, so she didn't worry about money. She had taken the children's need for a private school education for granted because she and Mark had decided it was preferable to the education provided by the public schools. For Diane, whether or not the children went to private schools was unrelated to cost—that had always been Mark's department. She was beginning to recognize that it was that way about everything related to finances.

A part of Diane wished she could return to her former mode of functioning, but another part of her resented the fact that she had allowed herself to be treated like a child when it came to anything financial. She could still see Mark seated at his desk in the den paying the bills and telling the children, if they interrupted him, he couldn't talk to them right then because he had bills to pay. As disloyal as she felt, Diane realized she was sometimes angry with Mark for leaving her in this mess. At first she couldn't tolerate anyone saying anything the slightest bit negative about Mark, but here she was finding herself angry with him for the financial mess with which she needed to deal. When she first heard the women in her widow support group talk about the anger they sometimes felt toward their husbands for abandoning them and leaving them to deal with all of life's problems, she couldn't relate to what they were experiencing. She thought they hadn't been fortunate enough to be married to someone like Mark. They told her she'd have similar feelings at some point in the grieving process, but she had rejected what they said as being something they were feeling because of their particular situations.

Here she was, several months later, having the very response she had defended herself against with her group. Actually, she didn't know how she would have managed without this group, and particularly Robyn, these past months. They had become such good friends. Robyn was so understanding. She could talk to her about anything. Jennifer Greenberg had also become a friend. She, too, always made the time to be helpful and available. Diane couldn't believe that now the majority of her social contacts were with people Mark didn't even know. She'd have to think about this further, but right now she had to look at private school education on a dollars-and-cents basis. Everything seemed to be so expensive.

At the urging of Dorothy Trumbull, her financial planner, Diane had gone to the Social Security office to ask what she could expect to receive from Social Security. It was difficult to understand because the amount of money she and the children would receive seemed to keep changing. However, she realized she needed to understand how it worked, so she wrote it down carefully in her notebook.

The bottom line was that Social Security was going to provide her and the children with a monthly income of about $3,500 for the present. However, as each child turned 18, the amount they as a family received would decrease. When the youngest, Alice, turned 16, Diane's survivor benefit would end, though she would still receive a benefit on Alice's behalf for two more years. This meant Diane would receive no Social Security benefits as Mark's widow from age 51 until she turned 60, at which time she would receive a widow's benefit equal to 71.5 percent of Mark's Social Security retirement income. On the other hand, under current Social Security regulations, if she were to wait until age 67, she would receive 100 percent of his annual benefits. The idea of having no income from Social Security for those nine years was scary, but it looked as if she really should wait 15 years to start receiving full benefits. This was all so confusing—what should she do? She couldn't think that far ahead. Even worse, Diane discovered she could lose her portion of the benefits if she worked and earned too much.

Diane's head began to swim. She really didn't know how she could handle all of this complexity. She knew she had to understand it for the children's sake, so she promised herself that she'd review the information she had obtained to date.

The life insurance agent had told Diane that the $800,000 policy Mark had from the firm could provide her with a lifetime annuity income of $3,454 per month. A possible alternative, called

"20 year certain," would pay her $3,425 per month. The meant that if she died anytime during the next 20 years her children would continue to receive these payments. In view of Mark's premature death, Diane thought it might be worth $29 less in monthly income to know these payments would be paid to her children.

Her mortgage payments were just about $3,000 per month, so if she picked this option, it looked like the family would have to live on the difference ($425) plus the Social Security payments ($3,500) for a total of $3,925 monthly income.

The three children's private school bills totaled $50,000 per year, and then there were camp and piano lessons. Maybe she should just pay the tuition for the next year and worry about it later. This was all too much! She had just received the annual real estate tax bill for $4,800. How would she ever work this all out? Diane wasn't a financial genius, but she didn't think they could live on $3,925 a month—especially with the tuition payments. The only other money she had was the $100,000 capital account from the firm and the $200,000 from Mark's personal insurance policies. She knew she didn't want to touch Mark's retirement account because of the IRS penalties. That was one thing she did comprehend. Perhaps she didn't have a choice. She made an appointment to see Dorothy right away to find out how she could cover her expenses.

Diane and Mark had put a deposit on a beach home for a couple of weeks for the summer (total cost: $4,000). This would be an opportunity for the family to be together, so that seemed to her to be a necessary expense. She dreaded the thought of going through Christmas without Mark; it was his favorite holiday. They had planned to take the family skiing. She was tempted to do it anyway so they wouldn't be haunted by the memories of Christmases past. Enough. She had to focus on her financial situation.

Based on the information Diane had provided to her, the expense statement Dorothy prepared for Diane and the children showed their total expenses were $70,000 per year.

Dorothy gave Diane a second statement called a *cash-flow statement,* which she emphasized was very preliminary. Under the category of income, Dorothy had factored in the Social Security payments ($42,000) and the proposed annuity ($41,100). These totaled $83,100 in annual income.

Then Dorothy looked at the money Diane would receive from the capital account ($100,000) and insurance money ($200,000), which totaled $300,000. She assumed these accounts were earning 3% interest. Altogether these funds would provide $9,000 annual income.

The good news was that because part of the projected annuity payment was not taxed (47 percent) and her mortgage payments were relatively high, she would not have to pay any income taxes! The bad news was that, according to Diane's estimate, her expenses would exceed her income by almost $77,000. Needless to say, Diane was really upset when she saw this, as she thought the expense estimates she had given Dorothy were very low. They certainly were less than the family had spent when Mark was alive.

Her situation was obviously a lot worse than she thought. Diane tried not to panic. Her biggest expense was private school tuition for the children ($50,000 a year). Perhaps they would have to go to public school. She might even have to sell their beautiful home and move to a less expensive one. Maybe her father could help out with the expenses, although she certainly didn't want to admit to him that Mark had not provided adequately for her and the family (even though it was beginning to look that way). The fact was that they had no idea he would die so young—had they known they would have bought more insurance! (*Editorial comment:* The reason many younger couples are underinsured is that they refuse to accept the possibility they may die prematurely!)

Dorothy suggested that Diane review her expense estimates to see if she couldn't reduce them. For instance, if she paid off her credit card debt of $15,000, she would not have to pay $2,700 in annual interest. Dorothy had some ideas about selecting other investments that might provide more income than the annuity and the money market accounts. She would work on increasing the income side of the cash-flow statement while Diane agreed to work on decreasing her expense estimates.

Dorothy said that she hated to be the bearer of such bad news, but if they both worked hard trying to solve this cash-flow problem, she knew that they would be successful. She also suggested to Diane that in fact she was more fortunate than some widows because she did have money available to her. It was their mutual goal to maximize how it would be used. It was difficult for Diane not to be disheartened as she left the office, but she resolved to review the budget once again. Although she didn't want to worry them too much, she thought the time had come to discuss the situation with the children.

Diane's Preliminary Annual Budget

Annual Income

Social Security	$42,000	
Proposed annuity	41,100	
Money market income	9,000	
Total		$92,100

Annual Expenses

Mortgage	$36,000	
Car loan	5,500	
Credit card interest	2,700	
Tuition	50,000	
Income taxes	None	
Other	70,000	
Property taxes	4,800	
Total		$169,000
Annual Negative Cash Flow		**($76,900)**

Susan

Reactions to the Budgeting Process

Susan had managed her own finances, including her investments, before marrying Lance, but that was 12 years ago, and she realized her previous budget would be vastly different from her present one. She needed to locate the records of their expenses as a couple so she could determine what her new budget would be. She knew that Lance had put all that information on the computer, and she had asked Sarah's help to access these expense figures.

Sarah had located the information on Lance's computer, but, as she explained to Susan, Lance's system appeared incredibly complicated. After discussing it further, Sarah helped Susan transfer the relevant information to the more basic program that Harry had given her. It would be much simpler to understand and maintain.

Susan was still worried about supporting her mother. The retirement home was costing $2,400 per month. Her mother was receiving pension payments from her father's retirement plan and

Social Security income, which totaled about $1,400 a month. Lance and she had been paying the monthly difference of $1,000.

Mr. Stepstone, her bank trust officer, told her that the trust would provide almost $1,700 of income per month; however, this income would be taxed to her, so the actual after tax income she would receive would be closer to $1,450 per month. Susan was comforted by the fact that with this trust income she could continue to help meet her mother's financial needs for the present. However, she was concerned about meeting higher living costs for her mom in the future when and if she needed assisted living care.

In her sessions with Dr. Coleman, Susan was beginning to identify the various ways she dealt with stress and life in general. She had become aware of her tendency to assume full responsibility for things when there was no need to do so. Her mother's financial support was a good case in point. Why had she assumed all of the responsibility for her mother? Her brother, Ron, was single and had no financial obligations other than his own expenses, yet she had never considered discussing with him either the selection of a retirement facility or its cost. Although Ron had never assumed responsibility for their mother on either a financial or personal level, she thought it was time to make him aware of their mother's monetary needs. She decided to ask him to help her financially; his contributing even a small amount would be helpful.

Susan had not been particularly effective in her job recently, but her boss and co-workers had been very understanding. She found herself working longer hours but accomplishing less. In this area, too, it had been helpful to discuss her feelings with Dr. Coleman. In the past, if she was not working to capacity at all times, she felt guilty. Dr. Coleman was helping her realize that she placed unreasonable demands on herself. Using the analogy of a machine, she reminded Susan that only machines worked at a constant pace, completing the same process without variation. She stressed to Susan that she was not a machine but a human being. There was no need to feel guilty about her decreased functioning on the job. She had suffered a major loss with no warning.

Susan was surprised that Dr. Coleman felt her employer and co-workers would not expect her performance on the job to be quite what it was before Lance's death. Dr. Coleman assured her that what she perceived as job inefficiency was not a permanent condition and she would return to her normal functioning as time passed. Susan was beginning to accept the fact that she had always been exceptionally demanding of herself, and she wondered what factors in her life had led her to act this way. She would have to explore this issue further, but for now she needed to address her financial situation.

When Susan put together her current budget, she had a negative cash flow of about $23,450. Given these figures, it was pretty obvious she could not afford to keep the lake cottage she and Lance had bought. Emotionally, she did not want to sell it because it held so many memories of the happy times she had there with Lance, but the basic cottage costs (mortgage and real estate taxes) totaled $11,250. Perhaps she would also have to sell their condominium, which she really loved. She had become attached to the beautiful view and the space of two bedrooms. It certainly was much more comfortable than the one-bedroom apartment she lived in before marrying Lance.

But facts were facts. It appeared she did not have enough income to support her current lifestyle. Maybe she could find a smaller apartment in the same building, or maybe she should look for a better-paying job—a thought that had not previously crossed her mind. In any case, Susan resolved to keep careful records of how she spent her money.

Thank goodness the association where she worked paid her insurance premiums (medical, disability, and life). It also matched her contributions to her 401(k) savings plan 25 cents on the dollar for the first $4,000 she contributed. She knew she was allowed to contribute more to her 401(k) than she had been doing. Up to now, she had only contributed the $4,000 that the association matched since she knew Lance had a good retirement fund. Now it appeared she couldn't even afford to contribute that much.

As for her personal income, Susan thought her salary was pretty secure at $55,000. She had been at the association for ten years and had received regular raises.

Susan's Preliminary Annual Budget

Annual Income

Salary	$55,000	
Trust income	20,450	
Total		**$75,450**

Annual Expenses

Mortgage, condominium	$24,000	
Mortgage, cottage	10,000	
Mother's retirement home	12,000	
Property taxes (condominium + cottage)	3,850	
Income taxes, FICA	8,400	
Other	40,000	
401(k)	4,000	
Total		**$102,250**
Annual Negative Cash Flow		**$(26,800)**

Audrey

Reactions to the Budgeting Process

Audrey looked at her sources of income, and it seemed as if she had enough to pay her expenses. John's pension would provide her with $3,500 per month for the rest of her life. Since she was only 62 years old, she would also receive 82 percent of his Social Security payment, which would be $1,167 per month. The Social Security representative told her this payment would increase the beginning of each year in accordance with the cost of living adjustment (COLA).

Audrey reviewed her checkbook for the past year and put together her expenses for Mr. Silver to review. It was obvious to her that they would be higher in the future since she had done little else besides care for John over the past couple of years. She had not spent much on clothes, they had done no entertaining, she had not had the time or inclination to go to their club, and they had taken no vacations. These were all expenses she expected would increase in the coming year.

Thinking about her lifestyle reminded Audrey of the invitation she had reluctantly accepted to attend a small dinner party given by one of their closest friends. It had felt very different going to a dinner party by herself. She realized not being part of a couple was an adjustment. She didn't really feel terrible—it was just a new role and one to which she would need to become accustomed. Everyone had been very nice, almost too solicitous. As always, Peg had prepared a great dinner. The only really awkward note was the undue attention paid to her by Walter and his wife Jane's very negative response to his behavior. Audrey thought Jane acted as if Audrey was going to take her husband from her! However, Audrey did have to admit that Walter almost made a fool of himself being attentive to her. Their other friends treated her as they had in the past, but she knew she wasn't the same person. She was sure this type of social activity would feel better to her as time went on and she was more comfortable with herself.

Audrey was also pleased with herself for deciding to do volunteer work for the symphony. She was working on membership. One of her close friends, Claudia, had always worked to raise money for the symphony and had encouraged Audrey to volunteer some time to this group. She had enjoyed meeting the women and getting out one day a week to work with them. She became friendly with Heather, another widow with whom she worked. Often they went out to lunch following their work, or she and Claudia would plan to do something.

Audrey was feeling better about the way she was spending her time. Her next step was to call the "Reading Is Fundamental" people. She had seen a small piece about this children's literacy organization on TV and the concept really appealed to her. However, none of her friends or acquaintances did any work with RIF, so she would be going into it cold—on her own. It felt like a big step. She would be trying something totally new. She knew she was almost ready to contact the group.

On the activity side, she had been pleased to learn from Mr. Silver that she would have no problem maintaining her country club membership. The dues were not high, and she could easily manage the expense. She had gotten back into playing golf, which she had been forced to give up during John's illness because of time constraints. She had forgotten how much she enjoyed it. The women in her former foursome were pleased to have her back since the woman they had added in her absence had not worked out. They were now talking about taking a golf clinic at some place such as Hilton Head. She liked the idea; it would be great to get away for a while. She hadn't been anywhere in at least a year and a half. She didn't think it would be difficult for her to go on this trip because she had been friendly with these women for most of her adult life. They had raised their children together and shared the joys as well as the trials and tribulations of daily life as wives and mothers. They all knew each other very well and usually had a lot of fun. She remembered a time about two years ago when a group of them had gone off for a sports weekend and spent most of their time laughing.

Because it appeared that she had more than enough income to live on comfortably, Audrey thought about helping educate Joanne's children. John Jr. could more than provide for himself and his family, but Joanne's husband, Keith, didn't make much money, and his prospects for promotion didn't look good. Joanne wanted to send both the younger children to preschool. Earlier, before John had become so ill, Joanne had asked if her parents could help out with the payments for Heidi's preschool. Audrey knew things must have been bad for Joanne to admit she needed assistance. She decided to ask her to be more specific about how much preschool would cost. Audrey wanted to help Joanne, but she also wanted to be fair to John Jr. and his children. She thought she could afford to give them both some money each year without sacrificing her lifestyle but wasn't sure of the best way to go about this. She decided to ask Mr. Silver for his advice.

When Audrey met with Mr. Silver, she gave him her expense figures for the past two years and told him she anticipated spending more in the future on food, clothes, entertainment, and vacations. She also told him she wanted to become more involved in charitable work and give more to charities if she could afford to do so.

Audrey asked Mr. Silver about the best way to help pay for the education of Joanne's preschool-age children. He said he wanted to look at Audrey's estimated income and expenses more closely, but it looked as if she could give Joanne and John Jr. each $6,000 annually. Mr. Silver felt gifting money was a sensitive subject. Even if John Jr. didn't need the money, it had been his experience in cases like this that it was important to treat both children equally. It avoided family arguments later.

Audrey had indicated to Mr. Silver that Keith might be sensitive about her giving them money. Mr. Silver suggested it might work best if Audrey paid the tuition and child care bills directly instead of handing them a check for $6,000. In John Jr.'s case, they could discuss the best way for her to give him the money. For instance, he might want to use it to add to his children's college savings.

Mr. Silver pointed out that under current tax law she could give as much as $12,000 each to John Jr. and Joanne annually. Audrey would not get a tax deduction for giving it, but John Jr. and Joanne would not have to pay taxes on receiving it. He recommended she start by giving each of her children $6,000 this year. This amount seemed more appropriate for her budget at this time. He also suggested that when Audrey spoke to her children about her desire to gift them annually, she should tell them that she was able to do this now because she had more than enough income to cover her expenses. However, because the major source of her income was John's pension money and the payments would not increase from current levels, she should explain to them there might come a time in the future when she could not be as generous.

Audrey decided to talk this over with Joanne and John Jr. and made another appointment to meet with Mr. Silver. He wanted to discuss a more realistic budget for her once she provided him with better expense estimates.

Audrey's Preliminary Annual Budget

Annual Income

Pension	$42,000	
Social Security	14,000	
Stock dividends	4,000	
Money market account	1,800	
Total		**$61,800**

Annual Expenses

Mortgage	$ 3,156	
Other	30,000	
Gifts to children	12,000	
Income taxes	12,000	
Real estate taxes	2,000	
Totals		**$59,156**
Annual Positive Cash Flow		**$ 2,644**

Elizabeth

Reactions to the Budgeting Process

It appeared to Elizabeth that her situation was pretty simple. She had two primary sources of income: Social Security and income from Ben's stock portfolio. The nice woman at Social Security had told her she would receive Social Security income of $1,666.66 per month. She also said this payment could be paid directly to her bank each month, which Elizabeth thought was an excellent idea. Ben's $500,000, which she now knew was referred to as a portfolio, was handled by someone called an investment manager. He told her that Ben's stocks were paying about $10,000 per year, or $833.33 per month. Ben had never set up a retirement fund at his company, so there was no income from that source.

Mr. Grossfeldt, her new lawyer, gave her a form to complete so he could help her estimate what her expenses might be in the future. She took out her and Ben's checkbook and reviewed their past expenses. She knew that future expenses would be different. While Ben was sick, she had bought no clothes, they rarely went out, and they never entertained—so they spent very little money. She couldn't remember when she had last spent time with the "girls." She had let all her friendships lapse over the past few years because watching out for Ben had taken up all of her time. She had really enjoyed her sewing circle and now realized how much she had missed those get-togethers.

Elizabeth had tried to keep her church activities up but had not been very successful in doing so. Ben didn't like her to be away from him for any longer than an hour, and it was easier to comply than argue. She was beginning to reconnect with the church but didn't know how much time she would spend on church-related activities.

There was no mortgage on the home, so she didn't have that expense. On the other hand, she would need to hire someone to help her with the yard work. A neighborhood boy who had been taking care of their small garden was going off to college in the fall. All in all, it appeared she could afford to continue living in her home, but she wondered if she wanted to do so. She felt as if she were rattling around in all those rooms.

Her older sister, Abigail, enjoyed living in her retirement community in Florida and was urging Elizabeth to visit her. The idea of warm weather after the bitter New England winters appealed to Elizabeth. Ben had refused to visit Abigail, to the point where the effort of convincing him to take the trip outweighed the pleasure of visiting with her sister.

In the past few years, because of Ben's deteriorating health, the couple had spent most of their time at home. Although she was basically a homebody, Elizabeth secretly yearned to take a cruise. She wondered if it were foolish of her to consider taking such a trip. She didn't think she had the courage to take one alone, but maybe she could talk Abigail into joining her. During their marriage, she and Ben never took trips—he always said he couldn't be away from work that long—but she suspected he really didn't like the idea of being someplace unfamiliar.

When Elizabeth added up her projected annual income, including the money she had in the savings account, it totaled $30,750. Her general living expenses were $19,500, her property taxes were $1,500, and she gave $1,000 to the church each year; her total expenses were $22,000. Thus it appeared she would have enough income to cover her expenses.

Mr. Grossfeldt gave her the name of an accountant he used, Mrs. Greenfield, to see about her taxes. Mrs. Greenfield determined that Elizabeth's total federal and state taxes would be $408 annually. She also told Elizabeth she would be in the 5 percent tax bracket—which sounded pretty good to her! Subtracting the taxes, Elizabeth had $7,934 left over to spend on herself.

Mrs. Greenfield suggested Elizabeth apply for a credit card, one that would earn her miles on an airline. She recommended that she charge everything she could on this card and then pay it off once a month (thus avoiding interest charges). That way she could keep track of what her expenses actually were as well as get credited with air miles and thus possibly earn a free air ticket to Florida.

Elizabeth had had more meetings and discussions with people related to money matters since Ben died than she had had in her entire life. She appreciated the fact that none of these people made her feel stupid. They all treated her considerately and took the time to explain things to her. She felt she had learned so much these past few months. She had even developed a new friendship with another recent widow, Lucy. Since Lucy looked at life and death in a positive way she was a good role model for Elizabeth. For the first time since Ben's death, she started thinking positively about her future.

Abigail had continued to press her about visiting her in Florida. Now that it appeared she could afford to do so, she decided she was ready to travel. Visiting her sister in Florida, taking a cruise, possibly moving to a warmer climate—all of that sounded pretty good to her.

She felt so fortunate that it appeared that financially she had so many options!

Elizabeth's Preliminary Annual Budget

Annual Income

Social Security	$20,000	
Portfolio income	10,000	
Savings account	750	
Total		**$30,750**

Annual Expenses

General	$19,500	
Taxes	408	
Property taxes	1,500	
Charities	1,000	
Total		**$22,408**
Annual Positive Cash Flow		**$ 8,342**

8
Calculating Your Net Worth

The moving finger writes; and, having writ,
Moves on: nor all thy Piety nor Wit
Shall lure it back to cancel half a line,
Nor all thy tears wash out a Word of it.
—Omar Khayyam

WHEN YOU CALCULATED your expenses and income, you might have discovered (as Diane and Susan did) that there does not seem to be enough income to cover your expenses. The next step is to determine what assets you have that might provide you with sources of income besides Social Security and pension income. To do this, you need to figure out your net worth. Calculating your net worth is simply listing what you own and then subtracting from that number the amount you owe.

Assets are defined as anything you own that has commercial or exchange value if you sell it. Thus, when you value personal assets such as jewelry and furniture for the purposes of an asset statement, think in terms of resale value rather than replacement value. If you are itemizing personal assets for insurance purposes, you would list them at replacement value. When you list your assets, it is a good idea to indicate ownership as well—that is, your assets (P = Personal), your husband's assets (E = Estate), and your joint assets (J = Joint).

In this chapter we have provided the basic format for listing each different kind of asset. We realize you may have more of one kind of asset than we have provided space for, but we want to provide the format for each kind of asset.

PERSONAL ASSETS

Your Home

For your residence, you should indicate ownership, approximate market value, original cost, and any major improvements you have made. (If you don't know the cost of improvements, approximate the cost.)

If the home was held in your husband's name, then the cost will be increased to the valuation given it in the estate. As we indicated previously, if the home was held jointly, one-half the cost is based on the original cost plus improvements, and one-half is the current value in the estate. Taking advantage of this so-called stepped-up basis for the cost of your home can be helpful in reducing or eliminating any capital gains tax you might incur if and when you decide to sell your home.

Location _____

Ownership _____

Original cost _____

Market value_____

Improvements_____

Second Home

If you have a second home that is primarily for personal use and/or if you own time-shares in a vacation home, you need to list similar information for these assets here. If the property is primarily a rental property, you would list it later, under "investment real estate."

Location _____

Ownership _____

Cost _____

Current market value _____

Time-shares should also be listed under personal assets:

Location _____

Ownership _____

Cost _____

Current market value _____

Personal Property

Personal property includes your cars, home furnishings, jewelry, furs, antiques, Oriental rugs, and art in your home. At a later date, you might decide you don't need as many cars as you now have, but at this point you are just identifying what you currently own. (You may find that your car is worth less than the amount you owe on it.)

If one or more of your cars are leased, you should indicate the terms of the lease, which would appear on your lease agreement. If you are unable to find this agreement, call your leasing agent to obtain a copy of the agreement.

A rough estimate of your personal property will do. Under the category "Other" we are including jewelry, furs, antiques, Oriental rugs, or art you may have in your home.

	Description	Owner	Value
Car no. 1	_____	_____	$_____
Car no. 2	_____	_____	_____
Car no. 3	_____	_____	_____
Furnishings	_____	_____	_____
Other	_____	_____	_____

PERSONAL INVESTMENTS

Cash

Here you would list your checking accounts, savings accounts, money market funds, certificates of deposit, U.S. Treasury bills or notes, and any money due to be paid to you in the next 12 months. This would include the proceeds of any insurance policies payable to you, a trust, or the estate.

A rule of thumb is to keep a cash reserve that equals three to six months' expenses. However, we have found the actual amount of cash reserve you would like to have is an emotional as well as financial decision. Some people are not comfortable unless they have a lot of cash available. Others require smaller amounts. At this point of uncertainty and change in your life, you may prefer to have a larger cash reserve. Once you have a better idea of your expenses, you may choose to decrease the amount of cash reserve you feel you need.

Once you have determined how much you need to have in your cash account in order to feel comfortable, keep this amount in a savings account or invested in a money market account, where it is readily accessible and earning interest. This cash reserve would be available to cover any expected or unexpected large expenses, such as replacing your furnace or repairing your car. Having this cash reserve prevents your having to liquidate an investment at an undesirable time. Besides, having a cash cushion should give you peace of mind.

Place Held	Owner	Balance	Interest Rate
Checking account		$	
_____	_____	_____	_____
_____	_____	_____	_____
_____	_____	_____	_____
_____	_____	_____	_____
Savings account			
_____	_____	_____	_____
_____	_____	_____	_____
_____	_____	_____	_____
Money market accounts			
_____	_____	_____	_____
_____	_____	_____	_____
_____	_____	_____	_____
Notes receivable			
_____	_____	_____	_____
_____	_____	_____	_____
_____	_____	_____	_____
Life insurance policies			
_____	_____	_____	_____
_____	_____	_____	_____
_____	_____	_____	_____
_____	_____	_____	_____

Bonds

Here you want to indicate what kinds of bonds you own: U.S. government bonds, tax-free municipal bonds, or corporate bonds. Basically, a bond is an I.O.U. to you from the U.S. government, a municipality, or a corporation. The certificate states to whom you are loaning the money, when you will be repaid, and the rate of interest you will receive from the borrower. The way you can determine to whom you are loaning the money is to look on your statement from a bank or brokerage firm or at the certificate itself.

For instance, if the statement or certificate reads "$10,000 IBM Corporation 6% 5/1/20," this means IBM is the corporation borrowing the money from you, so it is a corporate bond. The $10,000 is the amount IBM has borrowed from you. IBM has agreed to pay you back the money on the date it comes due—the maturity date. In this case, the corporation will pay you $10,000 on May 1, 2020 (5/1/20). The 6 percent is the amount of interest IBM will pay. In this example, you will receive $600 a year ($10,000 x .06). IBM will pay you one-half this amount ($300) every six months—on May 1 (the month of the due date) and November 1 (six months later) in this case.

If the borrower was the U.S. government, then it is a U.S. Treasury bond; if the borrower was a municipality like the city of New York, then it is a municipal bond. We will discuss bonds in greater detail in chapter 13, but in the meantime, you want to list what you own, indicating for each bond the borrower, the amount of the bond, the interest rate it pays, the date it is due, and the ownership.

Borrowing Entity	Face Amount	Interest Rate	Due Date	Owner
_____	$_____	_____	_____	_____

Notes Receivable

These would include any personal notes due you or your husband. List the amount owed, by whom, when the note is due, the interest rate being paid, and how often the interest is paid. You might also indicate the likelihood of repayment. For instance, if your husband loaned a friend some money and the friend has failed to repay the money in the past, you may not want to count on this as an asset.

Amount Owed	By Whom	Interest Rate	Due Date	Repayment Schedule
$_____	_____	_____	_____	_____
_____	_____	_____	_____	_____

Deferred Annuities

These are investments made with insurance companies. Deferred annuities may be fixed or variable. A fixed annuity pays a set rate of return for a specified period of time. A variable annuity has a variable return depending on the investments held in the annuity. (A more detailed discription of annuities can be found in chapter 13).

If you are not receiving current income from a deferred annuity, the income accumulates in a deferred annuity for you on a tax-deferred basis. In other words, you don't pay tax on what your money earns. At the end of each year, the insurance company provides you with a statement of the value of the annuity.

If you are the beneficiary of a deferred annuity your husband bought, you should write the company informing them of your husband's death. Someone from the company will let you know what the current value is and how you can access this money. If someone else is the beneficiary, the insurance company will notify him or her accordingly. Right now all you need to know is the current value of the annuity, the name of the insurance company, and the interest rate the annuity is currently paying.

Current Value	Company Name	Interest Rate
$_____	_____	_____
_____	_____	_____

Stocks

List the name of the company held, number of shares, cost (if you know it), date purchased (if you have it), and ownership. If you are the owner (or the stock was jointly held), the cost and date purchased are relevant; if your husband was the sole owner, these are not relevant because the cost will be determined by the value on the date of death (or six months later), depending on the value selected for the estate tax return.

Company	# Shares	Cost	Date Bought	Owner
_____	_____	$_____	_____	_____
_____	_____	_____	_____	_____

If your husband had some unexercised stock options, list these here, with the terms of how and when they should be exercised (this information would be provided to you by his company).

Value of outstanding stock options $_____

Terms of the stock options _____

Mutual Funds

Usually you don't have certificates for your mutual fund shares. These are held by the mutual fund company or by the stock brokerage firm. The most recent statement from the mutual fund company will list the number of shares you own, the name of the fund, and the owner of each fund. If you have been reinvesting dividends and capital gains generated by the mutual funds, the cost is difficult to calculate. We will discuss this in greater detail later.

Fund Name	No. of Shares	Cost	Date Bought	Owner
_____	_____	$_____	_____	_____
_____	_____	_____	_____	_____

Limited Partnerships and Non-Traded Real Estate Investment Trusts

If you or your spouse owned any limited partnerships or non-traded real estate investment trusts, list the name of each investment. In the first quarter of each year you should receive a tax statement from each company that should list the name and address of the general partner. For limited partnerships this statement is called a k-1. If you know the date the partnership was originally purchased and the cost, that is helpful but not essential information.

Name of Partnership	Name/Address Contact Person	No. of Units	Cost	Owner
_____	_____	_____	$_____	_____
_____	_____	_____	_____	_____

Investment Real Estate

List any real estate investments you or your spouse owned. Include rental properties as well as undeveloped land. These should be appraised to establish a tax basis. Your most recent tax return along with other data will provide your financial advisor with information needed to help you decide if you want to keep these properties or sell them. However, usually this is not a decision that needs to be made immediately.

Property	No. 1	No. 2	No. 3
Address	_____	_____	_____
	_____	_____	_____
	_____	_____	_____
	_____	_____	_____
Owner	_____	_____	_____
Market value	$_____	$_____	$_____
Amount of mortgage	$_____	$_____	$_____
Terms of mortgage	_____	_____	_____

Business Interests

Business interests would include your or your husband's ownership in any privately held business. "*Privately held*" means that the shares are not traded on a public stock exchange such as the New York Stock Exchange. A privately held business might have been your husband's business or an investment made in someone else's business. The valuation may be complex, but your professional advisors will help with this process. Right now, all you need to know is an approximate value of these business interests and how much cash you may receive from them.

Value of business interests $_____

Other

This category would cover anything we haven't previously discussed, such as stamp and coin collections, precious metals, commodities, or other "toys" such as boats or motorcycles. These are often worth less than you may think but should be listed in the asset statement.

Description	Ownership	Market Value
_____	_____	$_____
_____	_____	_____
_____	_____	_____

RETIREMENT ASSETS

Retirement Accounts

By now you should know what retirement income you will receive from your husband's previous employer(s). In addition, he may have other retirement accounts, such as IRA, Keogh, TIAA/ CREF, 401(k), 403(b), and SEP/IRA accounts.

If you are the beneficiary of these accounts, you can roll over these accounts into a retirement account in your own name. If you choose to receive the cash instead, then any amount you withdraw from a retirement account is taxable to you, and usually there are additional taxes due if you withdraw the money before age 59 1/2. Taking money out of retirement accounts is a complex decision, so be sure to get professional advice before you do it. If you don't, you may create adverse tax consequences that are irreversible.

	Current Value	Where Invested	Interest Rate (if applicable)
IRA	$_____	_____	_____
	_____	_____	_____
Roth IRA	_____	_____	_____
Nondeductible IRA	_____	_____	_____
Keogh	_____	_____	_____
	_____	_____	_____
SEP/IRA	_____	_____	_____
	_____	_____	_____

401(k)   _____   _____   _____
403(b)   _____   _____   _____
TIAA/CREF   _____   _____   _____
Other   _____   _____   _____

CHILDRENS' ASSETS

Custodial Accounts

Custodial accounts are set up for the purpose of holding assets for minor children. There are two very similar types of custodial accounts: Unified Gifts to Minor's Accounts (UGMA) and Unified Transfer to Minor's Accounts (UTMA). With either type of account, a child is the beneficiary and an adult custodian is named to oversee the account. Usually the custodian is the parent, but it could be any adult. All of the income paid by the investments in this account is taxed to the child each year.

Assets put into a custodial account are legally owned by the child, and when the child reaches the age of majority (either 18 or 21 depending on state law), the child has the right to spend that money any way he or she wishes. Of course, as the child is growing up, the custodian can spend the money on the child's behalf for things that directly benefit the child, other than food and shelter. This could include things like private schooling, camp, a computer, or a car.

Section 529 Plans (Qualified Tuition Plans)

Section 529 plans are college savings programs. The money in these plans must be used toward higher education, including graduate school. The owner of the account is usually a parent or grandparent, but it could be any adult. Unlike a custodial account, taxes don't have to paid on the interest and dividends or capital gains as long as the money stays in the 529 account. Section 529 plans differ from custodial accounts in another way: the owner of the account retains ownership of the assets even after the child reaches age 18 or 21. If the money is not needed for the beneficiary's college education, the owner can name another family member as the new beneficiary. Non-qualified withdrawals are subject to income tax, plus a 10 percent federal tax penalty.

We think college savings plans are a good idea for many people, but because of their complexity, we recommend you consult with a financial advisor before investing. The current laws that apply to Section 529 plans will expire after 2010 unless Congress extends them.

**Coverdell Education Savings Accounts
(formerly Education IRAs)**

This is another type of account that can be set up with a child named as beneficiary and an adult named as the custodian. An annual contribution of up to $2,000 can be made for each child under the age of 18 as long as your income does not exceed certain limits. Money in this account must be spent on the child's education, but under current law this education includes kindergarten through college. Like a custodial account, the money put into a Coverdell account is considered a permanent gift to the child. However, you do not have to pay taxes on the interest and dividends while the money remains in the Coverdell account.

If the money is not used by the time the child is age 30, it will be paid out to the child and any gain in value of the account would be taxed as ordinary income. However, the owner can change the beneficiary to another member of the family before that time.

Other Types of Childrens' Accounts

There may be assets in a trust set up for a child, or you may have a joint account with a child named as one of the joint owners. Regardless of the type of account, if you have any accounts that were set up for the benefit of a minor child, you should work with your financial or tax advisor to help you sort out the rules. Each type of account has special tax rules that apply as well as different rules regarding how much money can be put in, how much can be withdrawn, and who acually owns the assets in the account. Each type of account may also have a different impact on the child's ability to qualify for financial aid.

LIABILITIES

Now that you have a list of your assets and their approximate value, you can begin listing the money you owe other people. These debts are your liabilities.

Mortgages

Once you have estimated the value of your home, condominium, or co-op, it is important to determine how much you owe the mortgage company. Your mortgage holders will be glad to provide you with the following information:

Amount of current mortgage	$_____
Current interest rate (fixed or adjustable)	_____
Monthly payment (principal and interest)	_____
Years remaining on the mortgage	_____
Amount of second mortgage	$_____
Current interest rate (fixed or adjustable	_____
Monthly payment (principal and interest)	_____
Years left on second mortgage	_____

Mortgage on second home, condominium, or co-op

Current mortgage	$_____
Current interest rate (fixed or adjustable)	_____
Monthly payment (principal and interest)	_____
Years remaining on the mortgage	_____
Loan due on time-shares	
Current amount	$_____
Current interest rate (fixed or adjustable)	_____
Monthly payment	$_____
Years remaining on the loan	_____

Home Equity Loan (HEL)

As we previously stated, a home equity loan is a line of credit against your home. The bank has loaned you and your husband all or part of a preapproved amount. The usual maximum amount is $100,000. Repayment schedules vary. You may have agreed to pay certain amounts each month for five or ten years, or you may be paying interest only on the debt. The interest rate you pay can be fixed or variable. Be forewarned, however: now that your husband is deceased, this loan may be reexamined by the bank's loan officer, who may be concerned about your ability to repay.

Amount of home equity loan approved	$_____
Amount of current loan	$_____
Current interest rate	_____
Repayment terms	_____

Outstanding Debts

List here any debts you owe to anyone: the amount you owe, the interest rate you are paying, how often you make payments, and to whom you make payments. Include the amount you currently owe on your credit cards, on car loans, or to anyone else.

Kind of Debt	No. 1	No. 2	No. 3
Owed to whom?	_____	_____	_____
Current amount outstanding	$_____	$_____	$_____
Payment amount	$_____	$_____	$_____
Due date	_____	_____	_____
Interest rate	_____	_____	_____

CONTINGENT LIABILITIES

This is a potential obligation to pay a debt. For instance, your husband may have personally guaranteed a loan your son took out to start his business. If your son fails to make payments, your husband's estate may be liable.

Your husband may have signed a pledge to a charity, such as his college's Capital Campaign Fund but failed to mention this in his will. Depending on local law, the charity may be entitled to be paid.

Before your husband's death, you both may have agreed to pay for the education of your children or grandchildren. After looking at the total picture, you may find that you are unable to do this. List any such promises with the idea that you may have to amend them.

A Word of Warning Regarding Making New Loans to Family or Friends

Widows are prime targets for people seeking loans. If family or friends believe you have inherited a considerable amount of money, they may ask you to lend them some for various purposes. For example, they may want you to help them finance a "sure-fire" business venture, educate a child, or help them purchase a new home. Although this advice may seem harsh, we would strongly recommend that you make no loans, no matter how worthy the project appears—at least until you have determined your financial situation. If you feel that you must make the loan, we believe you should lend only the amount of money that you never expect to see again and that is relatively small in relation to your net worth. Always require a written agreement with stated interest rates and repayment terms. That way, if it is a business loan and you are not repaid, you can deduct it as a loss on your income tax return.

SUMMARY AND CONCLUSION

You now have a comprehensive list of your assets and liabilities. With this information, your financial advisor will prepare a statement of your current financial condition, also called a *net worth statement,* as outlined in figure 8.1. In the previous chapter, you estimated your income and expenses. Now you are ready to review all this information with your financial planner. Your goal is to make sure that you have sufficient income both now and in the future. This may involve changing some of these assets. Finally, you are ready to do some longer-term planning.

FIGURE 8.1 Net Worth Statement

Net Worth Statement as of _____

For:_____

I.	Personal Assets	$ _____	
	Home Value	_____	
	Second home(s) value	_____	
	Time-share(s) value	_____	
	Cars	_____	
	Total		$ _____
II.	Cash		$ _____
III.	Personal Investments		
	Bonds	$ _____	
	Notes receivable	_____	
	Deferred annuities	_____	
	Stocks	_____	
	Mutual funds	_____	
	Limited partnerships	_____	
	Business interests	_____	
	Real estate	_____	
	Other	_____	
	Total		$ _____
IV.	Retirement Investments		
	IRA	$ _____	
	IRA rollover	_____	
	Nondeductible IRA	_____	
	Roth IRA	_____	
	Keogh	_____	
	SEP/IRA	_____	
	401(k)	_____	
	403(b)	_____	
	TIAA-CREF	_____	
	Other	_____	
	Total		$ _____
V.	Liabilities		
	Mortgage loan on home	$ _____	
	Home equity loan	_____	
	Mortgage(s) on second home(s)	_____	
	Loan due on time-shares	_____	
	Car Loan	_____	
	Credit card debt	_____	
	Other debt	_____	
	Total		$ _____
	Net Worth		
	(I + II + III + IV −V)		$ _____

DIANE

Reactions to Calculating Her Net Worth

Diane had about $320,000 in available cash. The insurance companies had informed her that they were holding $200,000 for her in interest-bearing accounts, which she could access at any time. Karen Hutchinson, at Mark's firm, had been kind enough to arrange for the $100,000 from the firm's capital account to be paid to her right away. Diane had deposited the money immediately in an account at her bank that she had opened in her name. She also had a total of $20,000 in their checking and savings accounts at the bank.

Dorothy had suggested Diane pay off her credit card debt as soon as possible from this money in view of the 18 percent interest she was paying on the unpaid balance. The current bills seemed to total about $15,000. How had they gotten so high?

She had not had the home appraised yet but knew it was worth about $900,000. Her neighbor across the street had recently sold her home, which was similar to theirs, so she knew her estimate was about right. Values of homes had really increased since they bought theirs ten years ago for $400,000. The mortgage officer informed her that they had refinanced their home a couple of years ago, their current mortgage balance was $500,000 at 6 percent, and they still had 28 years of mortgage payments. Diane realized that by the time she paid the mortgage off she would be 70 years old! One solution to her negative cash flow might be selling their beautiful home she loved so much. She hoped she could avoid doing that.

Diane knew she needed to make the decision about whether or not to invest the $800,000 from the firm's insurance policy on Mark in the fixed annuity pretty soon because she needed to know how much income she could count on to pay her expenses.

Mark's retirement account was worth $300,000, but the stockbroker, her dad, and Larry all told her she shouldn't touch this because she would need it for her retirement. At this point, she felt she couldn't worry about retirement. There were too many other immediate needs to worry about. She needed to find money now to educate her children.

It was obvious to Diane that she had better get back together with Dorothy right away to see what she should do. Even to Diane's nonfinancial brain, things looked pretty grim!

Diane's Financial Statement

Assets

Cash in bank	$ 20,000	
Home	900,000	
Insurance (firm)	800,000	
Insurance (other)	200,000	
Capital account	100,000	
Retirement account	300,000	
Van	15,000	
Mark's car	10,000	
Total		**$2,345,000**

Liabilities

Mortgage	$500,000	
Van loan	15,000	
Charge accounts	15,000	
Total		**$ 530,000**

Net Worth	**$1,815,000**

Susan

Reactions to Calculating Her Net Worth

After reviewing her income and expenses, Susan realized that she did have a cash flow problem. It was important that she review her assets more carefully to see if they could produce more income.

Lance and Susan had a money market account with $15,000 in it. Their condominium had appreciated greatly in recent years; it was now worth about $500,000, and the mortgage was $350,000. Their cottage was worth $250,000, and the mortgage was $150,000. They had no credit card debts because Lance paid the bills monthly and really didn't like having any debt. The more Susan looked at the situation, the more obvious it was that the cottage was a luxury she could not afford. She decided to call the realtor who had sold it to her and put it up for sale.

Bob O'Brien, Lance's stockbroker, sent Susan the list of Lance's stocks, which were worth $200,000, together with his recommendation of which ones to sell to raise the $50,000 she needed for Lance's children. She met with Bob to finalize these sales and figure out a strategy for the future. Bob explained that the stocks Lance owned paid no income because they were growth stocks. She discussed with Bob the advisability of changing these stocks to ones that would produce more income. In view of her relatively young age, he told her he was reluctant to recommend moving too far in this direction; he wanted her portfolio to have the potential to grow in value. It had been his experience that most stocks that pay a high level of income don't grow much in value.

Susan had asked her brother, Ron, about helping out with their mother's financial support, but he was not reassuring. He told her that his salary was not high, and he had his own financial problems. At best, he would be able to contribute $200 per month toward their mother's expenses. However, he realized that it wasn't right for Susan to take on all the responsibility. If he could not help much financially, at least he could help personally. He offered to visit Mom weekly in the future and occasionally take her out for lunch or another activity. Susan was grateful he could help out with the monthly payments; this meant she had to pay only $800 a month.

Susan knew that she could withdraw money from Lance's pension fund (worth $500,000) if she really needed the money to make ends meet. However, because any income she withdrew would be taxable to her, Susan wanted to avoid doing that. Also, because she didn't have a very large retirement fund of her own, she thought taking money from this fund was really her last resort. This pension plan was invested at Lance's firm. Harry told her she could leave these assets with the firm's pension manager for the time being. Eventually, she would have to make a decision about managing this money, but it was not necessary to do this right now.

Susan's own retirement fund at the association was invested in a fixed-income investment held by an insurance company. It had seemed to be a safe place for her to invest her money, and she had never paid much attention to it. Susan thought to herself, now that she was dealing with larger amounts of money, it would be a good idea to learn more about investments.

Susan was also the income beneficiary of the trust fund Lance had set up for his two children, but she could not list the trust as her asset because she did not own it. For the present, the trust owned the assets. According to the way the trust was written, Susan was entitled to receive the income from the trust for her lifetime. Actually, she also had the right to invade the principal if necessary. However, since her stepchildren were already upset about the fact they felt they'd been cheated out of their inheritance, she didn't want to take anything except the income out of this trust, which ultimately went to them, unless it was absolutely necessary.

On reviewing her situation, Susan seriously considered the thought that she might have to look for a better-paying job. Maybe she should talk to her boss at the association about raising her salary. Everyone at the association had been so good to her during these recent painful months that she hated to make a change. However, she had to be realistic about her situation. It was clear she needed more income than she currently had if she was going to keep the condominium.

Susan wanted to discuss these feelings and options in her next session with Dr. Coleman. She realized she was truly benefiting from her sessions with Dr. Coleman.

Susan's Financial Statement

Assets*

Cash	$ 15,000	
Condominium	500,000	
Lake cottage	250,000	
Stocks	200,000	
Lance's pension plan	500,000	
Susan's pension plan	25,000	
Car	10,000	
Total		**$1,500,000**

Liabilities

Mortgage, condominium	$350,000	
Mortgage, cottage	150,000	
Money due stepchildren	50,000	
Total		**$ 550,000**

Net Worth	**$950,000**

*Trust assets do not appear as Susan's assets because she is entitled to receive income only from the trust.

AUDREY

Reactions to Calculating Her Net Worth

Audrey reviewed her assets. She had about $20,000 in a savings account. The home was worth $400,000, and it was really too big for her. It was the home she had lived in most of her married life; now she wanted something newer and easier to take care of than her present home. On the other hand, she wasn't in any rush to move. She liked the location, particularly because it was close to Joanne. She wanted to help Joanne as much as possible and didn't want to miss the opportunity of seeing her grandchildren grow up.

In addition to the $20,000 in her and John's joint savings account, Audrey had received $40,000 in insurance money. She didn't know where to put it, so she added it to her savings account at her local bank. The manager certainly had been nice to her when she made the deposit.

Shortly before John was diagnosed as having cancer, they had decided to redo the kitchen and had applied for a home equity loan of $20,000. Fortunately, they hadn't started the work, although they had made all the plans with the contractor. She wondered if she should go ahead with this project. She decided to ask Mr. Silver if she should use the home equity loan or some of the insurance money to finance this expense if she did decide to fix up the kitchen.

The thought of dealing with all the workers and the mess involved in redoing the kitchen was not appealing to Audrey, especially if she might move sooner rather than later. The idea of spending money on a much-needed vacation was certainly more attractive. The prospect of going to a golf clinic at Hilton Head was becoming increasingly desirable—it would also be a good way to brush up on her skills! She knew Dr. PaPadisio would think it was a good idea. She needed to give more thought to how she wanted to spend her time and money. She was not in a rush but did not want too much time to pass without formulating a plan.

There was also the question of the company stock held in John's name, which was worth about $200,000. It paid her $4,000 per year in income, which wasn't much (2 percent), but John never wanted to sell it because he loved the company so much. Besides, he said, the taxes on the gain would have been prohibitive because his cost for the shares was so low. The lawyer had mentioned something about the fact that because the shares were part of John's estate, the cost basis would be increased to reflect current market values. That meant she could sell these shares without worrying about paying tax on the gain. But she knew John would not have approved! She would have to think about this further in terms of her needs. For now, she would make no decision, but she would discuss it at greater length with Mr. Silver.

By the time Audrey had completed her asset and liability statement, it was time to get ready for her lunch with Joanne. They had begun to meet for lunch regularly on Wednesdays, and both women looked forward to it.

When Audrey had last seen Dr. PaPadisio, he was very pleased with her because she had gained five pounds. She attributed this gain in part to the efforts she had been making to include a lunch out with friends in conjunction with her volunteer work as well as her regularly scheduled lunches with Joanne. Today she was looking forward to discussing the preschool issue with her daughter.

Audrey was also pleased with the results of her conversation with John Jr. He called when he was about to leave for the office a few days ago and asked if he could drop by to see her. He said they hadn't had much time to talk, and he didn't want her to feel neglected by him. She assured him she wasn't feeling neglected and encouraged him to stop by the following week on his way to work. She thought this meeting would provide her with a wonderful opportunity to discuss her financial situation with him.

When John Jr. arrived, he looked somewhat more tired and older than Audrey remembered. She guessed she'd been so preoccupied with John's care and then her financial situation that she hadn't given much thought to how the loss of their father had impacted the children. She looked at John Jr. as though she hadn't seen him in a long time even though he had been present throughout the planning for the funeral and at the funeral itself. He looked as though he had the weight of the world on his shoulders. Somehow, this older, more vulnerable look made him appear less formidable to her.

She offered him a cup of coffee, and they sat at the kitchen table in the comfortable, well-worn chairs. After telling him about her decision to become involved with the Reading Is Fundamental organization, Audrey told him she was really pleased he had decided to stop over because she had been meaning to talk with him about her financial situation. She could see him imperceptibly stiffen. She immediately went on to say that his father had provided very nicely for her, and she anticipated no financial problems. She laid out the various sheets she had been working on—her assets and liabilities sheet and a summary of her monthly financial needs. She told him about her work with Mr. Humphrey, her lawyer, and with Mr. Silver, the financial planner. She explained that after reviewing her total financial status with these men, she found that she was in a position to give some money to each of her children and wanted to do so on an annual basis.

John Jr. was somewhat taken aback by both her understanding of her financial situation and her generosity. She could tell that he was also relieved that he wouldn't have to help support her. She could see him visibly relax. He was generous with his praise of all she had accomplished, and he seemed to view her with greater respect. She went on to tell him that she had decided on $6,000 per year per family. He tried to dissuade her from making that sum available to him in view of the disparity in income between his family and Joanne's. She assured him that she had taken all that into consideration but had decided on giving each of her children the same amount. If he wanted the money to go directly to his children, that was all right with her. She told him she would discuss the best way to accomplish this with Mr. Silver. Audrey also asked John Jr. if he would be willing to meet with her and Mr. Silver to review her financial plans for the future. He was most agreeable to doing that and told his mother to make an appointment for them in the next two or three weeks.

Both mother and son realized they had gotten beyond the barrier that had existed between them for such a long time now, although neither one verbally acknowledged it. He invited her over for dinner the next week, and they hugged each other when they parted. Audrey thought she might make more of an effort to see John Jr. than she had done in the recent past. She realized he really wasn't pompous; it was just that he didn't know how to express his concern for her.

She hoped things would go as well with Joanne, with whom she was having lunch. She was running late and called Joanne to take the table she had reserved for them at a new restaurant about which she recently had heard many good things. She was really excited about sharing with Joanne what she had discussed with Mr. Silver. As soon as they ordered, Audrey elaborated on her discussion with Mr. Silver regarding the $6,000 a year to each of her children. Audrey could see that Joanne was surprised and somewhat defensive. She apologized to her mother for being a burden and told her she felt like a charity case, which made her very uncomfortable. However, not wanting to hurt her mother's feelings, Joanne went on to tell her how very grateful she was for making the money available. Audrey reassured her and was pleased she could tell her she was doing the same thing for John Jr. and had already discussed it with him. Joanne appeared greatly relieved and perked up considerably.

Audrey's Financial Statement

Assets

Savings account	$ 60,000	
Home	400,000	
Stock	200,000	
Car	20,000	
Total		**$680,000**

Liabilities

Mortgage	$20,000	
Total		**$20,000**

Net Worth		**$660,000**

ELIZABETH

Reactions to Calculating Her Net Worth

Elizabeth had $25,000 in a savings account, and since it appeared her expenses were about $22,408, she thought that should tide her over until she worked out the rest of her financial situation. Her home was worth about $300,000, and Ben was proud of the fact that they had paid off their mortgage several years ago. She had received a $10,000 check from a small life insurance policy and used that money to pay for the funeral and some outstanding bills. She also had some land in Vermont that Ben had bought years ago with the idea they might someday build a home on it. Somehow they never got around to it. The appraiser said it was worth $50,000

Elizabeth was having trouble dealing with the portfolio Ben owned. She was torn between leaving it with the money manager Ben had worked with all these years and taking it to a trust department of a bank to be managed, as Mr. Grossfeldt had suggested. She really didn't know enough to make an intelligent decision in this regard. She hated to impose on Sam Weatherly once again to help her, but she didn't know where else to turn. Her friend Mabel told her that municipal bonds were wonderful. They paid tax-free income and were safe. Perhaps she should sell everything and buy them—certainly life would be simpler that way.

Making financial decisions wasn't easy for her, but Elizabeth knew she needed to make some decisions. For example, she had to decide where she wanted to live for the remainder of her life. She had never really given much consideration to major decisions during her marriage. Ben would usually come home and say something like, "I've been thinking it's about time we did such and such, Liz. What do you think?" Her predictable response was, "Whatever you think, dear, is fine with me." She had always thought of herself as somewhat timid. As a child, she had allowed her older sister, Abigail, to make decisions for her and, later, Ben. She had been grateful to them for not expecting anything more of her on this level. Now her new financial advisors expected her to make certain decisions after they provided her with the advantages and disadvantages of each of her options. It was a new and uncomfortable role for her. She would have preferred to do nothing, burying her head in the sand and allowing others to decide for her. Unfortunately, she knew all too well that it was no longer appropriate to allow others to make her decisions. There was no one to turn to but herself.

Elizabeth was frightened by the thought of living any place other than her home, yet the harsh winters in Boston were beginning to bother her. The idea of moving to Florida was becoming more and more appealing. She enjoyed her church work and her friendship with the Weatherlys, Lucy, and Mabel, but many of her friends had moved away when they retired and some had died. Actually, if she were truthful with herself, she would have to admit she was often lonely, even though she now had Mittens to keep her company. It would be good to be near her sister.

Elizabeth realized that in order to make a change of this magnitude, she really needed to visit Abigail. Then she could see where she was living and meet her friends. Her sister had been encouraging her to come for a visit for years and had been insistent in their recent phone conversations. Elizabeth wondered why it was so hard for her to initiate anything. She had dealt with so many new people and money matters since Ben's death. She was becoming annoyed with herself over her ambivalence and lack of action. Mabel had already volunteered to look after Mittens while she was in Florida.

As she mulled over what to do about a visit to Abigail for the umpteenth time one gray morning, Elizabeth became irritated with herself for her own inaction. With resolve that she wasn't feeling, she picked up the phone and called a travel agent. She was surprised at how simple it was to arrange a direct flight to Miami. After making the necessary arrangements, she shocked herself by asking the travel agent to send her some information on one-week cruises that left from Ft. Lauderdale or Miami for the Bahamas.

As soon as she hung up, she called Abigail to tell her when she would be arriving. She decided not to mention the cruise until she got there. She wasn't sure how serious she was about it just yet. Somehow it seemed too daring—but maybe not.

Elizabeth's Financial Statement

Assets			
Cash	$ 25,000		
Home	300,000		
Land in Vermont	50,000		
Portfolio	500,000		
Total		875,000	
Liabilities	$ 0		
Total		$ 0	
			$ 875,000

9

Identifying Today's Financial Attitudes and Realities

Time is a dressmaker specializing in alterations.
—Faith Baldwin

The time has come to make sense of all the information you have accumulated. By now you should have a pretty good idea of whether you have enough income to cover your expenses. Whatever your circumstances, your advisor may be able to improve your situation by recommending changes in your investments.

Before making any adjustments, you need to review the attitudes you formed in childhood about money, your risk tolerance, your investment goals, and your investment objectives. In chapter 2 we discussed how your financial attitudes are formed. In this chapter we will review these factors in relation to where you are now.

FINANCIAL CONDITIONING

As indicated in the statistics in chapter 1, most women are widowed between the ages of 55 and 84. Most women born before World War II are likely to be affected by beliefs and myths associated with images of the traditional Ozzie and Harriet family. Parents had distinct roles: Father was head of the household and the decision maker outside the home, and Mother made most of the decisions about the home and the children. Women were not supposed to "worry their pretty little heads" about numbers. That was the man's job.

Talking about money was taboo. In fact, money was not to be discussed at the dinner table. It was a subject left to the men—father to son. Women were not encouraged to ask questions about finances. It was not considered ladylike for a woman to be competitive. In some families, this view carried over to the area of achievement. For example, if a young girl was better at a subject or a sport than her brothers or her boyfriend, she was encouraged to appear less competent and to make mistakes in order to allow the male to feel better about himself in general. The message was loud and clear: Women were not supposed to seek knowledge or success for themselves; it was unimportant for them to achieve.

Over the years, concepts such as these have been passed down from generation to generation without recognition of the consequences. Many women were therefore conditioned to be dependent rather than independent, particularly financially. To be independent might be viewed as unfeminine. To strive for independence might make you appear to lack confidence in your husband's ability to provide for his family and make decisions on their behalf. Regardless of the skills the man possessed, he was not to be challenged. It wasn't necessary for a woman to have knowledge about the family's finances.

These concepts were reinforced in school. As a generalization, women earn lower grades in high school math than do men. Studies have shown that the "math anxiety" that contributes to this picture is due more to conditioning than fact. What is true is that women and men learn differently. Men do better when material is presented concretely; women do better when material is presented verbally. Traditionally, math is presented in a matter-of-fact manner. This is not surprising considering that most people attracted to math prefer to focus on nonverbal activities and do not have strong verbal skills. Therefore, math teachers are often weaker on a verbal level than are other teachers. However, studies have shown when math is taught by someone with strong verbal skills, there is no difference between the achievement levels of males and females.

Women brought up in this era may also have incorporated into their thinking, unconsciously or consciously, the idea that it is unacceptable for a woman to take a job or have a career where the woman's earning power (present or potential) is greater than her husband's. The spoken or unspoken thought here is that this is emasculating and will make the man feel less adequate. Note that all of this suggests that the woman is the caretaker of the man, responsible for ensuring that he feels good about himself regardless of the reality, the effect on the family, or the personal toll. The younger widow may not have been so conditioned as a child and therefore it may be easier for her to take charge of her finances.

These are difficult thought patterns to break, but it is essential that you do so in order to take control of your financial life. If this is your background, you need to overcome it. If you do not do so, you are powerless. If you need help, consult a mental health specialist, a financial planner, or both. Without control over your money—and therefore over your life—you are enslaved to those who do understand money.

YOUR CURRENT ATTITUDE TOWARD MONEY

It is a good idea at this point to assess how your attitude toward money has changed since you were widowed. Over the past six months to a year, you have gathered a considerable amount of financial information and have been forced to make some financial decisions. Now is a good time to review what you have learned and what areas you have had a difficult time comprehending. Remember: This list is for your eyes alone and to be used only to help you identify where you are with regard to your financial attitude.

In completing your "Who Am I Today Financially?" form (figure 9.1), list under "Financial Strengths" those financial tasks you feel competent to handle. Under "Financial Weaknesses," list those tasks you are still having difficulty managing. Under "Financial Needs," indicate those areas where you would like to have more knowledge.

YOUR RISK TOLERANCE

Webster's Dictionary defines risk as "the possibility of loss or injury." It has been our experience that the majority of widows (regardless of wealth) say they don't want to take any risk because they are worried about having sufficient income and don't want to lose any of the money they have. After the first year, the widow usually has a better understanding of her situation and is more willing to take some risk. As the years go by and her financial knowledge increases, she may find she is ready to take even more risk. It is like learning to ride a bicycle. At first you are unsteady, but as you become more skilled, you gain self-confidence. The more you ride, the more venturesome you become.

There are different kinds of risk. Most people equate risk taking to gambling. However, all life entails taking chances. You can't even cross the street without some risk! What you *can* do is try to limit that risk by taking educated risks—in this example, you wait for the light to turn in your favor so you can cross the street safely.

The primary kind of risk you need to be aware of as a widow is the risk of loss of principal. If you don't have much money, you can't afford to lose any principal. Therefore, you should try to limit the amount of risk you take. We have all heard about women who run through their inheritances within a couple of years of being widowed. In some cases, these widows have spent more money than they should have because they didn't grasp the fact that this money wouldn't last forever. In other cases, the widows took more risk than they should have.

FIGURE 9.2 Risk Scale

Investment Risk Comfort Level		
Conservative	Middle of Road	Aggressive
1 2 3	4 5 6 7	8 9 10

How much risk are you willing to take? Later on, in chapter 13, we talk about how much risk different kinds of investments entail. In chapter 14 we give you some guidelines on how to reduce risk, but right now we

FIGURE 9.1 Who Am I Today Financially? Financial Strengths

1. _____
2. _____
3. _____
4. _____

Financial Weaknesses

1. _____
2. _____
3. _____
4. _____

Financial Needs

1. _____
2. _____
3. _____
4. _____

are talking about how much risk you can handle *emotionally*. On the scale in figure 9.2, circle the number that indicates how much risk you are comfortable taking when you invest. Circling 1 indicates that you want to take very little risk, while circling 10 indicates that you are willing to take a high degree of risk. This helps you and your advisor understand your risk-tolerance level.

INVESTMENT GOALS

You undoubtedly have certain financial goals you want to achieve with your money. Typical goals include educating children (or grandchildren), retiring in comfort, building wealth, and reducing income and estate taxes.

For example, a younger widow like Diane is primarily interested in educating her children; the concept of retirement seems very remote to her. On the other hand, the primary concern of an older widow such as Audrey is likely to be to remain self-sufficient for the rest of her life and also be able to leave a reasonable inheritance to her children when she dies.

On the following chart we have listed five common goals and left a place to add your own goals under "Other," which might include buying a new home or another similar goal. Write down your goals and then prioritize them in order of importance to you.

Educating children or grandchildren   _____
Having sufficient income for life   _____
Building wealth   _____
Reducing income taxes   _____
Other   _____

INVESTMENT OBJECTIVES

After you have determined your risk attitude and listed your investment goals in order of importance, you need to determine which investment objectives are most important to you.

Ask yourself what your highest investment priority is. Is it preserving principal, obtaining the highest current income, or having your principal grow? Most of us want to achieve all three objectives in one investment, but it is important to recognize this is not possible. An investment that has more of one advantage—such as safety of principal—will have less of another—such as potential for growth.

You need to decide which investment objective is most important to you and what you have to give up in order to attain it. Basically, it is an issue of trade-offs. For instance, if you want high current income, then the investments you select will have limited potential for growth of principal. If growth of principal is your priority, usually the income you receive from this investment will be low and you will have to take more risk. Even if your stated investment objective is high current income, your advisor will probably select different kinds of investments for you so that there is balance between investments with growth potential and those that provide high current income.

For instance, you might feel very comfortable investing in certificates of deposit (CDs) because they are issued by a bank, are fairly liquid, and, if less than $100,000, are guaranteed by the Federal Deposit Insurance Corporation (FDIC). But let's look at an example that might convince you otherwise.

Let's say you invest $10,000 in a one-year CD that pays 6 percent. This means you will receive $600 of income during the first year. On this income, you will pay federal and local taxes. If your combined state and federal tax bracket is 30 percent (ask your accountant or financial advisor what your tax bracket is), to find what you owe in taxes on this income multiply 30 percent by $600, which means you will owe $180 in taxes on this income. Thus, your after-tax income from this CD is $420 ($600 income minus $180 taxes).

In addition, if the inflation rate is 3 percent during the year you hold the CD, the $10,000 the bank will pay you at the end of twelve months will buy 3 percent ($300) less than it would have at the beginning of the twelve months, because the goods you buy will cost 3 percent more than they did when you invested in the CD a year ago.

When you combine the taxes you will owe and the loss of principal due to inflation, your real rate of return would be substantially less than 6 percent. Subtracting $300 from $420, your real rate of return after taxes and inflation would be $120, a yield of 1.2 percent on the $10,000 investment.

Details of the Explanation

$10,000 earns	$600 in a year
minus	$180 taxes (30%)
minus	$300 inflation (3%)
leaves you with	$120 net income from your investment

Rank the three investment objectives listed here in order of their importance to you. Number one would indicate the most important objective for you.

Preservation of principal	_____
Growth of principal	_____
High current income	_____

REVIEWING YOUR
FINANCIAL STATEMENTS

At this point, you have determined and told your financial advisor what your attitude toward money is, your risk tolerance, and your investment goals and objectives. Your advisor also knows your various sources of income and estimated expenses as well as your current assets and liabilities. The next step is to review three statements that will help you plan a secure financial future. These are your taxable income statement, your cash flow statement, and your balance sheet.

Taxable Income Statement

This statement lists your various sources of taxable income and gives you an idea of what your federal and state taxes will be for this year and the next two. At this point, it is still an educated estimate because the estate is not settled and you are not sure what all your sources of income or actual expenses will be. You might owe estate taxes and estate settlement fees, which will reduce the amount of the assets you inherit. In addition, income tax laws could change at any time. However, this statement will give you an idea of what you will owe in taxes under current law.

The taxable income statement is helpful because your tax status may change over the next few years. For instance, you will file as a "married" taxpayer the year in which your husband died but as a "married," "head of household," or "single" taxpayer the following year. These three categories involve three different tax tables.

The taxable income statement is also useful because it identifies your tax bracket, which will help your advisor determine whether you need to select investments that generate taxable or tax-free income. If you are in a lower tax bracket, you might be better off investing in something that generates taxable income. We find many widows are obsessed with reducing their income taxes, but when we compute what they actually will owe in taxes as a percentage of their total income, they aren't paying that much in taxes. Thus they might be better off with more taxable income. If this is true for you, selecting tax-free investments may not be your best choice.

Cash Flow Statement

On this statement will be listed all your estimated sources of income and expenses, including state and federal income taxes. (A few states do not have a state income tax.) The bottom line will show you whether you have more income than expenses or vice versa at the end of each year.

If the bottom line number is negative, then you need to reexamine your expenses to see if you can reduce them. Your advisor can also look at your investments to see if they can be changed to generate more income without sacrificing too much in the way of future growth potential. For instance, you may be able to increase your income by renting out a room in your home, or you may have to face the fact that your current home is too expensive for you to keep. After looking at your expenses, it may become apparent that you may have to go to work (if you are not already working). If you are currently working, you may have to find a better-paying job or work at more than one job. If you have children, you may have to talk to them about their getting part-time jobs or reducing their expenditures.

The most important thing is to look at your income and expense situation for the long term as well as the present. *Remember that your income has to keep pace with your expenses for the rest of your life.*

Net Worth Statement/Balance Sheet

In the last chapter, we showed you a typical net worth statement (sometimes called a balance sheet) for each of our hypothetical widows. It is nothing more than a listing of everything you own and everything you owe. The difference between the two numbers is your net worth. In the future, this number should be computed annually to determine whether you are building your net worth or losing ground.

SUMMARY AND CONCULSION

Now you are more aware of how your family's attitude about money has affected you. You have assessed your financial strengths, weaknesses, and needs. You have indicated how much risk you feel comfortable taking with your money. You have prioritized your financial goals and your investment objectives. You have reviewed your taxable income statement so you have a better idea of what your state and federal income tax bill will be as well as your tax bracket. You know whether your current income is sufficient to pay your estimated expenses, and you have a current balance sheet. With this information, your advisor can now help you do some short-term and long-term planning for your future.

DIANE

Reactions to Identifying Today's Financial Attitudes and Realities

Diane completed her "Who Am I Today Financially?" form as follows:

WHO AM I TODAY FINANCIALLY?

Financial Strengths

1. Better understanding of finance
2. Capable of putting together a budget
3. More aware of the interrelationship of financial decisions
4. Have an organized set of files

Financial Weaknesses

1. Hard time adjusting to the reality of my financial situation
2. Have trouble saying no to the children because of lack of money
3. Difficulty comprehending the advantages and disadvantages of different types of investments
4. Want to spend more than I can afford

Financial Needs

1. Need more financial knowledge
2. Rationale for financial decisions made
3. Children to become more financially aware and responsible
4. Discipline myself to review financial situation on a regular basis

Diane told Dorothy when they met that she didn't want to take any risk. In fact, she circled number 1 on the risk scale. The security of receiving fixed payments from the insurance company for the rest of her life looked very attractive to her.

Her *primary financial goal* was to *educate her children.* She thought she could worry about retirement later—after all, she had 20 years before she was 62, and by that time her youngest child would be 27 years old.

Her *investment objective* was to have *high current income* so she could keep her children in private school and not have to sell the home.

Diane's Budget

Diane proudly showed Dorothy the revised budget she and the children had worked out together. After her last visit with Dorothy, she had sat down with the children and explained the situation to them. She told them that she thought the family should determine as a unit what to do. She had several ideas as to which expenses could be eliminated from the budget but wanted to hear what the children had to say.

When they reviewed the budget, they all agreed that they didn't need to belong to the country club, which eliminated $2,500 in dues. Much as she wanted to go to the beach for two weeks, the idea was unrealistic. They all agreed to compromise and go for one week instead of two ($2,000 savings). They also agreed to forget the Christmas trip ($2,000). She needed a maid once a week to help out with the heavy housework, but the older children could certainly pitch in; they could baby-sit when necessary ($1,000 savings) and help with the yard work ($1,500 savings). Much as she didn't want to, she would have to reduce her charitable contributions by $1,000—after all, charity begins at home! Those items together would save $10,000, so she was making progress. She had figured her expenses were $70,000. Now she had reduced them to $60,000. She couldn't eliminate Jeremy's orthodontia—he really needed braces.

Diane thought she could make up the remaining negative cash flow each year by drawing down the cash she had received from Mark's personal insurance policies ($200,000) and the firm's capital account ($100,000). Dorothy gently told Diane that even though she had lowered her expenses by $10,000, if she spent the $300,000 from these two sources to cover the almost $67,000 negative cash flow each year, that money would last only four and a half years ($300,000 divided by $67,000) and that solution would work only if none of her expenses increased, which appeared highly unlikely. She also pointed out that Diane had to consider college education costs for the children.

College Education Projections

Dorothy told Diane that college expenses had increased 6 percent annually over the past few years. She projected what it would cost to send her children to college and showed the numbers to Diane. Diane had been so concerned about covering their current education expenses she had not even thought of the cost of their college education.

In these projections, Dorothy assumed that college costs would continue to increase 6 percent annually, as they have in recent years. If this were true, Diane would need the following amounts of money accumulated by each child's freshman year:

	Public*	Private*
Erin (15)	$ 69,000	$143,000
Jeremy (11)	$ 87,000	$180,000
Alice (7)	$110,000	$227,000

In other words, if Diane were going to send all three to private college, it would cost about $550,000—a mind-boggling figure. If she wanted to put aside sufficient money now to cover this future expense (assuming it earned 7 percent after tax annually), she would need to invest:

	Public*	Private*
Erin (15)	$56,000	$116,000
Jeremy (11)	$54,000	$112,000
Alice (7)	$52,000	$108,000

*These numbers are taken from the 2004 College Board Annual Survey of Colleges and represent the national average cost of tuition, fees, room and board, books, supplies, transportation, and other personal expenses.

Now Diane was really depressed. She had known vaguely that college would cost a lot, but Mark made a lot of money, so she had never worried about paying for the children's college education. Now she had something new to be concerned about. The idea of being able to keep the children in private schools throughout high school was becoming less and less feasible. Clearly, this was a case of choosing between long-term and short-term economic goals.

Dorothy's Revised Cash Flow Statement for Diane

Dorothy told Diane that she was not at all comfortable having Diane choose the immediate annuity approach with the $800,000 life insurance money. While she realized that Diane would find the certainty of receiving $3,425 per month comforting, it worked out to only a 5.14 percent return on $800,000. (To find the return on an investment, take the annual income [$41,100] and divide it by the principal invested [$800,000]). Further, this monthly payment would be the same amount annually for the rest of her life. If Diane's expenses remained fixed, then it would be all right to receive fixed income. But because they were bound to increase, her income also needed to increase. If she invested in this annuity, she would have no access to the principal in the future This would b a problem for Diane if she needed additional money to cover expenses, which was highly likely.

As she had promised, Dorothy had worked on Diane's net worth statement. After paying off her credit card debt of $15,000, Diane had $5,000 cash left in the bank. She also had available $200,000 from Mark's personal insurance, $100,000 from the firm's capital in a money market fund, and $800,000 from the firm's insurance. Altogether she had $1,105,000.

Dorothy told Diane she should also pay off her loan on the van ($15,000). Diane was grateful that they had paid off Mark's car only a few months ago. If she paid off the van loan, she would be left with only one long-term debt—the mortgage on the home. She would lower her monthly expenses because she wouldn't have to pay the interest on the credit card debt and van loan, which were not tax deductible. Dorothy urged her to try to keep her monthly bills current so she didn't run up any more debt.

Diane asked Dorothy if she should use some of the remaining money ($1,090,000) to pay off the home mortgage ($500,000). Dorothy recommended that she not do this right now because the interest rate she was paying was relatively low (6 percent) and the interest payments on the mortgage were tax deductible.

Diane had been worrying about how to meet her monthly expenses, so she readily agreed to pay off the loans. By paying off the van and the car loans, the current values of these vehicles ($25,000) would now be considered assets. She could now adjust her net worth statement accordingly, removing the $15,000 more from her liability column.

Dorothy advised Diane to put aside $90,000 of her cash in a money market fund earning 3 percent. This would be a cash reserve so that Diane would have cash available to pay expenses as they occurred. After six months, they should look at this reserve to see if Diane needed that much. However, initially Dorothy thought it would be a good idea to have a large cash reserve. She emphasized this was a cash reserve to be used for necessary expenses, not for "splurges."

Dorothy recommended investing the remaining $1,000,000 so that it would pay Diane $50,000 (5 percent) annually. She reviewed Diane's revised budget but added one additional expense—the premium for a fifteen-year, level-term $1,000,000 life insurance policy. The annual premium ($550) would remain the same for fifteen years. She thought this was a necessary expense to provide for Diane's children until Alice, the youngest child, had completed college, in case something happened to Diane.

With these adjustments, the annual negative cash flow number had been reduced to $53,500. They were making progress, but they had to do more.

Diane was confused. Jack Blafford, the insurance agent, seemed so sure when he proposed the annuity to her—it seemed like the solution to all her problems! Dorothy explained to her that Mr. Blafford had not had an opportunity to look at Diane's total situation and review these cash flow projections. Receiving an immediate annuity payment might be a very good solution for some people, but in view of her comparative youth and high expenses, it was not a good choice for her. Diane was right to want the highest possible income, but she also needed to invest where there was a chance for her principal to grow. If her principal grew, then the income should increase and would hopefully keep pace with inflation.

Dorothy pointed out that if Diane were to die prematurely, the principal invested in the annuity would not be available to her children. On the other hand, if the cash were invested in something other than an immediate annuity, on Diane's death the full amount of the remaining principal would be available to provide for her children.

Dorothy indicated that because Diane's Social Security income would decrease as the children grew older, she needed to figure out how to increase her income over the years ahead. She also had to cover future college costs. Her two biggest expenses kept staring Diane in the face—the children's tuition and the mortgage payments. These two items represented almost half of her expenses.

Dorothy told Diane that because she still had a negative cash flow of around $58,000, she had to make some choices to reduce her expenses further. One option was selling their home and buying a less expensive one. Another was to consider sending the children to public schools. She pointed out that the public schools in Diane's area had a good reputation and her children might do very well there. She suggested that Diane visit the local schools and talk with the principals about the curriculum and the facilities available to the students.

Although Diane didn't like to hear what Dorothy was telling her, she knew Dorothy was right. Changing her children's schools would be disruptive but so would moving out of their home of many years. Diane decided to call Robyn, her new friend from the widow support group who was a teacher in the Montgomery County School System, and learn more about the schools in her area. If she was going to change her children's schools, she would like them to start at the new schools in the fall. She also wanted to talk to a real estate agent about what their home was really worth. If they moved to a less expensive home in the Washington, D.C., area, where would they have to go? Dorothy had told her to consider something in the $600,000 range. Maybe they should rent.

Diane realized that going back to work was no longer optional. She really had to do it—but it had been so long since she had worked. What was she qualified to do? She had enjoyed her former career as a paralegal. Perhaps she could take a refresher course and go back to working at a law firm. But all of this would take time, and it would be a while before she would be earning a salary.

Making all these major decisions was overwhelming. Although Diane had avoided talking with her dad in an effort to be self-sufficient, she thought the time had come to do so. She thanked Dorothy for all her help and said she would be back to her as soon as she gathered more information. There was so much to do! Diane was tempted to give up, but, for the sake of the children, she knew she couldn't.

Diane's risk tolerance: Very low
Diane's primary financial goal: Children's education
Diane's investment objective: High current income

Diane's Revised Financial Statement

Assets

Money market account	$ 90,000	
Investments	1,000,000	
Home	900,000	
Retirement account	300,000	
Van/car	25,000	
Total		**$2,315,000**
Liabilities		
Mortgage	$ 500,000	
Total		**$ 500,000**
Net Worth		**$ 1,815,000**

Diane's Revised Annual Cash Flow Statement

Income

Social Security	$ 42,000	
Investment income	50,000	
Money market account	2,700	
Total		**$ 94,700**

Expenses

Mortgage	$ 36,000	
Tuition	50,000	
Life insurance	550	
Other	60,000	
Taxes (income)	1,522	
Property taxes	4,800	
Total		**$ 152,872**
Annual Negative Cash		
Flow		**$ 58,172**

SUSAN

Reactions to Identifying Today's
Financial Attitudes and Realities

Susan completed her "Who Am I Today Financially?" form as follows:

WHO AM I TODAY FINANCIALLY?

Financial Strengths

1. Aware of present financial situation
2. Able to assume responsibility for financial decisions
3. Confident about implementing financial decisions
4. Recognize the necessity of looking at the long-term as well as the short-term financial future

Financial Weaknesses

1. Reluctance to focus on career in terms of needed income
2. Ongoing lack of comprehensive knowledge of investments
3. Unwillingness to accept a lifestyle that fits my budget
4. Not comfortable earning more than a man

Financial Needs

1. More knowledge regarding different types of investments
2. Exploration of personal risk tolerance
3. Assistance from brother with regard to mother's support
4. A realistic budget

Susan was comfortable *taking some risk* with her investments. Although she detested gambling, she had come to realize that she had to take a certain amount of risk in order to make money. She probably wasn't as venturesome as Lance had been because she was not as knowledgeable, but she was willing to take some risk with professional guidance.

Her *primary financial goal* was to *take care of herself.* However she was also very concerned about making sure her mother's costs were covered. It appeared that the trust income she would receive would more than meet her mother's current financial needs, but she was worried about her mother needing additional care in the future. Susan's *secondary goal* was to *figure out a way she could stay in their condominium,* which she loved so much.

Her *investment objective* was *growth of capital.* Although her current income picture did not look that good, she thought she could improve it by rearranging some assets.

Susan knew a widow was not supposed to make momentous decisions, such as selling a home, in the first few months of widowhood, but it had become painfully obvious she could not afford to keep the lake cottage. She was fortunate that the real estate agent had been able to sell the lake cottage fairly quickly for her full asking price of $250,000. Susan wondered if she should have asked more for it, but it was a great relief not to have to worry about meeting the monthly expenses. After paying the realtor's commission, she netted $235,000. She and Lance had paid $175,000 for the cottage and had made $30,000 in improvements. It appeared that she would owe about $5,000 in taxes on the gain. After paying off the $150,000 mortgage and these taxes, she would have $80,000 left.

Susan would be glad to have this cash. At this point, she only had $5,000 left in her money market fund and was eager to replenish it. When she refigured her balance sheet, she realized that after she sold the cottage her net worth would actually be reduced by $30,000. On the other hand, she would have eliminated the expense of maintaining the cottage. Although she had reduced her negative cash flow, it appeared that her expenses this year still would exceed her income by $12,000. She decided to keep $35,000 in a money market account to cover this shortfall as well as any unexpected expenses. This meant she would have $50,000 of the $80,000 from the cottage sale to reinvest.

Susan didn't like to think about it, but she had noticed that her mother's short-term memory was getting worse. She had postponed taking her mother to the doctor to be further evaluated because she had been so preoccupied with her own situation. She decided she should probably make time for that in the near future so she would have a better idea of her mother's overall health, which in turn would have an impact on her housing needs. If her mother needed an environment that provided progressive care, it would be a lot more expensive. Susan thought she would have to factor these financial implications into her planning. She realized that there was some urgency in doing so, because her mother might have to move to a more expensive facility sooner rather than later. The women in her mother's family historically had lived long lives. Her mother might live to be 95 or 100, and she needed to plan for that possibility.

Susan knew she had to be realistic about her financial future. She knew she couldn't depend on finding a husband to support her. Although she was attractive enough, she was picky. After all, she hadn't found

Lance until she was 37 years old, and she didn't think there were many other Lances available. She had been comparatively happy living on her own before, and she imagined she would be again.

As long as she and Lance had been married, money was not a problem. He earned more than enough to keep them comfortable, so she never considered looking for another job. It was funny how quickly she had become accustomed to having the comfortable lifestyle that Lance's income made possible. She decided she better seriously consider the idea of looking for a higher-paying job. A new situation might even provide her with some positive challenges. On the other hand, she already had experienced a lot of change, and a job shift might be more than she could handle right now. Although the thought of a better-paying job was appealing, she felt a little guilty thinking about leaving her present job, where everyone had been so nice to her.

Right now she had to focus on making an appointment to see her mother's doctor. Next on her list was to review Lance's stock portfolio and invest the $50,000 from the cottage sale as well as pension assets.

Susan's risk tolerance: Moderately high

Susan's primary financial goal: To be financially independent

Susan's investment objective: Growth of capital

Susan's Revised Financial Statement
(reflects sale of lake cottage)

Assets

Cash	$ 85,000	
Condominium	500,000	
Stocks	150,000*	
Lance's pension plan	500,000	
Susan's pension plan	25,000	
Car	10,000	
Total		**$ 1,270,000**

Liabilities

Mortgage (condominium)	$ 350,000	
Total		$ 350,000
Net Worth		**$ 920,000**

*Net of $50,000 to stepchildren

Susan's Revised Annual Cash Flow Statement

Income

Salary	$ 55,000	
Insurance trust	20,000	
Income from stocks	3,000	
Money market account	2,250	
Total		$ 80,250

Expenses

Mortgage (condominium)	$ 24,000	
Mother's retirement home	9,600	
Income taxes, FICA	12,195	
Other	40,000	
401(k)	4,000	
Real estate taxes	2,500	
Total		$ 92,295

Annual Negative Cash Flow	**$ 12,045**

AUDREY

Reactions to Identifying Today's
Financial Attitudes and Realities

Audrey completed her "Who Am I Today Financially?" form as follows:

WHO AM I TODAY FINANCIALLY?

Financial Strengths

1. Able to feel comfortable making financial decisions
2. Recognize need to plan ahead
3. Appreciate the importance of diversification in investments

Financial Weaknesses

1. Inclined to procrastinate regarding investment decisions
2. Overly concerned about making financial errors
3. More concerned with my overall financial picture than my monthly budget

Financial Needs

1. Willingness to take some risk
2. Be able to contribute to my grandchildren's education
3. Be in a position to improve my daughter's financial situation

Audrey didn't consider herself much of a risk taker. She had no experience investing, so she didn't want to "gamble" her money. Her *investment objective* was both *growth and current income*. Although she had ample income, she liked the idea of investing more for income than growth. She told Mr. Silver she also wanted to preserve her principal.

Her *primary financial goal* was to be *financially independent.* Her *secondary objective* was to *help educate her grandchildren.*

Audrey had assessed her financial situation with Mr. Silver and felt very comfortable with where things were. Her income situation appeared to be fine. Her expenses were not that high, and her income from John's pension plan was secure. Mr. Silver estimated the amount she needed to reserve each month for tax payments.

They discussed the mortgage situation, and he explained that the interest on a mortgage provided a tax deduction. However, because she and John had owned the home for 22 years now, most of what she paid each year was principal payments, not interest, and thus was no longer deductible. Because the tax deduction was low and she preferred to have the mortgage paid off, Mr. Silver recommended she do that. With a sigh of relief, Audrey called the bank and asked for the necessary papers.

After Audrey paid off the $20,000 mortgage, she had $240,000 in liquid assets. This included the balance in her savings account ($40,000) and stocks ($200,000). Her home was worth $400,000 and her car $20,000. She had no debt. Altogether she was worth $660,000.

Mr. Humphrey told Audrey that, as things stood now, John's estate was under $2 million. Since all his assets had been left to her, there would be no federal estate taxes due.

Because the estate would not be taxable, Audrey questioned whether it was worthwhile to have the home appraised. Couldn't she just make an educated guess? Both Mr. Humphrey and Mr. Silver were adamant that she needed to have it appraised. They explained that if she had a professional estate appraisal, the IRS would not be able to question her cost basis when she wanted to sell the home. Because the home had been held in both their names, the cost for half of the home would be based on half of the original cost (plus improvements). The cost for the other half would be based on half of the estate value (the current market value). Audrey knew the original cost was $50,000. She didn't expect to sell the home right away, but she now understood why she needed an appraisal. She would add that to her list of things to do.

John's company stock had always been registered in his name because it was acquired primarily through stock options. Audrey had always been a little annoyed that it was not jointly held. After all, she helped John be the success he was at the company, so she thought her name should be on the stock, too. However, Mr. Silver explained to her that it really was better this way. Because it was part of John's estate, the stock would be valued at the date of his death (or six months later). This estate value would become her cost, and the difference between this price and the price of the stock when it was sold would determine the amount of her taxable gain.

Audrey quickly realized that this was a big benefit. If she wanted to sell this stock, she would pay a relatively small capital gains tax (maximum 15 percent of the gain). Apart from the sentimental attachment John had for the company stock, he always told her they couldn't afford to sell it because he, as an employee, had purchased it at lower prices; if it were sold at market value, substantial capital gains taxes would be due. Now that she no longer had to worry about paying taxes on the gain, Mr. Silver told her he thought it was unwise to have all her investments in one company. He felt strongly that diversifying her investments was important in order to protect her principal, so he would advise her to sell at least part of her stock in the not-too-distant future. Audrey thought it was a little too soon for her to take the big step of selling John's stock now, but she thought she would be willing to do so eventually. Mr. Silver suggested she consider selling it gradually, and that made sense to her.

Audrey asked Mr. Silver what she should do with the $40,000 she had left in the savings account after paying off the mortgage. He suggested she maintain $20,000 of this money as a cash reserve. This would leave $20,000, which they could invest at a later date. Until she knew what her expenses were going to be, he suggested she keep this money in a savings or money market account, where it would earn interest. He told her to use her checking account at the bank to pay her monthly bills and suggested her Social Security and pension checks be deposited in that account automatically. She should use her savings account as her investment account and emergency reserve.

Audrey spoke to Mr. Silver about redoing the kitchen, and he agreed with her that it might be a little too soon to tackle such a major renovation. Perhaps six months from now she would be better able to face it.

As for vacations, he encouraged her to consider them. In addition to the possible golf clinic, a widow friend of hers had asked her to consider going to London with her on a theater tour four months from now. Audrey thought that might be a very good idea. Because of John's illness, they had not traveled in a long time, and she would welcome any change of scenery. Besides, it would give her things to look forward to. Maybe she would even buy some new clothes!

Audrey's risk tolerance: Middle of the road

Audrey's primary financial goals: Continue to be financially independent and educate Joanne's children

Audrey's investment objective: Preservation of principal

Audrey's Revised Financial Statement

(after mortgage is paid off)

Assets

Cash	$ 40,000	
Home	400,000	
Stock	200,000	
Car	20,000	
Total		$ 660,000
Liabilities	$ 0	
Total		$ 0
Net Worth		**$660,000**

Audrey's Revised Annual Cash Flow Statement

Income

Pension	$ 42,000	
Social Security	14,000	
Stock dividends	4,000	
Savings, insurance	1,200	
Total		**$61,200**

Expenses

Living expenses	$ 30,000	
Gifts to Joanne and John Jr.	12,000	
Income taxes	12,000	
Real estate taxes	2,000	
Total		**$56,000**
Annual Positive Cash Flow		**$ 5,200**

ELIZABETH

Reactions to Identifying Today's Financial Attitudes and Realities

Elizabeth completed her "Who Am I Today Financially?" form as follows:

WHO AM I TODAY FINANCIALLY?

Financial Strengths
1. Beginning to make my own financial decisions
2. Recognize my need for professional help
3. Becoming financially responsible
4. Have an understanding of my monthly income and expenses

Financial Weaknesses
1. Still fearful of making independent financial decisions without support
2. Continue to be uncertain about my ability to understand finances
3. No tolerance for risk
4. Prefer to handle as little as possible financially

Financial Needs

1. Financial security
2. To be able to travel
3. To focus on estate planning and housing issues
4. To review my feelings with regard to risk

Elizabeth was definitely *risk averse*. Although most people thought business owners such as her husband Ben were risk takers, his had been a pretty traditional business—owning and running a hardware store. Neither she nor Ben liked to take chances.

Her *primary financial goal* was to have *sufficient income to continue living comfortably*. After reviewing her budget, she decided that because her home was paid for and her needs were small, she had sufficient income to pay the bills.

Her *primary investment objective* was to *preserve principal*—that is, to make her money last for the rest of her life. She and Ben had no children, so she didn't have to worry about leaving anyone a lot of money. Having taken care of Ben in his declining years, she was well aware of the medical expenses involved in long-term care. She wanted to be financially independent and able to take care of herself.

Next, Elizabeth decided to meet with Mr. Samuels, the trust officer whom Mr. Grossfeldt had recommended to her. Sam Weatherly agreed once again to accompany her. Mr. Samuels had reviewed Ben's portfolio report, which Mr. Grossfeldt had sent him before their meeting. He explained to her that it contained blue chip stocks that paid an annual income of about 2 percent. This return didn't seem very high to Elizabeth because she knew her savings account paid higher income than that. Mr. Samuels reviewed the list of stocks Ben owned and told Elizabeth he thought there was no urgent need to make any changes in the portfolio because the stocks were good quality. He said that if he managed the portfolio, he would recommend she invest in what he called a balanced portfolio, partially invested in corporate and government bonds and partially in good-quality stocks paying dividends. He indicated that with this mix she could increase her income from its present rate of 2 percent to 4 percent. This meant that her income would increase from $10,000 to $20,000 annually.

Sam asked Mr. Samuels about the fee the trust department would charge and the services it could provide. He said that it would be 1.5 percent of assets managed and would be deducted from the account, so Elizabeth would not have to pay a separate bill. She was pleased to hear this, as she wanted her financial life to be as easy as possible.

Mr. Samuels also suggested that she discuss with Mr. Grossfeldt the idea of putting this portfolio into a living revocable trust in her name. If she did this, she could be her own trustee, but the bank could act on her behalf if she wished to travel or became incapacitated. In addition, when she died, the assets would go directly to her heirs without going through the probate process. He said she did not have to make this decision right away, but several of his widow clients had found it to be a good solution.

Elizabeth left the trust department feeling reassured. It appeared that Mr. Samuels clearly understood that she didn't want to take much risk and that her investment objectives were to preserve her principal as well as provide sufficient income to take care of herself. The fact that Mr. Grossfeldt had recommended Mr. Samuels was comforting to her. She liked the fact that they were used to working together.

After discussing the meeting with Sam Weatherly, Elizabeth decided she would make the change. The current portfolio manager may have done a terrific job for Ben, but she didn't know him at all, and she felt much safer working with a bank trust officer. The next step was to transfer the portfolio to Mr. Samuels' bank.

Mr. Grossfeldt told her all that was necessary was to write a letter to the current portfolio manager telling him of her decision. Ben's contract with the manager stipulated that 30 days' written notice was required in order to transfer the account. Mr. Grossfeldt provided her with a letter to send to the manager. In it, she asked for a final bill, a statement of the portfolio value on the date of Ben's death, and a statement of any purchases or sales that had taken place in the account in the calendar year before the date of Ben's death. She also needed a statement of any dividends collected and fees charged during the calendar year. Mr. Grossfeldt explained that her accountant would need all these numbers. He also warned her that the portfolio manager might try to talk her out of her decision, because no one likes to lose an account. He urged her to tell him that the decision was final, and if the manager continued to object. Mr. Grossfeldt would be glad to talk to him on her behalf.

Mr. Grossfeldt suggested Elizabeth call Mr. Samuels to tell him of her decision so he could send her the forms she needed to sign and make sure that the transfer occurred. Mr. Grossfeldt made it clear to Elizabeth that this did not have to be an irrevocable decision. If at any time in the future she decided she no longer wanted the bank to manage her money, she could move her assets elsewhere. In addition, he said that he thought setting up this account in a revocable trust was a good idea.

Elizabeth's risk tolerance: Low

Elizabeth's primary financial goal: Maintain financial independence and comfortable lifestyle

Elizabeth's investment objective: Preserve principal

Elizabeth's Financial Statement

Assets

Cash	$ 25,000	
Portfolio	500,000	
Vermont land	50,000	
Home	300,000	
Total		**$ 875,000**
Liabilities	$ 0	
Total		$ 0
Net Worth		**$ 875,000**

Elizabeth's Revised Annual Cash Flow Statement

Annual Income

Social Security	$ 20,000	
Portfolio income	17,500	
Savings account	750	
Total		**$ 38,250**
Annual Expenses		
General expenses	$ 19,500	
Property taxes	1,500	
Charities	1,000	
Income taxes	1,400	
Total		**$ 23,400**
Annual Positive Cash Flow		**$ 14,850**

10

Identifying Today's Personal Attitudes and Realities

Above the titles of wife and mother, which, although dear,
are transitory and accidental, there is the title human being,
which precedes and outranks every other.
—Mary Livermore

Many widows find themselves looking at where they are personally about six months to a year following the occurrence of their loss. Again, there are no exact time frames when this is likely to take place, and there is nothing amiss if you find it takes more or less time. Some widows, out of economic necessity, are forced to deal with these issues in a much shorter time frame. Others take longer because they are financially able to do so. The ability to take a new look at where you are in life usually results from the passage of time, a better acceptance of your widowed state, and the courage to face a future without your spouse. Regardless of your financial knowledge at the time of your husband's death and your emotional response to facing financial issues, by this time you have had to address certain realities in your financial situation. Now you are ready to look in a comprehensive way at other issues that affect your life both now and in the future.

Depending on your age, physical and mental health, financial resources, responsibilities, and education, you need to make certain decisions about your future. Such things as life expectancy, financial security, personal goals, dreams, hopes, and fears need to be reevaluated. Whatever your patterns have been in the past, give serious thought to whether or not you wish to maintain these patterns in the future. Surprisingly, on reflection, a number of widows find themselves drawn to activities other than those they previously thought to be of critical importance.

At this juncture in your life, we suggest, it is essential for you to assess both your skills and needs. You need to identify for yourself what you might want to do with your life to experience some fulfillment, acknowledging that your husband is no longer there to help you meet your needs or participate in your realizing any objectives you may have set for yourself. Although your life has changed dramatically because you have lost your husband, it has not ended,

In this book, we have not focused on widows who were unhappily married and felt trapped in their marriage for financial, religious, or family reasons. Widows making up this group are those who were physically and/or psychologically abused, those who found themselves in a marriage devoid of emotion, or those whose beliefs about duty to husband and family predominated over any other considerations. This widow's reaction to her loss may be complicated by feelings of relief. She may therefore feel guilty because she is unable to experience the feelings of sorrow she believes she is expected to feel.

If this is your situation, accept where you are and look ahead to what you may realize in the future. You did what you did. The past is now over, and you have the opportunity to focus on yourself and obtaining your personal goals. At long last, you can attempt to meet your personal needs. For some widows, just the cessation of the fear, stress, and tension will be sufficient. As you heal, think about your needs and where you are in life. This approach will enable you to move forward. For some, the pace may be rapid, while for others it is interminably slow. The important thing to remember is, despite the pace, you are making progress down your personal path to a new you.

If for any reason at this point in the grief process you are unable to move forward, you may want to seek the services of professionals or groups described in chapter 3, whether or not you did so at an earlier time.

WHO AM I TODAY PERSONALLY?

Regardless of your circumstances, you are emerging from what is likely to have been the most painful experience of your life. You have survived, and you are now ready to move forward personally. To help you identify who and where you are, we have developed the "Who Am I Today Personally?" form (figure 10.1).

FIGURE 10.1 Who Am I Today Personally?

Personal Strengths

1. _____

2. _____

3. _____

4. _____

Personal Weaknesses

1. _____

2. _____

3. _____

4. _____

Personal Needs

1. _____

2. _____

3. _____

4. _____

In completing your "Who Am I Today Personally?" form, consider as "Personal Strengths" characteristics people admire about you or things that come easily to you. Under "Personal Weaknesses," identify those areas where you have had more difficulty than others you know. We all have strengths and weaknesses. Personality traits should be viewed on a continuum from least to most. Most people have more or less of a certain characteristic, which leads people to say they are outgoing or shy, overly emotional or stoic, or whatever. It is the combination of these traits in a given individual that results in the image the individual presents to the world.

It is time to clarify your "Personal Needs." Are you a person who requires a great deal of emotional support to feel good about yourself? Do you thrive on social contacts, or do you prefer a quiet life with little intrusion from the outside? Is learning, whether from exposure to cultural events or in an academic environment, important to you? Is travel for recreation or the expansion of horizons important to you? Do you feel best when you are working or volunteering?

What you are attempting to do here is define where you are personally at this time in your life. Once you have identified your strengths, weaknesses, and needs, you are ready to move forward.

FAMILY ISSUES

If you live in close geographic proximity to your family—whether parents, children, or grandchildren—they may encourage you to spend more time with them. If you enjoy your family, you may be willing to do so. You may also feel closer to your children now and want to be surrounded by their families as often as possible.

If you don't have family nearby, as part of the healing process you should make a concerted effort to participate in social activities.

Elderly Parents

If you have elderly parents in need of your attention, you may now find yourself more focused on their needs. Many of you were unable to do this for a period of time before your husband's death, and perhaps you feel guilty about having neglected them. Elderly parents likewise present financial needs that most children, widowed or not, feel obligated to meet. As the elderly population continues to grow, so do their economic needs. It is not uncommon for elderly parents to have insufficient financial resources. This is illustrated in the case of Susan, who is concerned about her mother's situation. She truly feels the need to help her mother and provide her with the best care possible.

Dependent Adult Children

Perhaps the most complex emotional issue on a family level that a widow may confront is that of the dependent adult child. Increasingly, adult children are staying at home longer, marrying later, and seeking their parents' financial support for a variety of reasons, including more and more education. Parents often feel guilty about adult children who are not self-supporting. They may feel having a child who has not found herself or himself by this time in life suggests they have not done a good job of parenting. This tends to increase the likelihood of the widowed mother providing the adult child with money for whatever need is presented to alleviate her guilt. It might be additional education, a business venture, or a place to live.

Consider the family issues presented here and make an effort to evaluate them with respect to what you feel comfortable doing, not what you feel obliged to do. Decide for yourself what you need to do for yourself to best meet your own needs before any other considerations. Do not view this as being selfish. Your primary goal is self-preservation.

SOCIAL CONTACTS

It is quite usual for recent widows to surround themselves with family members and friends if they are available. Initially, seeking comfort from people you know is appropriate and helpful. After six months to a year into your widowhood, however, this approach is too exclusionary. Despite the fact that you may have little or no energy to devote to something or someone unfamiliar, try to do something in your daily life that will bring new people into your world. Determine your comfort level and then work toward some new contacts. You might start with something as simple as a conversation with someone you've met casually or in conjunction with your new responsibilities, such as a salesperson or a member of your congregation with whom you are unfamiliar, or more formally by contacting a group of widowed persons. Although we have introduced this concept earlier in the book, you may not have been ready to venture beyond your circle of family and friends. Our goal here is to broaden your existing support group. Looking ahead to new activities makes a positive contribution to one's mental health.

Existing Friends and Acquaintances

Widowhood sometimes creates serious shifts in existing friendships. You and your husband may have had a few close couple friends with whom you did most of your socializing and vacationing. Now you may find yourself uncomfortable with these coupled activities and instead choose to share social activities only with the wives during the day. Some widows report they detect a difference in the attitude of their close women friends. Sometimes these women, whom they had thought of as close friends, now act as if the widow is a threat to their own marriages and are reluctant to include her in activities that may lead to additional exposure to their husbands. Needless to say, if this occurs, the widow is not eager to continue to socialize with these friends in the way she had in the past.

On the other hand, some widows have friends who go out of their way to encourage them to continue their former social life. They deal directly with their concerns about picking up a dinner bill or paying for a ticket. Still other widows had few contacts outside their home and their husband and find themselves at a loss as to how to occupy their time.

Reflect on previous patterns in relation to what you would like for yourself now. You may want to maintain your existing patterns, but you may also want to make some changes. There are many groups one may join to develop new social contacts based on age or interest. Consider joining such a group. This does not mean you are committing to participating with people you don't know that well. Rather, it is exposing yourself to new people while focused on some personal interest or activity. If, for whatever the reason, you find that the group doesn't work for you, do not feel obligated to remain involved. Feel comfortable establishing your personal boundaries from the outset.

Becoming active in a new activity does not preclude maintaining your previous social activities. It is a way of adding to your existing network of friends. Take this opportunity to expand your contacts and knowledge.

New Friends

Perhaps you find yourself sitting in your home or apartment wondering what you are going to do about developing new social contacts. Will you need to find all new friends? Will you or should you think about male social contacts? Will anyone find you attractive again? What if someone did ask you out? How would you respond to the introduction or expectation of some physical relationship between yourself and this new person? Could you ever have sex with a man other than your husband?

These questions may seem overwhelming at first, but in time they will be answered in what is a natural progression for each widow. Now, as in the past, you will make decisions about your life when you are ready. Decide which areas you feel comfortable exploring first and get started. If you decide to investigate widow support groups, do so. Again, a friend, spiritual leader, physician, or a widowed persons group might be helpful in identifying an appropriate group for you. We have found that the attitudes and needs of the divorced population differ from the attitudes and needs of the widowed population. However, many of these groups feature discussions on various topics dealing with aspects of relationships between men and women following separation and divorce that are applicable to both the widowed and the divorced. You can usually contact a given group and find out about its structure and the topic to be discussed on a given evening. If you are affiliated with a church or synagogue, it may offer group meetings for the widowed or single population.

If a group approach does not appeal to you, think about something you might like to do for personal satisfaction. You might enroll in a class at a local community college, taking anything from flower arranging to Chinese. You might want to join a health club where you can arrange your own routine. Check out classes offered by universities and museums as well as adult education classes sponsored by the library, the public school system, the YWCA/YMCA, your church or synagogue, or senior citizen organizations, just to name a few. Many areas have a variety of singles activities that are advertised in the local newspaper. Some of these may be of interest to you.

If you are going to develop a new you, you need to let go of any excessive ties to the past and move into the future. One way to accomplish this goal is to allow yourself to meet new people, acquire new knowledge, and broaden your horizons. Not dwelling on the past and instead adding new dimensions to your life will enable you to find greater satisfaction in the years ahead.

Widowers

Just as not all widows are the same, neither are all widowers. However, be aware of some societal factors that often impact the widowers' mourning process that makes it different from yours. Many men have been raised with the belief that it is unmanly to express emotion. Expressing emotions is frequently thought of as something that is acceptable for girls and women but not for men. It is not uncommon for a widower to view expressing emotion as a weakness. A man is supposed to be tough and not express his pain to those around him. If he is an older man, he might think of himself as a rock or a tree upon whom his family can lean.

These distorted views make the healing process more difficult for the widower. He may find himself unable to shed tears. He may not allow himself to seek the solace he so desperately needs. As a result, he may attempt to drown his sorrows in alcohol or other destructive behavior. Basically, he is running away from the emotion that he must express in a healthy way in order to heal and move forward. He may appear insensitive and caught up in pretending that he is strong and able to deal with anything. The death of a wife also reminds a man of his personal vulnerability and mortality. It is not unusual to read stories in the media about a visible public figure behaving in very destructive ways following a loss. Years after the incident, this person may come to terms with what was experienced and attempt to help other men by sharing his personal agony and suggest that these men who are experiencing loss attempt to mourn. They are encouraged not to follow in his footsteps.

Men are conditioned by our society to consider themselves to be in control, even powerful. Nothing challenges this belief system as much as the death of a wife. In place of strength, they feel loneliness and emotional isolation. Perhaps because men often have so much difficulty expressing their emotions, they experience more physical effects as widowers than do widows. They report having a variety of illnesses, most commonly of a cardiac nature. Sometimes they express these concerns to their physician, but equally often they attempt to medicate themselves with over-the-counter drugs.

Widowers are also likely to experience mental health problems such as depression. Unfortunately, they are also more resistant to seeking professional help, which, after all, could be interpreted as a sign of weakness. Refusing to seek help may complicate further the children's recovery because the widower is not able to deal with their grief problems either. There is little likelihood of his arranging for them to see an appropriate grief counselor.

The U.S. Census indicates that, on average, widowers will remarry within three years of the death of their wives. It is not uncommon for a widower to attempt to deal with his grief by seeking female companionship. One widower shared with us that, after his wife died, he experienced no emotion but decided he did not want to face an empty home another night. At that moment he decided to contact a female acquaintance and invite her to dinner. She accepted and within a relatively short period of time he was reattached, committed, and subsequently married. This remarriage took place less than a year after his wife had died. It should not surprise the reader that the relationship did not last. Once again this widower found himself alone, albeit wiser in terms of recognizing the need to deal with his loss.

Other widowers deal with their grief by not allowing themselves to take the time to grieve. These men make every effort to keep themselves frenetically busy by taking on even more work responsibility or spending more time with male friends in various activities such as golf and tennis. In this way they attempt to mask their grief by remaining in constant motion and often fall asleep in a state of total fatigue. This approach rarely works and will most likely lead to other problems.

Sometimes, widowers feel it is not appropriate for their children to see them in a weakened condition. They have bought the myth that they need to be strong for the children. In reality, it would help all family members if they could mourn together, sharing memories, heartaches, and special moments.

Widowers, like widows, experience sexual anxieties. The loss of a wife might make a widower feel impotent because he was unable to prevent his wife's death. This sometimes leads to a need to become sexually active as soon as possible. On the other hand, the widower may have had no sexual experiences with anyone other than his wife in so many years that he is anxious about his ability to perform and please another woman.

There is no one pattern that fits all widowers any more than there is one pattern that fits all widows. Neither widow nor widower is able to replace that which has been lost. Both must accept the need to mourn their loss and move on, gradually allowing themselves to redefine who they are over time. If you as a widow find yourself socializing with a new widower, keep in mind that he is probably experiencing many of the same emotions that you are experiencing but may express them very differently. As always, open communication is recommended.

PHYSICAL HEALTH

Your physical health is of particular importance at this point in your life. It is crucial both to your recovery and to your future health. Studies show that physical fitness programs are essential to physical and mental well-being. Exercise programs are known to reduce stress and tension, and certainly this has been a time of considerable stress for you.

If you have been involved in an exercise program, make every effort to maintain it in some form. If you have not been involved in an exercise program, try to develop one that is suitable for your age and present physical condition. Your efforts will be rewarded. You will relieve stress and feel better about yourself.

Walking is a great way to begin. In some areas, group walks are sponsored by various agencies or organizations. Many different facilities provide advice on exercise in relation to health. Some are free or charge a minimal fee, such as a hospital or senior citizen group, while health clubs, country clubs, the YMCA, YWCA, and JCC charge a stated fee for participation in their programs and the use of their equipment and facilities. You might consider joining a local athletic club, where an instructor will show you how to use the equipment. You might also consider taking physical fitness classes on a regular basis, which may be the best way to motivate yourself to maintain a sustained exercise plan.

If in the past you were an avid or even casual player of a particular sport, your health allows you to remain active in that sport, and it still interests you, maintain this activity. You might need to find a new group of people with whom to share your interest. Most municipalities offer group programs in various sports. If you belong to a country club, discuss your situation with the appropriate pro, and he or she will help you find someone to play with on your level.

Groups such as the Sierra Club offer different levels of activities for environmentally oriented hikers and campers. Most areas will have some group focusing on skiing or tennis. Read the papers; ask your friends and relatives about groups in which they have had a successful experience. If you are shy and uncomfortable at the thought of entering some activity on your own, work at overcoming these feelings. These groups are designed to meet your needs, and the members will usually extend a warm welcome to you. You'll find, to your surprise and comfort, others in the group may have had feelings similar to your own.

The most individualized approach is the personal exercise trainer. This person will work with you either in your home, if appropriate, or in a given facility to create an exercise regimen tailored to your needs. Again, information about qualified personal trainers may be obtained from newspapers, the yellow pages, a health club, or friends.

For women with sufficient funds and desirous of trying to work on a personal health and exercise program, a trip to a spa is a wonderful way to refocus. For one thing, many people go alone. Being there without a friend or mate is not at all awkward. Some spas have a dining structure designed to promote conversation for those by themselves. Everyone is friendly, and you are able to do as much or as little as you want on the physical side while being pampered. All sorts of beauty and health treatments are available and often classes in meditation, yoga, stress reduction, nutrition, and other health-related topics. The focus is on inner and outer recovery, the very process you need.

SEX

Many widows with whom we have worked are most sensitive and awkward about dating and the thought of a sexual relationship with another man. Sentiments such as "I can't go back to dating the way I did when I was younger," "I feel ridiculous," and "I can't imagine myself in bed with another man" are frequently expressed. Keep in mind that any man whom you might meet at this stage of your life has similar anxieties and feelings—perhaps even more so because of his concerns about sexual performance.

It is often advisable to discuss these feelings with a friend or in a group with others who are in a similar situation. You will be able to articulate your fears and questions, and you will recognize that what you are experiencing is probably not unique to you but shared by others. After a while, you will be ready to envision spending time with a man and to think of him as a person with feelings and a lifetime of experiences, just like yourself. If you should meet a man or be introduced to a man you may be interested in, you will begin this relationship by getting to know each other. This process is much the same as when you were younger but now with the addition of maturity and, it is hoped, a better sense of self.

There are no givens! If the relationship progresses, there will come a time when both of you are ready for it to become a sexual one. Many women feel embarrassed and uncomfortable at first because they feel they are betraying their husband or family. It is not uncommon to struggle with the issue of loyalty. Do not feel awkward if the only man you ever slept with was your husband. This should not prevent you from seeking a new relationship. The new man in your life will not replace your husband but he may very likely provide you with an equally positive sexual experience.

If you have successfully progressed through the mourning process, you should now be able to get past these normal feelings of discomfort and move forward with your own life in whatever way feels right for you. Some widows have no desire for any new sexual experiences. Others miss sex a great deal and do not know what to do with their feelings. Sex, in addition to exercise, for example, often provides an emotional release for the tension that a widow experiences in her new state. The lessening of tension and stress is something most widows need.

We are all sexual beings, and self-satisfaction is also an option. Some young widows—and some not so young—find themselves seeking sexual encounters early on in their widowhood just to affirm their femininity and sexuality. Others have no interest in pursuing this approach. Once again, there are no real guidelines here. Do what is right for you. For many widows, more important than the need for sex is the need for the warmth, closeness, tenderness, and affection previously provided within the marital relationship. Some women feel a greater loss on this level than they do on the sexual one. The familiar pat on the head, occasional peck on the cheek, or hug when needed—all that is gone. The absence of these shared intimacies creates a major void. Some widows would be most grateful to have this need met without any sexual component.

For some women, socializing with other widows or friends is satisfactory. They feel no strong desire for another man in their life. They feel too old or are uncomfortable trying out new experiences that expose them to new people. If such is your case and you are content with your decision, go ahead with it. If your decision is based on feelings of inadequacy or uncertainty and you are aware of that, seek group or professional help to move forward (see chapter 3).

SUMMARY AND CONCLUSION

After you have dealt with the feelings and issues associated with initial loss, you will find yourself at a point where you need to review your own present and future. It is time to think about yourself in a new light, to explore new horizons. Perhaps being in a position to maintain your existing activities and contacts is sufficient. Perhaps you are still uncertain as to what you would like to do in the future. Whatever you are experiencing, it is essential to allow yourself to think about your own needs, desires, and aspirations in a new light. It is time to make the most of what has been for you such a painful experience. As with childbirth, out of pain can come a rewarding new beginning.

Diane

Reactions to Identifying Today's Personal Attitudes and Realities

Diane completed her "Who Am I Today Personally?" form as follows:

WHO AM I TODAY PERSONALLY?

Personal Strengths

1.   Outgoing
2.   Better organized
3.   Better able to address and solve problems
4.   Becoming more self-confident

Personal Weaknesses

1.   Seek excessive approval for personal decisions
2.   Underestimate my intelligence
3.   Tend to spoil children (to compensate for loss of father)
4.   Preoccupied by children's needs

Personal Needs

1.   Affection
2.   Approval from others
3.   Friends
4.   Financial security

As she reviewed her responses, Diane realized how much she had personally changed since Mark's death. She had learned so much. Now, for the first time in her life, she was responsible for herself and—even scarier—her children.

She reflected on her general acceptance of what anyone she viewed as an authority in the financial area told her shortly after Mark died. She remembered how willing she was to accept the advise of Jack Bradford, the insurance agent, regarding putting all her money into an annuity. What if she had gone ahead and done that? She now knew that would not have been a good decision for her. It was now difficult for Diane to relate to the woman she was when she was married to Mark. Why was it that she had never questioned him about anything?

In her widow support group, Diane had identified that she had resisted growing up and Mark had assumed the role of her father, especially in the financial area, probably because he thought it was expected of him. Sometimes when she thought about her ideas about things when Mark was alive, she wondered why she had adopted certain views without any appropriate investigation. In her musings, she thought that she would be a much different marital partner today than when she was married to Mark. She also wondered, when she allowed herself to, whether Mark would have loved the person she was today. They had obviously done so well together because they fulfilled each other's needs at the time they met. Did he enjoy having her so dependent on him? She'd never know the answer to that question.

Diane and Robyn had become such close friends that Diane had no trouble turning to her to discuss her dilemma about the children's education. Robyn told her about the various programs the public schools offered to children depending on their needs. Diane was surprised to learn that they made an effort to identify children who were particularly bright as well as those with learning difficulties. There were specialized enrichment programs in what were designated as magnet schools; there were schools in which the children were instructed in English plus one of two foreign languages; there were various honors classes, advanced placement classes, and so on. Some schools had school counselors and even support groups for children living in a single-parent home.

Diane had no idea the public school system provided its students with so many different options. Robyn encouraged her to make appointments to meet with the principals of the schools the children would attend if they went to public school. She assured Diane these professionals would be very cordial and wouldn't mind discussing their particular school with her. Robyn told Diane it was not uncommon for prospective students to spend a day at the school before they actually enrolled. The school would designate a student in the same grade to spend the day with each of Diane's children. This way they would get an idea of what the school day would be like if they attended that school. Diane followed Robyn's advice and was very pleased with the outcome of her meetings with the principals. If she had to go this route, she would now be comfortable with the quality of the instructional programs that would be available to the children.

Dorothy Trumbull had been very definite with Diane about her financial options: She would have to either sell her home and buy a less expensive one or remove the children from their private schools and place them in public schools. She might even have to do both. In addition, she would have to go back to work. Diane knew she had resisted dealing with this issue long enough. She knew she needed to discuss this with the children the way she had earlier discussed the budget. Before doing so, however, she decided to talk with her dad. She had avoided getting him involved in her financial problems, but she knew how much he loved and cared about the children. She could no longer worry about what he thought of Mark. She had to resolve this matter now.

She called her dad and asked him if he would meet her for lunch at a local restaurant because she wanted to go over some things with him. Diane had always talked to her parents in the home in which she had grown up, and she wanted this to be different. She was making progress toward the personal security she hoped she'd eventually achieve when it came to money matters, and she didn't want to regress to her former dependency.

After they had ordered their lunch, Diane brought out the most recent financial statements she had developed with Dorothy. They clearly indicated her assets and liabilities as well as a negative cash flow. Diane told her dad about her visits to the schools. She had reconciled herself to the idea of putting the children in the local public schools but wanted his input as to the advisability of selling the home. She really felt the stability provided by staying in the home was exceedingly valuable for the children.

After Diane had laid all of this out for her father, she sat back somewhat nervously to hear his response. For a few seconds, which seemed much longer, her dad said nothing. She looked up at him expectantly and was shocked to see a tear in his eye. What had she said or done to sadden or upset him? She couldn't think of anything. At about this point, her dad reached across the table and took her hand. "Diane," he said, "I can't believe how much you've changed since Mark died. You'll always be my little girl, but now you are an adult woman, and I am so proud of how much you've grown. I don't know this financial planning woman you've been seeing, but she has certainly given you good advice. I basically agree with the direction in which you are moving and think you should stay in your current home. But I am really concerned about Erin. She'll be going into her junior year next year, and I would hate to see her have to adjust to a new school during a year that's so critical to college preparation. I know I don't need to tell you this, but Erin will always have a special place in my heart because she was my first grandchild. In any case, I'd like you to allow me to pick up the financial responsibility for her tuition for the next two years. I'm sure your mother will agree."

Diane smiled to herself, thinking her mother would go along with anything her father suggested, just the way she would have with Mark. She wasn't sure how she felt about this offer. Was it fair to Alice and Jeremy? How would they feel about their sister having the opportunity to remain in her school while they had to go to a public school? On the other hand, she had the same concerns about Erin her dad had expressed. Before she could reply and thank Dad for his generous offer, he went on to say he wanted to do something for the other two children, but it would have to be at a later date. Perhaps he could pay for one year of college tuition for each of them. Diane thanked him profusely but said she would have to discuss it with the children.

Seeing his quizzical look, she explained that they functioned differently as a family now and discussed as a unit decisions that involved all of them. Diane realized this was the first time she had eaten a meal with her dad by herself since she graduated from high school. She felt good about it. She recognized from the way he looked at her that he had a new respect for her. She didn't have a problem with his paying for the lunch; it was just the way it was. He hugged her extra hard when they parted in the restaurant parking lot.

That very evening Diane resolved to discuss with the children the financial realities that prevented them from continuing in their present schools. She had expected a big fuss and lots of tears. She was pleasantly surprised. The children all said, given the choice, they would rather stay in the home than attend their present schools. However, Erin did not feel it was fair for her to continue at her school if Jeremy and Alice had to go to public school. Jeremy told her she was being ridiculous. He could accept what his grandfather proposed and was willing to risk that his grandfather would be willing and able to help him when he entered college. Alice said she was scared, but if

Jeremy could deal with public school, she guessed she could too. She wanted to know if she could still see her present school friends. They had a good discussion about the schools. In the end, everyone agreed that Erin should finish her last two years in her present school.

Diane was so proud of her children. She was pleased with their family meetings. When Mark was alive, all of them seemed to function individually, although she never looked at it that way at the time. They had all matured. It was hard for Diane to acknowledge that they worked better as a family unit now than they ever had in the past. She thought the change was healthier, too. Erin asked if she could call her grandfather to thank him and tell him that they had talked it over and she was going to accept his generous offer. Diane thought that was a nice idea.

Diane felt relieved when the discussion about schools was over. She had been preoccupied with the question of the private schools since she had "come to" following Mark's sudden death. She was now ready to pay attention to her own needs. She decided to investigate whether the University of Maryland had a paralegal brush-up program. If they didn't offer one, they might know of a course that was offered by another school in the area. Maybe Erin could help her find information on the Internet. She had heard that it was now possible to enroll in classes with certain universities totally online. She wondered how she would feel about working again. It would all be so different now.

Diane called Robyn because she wanted her to be the first to know she had resolved the school issue. She had never had a friend like her before, yet they might never have met and become friends if it weren't for the widow support group. Robyn was so pleased to learn of Diane's decision.

Robyn told Diane she would not accept any more excuses from her about not going to the health club. Robyn knew Diane had played tennis when Mark was alive but that she had not been ready to do anything on a physical level since his death. Robyn had often told her how working out at the health club had enabled her to survive after her husband's death. She would no longer accept no as an answer because of this or that—she was going to take Diane as her guest this coming weekend!

Diane laughed and said, "Okay, you win. I'll go with you and see what I think. I'm so out of shape I would be embarrassed to be seen in shorts and a T-shirt!" Robyn told her, no matter what, she would look better in those clothes than Robyn did, and Robyn really benefited from her exercise program. She assured Diane the other people would make her feel welcome and comfortable. As always, Diane felt good about her conversation with Robyn.

Next, Diane called Dorothy to update her on where she was with regard to the schools and the home. She had checked with the University of Maryland, and they did have a brush-up paralegal course. The counselor there had been very helpful about what courses she would need to take to qualify for a job. It appeared that she could go to school at night and that it would take about two semesters. The current cost was $1,400 per semester. She could even take the classes online. She and Dorothy agreed that this was a necessary investment in her future. Then Diane somewhat reluctantly told Dorothy that she really wanted to join the health club. The club had this promotional offer and she wanted to take advantage of it. She realized it was an extravagance, but she thought it was necessary for her mental and physical health. Could she afford it?

Dorothy reviewed Diane's budget once again. Needless to say, eliminating the tuition costs ($50,000 annually) had helped a lot. She had to add the expense of $1,400 a semester for the paralegal course and $1,000 for the health club plus the money necessary to purchase the home computer Diane would need to help her complete her course work and keep better track of any number of other things. The result was that Diane still had a negative cash flow of about $11,000 in her projected annual budget. This discouraged Diane, but Dorothy reassured her that this figure was much better than the previous negative cash flow of $58,000.

The reason she had advised Diane to set aside the large cash reserve was so she would be in a position to cover this negative cash flow. Next year, assuming she was able to get a job as a paralegal, she should be able to cover expenses and replenish her cash reserve. However, it was obvious to Diane she would need to continue to try to reduce their expenses. Time for another family meeting!

Susan

Reactions to Identifying Today's Personal Attitudes and Realities

Susan completed her "Who Am I Today Personally?" form as follows:

WHO AM I TODAY PERSONALLY?

Personal Strengths
1.   More self-confident on a personal and professional level
2.   Actively involved in understanding my own social and emotional needs
3.   More in touch with my feelings

Personal Weaknesses
1.   Sometimes insensitive to feelings of others around me
2.   Reluctant to delegate responsibility both personally and professionally
3.   Difficulty establishing friendships

Personal Needs
1.   Physical and emotional affection
2.   Regular fitness program
3.   Need to be perceived as a good daughter

In contemplating her responses to the "Who Am I Today Personally?" form, Susan realized that Lance's death and her work with Dr. Coleman had impacted the way she saw herself. She now saw herself in her personal life as someone capable of being proactive, whereas before she would have described herself as reactive—in other words, waiting for something to happen and then responding. Today, she was more likely to analyze a situation, giving thought to possible actions she might initiate to resolve the matter as opposed to waiting for she knew not what. Her increased understanding of her financial situation had made her aware of her need to earn more money. Her sessions with Dr. Coleman had increased her sense of self-worth. They had discussed her functioning at her job. She now realized she was underpaid for the work she was doing in her present job. The association had given her regular salary increases; however, if she was honest with herself, she had to acknowledge that her pay was not commensurate with her job responsibilities. She also realized she was capable of assuming greater responsibility than her current job entailed.

Susan knew she would be attending the American Society of Association Executives (ASAE) convention in two weeks. She found herself actually looking forward to having the opportunity to talk with her peers about the current job market. As she boarded the plane for the convention, she surprised herself with the realization that she was no longer afraid to think about the future without Lance. The time away from home and the demands of daily life would allow her to reflect on her options in a more leisurely fashion. She noted, as she seemed to do with most events that had occurred following Lance's death, that this was the first flight she had taken since Lance died. Before she knew it, she had landed, transported herself to the hotel, and checked into her room.

After getting settled in her room, she went downstairs to register for the convention. Susan found herself in a short line in front of a man about her age who began to chat with her while they waited. He asked which association she represented and identified both the city in which he lived and the association with which he was affiliated. The line moved very slowly. Apparently, one of the registrants in front of them had lost his badge. It took some time for the registration personnel to locate the information and replace the badge, delaying the registration process for those in line behind him.

Susan and the man, who had now identified himself as Andrew Neily, commiserated about the interminable pace at which their line was proceeding. By the time Susan reached the head of their line, Andrew had asked her to have a drink with him later on that day. Both of them were attending the convention without coworkers. Susan found herself hesitating. She had never considered the possibility of having this type of social contact at the convention. She had been exclusively focused on her career and business concerns. Her lack of response caused Andrew to inquire if something was wrong. She assured him no, and without further thought accepted the invitation.

When she returned to her room, she was panicked. What had she done? What would this outwardly friendly guy think of her? How could she socialize with a man other than Lance? She wanted to escape but realized Andrew had caught her so off guard she had neglected to find out which hotel he was staying at, so she could not call him to cancel. Oh, well, she guessed one drink couldn't hurt. As the time to meet Andrew approached, Susan found herself thinking about what she would wear. She felt almost girlish yet simultaneously was ashamed and guilty about her feelings. She put on what she thought was a professional-looking dress, softened somewhat by a scarf. "Well," she thought, "If I'm going to do this, I'm going to put my best foot forward."

Andrew was waiting for her in front of the bar—she was relieved she wouldn't have to wait for him. They found a table and placed their order. Susan was unprepared for how easy it was to talk to Andrew. She told him about Lance, and he told her he was recently separated from his wife and was having a difficult time dealing with it. Drinks led to dinner in the hotel. Andrew insisted on paying for the drinks but was amenable to each paying separately for dinner. The evening seemed to fly by, and Susan realized how much she had missed talking to a man about anything other than Lance's estate, varied financial matters, her mother, or her work. She wondered to herself if she would ever find another man with whom she could have a relationship. This was the most pleasant evening she'd had since Lance died. Until now, she had taken for granted that there would not be another man in her life. She experienced a twinge of guilt when she returned to her room and made a note to herself to discuss these feelings with Dr. Coleman. As she prepared for bed, she returned to her earlier thoughts about taking advantage of this convention to get a better sense of what was going on regarding career and salary advancement opportunities in the association world.

Over the next several days, she reestablished some former contacts and made some new ones. She was busy and had little opportunity for socializing other than on a work-related basis. On the evening of the banquet she found herself chatting with Andrew again. They exchanged business cards and agreed to keep in touch, although Susan doubted there would be much opportunity for them to meet again since she lived in Seattle and he lived in Chicago. Perhaps it was just as well. Susan knew that Andrew would have liked to pursue a relationship with her. Although he had made her realize she was not dead as a woman, she was not yet ready for a relationship with a man. She was glad she had met Andrew but was also grateful for the geographic distance between them.

Susan was very pleased with what she learned about job opportunities. One of the people she met had talked to her about a job that would be opening up soon for an executive director with an association based in Seattle. The salary would be $70,000, which was $15,000 more than her current annual income. Susan thought this possibility sounded interesting—at this point she was about ready to take on a job with greater responsibility. However, before making a final decision, she knew she would discuss her options with Dr. Coleman. Her inclination was to move ahead to something new with greater responsibility, but she wondered if Dr. Coleman would think she should first investigate a raise with her present association. Even if she was able to get the raise, she wasn't sure she wanted to maintain her present role. The prospective job was a greater challenge, and she felt ready for it.

On the plane back to Seattle, Susan allowed herself to contemplate where she was in her life in a somewhat new light. Since Lance's death, she had devoted more time to her mother than ever before. Dr. Coleman had suggested to her that she was becoming preoccupied with her mother's situation in order to delay facing more painful personal issues. She knew just how important Susan's mother was to her but emphasized that she could not be all things to her mother. Dr. Coleman did not feel it was healthy for her to assume the role she had in the past to the exclusion of her brother. She was pleased that Susan had spoken to Ron and he had agreed to take on a more active role with her mother. His help would be particularly helpful if she pursued this new job.

As the plane brought her back to Seattle, Susan recognized that her psychological need to order her life was causing her to review just about every aspect of her life. Having dinner with a man had caused her to think about her physical being. She and Lance had been fairly active people, but she realized she hadn't done anything physical since his death. She wondered if she could bear to go bicycling. This was an activity from which she and Lance had derived much pleasure. She knew her memories of their rides together would be too painful if she attempted to ride on any of the bicycle paths they had taken. Once, Lance had investigated a cycling club because they had given some thought to taking a bicycle tour through France. Without warning, tears came to her eyes as she thought about the trip they would never take. However, she thought she might be able to get back into her bicycling if she had the opportunity to do it with others. This was another area she needed to investigate sooner rather than later; she even thought she had seen the information on Lance's desk.

Thinking about the bicycle trips she and Lance had taken reminded her of the one they attempted with his children. She had not seen or even heard from Leslie and Adam in quite some time. She guessed they would no longer play a role in one another's lives; perhaps they would send each other perfunctory Christmas cards. In some ways, Susan wished things were different with them because they were a part of Lance. Both she and the children had shared a special relationship with him. Unfortunately, Susan knew all too well that wishing didn't accomplish anything. Instead of ruminating about something that would never be, she should pay more attention to something she did have control over—mainly her friends. Dr. Coleman had been stressing to Susan the need for her to reestablish relationships with some of her former friends and to investigate some new contacts. Attending the convention had moved her to the point where she was ready to deal with people. It felt good to talk to people and share common interests. She hadn't been ready before, but now she was, and she planned to do something about her social life on her return.

Dr. Coleman would be pleased with her response to the convention and her willingness to give serious thought to a new job. Her work with Dr. Coleman had resulted in Susan's seeing herself in a new light. She had contacted Dr. Coleman to help her deal with the aftermath of Lance's death, but in the process she had begun to look at herself in ways she never had before. She hated to admit it to herself, but her work with Dr. Coleman had gone far beyond the issues surrounding Lance's death.

Audrey

Reactions to Identifying Today's Personal Attitudes and Realities

Audrey completed her "Who Am I Today Personally?" form as follows:

WHO AM I TODAY PERSONALLY?

Personal Strengths

1.   Willingness to assume personal responsibility
2.   Socially conscious
3.   Desire to learn
4.   Enthusiastic about the opportunity for new experiences

Personal Weaknesses

1.   Tendency to become overly committed
2.   Neglect my health
3.   Tendency to be too cautious

Personal Needs

1.   To be my own person
2.   To be actively involved with my family
3.   To contribute to society
4.   To continue to seek new experiences and widen my horizons

Going to the golf clinic at Hilton Head with her friends had been just what the doctor ordered. The golf pros had improved her game considerably, but, even more important, she enjoyed being away with her friends. They were upbeat and teased her about finding a man. They even came up with elaborate schemes to attract one man they saw in the clubhouse. They thought he was just right for her and laughed themselves silly in the process.

In fact, they were all surprised when, having inquired about her marital status and learning that she was a widow, he approached her on his own about having a drink. Her friends insisted that she accept, and everyone had something to say about what she should wear. It was like getting ready for a prom. They all laughed so hard she didn't think she'd be able to walk to their designated meeting place. She wasn't sure how she felt about this, but all of her friends encouraged her, telling her it would be good for her. She didn't even know what she would say to a man at this point in her life. She felt strange but decided to go ahead with the meeting anyway.

When they met, she learned that Lionel, the man in question, was a recently retired corporate executive whose wife had died two years ago. She had also died following a lingering illness, which gave them something in common. In addition, he was charming and witty. He had lived in Atlanta, Georgia, all of his life and had four grown children, busy with their own lives. As Lionel spoke about his feelings following the death of his wife, Marian, Audrey began to realize that he had had some different adjustments to make than she had. He obviously understood his financial situation, but he was at a loss as to how to manage anything in the home. He shared with her his sense of inadequacy as to what to do about simple things, such as their cleaning woman asking him what he wanted to do about the rug-cleaning service. Apparently his wife had the rugs professionally cleaned once a year, but he had no idea whether or not he should continue with this service and, if so, when to have it done. He was embarrassed by the question because he felt the woman must have realized that he didn't even know what she was talking about. He remembered feeling like a fool and felt he had stood before her for an interminable amount of time, staring at the floor with his arms dangling at his sides. Finally, he told her to go ahead as usual, but both of them knew he didn't have a clue what that meant.

Marian had always made things appear effortless, and the household had run smoothly, something he accepted without question. Lionel said that in an odd way he felt he had been excluded from her life, which intensified his loneliness and sense of being at a loss as to what he was supposed to do. He mused to Audrey that somehow that moment with the cleaning woman humbled him in terms of all Marian had done in the management of their home and the children's lives. Audrey wondered whether John would have been able to share something like that with anyone or whether he had ever been aware of all she had done to make their home run smoothly.

As they shared their mutual experiences regarding their spouses' illnesses and the early days following the funerals, Audrey became aware of another disparity, yet also a similarity, in their social experiences. Lionel too had not known what to do about the couples who were mutual friends—but from a different perspective. As in her own case, Marian had managed the social calendar. When she was well and even toward the end of her life, if she was well enough to see friends, it just seemed to happen. He wasn't quite sure how. After Marian's death he didn't know what to do with their friends. He didn't want to impose on them and invite himself over to their homes. He didn't want to become the extra man to be paraded before a series of "wonderful" divorced, widowed, or never married women. He didn't want the women to feel sorry for him and feel he needed to be included because he didn't have the ability to prepare his own food, even though it was true that he was hopeless in the kitchen. He wasn't a hermit, and he hated eating alone. He found that he couldn't bear to be at home with the silence of the home crashing down around him. There was always this pervasive sense that he didn't belong anywhere.

Lionel found that his role even with his male friends had changed in subtle ways. For instance, he played golf with the guys on Saturdays, as he had done forever. However, now after having something to eat with them following the game, his friends would go off to do something else with their wives, and he would remain to linger over another glass of beer or cup of coffee and feel disconnected from life. He was no longer part of the group, nor was he removed from it. He described it as always feeling in limbo, of not quite belonging, of not being fish or fowl. It was odd, but until this moment Audrey had never given much thought to how the loss of a spouse might impact a man's life. He was never concerned with issues surrounding paying his share of the bill after a dinner out with mutual friends, as she had been, yet he too had concerns. Clearly, he had some different adjustments and some similar ones. Was it possible to determine which was more difficult? Probably not!

She found she was quite comfortable with Lionel, and drinks led to dinner. Her friends told her they had bet she would end up having dinner with him, but she had said the idea was ridiculous. They'd have a thousand questions for her when she got back to the suite, as well as "we told you so's." Before dinner was over, she had agreed to see Lionel again during her stay at Hilton Head. His interest in her was flattering, but she wasn't sure she was ready for a relationship or even that she wanted one. She guessed she hadn't expected anyone to be interested in her, so she hadn't focused on such an eventuality at all. She knew she would give the whole area of relationships more thought when she got back home.

So much had taken place since John's death. She was still dealing with all the changes in her life and attempting to make good decisions for herself as to how she spent her time. She was very positive about her current relationships with her children and grandchildren. She was closer to Joanne than she had ever been, and both women had benefited from the opportunity they had created to get to know each other better. The weekly lunches had really been a plus. They now shared things with each other they had never shared before. Audrey tried to be as supportive as she could to her daughter with regard to her marriage. She knew there was ongoing tension between the couple because of their financial situation.

She adored Joanne's children and they her. All of them looked forward to her day with them. Because she now had more time to spend with Heidi and Noah, she also made a point of doing extra things with the oldest child, Jamie, who was usually in school during Audrey's visits. She and "Gran Gran" had some special sleep-overs. Audrey always got a thrill out of having the chance to personally watch her grandchildren acquire new skills and proudly demonstrate them for her. Children learned so much in such short periods of time.

She was also pleased with her current relationship with John Jr. In his high school and college years, he and Audrey had been fairly close. It was not uncommon for him to come to her with a question about which course might be better for him or, more likely, a question related to a relationship he had with some girl. Their relationship changed when he entered medical school, as did his overall attitude. Audrey couldn't pinpoint when he developed what she called his superior attitude, but she hadn't found it attractive. It created more distance between them. The conversation she had with him in the kitchen about her financial situation had brought them back to where they had been in the past. She thought they both realized this was a turning point for them. John Jr. had gone with her to Mr. Silver's. He liked his approach to his mother's situation as well as his mother's understanding of her financial affairs. He realized he had never given much thought to his own financial affairs, and this type of approach would also be of value to him. Before he left the office with Audrey, he had made an appointment for himself and his wife to meet with Mr. Silver and took home with him various forms that Mr. Silver requested be completed in order to give him a full picture of his financial status.

After this, there had been more invitations from her daughter-in-law, of whom Audrey was fond, for dinner or an activity involving her grandchildren. She hadn't seen much of John Jr. and his family before now and felt she was just getting to know them. J.T., the older son, was a freshman in high school and all boy. His younger brother, Casey, was more sensitive and serious, spending all of his spare time poring over computer books and doing scientific experiments. She had both of them over to spend the night and was pleased with the way things turned out. They all seemed to be discovering one another.

Audrey was basically comfortable with her social life too. Some of the couples from her married days had remained friendly with her. They included her in their dinner get-togethers and other activities. There had been some rocky times in the beginning over money, but these had been resolved. At first the men didn't know what to do about her when it came to buying a ticket or paying a restaurant bill. They had tried to pick up her share and split it among them, but that made Audrey feel like a charity case. She had told them as firmly as she could that she wanted to join them but couldn't do it if they would not allow her to pay her own way; it was uncomfortable for her not to do so. They finally got the message and now treated her as an equal on that level. She realized she was the first widow in their circle of friends, so it was like breaking ground. Walter and Jane were still a problem sometimes because of Jane's reaction to her husband's attention to Audrey, but Audrey paid less attention to it, as did everyone else in their group.

Her new friends were more diversified and exciting to her. She had become quite friendly with Heather, whom she had met through her symphony volunteer work. She too was a widow, and they had gotten into the habit of getting together about one evening a week now to take in a movie, have something to eat together, go shopping, or whatever else appealed to them. She was probably her closest friend now, mainly because they were both widows. It did make a difference! She could discuss things with Heather that her other friends wouldn't understand. Heather was the one who had suggested the London theater trip, which Audrey was considering.

Audrey was most pleased with the friends she had made through her work with the Reading Is Fundamental (RIF) program. All the volunteers were concerned about motivating young children— particularly disadvantaged children—to read. They worked tirelessly to make sure the program worked in their community. Through the RIF program they were making sure each child had a book of his or her own to take home, read, and keep. For many it was the first book that they had ever owned. Audrey realized what a relatively sheltered life she had previously chosen to lead and enthusiastically embraced this new activity. Although initially intimidated by the group, she responded positively to their acceptance of her. They made her feel welcome very quickly, and she realized that her organizational skills were helpful to this involved group of women. They were also very complimentary to her about her contributions to the program. All this made her feel good about her decision to become active with this group.

Elizabeth

Reactions to Identifying Today's Personal Attitudes and Realities

Elizabeth completed her "Who Am I Today Personally?" form as follows:

WHO AM I TODAY PERSONALLY?

Personal Strengths

1. Becoming more outgoing
2. Beginning to make my own personal decisions
3. Recent ability to envision major lifestyle change without guilt or fear
4. Openness to new friendships

Personal Weaknesses

1. Lack self-confidence
2. Still dependent on the approval of others
3. Slow to change
4. Afraid of making mistakes

Personal Needs

1. Companionship
2. To be physically self-sufficient
3. To be closer to Abigail
4. To be more responsible about personal health

Elizabeth had a difficult time completing her "Who Am I Today Personally?" form because she wasn't sure she really knew who she was anymore. She wasn't the same person she had been when Ben was alive, but she hadn't changed a great deal either. She had amazed herself on the cruise she had taken with Abigail; she had participated in almost everything. She thought it was the most exciting experience she had ever had. She wished she had been brave enough to insist Ben take her on a cruise after he had retired. She had made comments about cruises, but he never picked up on the idea as something she really wanted to do. She wondered if he would have gone if he had known it was important to her. Well, she'd never know. She thought about the expression on Abigail's face when one of the crew members asked Elizabeth to dance and she had accepted. She smiled to herself just thinking about it.

The ports they visited were all interesting, and the heat hadn't bothered her. There were several senior citizens on the ship. By the end of the first full day on board, she and Abigail found themselves socializing with a small group who shared similar interests. She was surprised at how close they had all become in the course of one short week. She had discussed a variety of topics with these people, topics she had never discussed with the few friends she and Ben had known in Boston in all the time they had known them. One of the couples she had become friendly with on the ship lived near Abigail in Florida, as did another widow whose company she particularly enjoyed.

Elizabeth was giving more and more thought to relocating to Florida. Because she and Ben hadn't socialized that much, at this point she really had only acquaintances in Boston. The exceptions were her longtime friend Mabel and now her new friends the Weatherlys and Lucy. When she visited Abigail's retirement community, she was amazed at the number of activities offered to the residents. She sat in on Abigail's Wednesday afternoon bridge group and remembered how much she and Ben used to enjoy their bridge games before he became ill. Someone even asked her if she would take a hand for a while. She was reluctant because it had been so long since she played, but she agreed after the players assured her they wouldn't get upset with her if she made a mistake. She felt she hadn't done too badly, although she knew she was rusty. It would be nice to play bridge again.

Abigail had encouraged Elizabeth to attend some of the activities with her, and she had done so. She'd always wanted to take an advanced quilting class but had never gotten around to it. The class she visited at the retirement facility seemed perfect—it was neither beyond her sewing level nor too simple. The young woman teaching it seemed to be very pleased to answer any and all questions. When she saw other women about her age participating and asking questions, she felt more comfortable about undertaking such an activity herself. She was beginning to get frustrated with herself for always needing support from someone else. The senior citizens she saw in Florida didn't seem to need the same kind of approval and support she appeared to need. A part of her was tired of being this way, worrying about who she was, what others would think, and what she was going to do. Another part was reluctant to change.

Mabel and Lucy had suggested to her that she visit some continuing care retirement communities (CCRC) in the Boston area before she made a final decision about moving to Florida. Elizabeth thought this was a good idea. Mabel had a widowed friend living in a CCRC, and she suggested they go over for lunch. Mabel made the necessary arrangements with her friend, Caroline, who turned out to be very gracious. They had had a delicious lunch as Caroline's guests in the light, airy dining room. Afterward, she gave them the grand tour of the clubhouse complete with an indoor swimming pool and the grounds. She showed them the week's schedule of events and the menus. Elizabeth noticed that the day they were there a lecture by a well-known Boston antiques dealer was scheduled. Caroline's apartment was surprisingly spacious and tastefully decorated. Her son and daughter lived nearby, and the location enabled her to spend time with her children as well as on her own.

Elizabeth thought such a place would clearly be an option if she stayed in Massachusetts. Although, if she stayed in Boston, she didn't know if she was quite ready to give up her home—all these decisions! There was something about Florida that was more appealing, but she wasn't quite sure what it was.

She decided to invite Pastor Appletorn to tea. She thought it would be helpful to discuss her dilemma with him. She hadn't had much of an opportunity to talk with him personally since she had returned from her cruise. She attended church faithfully on Sundays, but that wasn't the same as speaking with him personally. She thought about how much more comfort she had derived from his sermons these past few weeks, and all because she had been fitted with a hearing aid. Now that she had adjusted to it, she readily admitted that she had needed one. Funny, she hadn't realized how much her hearing had deteriorated until Abigail had brought it to her attention.

When Elizabeth had gone for her physical, her doctor, Dr. Longworth, had said he hadn't seen her in so long he had forgotten what she looked like. He was pleased with her overall health but confirmed that she had a moderate hearing loss in definite need of correction. He was sure the type of loss he suspected would improve markedly once she was appropriately fitted with a hearing aid. He referred her to another doctor to handle the hearing problem. It turned out he was right—the hearing aid made a world of difference!

As she greeted Pastor Appletorn at the door, she was pleased to see his smiling face. He had a way of making all of his parishioners feel special. They had tea with some scones she had baked for the occasion. He complimented her on how good they were. He asked about her cruise and her sister. She told him all about the cruise, her sister, and where her sister lived. She made a special point of telling him she had attended church with Abigail in

Florida and had enjoyed the sermon but assured him it wasn't the same as attending his church. He reminded her that it didn't have to be just the same to be valuable—he was sure the Lord appreciated diversity among his flock. He added, as she knew all too well, that nothing stayed the same forever. Toward the end of the tea, Pastor Appletorn surprised her by saying, "Elizabeth, I've known you for a long time, and I hear something different and new in your voice when you talk about Florida. There is a spark, a greater sense of self-confidence that I have never heard before. I can't tell you what to do. If you do move, it will be a loss to our congregation, but I think you should give it some serious thought."

After he left, Elizabeth sat in her familiar comfortable dining room for some time. Mittens jumped up and sat in her lap, purring away. She really did enjoy having him. She would have to inquire as to whether or not they allowed pets at Northern Palms. She thought they did but wasn't positive. What really was keeping her in Boston? She guessed she felt disloyal to Ben because they had always lived here and Ben was buried here. It was as if she had decided Boston wasn't good enough for her any more. But Ben was no longer with her, and she was all alone. The winters were really hard on her, and she knew she would have to increasingly depend on Pastor Appletorn and other members of the congregation for one thing or another when the weather was bad. In Florida, she had been able to be something more than Ben's wife. She was Elizabeth in her own right, and she liked the feeling. She wasn't sure who she was quite yet, but she liked the way she had felt in Florida. Besides, she did want to be close to Abigail. She was getting closer to making a final decision every day.

PART THREE

Building a Secure and Rewarding Future

11

Developing Your
Long-Term Financial Plan

You have to have confidence in your ability,
and then be tough enough to follow through.
—Rosalynn Carter

WHEN A WOMAN BECOMES A WIDOW, she has to understand her financial situation and manage her own money in order to survive. Prior to becoming a widow, many women have not had the primary responsibility for controlling the family's finances. The recognition and acceptance of the fact that financial decisions now rest in your hands require a major adjustment in mind-set. It is not that widows are incapable of handling finances; it is more often likely they were not involved in the process—either by their choice or their husband's. Because they were accustomed to their husband's assuming responsibility for their finances, now their natural tendency is to find someone else to assume that role.

Delegating total responsibility to someone else frequently causes widows to run into financial trouble. It is understandable that you want to rely on someone else, just as you trusted your husband. Many new widows assume the "child widow" role because it is familiar, and they resent the fact that they are forced to manage their own money. Others resist dealing with finances because it is symbolic to them of the fact that they are widows—a state they did not choose and don't like. Perhaps not taking charge of their finances allows them to cling to the myth that their life has not really changed. They may also be reacting to feelings about money established earlier in life (see chapters 2 and 9).

Regardless of how you felt about money management in the past, as a widow you must now accept the fact that you and you alone have the ultimate responsibility for your financial future. To do this, you have to understand your financial situation from a short-term as well as a long-term point of view. Ultimately, you may decide to delegate all or part of the management of your money to someone else, but before you take that step you need to understand your situation.

UPDATING YOUR BUDGET
AND BALANCE SHEET

Now that you have been living on your own for a while, you have a better idea of what you are actually spending as opposed to what you estimated you would spend. In chapter 7, we presented a format to help you estimate the amount of money you need to cover your expenses. The temptation is to go through this exercise initially and then ignore it. However, it is essential to keep monitoring your expenses and income periodically to make sure you are not spending your principal. This is not easy to do while the estate is being sorted out. In these early stages, the difference between income and principal is not always clear.

As we have mentioned many times, the first year of widowhood is one of transition, one during which many mistakes may be made. We have tried to demonstrate how to avoid these mistakes. After you have gone through this initial stage of dealing with crises—both emotional and financial—your life should become more predictable, and new patterns will be established. Now is the time to look at your budget again. Are all your expenses necessary? We hope that you are past the splurges you might have indulged in initially—the special vacation, the clothes you bought, or the redecoration of the home—most of which were designed to cheer up you and your family. Are things costing more than you expected or less? Is your income sufficient to cover your expenses?

It is also advisable to update your balance sheet. Now that your husband's estate is settled or is closer to being settled, you should have a better idea of what you actually own and what debts you still owe.

It is a good idea to compare your current net worth with what it was last year. After this year, we recommend you calculate your net worth at least annually to see where you are. Note if you are making progress or losing ground. By now you should have sufficient information to make some major decisions about whether you want to sell your home or make any changes to your investments.

At this point, it is important to do some longer-range planning rather than the "getting by" approach of the early stages of widowhood. We have used the time frame of a year, but, as we said previously, this settling-down period may take a shorter or longer time for you to reach.

In the early stages of widowhood, you probably worked with your husband's advisors. Assuming that you now feel more in control of your situation, we recommend you review your relationship with these advisors. Were they helpful to you and responsive to your requests? If not, you may want to change them (see chapter 5). If your experiences were good, make appointments with them to discuss your future financial plans.

ESTATE PLANNING WITH YOUR ATTORNEY

Your Will

The attorney who handled the settlement of your husband's estate probably reviewed your will or created one for you to ensure your estate would be in order. However, you should reexamine the will that you approved when you first were widowed. It may not accurately reflect your intentions now that things have quieted down somewhat and you have had more time for reflection.

Questions to consider when drafting a will include the following:

- Who will inherit your assets?
- Who will supervise the distribution of these assets and the winding up of your affairs?
- How will your assets be distributed? Outright gift or trust?
- When will the distribution be made?
- Who will be the guardian for your children if they are minors?
- Do you want the personal and financial guardian of the minor(s) to be the same person?

On this last question, if you don't have a valid will and you have minor children, your probate estate will be divided equally among them. The court will appoint a guardian for them as well as an administrator to settle the estate. To avoid this, you need to designate a guardian or personal representative in your will.

Make sure the person you select agrees to assume that role. The person you have in mind may not want to take on that responsibility. Be sure that the person you ask to be trustee for your children realizes that he or she doesn't have to be an expert in investment management. In fact, you should encourage this person to seek professional help managing the inherited assets. You might even decide to name a second trustee who is not involved with the care of the children but is financially knowledgeable. To avoid disaster, you might consider naming a *trust protector* who can discharge a trustee under some circumstances or even veto certain trustee decisions. You also may want to allow a change of trustee should the beneficiaries move out of state. Think through all of these issues and discuss them with your attorney.

It is a common misconception that if you are single and you don't have children, you do not need a will. This is not correct. The purpose of a will is to make sure that your assets go to the individuals or institutions that you designate.

We recommend that you use percentages rather than dollar amounts in your will. For example, if your will specifies that your six heirs should receive $100,000 each and your total estate is less than this amount, then your personal representative has a problem. If instead you had said each heir was entitled to one-sixth of the estate, it would be easier to divide your assets.

Under current federal estate tax law, when you die, $2 million of your assets will be excluded from federal estate tax (for the years 2006, 2007, and 2008). (This estate exclusion amount increases to $3.5 million in 2009, disappears in 2010, and reappears as $1 million in 2011).

Year	Estate Exclusion	Maximum Tax Rate
2006	$2,000,000	46%
2007	$2,000,000	45%
2008	$2,000,000	45%
2009	$3,500,000	45%
2010	Not applicable	0% estate tax rate; 35% gift tax rate
2011	$1,000,000	55%

If your assets exceed these amounts, your estate will be taxed according to an established formula. One way to avoid this tax is to leave all of your assets in excess of the estate exclusion amount to charity, which you might consider if you have no heirs.

Any assets you do not own in your own name will not be distributed according to the terms of your will. For example, assets you own jointly with another person with right of survivorship become the property of the surviving joint owner, regardless of what your will might say. Similarly, IRAs, pension benefits, and life insurance pass to the named beneficiary. If the named beneficiary is the estate and not an individual, what the will says determines how the assets are distributed. We recommend you name individuals rather than your estate to avoid adverse tax consequences for your beneficiaries.

Some people have very good wills drawn up but then mistakenly title their stock and bank accounts jointly with some member of the family. For example, your will may specify that your five children share equally in your $600,000 estate. If a part of the estate consists of a jointly held bank account of $100,000 with one of your children, this asset will go directly to that child and the balance of your estate ($500,000) will be divided equally among your five children. This probably was not your intention.

Some people assume that by titling all their assets in joint name they have done their estate planning and don't need a will. Under current tax law, this may work for estates under $2 million (at least until the end of 2008), but it is always advisable to have a will to make sure your estate is in order and to make appropriate arrangements for any assets going to young children.

You should consider changing your will if any of the following occur: you remarry or divorce, a tax law changes, you have a child or grandchild, someone mentioned in the will dies, you move from one state to another, or the size of the estate has changed significantly. In the past, you might have added a codicil to your will to reflect a desired change. Today, signing a new will that reflects any change costs about the same and will be less subject to challenge.

Once your will is drafted according to your specifications, your lawyer should make sure that it is signed, witnessed by the required number of people, valid in your state of residence, and put in a safe place, where the appropriate people can find it. This last piece of advice seems obvious but it is not. Often, someone dies and the family has no idea where the will is located. Make sure your family does not have this problem.

Powers of Attorney, Living Wills, and Advance Directives

In addition to having a will drawn up, you should designate someone to have what is called a durable *power of attorney* (POA). This allows that person to act on your behalf should you be traveling or become incapacitated. If you become unable to make financial or medical decisions and have not given anyone your POA, a family member or friend may have to petition the court to appoint a guardian for you. We recommend that you have two durable POAs, one to handle your financial affairs and the other to cover your health-care directives. You may want the same person to have both POAs, or you may want to appoint two different people.

The financial POA allows your agent to act for your benefit when handling your financial affairs. However, check with your bank and investment manager to make sure they will accept the document prepared by your lawyer. Sometimes they will honor only their own POAs, so you should sign both.

The health-care POA enables you to provide guidelines and instructions about the extent of medical care and intervention you would want under various circumstances. This POA will be effective if your physical or mental condition makes it impossible for you to understand, make, or communicate an informed decision about providing, withholding, or withdrawing treatment. In this document you would also appoint someone to act on your behalf. For example, the person you name would be able to talk with your doctors and nurses about your care. It is very important to have someone represent you in this capacity. Doctors and hospitals today have to follow very strict privacy rules designed to protect your personal information, but the unintended side effect is that without your written consent they may not be able to discuss your condition with your loved ones.

In your health-care POA you can describe what quality of life is acceptable to you, thus relieving your family and friends of the burden of making these difficult decisions. Today many hospitals are requiring that you have one of these in place before undergoing an operation. In some states, the individual designated for this responsibility must sign an affidavit stating that he or she will in no way financially benefit from your demise.

This health-care POA is different from a living will, in which you express your wishes to withhold or withdraw treatment if you are a candidate for life support and are considered terminal. For instance, if you were to develop Alzheimer's disease, a living will would not control medical decisions. For more information about living wills, contact the National Hospice and Palliative Care Organization, 1700 Diagonal Road, Suite 625, Alexandria, VA 22314; 800-989-9455; www.caringinfo.org.

Rather than having a health-care POA and a living will, many lawyers prefer to draft an Advance Medical Directive, which combines the two into a single document. In this case you would have an Advance Medical Directive and a financial POA rather than three separate documents.

We consider each of these documents as important as a will and suggest you ask your attorney to draft them at the same time as your will is being updated. Your signature on these documents should be notarized and witnessed by two disinterested persons. If you own property in more than one state, make sure the POAs will work in these states. And as with the will, make sure that there are plenty of copies in the right hands. Give copies to family members and friends.

Living Trusts

To further confuse you, there is another legal document called a *living trust*—which is totally different from a living will. (The only similarity is they are both legal documents.) A living trust is a written agreement that is established while you are alive (thus the name *living*). Typically, you name yourself as the trustee of your own trust and someone else (a relative, friend, lawyer, or bank trust department) as the successor trustee. This successor trustee can distribute the assets in the trust if you die but can also act on your behalf if you become ill and are unable to manage your own affairs.

A living trust can be revocable or irrevocable. A *revocable trust* means the person who establishes it can change the terms of the trust at a later date if desired. An *irrevocable trust,* once established, cannot be changed. Setting up an irrevocable trust has tax advantages, but they are rarely used because most people don't like to set up something they can't change later.

There are six reasons why you would consider establishing a living trust for yourself:

1. Assets in the trust will not have to go through the probate process, which in some states can be expensive. Even more important, having your assets held in trust will expedite the distribution of assets to your heirs.
2. Assets held in a trust are not a matter of public record when you die. With a will, the amount of your estate and the terms of the will are a matter of public record.
3. A trust is less likely than a will to be successfully challenged by unhappy relatives and friends.

4. Even though we think powers of attorney are effective, a trust is less likely to be questioned than a power of attorney.
5. In some states, transferring your property into a living trust may protect it against your creditors.
6. If you own real estate in more than one state and it is titled in the name of the trust, you can avoid your estate's having to be probated in another state.

Once you establish a trust, in order for it to have the desired effect you must transfer all your assets into the name of the trust. This procedure is fairly simple: Your bank and broker open a new account for you in the trust name, and you write a letter asking them to transfer your current holdings into it. Real estate should be titled in the name of the trust. You control the assets, just as you did when they were in your own name. However, some widows set up a living trust but never follow through with the next essential step of titling all their assets in the trust name. If you do not take this step, then the living trust is worthless.

Some advisors recommend that everyone have a living trust instead of a will. We think that the living trust can be a useful device, particularly for an elderly single person with an uncomplicated financial situation, someone who is suffering from a debilitating illness, or someone who travels extensively. However, just as no one investment is a panacea, neither is having a living trust to the exclusion of other legal documents. If you and your attorney decide a living trust fits your circumstances, we think you still should have a will to take care of other matters that are not included in the trust.

Selection of the appropriate successor trustee is very important and is similar to selecting a personal representative for your will. In fact, we would assume you would name the same person to take care of both responsibilities. (See chapter 5 for the list of duties of a personal representative.) If you select an individual, it is very important that this person be honest, financially knowledgeable, and younger than you are!

The Role of the Lawyer

You may be tempted to use the forms available in popular books or computer programs to set up your estate documents in order to save the lawyer's fees. We strongly recommend using an attorney to make sure that every legal aspect of your situation has been considered. An attorney will know how to prepare the appropriate documents required in the state in which you live and will make sure they stay valid if tax, probate, or property laws change. In addition, your attorney may bring up issues you should consider that you might not have thought about previously.

TAX PLANNING WITH YOUR ACCOUNTANT

The best time to do tax planning is in the late fall, when you have a good idea of what your income will be for the year. It is also usually the slowest time of year for accountants, so they have time to spend with clients on planning. By late fall you should have enough information so that your accountant can estimate your tax liability for the current year and project it for the next year.

If appropriate, your accountant will also make suggestions about what you can do to reduce your tax bill for the current year. By visiting your accountant in the fall, you will have enough time to implement any recommendations in that taxable year and for the next year. This is also the best time of year to find a new accountant should you so desire.

Your accountant will tell you what financial information you need to keep track of during the year and how best to organize this information. As with any other professional advisor, the better prepared you are for your meeting, the lower the fee you will be charged. If you appear with a shoe box full of receipts, you will have to pay someone else to organize them. If, instead, you have kept your records in a binder (as we suggested earlier) and present them in this organized form to your accountant, your fee will be lower.

In the future, you might even get to the point where you feel able to prepare your own tax returns without the services of an accountant. There are several computer tax preparation programs available if you are so inclined. If you do prepare your tax returns yourself, we strongly recommend that you have a professional tax advisor review them. Tax laws keep changing, and an accountant will be aware of any new action you should be taking in light of these changes. Also, if the IRS audits your return, it is very comforting to know that you have a professional who can represent you.

The Role of the Accountant

As we previously mentioned, the accountant's role is to prepare your tax return in a timely fashion and give you tax advice. Some accountants may also help you with budgeting and long-term financial planning. Sometimes, because they are asked or are so inclined, they may make investment suggestions, but be careful about taking this advice without consulting your investment advisor. For instance, if you complain about the amount of taxes you are paying, your accountant might respond to your concern by recommending that you invest in tax-free municipal bonds. By making this recommendation, he or she is responding to your concern. Municipal bonds do produce tax-free income. However, from an investment point of view, your principal rarely grows when invested in municipal bonds and in fact can decline if interest rates rise after you invest (more on this in chapter 13). If your primary investment objective is growth of principal, this recommendation might be shortsighted.

FINANCIAL PLANNING
WITH YOUR ADVISORS

After getting your legal and tax situations in order, you should focus on your long-term financial planning. When you were first widowed, your major concern was whether you had sufficient income to cover your expenses. Now that you are past this initial stage, you should review your investments with your financial advisor to see if they meet your long-term needs. Managing your investments can be a monumental task. Some people feel investment management applies only to those with a lot of money. However, we think it is even more important for those of you with limited resources because you can't afford to lose them! Although eventually you may handle most of your financial affairs yourself, it is always useful to get outside opinions—objective advice by advisors whose job it is to keep current on issues. They can point out areas of concern you might not even know are potential problems for you.

Most widows realize they need help but don't know where to turn. There are many types of financial advisors—all of whom claim to be the one you should select as your primary, if not only, financial advisor. In chapters 5 and 6, we discussed how financial advisors can help you in the initial stages of widowhood. Now we will describe what long-term services each of these advisors can provide and what they will charge.

Thirty years ago, it was much easier to select a financial advisor. Back then, insurance agents ascertained how much insurance you and your husband needed. This would include life, disability, health, car, and home insurance. They were paid by the commissions earned on the insurance you bought. If you invested in stocks and bonds, stockbrokers would advise you as to what to buy or sell in your portfolio; they were paid by the commissions made on transactions. You kept your checking and savings accounts at the bank and went to your banker for a loan. The roles of these advisors were clearly defined. Insurance agents did not sell you stocks and bonds, and stockbrokers did not sell you life insurance. The term *financial planner* was nonexistent.

Today, the lines are blurred. There are many competent, well-educated, and experienced people who work for insurance companies, stock brokerage firms, banks, and independent financial planning firms who say they can provide you with financial planning advice. Deciding which one is best suited to give you advice is difficult. Your decision should depend on what kind of advice you need the most and the quality of advisors available to you in your area. Whichever financial advisor you select, it is essential that he or she has been personally recommended to you, works with a reputable firm, and has been advising individuals, including widows like you, for several years. When your financial future is at stake, there is no substitute for experience, expertise, and integrity.

Included under the category of *financial advisors* are financial planners, stockbrokers, money managers, investment advisors, life insurance agents, trust officers, private bankers, and real estate agents. Although each of these advisors can provide you with financial advice, each has his or her own area of specialization.

We have added two relatively new professionals to our list: the geriatric care manager and the daily money manager. Although these individuals do not, strictly speaking, fall under the description of a financial advisor, they can help you make some financial decisions and organize your records.

The Role of the Financial Planner

The financial planner's primary role is to review your overall situation and recommend specific actions to enable you to better achieve your long-term economic goals and objectives. The planner's initial focus is to give you advice on your overall situation and then to make specific remedial recommendations. The planner usually charges you a fee to prepare a written financial plan. Typically, this fee is based on the planner's hourly rate. Some firms will provide financial plans at a nominal charge or even for free. However, these firms expect you to do some other business with them, which will provide them with other revenue. In other words, one way or another you will pay for the advice. This is why you want to make sure that you select a financial planner who is experienced and knowledgeable.

The planner's secondary role (once you agree on a course of action) is to make sure that you implement the recommendations in your plan. This may include helping you make investments and/or buy insurance. The planner may refer part or all of this business to another financial agent, such as a stockbroker, money manager, or insurance agent. If the planner refers you to someone else, he or she may share in the fee or commission that individual charges you.

Some financial planners will manage your portfolio themselves and charge you an annual fee (usually computed as a percentage of assets managed). Others will select money managers for you, monitor their performance, and share the fee you are charged. Still others will invest your money and/or buy insurance for you and be paid a commission. In some cases, the financial planner may also prepare your tax return, charging you an hourly fee.

If the planner is involved in implementing your financial plan, he or she will receive some kind of financial compensation. Whatever your costs are, the planner should fully disclose to you (preferably in writing) what they will be before you agree to be a client.

During the first year of widowhood, typically you will meet and talk with your financial planner several times as you get your financial life in order. Subsequently, you should meet in person with your planner at least annually. Often, your planner becomes your primary financial advisor—you will not make a financial decision without talking to this advisor first.

The Role of the Stockbroker

The full-service stockbroker's primary focus is to manage your investments in order to enable you to achieve your investment objectives. After reviewing your current holdings, your stockbroker will advise you about what to keep and what to sell. Stockbrokers can also purchase insurance for you and in many cases can provide you with a financial plan or even obtain mortgage financing for you.

The stockbroker can be compensated in several ways. In the past, stockbrokers have been compensated only by the commissions earned on the transactions in your account. More recently, stockbrokers will select money managers (for fuller description see the discussion on the role of money managers later in this chapter) to manage your assets. You will be charged a percentage fee based on the value of your assets, and the broker will receive part of the fee for monitoring the performance of the money managers. Some brokers will charge you a fixed annual fee and then nominal or no commissions on transactions.

Your stockbroker should keep in touch with you on a regular basis, providing you with regular reviews and suggestions for your portfolio. As with all your advisors, it is important to sit down at least once a year with your stockbroker to review your portfolio to make sure it is structured to meet your investment objectives.

Initially, we think it is important you select a stockbroker who has a reputation for being conservative. Later on, after you have your feet on the ground, you may want to be more venturesome with some of your money, but until or unless you are an experienced investor, now is the time to be careful. The money you have inherited may have to provide for your financial needs for the rest of your life. It is important to invest it wisely!

The Role of Discount Stockbrokers

With a discount brokerage firm, you make your own investment decisions and call the firm to execute the transaction you want to make. The commissions are lower than you would pay with a full-service stockbroker because you are not paying for advice.

You can also deal directly with a discount broker via the Internet. If you use this approach, make sure you select a reputable firm that will execute your trades in a timely fashion.

Unless you are a sophisticated, knowledgeable investor, we would not recommend using either of these approaches, particularly in the first year of your widowhood. Even the most experienced investors often retain the services of a professional financial advisor to get a second opinion.

The Role of the Money Manager (Also Called an Investment Advisor or a Portfolio Manager)

A money manager's job is to manage investments primarily for wealthy individuals. He or she requires a minimum investment of a certain amount ($50,000 or more). Typically, the investor will receive quarterly statements of the portfolio accompanied by a letter that reviews the current status of your holdings, explains any transactions that took place during the last quarter, and recommends any changes to be made now. Usually, this manager requires that you give him or her total discretion to make changes in the account whenever necessary without consulting you first.

In the past, money managers managed only individual stock and bond portfolios. Today, many managers (and financial planners) put together portfolios of mutual funds. These managers select mutual funds that invest in different kinds of stocks and bonds with different management styles (see chapter 13 for more detail).

Whichever type of money manager you select, you pay an annual fee based on the value of your account. Fees vary, but there is usually a volume discount. In other words, the larger the amount of money managed, the lower the percentage fee you pay. For instance, you might pay 1 percent on the first $1 million, 0.75 percent on the next $2 million, and 0.6 percent on amounts between $3 and $5 million.

Usually there is a minimum annual fee of $1,000. There are usually no, or very low, commissions charged on the transactions in your account, and the money manager does not receive any of that revenue.

This amount is computed as an annual amount but is billed quarterly retroactively. For instance, if your account was worth $100,000 on March 31, you would receive a bill for $250 on April 1 to cover management of your portfolio from January 1 to March 31 ($100,000 × .01 = $1,000 ÷ 4 quarters = $250). You will sign a contract spelling out the terms of the arrangement with the money manager. Make sure you keep a copy in your files.

Investment advisors should be registered either with the Securities and Exchange Commission (SEC) or in the state where their main office is located. Where these advisors are registered depends on the amount of money they manage. If they manage $25 million or more they must register with the SEC and fill out a form called an ADV form, which has two parts. This form will provide you with a lot of background about this advisor, so ask to see both parts.

Registered investment advisors who manage less than $25 million must register in the state where their main office is located. For these advisers, the state regulators may have different registration and qualification requirements that vary from state to state.

If you are not sure whether you want to invest all your money with a money manager, you can start out investing a portion of your assets. Then, after a year, you can determine if this manager has met your expectations and decide if you want to add more to this account or consider other advisors.

The Role of the Life Insurance Agent

The primary role of a life insurance agent is to make sure that you and your family have sufficient life insurance protection. In the past, these agents recommended only life insurance policies, usually whole life. Today they offer several different kinds of life insurance as well as deferred annuities and mutual funds. Health insurance is usually available from life insurance agents or from agents who concentrate exclusively on health policies. A life insurance agent usually does not take care of your car or household insurance; other agents specialize in those areas.

The more experienced life insurance agents have passed a series of rigorous tests to become a Chartered Life Underwriter (CLU). These courses cover in depth various types of insurance as well as estate and financial planning.

Insurance agents are usually compensated by the commissions earned on the policies you buy. Premiums (the amount you pay for the insurance coverage) vary widely from company to company and by the type of coverage you buy. As with your other advisors, make sure you are working with an experienced agent who is with a large, well-established agency or insurance company whenever you buy insurance. (See chapter 12 for further discussion on buying insurance.)

The Role of the Traditional Trust Officer

Your husband's will may have named a bank trust department as trustee to manage a trust for part or all of the assets he left you. The trust officer performs the same role as the independent money manager—that is, managing your investments. Unless the language in the will or trust specifically allows you to change banks, you must keep these assets in the designated bank. Be aware that even if you can change banks, the bank may charge a termination fee to move your assets to another bank. Therefore, you should review all fee schedules before making a change.

If a trust department is designated to manage your investments, a fee will be charged usually based on the amount of money managed. In addition to a management fee, you also may be charged an administration (fiduciary) fee. Under the new Uniform Principal and

Income Act, effective January 1, 2000, trust fees must be taken one-half from income and one-half from principal regardless of how the fee may be calculated—on market value and/or income received.

Like an independent money manager, the bank sends you periodic (monthly or quarterly) written reports of your account that show the current market value of your trust assets as well as an itemization of income received and distributed during the period. The bank also provides you with an annual report of capital gains and losses taken in the portfolio during the year (which is typical of all your financial advisors). You can arrange to have the income from this account transferred to your checking account on a regular basis.

Trust accounts worth $500,000 or less are often invested in the funds managed by the bank to meet your stated investment objectives. From the bank's point of view, this is a more efficient way to manage accounts because it provides diversification, which in turn reduces risk to the portfolio. However, you may be able to arrange to keep your portfolio of stocks and bonds. This is an issue to discuss with your trust officer.

Be aware that in most cases the trust officer has two legal obligations in managing your trust: to produce a competitive level of income for you and, at the same time, to preserve the principal for the trust's ultimate heirs. To achieve these two objectives, the trust officer might invest half of the trust's assets in bonds and half in stocks. If you have a trust account, we suggest you ask the trust officer to review and explain the terms of your trust with you.

If you have an irrevocable trust, you can't tell the bank officer how to manage the assets. However, it is worthwhile to visit with your trust officer annually to discuss the current status of your portfolio. If you have a financial planner, ask him or her to periodically review copies of your trust statements. You may even ask your financial planner to talk to your trust officer on your behalf or actually accompany you on some of your visits to the bank.

Trust officers have been criticized for being too conservative as investment managers. Because their mandate is to preserve your principal for the ultimate heirs as well as provide you with current income, they are prohibited from taking undue risks. This approach has merit. Although you may not make as much money as you might with an independent money manager, there should be less chance of losing money.

Even if your husband has not set up a trust for you with a bank, you may decide to have all or part of your investments managed by a trust department of a bank. This approach is sometimes a good choice for someone who is disinclined or unable to handle her own investments. The trust officer can assist you with paying bills as well as provide you with a buffer from unreasonable requests for money from family members. If the assets are held in a trust account, the widow can position the trust officer as the "bad guy" to say that she doesn't have sufficient income to lend or give away any money, or she can say that she would like to help but that all her money is tied up in trust.

The Role of the Private Banker

Many banks offer their preferred customers—those with substantial assets—the services of a private banker. This person will take care of your investments just as the financial planner or stockbroker might. Private bankers can also handle your banking needs (checking accounts and loans) and may work with the trust department of their bank or with other money managers. These private bankers may be compensated by commission or by a percentage of the assets managed. They also may be qualified to prepare financial plans or provide financial planning advice for a fee.

The Role of the Real Estate Broker

The real estate broker's role is to assist you should you decide to sell your home, buy a new one, or both. As in choosing any other professional advisor, select someone from an established, well-regarded firm familiar with the area in question. This is not a time to make a sentimental choice. Don't give your business to a neighbor who has been particularly nice to you but is lucky to sell one home a year. You want to select someone who is actively involved in real estate transactions on a regular basis. The real estate agent is paid a percentage of the sale price of the home.

If you are selling, your agent should provide you with a list of recent sales of comparable homes in your area. The agent should market your property through the multiple listing service (MLS), newspaper ads, and open homes and should also be able to help the potential buyer locate financing. You should avoid helping the buyer finance the transaction. A buyer who is unable to obtain financing is usually a poor financial risk.

Your real estate agent should be a member of the National Association of REALTORS®. The agent should disclose to you whether he or she is representing the buyer, the seller, or both. Ideally, you want the agent to put your interests first. The REALTOR® should provide you with all the documents to list the property and all contract documents and explain to you the typical time frames involved (such as how long before you actually will receive the money after you agree to a sale).

The Role of the Geriatric Care Manager

A relatively new profession has developed to meet the needs of senior citizens and those responsible for their welfare. At a minimum this person holds a baccalaureate degree in nursing, social work, gerontology, health and human services, or other related fields of human services delivery; is primarily engaged in private practice, administration, or supervision of client-centered services to the elderly and their families; and has two years of supervised experience in the field of gerontology after obtaining his or her degree.

The geriatric care manager can help you or a family member sort through the various levels of care and the type of living accommodations most suitable for you or a loved one on the basis of the individual's current state of health. To obtain a list of managers in your area, call the National Association of Professional Geriatric Care Managers (520-881-8008) or visit the Web site www.caremanager.org.

The Role of the Daily Money Manager

Earlier in this book, we referred to daily money managers who could help you organize your estate paperwork for an hourly fee. If you think you need help keeping your financial papers in order on an ongoing basis and/or paying your bills, the daily money manager can be of assistance. For more information, contact the American Association of Daily Money Managers (301-593-5462) or visit the Web site www.aadmm.com.

SUMMARY AND CONCLUSION

You may conclude that one person is unable to meet all your financial needs and that it is best to work with more than one financial advisor. If you make this decision, we think you should select one advisor to function as the "quarterback." This advisor may be a lawyer, an accountant, or a financial planner, but it is his or her job to supervise your total financial picture to make sure all your advisors are working together on your behalf. We think the best advisor to function in this capacity is a financial planner, but this choice must be based on your particular situation and the quality of advisors available in your area.

ONE FINAL ISSUE:
PREPLANNING YOUR FUNERAL

In the next few chapters we will discuss various kinds of investments and some basic guidelines on how to manage your investments wisely. However, there is another aspect of long-range planning we think you should consider: preplanning your funeral.

It is our experience that many individuals procrastinate having a will drawn up or buying life or long-term care insurance because psychologically they think that by avoiding preplanning for death they can prevent death. The obvious fact is that none of us can avoid death, so why not consider making things easier for your family by preplanning your funeral? Recent statistics indicate over 50 percent of people preplan their funerals. On the other hand, do not feel that it is essential for you to take on this kind of planning. You need to make a personal choice in keeping with existing religious practices and personal preferences.

Your husband's funeral may or may not have been preplanned. If it was, you know what a relief it was to know that you were following his wishes. If you were happy with the arrangements, you may want to work with the same funeral director. If you want to make a change, just as with any other financial choice, ask for recommendations from well-informed relatives and friends. Should you wish to preplan your funeral, select a well-established firm with a good reputation in the community.

There is no charge for making funeral arrangements before the occasion arises. Now that some time has passed since your husband's death, you can discuss with the funeral director all aspects of your eventual funeral service, make the appropriate decisions, file your prearrangement instructions at the funeral home, and inform your family where to call when you die. You may choose to fund your funeral when you make the arrangements. This is accomplished by the funeral home manager putting the money into a pooled trust, or you can buy insurance offered by the funeral home. This prepayment plan will freeze most of your costs at today's levels and is generally transferable to other states. This could be a wise financial choice, as these costs double on average every ten years.

Burial arrangements are separate. The arrangement with the cemetery would include buying the plot as well as its perpetual care and maintenance. These costs can also be prepaid, and you can take title to the plot.

Although most people have difficulty discussing death, both prearranging and prefunding your funeral and burial plot can lift a great financial and emotional burden from your family when you die. You might even put together a draft of your own obituary to give to a family member. Often at the time of your death, members of the family are unable to recall the history of your life as well as you can now—after all, who knows the details better?!

Diane

Reactions to Developing Her Long-Term Financial Plan

A year had gone by since Mark had died. It was hard for Diane to believe. She had completed the first semester of refresher courses at the University of Maryland for her paralegal program. She was amazed at the new developments in the paralegal field, particularly in the computer area. She had thought it would be difficult to master the different computer programs, but she found that after a while it all made sense. Best of all, she was enjoying the classes as well as the people she met.

Dorothy had called Diane and suggested they get together to update her budget. Diane had been able to keep fairly reliable records of what the family had spent over the past six months, using the forms Dorothy had given her. When she totaled her expenses for Dorothy, she realized that although they had spent more money in some areas than she had estimated, they had spent less in other areas, and it all seemed to equal out. She was proud of the children, who had really pitched in and helped. Adjusting to the new schools had not been easy for Jeremy and Alice, but, after an initial period, they seemed to be doing well and making new friends. It looked as if they had made the right decision to stay in the home instead of keeping all the children in private schools.

When Dorothy met with Diane, Dorothy urged Diane to review her will. She knew that Diane had put the will together in a hurry after Mark's death and thought it would be advisable for her to look at it again.

Following her advice, Diane met with Mary Sue Ryan, the partner at Mark's firm in charge of estate planning. Mary Sue reviewed the will with Diane. Diane had appointed her father as guardian for the children, and that still seemed to be a good idea. She and her dad had discussed her parents' ages in relation to the task of raising the children. Dorothy had drawn to Diane's attention the need to give consideration to age when determining a guardianship. Dorothy pointed out that sometimes it is better to have a younger family member or good friends closer to the age of the parents assume this responsibility. Because her parents were still comparatively young, Diane had decided to ask them to be guardians for her children. She viewed this as her best option, at least for the time being.

Mary Sue told her that, in addition to the will, she also needed to give her father a power of attorney so he could act on her behalf should anything happen to her. She should also have a health care power of attorney and a living will. Diane vaguely remembered that Mary Sue had mentioned these issues to her when they had met shortly after Mark's death. However, at that time, she was in no condition to comprehend the information given to her. Now, because she had covered these issues in her paralegal class, Diane understood why these documents were important. She would have to check with her father to see if he was willing to be the designated person for these powers as well as guardian for her children, but she was sure he would agree.

Diane had initially resented her father's advice on financial matters, but now she realized how valuable it had been. She felt fortunate she had located such a good financial planner. So far, Dad had agreed with her advice and in fact was considering going to Dorothy himself. He didn't think he needed any help with his own financial planning, but Mark's death had made him worry about what her mom would do if she were widowed. He realized that she would be as ill prepared as Diane had been to handle her finances.

At this meeting with Mary Sue, Diane took the opportunity to tell her about the paralegal course she was taking. Mary Sue was interested and encouraged Diane to talk with her when she finished taking her refresher courses. They might have a job opening. If they didn't, she might know another firm that might need a paralegal. She herself had found the estate planning area very rewarding. She especially liked it because, unlike some other kinds of law, you could actually see how you helped people.

A few months later, Diane called Dorothy and told her that with Mary Sue's help, she had gone on a couple of interviews and had received a job offer to start at the end of June with a salary of $35,000. The law firm would pay half her medical insurance premiums and all her disability insurance premiums. It also offered a 401(k) retirement plan, which meant that she could contribute up to 20 percent of her salary to her own retirement plan. She asked Dorothy to see how much her salary would improve their cash flow situation. Maybe the family could afford to take that Christmas vacation this year after all! She was concerned because she had spent $10,000 of her cash reserve as a result of her expenses of the past year.

Dorothy put Diane's new numbers into her computer. She was gratified to see that even though Diane would pay more in taxes when she began working, it appeared that finally she would have an annual positive cash flow of a little over $10,000. In putting together these numbers, Dorothy had even factored in her health club dues, the life insurance premium, and a contribution of $7,000 a year to the 401(k) retirement plan. She knew how happy Diane would be when she finally saw a positive cash flow instead of negative numbers!

When Dorothy showed these projections to Diane, she warned her not to get too excited because there would always be unexpected expenses. She advised Diane to try to save any excess income for these expenses or a special event rather than spend it all. She might be able to start a college fund for the two younger children. Diane was really pleased to see these new budget numbers. She knew that there would be extra expenses caused by her working, but it would be such a relief not to have to worry about every penny!

Dorothy told Diane that because all of her children were eligible for their own Social Security benefits, they would not be affected by Diane's new salary income. However, Dorothy explained to her that once Erin turned 18, there would be some reduction in the family Social Security benefits.

Susan

Reactions to Developing Her Long-Term Financial Plan

Susan had interviewed for and had been offered the job of executive director at another association. The pay was considerably higher ($75,000) than her current income ($55,000), and so was the responsibility. There had been many applicants and being selected for this challenging job gave her a sense of accomplishment. After considerable thought and discussion with Dr. Coleman, she decided to accept the job. She hoped she had not taken on more than she could handle.

Susan had gone back to the lawyer she and Lance had previously used, Tim Longwood. She realized that her mother would have some real problems paying for the retirement community if anything happened to her. If Susan died, the trust assets would go to Lance's children, so this income would no longer be available for her mother. Because of estate tax considerations, she decided to leave her assets to her brother, Ron. She would have to discuss this idea with him because she wanted to make very sure that he would use the money to take care of their mother as long as she lived.

She talked her idea over with Ron, and he agreed to provide for their mother if Susan died. He was somewhat concerned because he really did not have much experience managing investments. She suggested that he might want to use the bank trust department to help him. They both hoped this was a problem he wouldn't have to worry about, but Lance's premature death had certainly affected all their thinking.

Susan returned to Bob O'Brien, the stockbroker, to update him on recent developments in her life. She was now clear about her investment objectives. In view of her increased salary, she no longer would need the stock portfolio to generate as much current income but instead could concentrate more on growth of principal. She told him that now that she intended to add $50,000 to this account using the excess proceeds from the lake cottage sale. Bob was glad to hear of her change of investment objectives and agreed to make recommendations for the portfolio she had inherited as well as the new money she was adding to the portfolio.

Susan also showed Bob the statements she was receiving from Ms. Peabody, the trust officer. He reviewed them for her and explained that she really had no control over this account because the bank had been named by Lance to manage the trust. He went on to tell her the bank's obligation as trustee was twofold: It had to provide her with sufficient income but at the same time preserve the principal for the ultimate beneficiaries, her stepchildren. Given these dual objectives, it appeared the trust officer was doing a good job—the principal and the income had both increased during the time she had managed the account. Bob said he would be glad to review the account with her once a year to make sure the trust objectives were being met. He pointed out that, according to the terms of trust document, she did have the option of moving the account to another bank trust department if over a reasonable period of time they were not pleased with the performance of the portfolio.

Audrey

Reactions to Developing Her Long-Term Financial Plan

At Mr. Silver's request, Audrey had reviewed her budget one year after John died. As she had anticipated, her expenses were higher this past year than they had been when John was ill. However, she had sufficient income to cover her expenses. She felt it was time she enjoyed herself rather than focusing on the care of everyone else.

She did think she should pursue further the idea of moving to a smaller place. Because she had lived in the same home for the past 23 years and John had handled the original purchase, she really wasn't sure where to start in either putting her home up for sale or buying a new one.

One of her friends from the club, Georgia Brown, was an active REALTOR® with a leading firm in her area. Audrey decided to call her and talk to her about a potential move. She wanted to ask this friend how much the home would sell for and if she should look for a new place now or concentrate on selling her home first.

Georgia came to her home the following week and was very helpful. A couple of comparable homes had sold in the neighborhood recently—one for $435,000 and the other for $465,000. After looking at the home, Georgia suggested Audrey ask $450,000 for it, because he had concerns about the kitchen needing renovation. Audrey asked if she should redo the kitchen before she put the home up for sale. Georgia said no as she thought that the additional money Audrey was likely to receive for the updated kitchen wasn't worth the aggravation. The purchasers would probably have their own ideas about what they wanted in a kitchen, and it was better to let them deal with renovating it. However, it did mean she would have to accept a somewhat lower price than if the kitchen was up to date. Georgia felt the home would sell quickly. The neighborhood was a good one, the garden looked particularly pretty at this time of year, and it was perfect for a young family.

Audrey knew she should talk to more than one REALTOR®, but she really liked and trusted Georgia and felt she would take a personal interest in the sale because they were friends. She had accepted the maxim of not making a major move in the first year of her widowhood and had not done so, but she was ready to do so now. The question was: What type of home should she buy?

One thing she was sure about was that she wanted to stay geographically close to Joanne, her friends, and the golf club. She also wanted to have three bedrooms so her grandchildren would have a place to stay when they visited. She asked Georgia to help her find the right place. She had looked at town houses, smaller single-family dwellings, condominiums, and even retirement communities. She had made multiple lists of the pros and cons of each and finally decided that a town house would be best. She soon located one that suited her needs. The space was manageable, and it had the requisite number of bedrooms. The yard required minimal upkeep, and she could go outside and barbecue if she wanted to do so. The kitchen was well designed, modern, and cheerful. All in all, it suited her needs and the price was right—$325,000.

Audrey consulted with Mr. Silver, and he concurred that the move appeared to be a good one, both personally and financially. Knowing her aversion to debt, he recommended that she pay cash for the home.

She was surprised at how quickly her home sold. She had accepted an offer for a little less than she had asked ($425,000) but the young family who bought it seemed perfectly suited to the home. In addition they were willing to settle in 60 days. She hoped they would enjoy living there as much as she had. After she paid Georgia's commission, she would have about $400,000, which was more than enough to buy the town house.

Now that she knew she had the money in hand for the purchase of the town house, Audrey spent many hours deciding which pieces of furniture to move, which to replace, and which to give away. When she moved into her new home, the end result was a tastefully decorated home that combined new purchases with valued pieces from her former home. Much to her surprise and relief, Audrey found that she was immediately comfortable in her new home. It certainly was a lot easier to take care of, and she loved the fact that everything was brand new. She didn't have to worry about maintenance problems the way she did with the old home. Achilles too seemed to have no difficulty adjusting to his new home.

The grandchildren liked it as well, which pleased her. She was much more involved in their lives now than when John had been alive. She valued these expanded relationships with her grandchildren and always made time for them.

Audrey had called her lawyer, Mr. Humphrey, for the name of a lawyer to handle her real estate transactions, and he had recommended someone to her. In the same conversation, he suggested they get together to review her estate planning.

As soon as Audrey was settled in her new home, she made an appointment to see Mr. Humphrey, as he had suggested. She was concerned about the education of Joanne's children should anything happen to her. She was also a little worried about the stability of Joanne's marriage. Mr. Humphrey pointed out that in her will she could set up a trust for the grandchildren that specified it was to be used for their education. If anything was left in the trust after they were educated, Joanne would receive it. Audrey said that although she had a comfortable income from the pension and Social Security, she didn't have a lot in assets to leave to the grandchildren. Mr. Humphrey explained that although it might not seem like that much now, hopefully her investments would grow over the years so he thought there should be sufficient funds to take care of the children.

Once again, Audrey expressed her wish to treat John Jr. and Joanne equally in her will, even though John Jr.'s financial situation was much better than Joanne's. Mr. Humphrey suggested that Audrey discuss her concerns with John Jr. In fact, he might be a good person for her to name as the trustee for the education trust because he was more financially astute than Joanne. John Jr. might not have as warm a personality as Joanne did, but Joanne was his sister, and if she needed financial help, Mr. Humphrey was sure that John Jr. would take care of her and the children.

Mr. Humphrey also discussed with Audrey to whom she should give her financial power of attorney as well as her health care power of attorney. She thought that John Jr. was the best choice for the financial power of attorney but wanted to give Joanne the health power of attorney because she felt emotionally closer to her. Audrey thought that as tough as the decisions Joanne would have to make would be, she had seen her father suffer and would do the right thing for Audrey. She knew that her daughter would consult with her brother, as he was a physician, before making any final decisions on her behalf. She also wanted Mr. Humphrey to prepare a living will for her.

Rather than being depressed by all this preplanning for her death, Audrey really felt good about the fact that her affairs would be in order. She decided to take it a step further and make an appointment to meet with Mr. Brown, the funeral home director who had been so helpful to her when John died. She had a pretty good idea of what she wanted in the way of a funeral service, and she thought it would be helpful to her children to make the arrangements ahead of time. In fact, after talking with Mr. Brown and reading the booklet he had given her, Audrey thought she would take the second step of prefunding the costs. By doing so, there would be no question as to how and by whom she wanted to be buried. Audrey and John had previously purchased adjacent plots in the Oak Tree Cemetery, so she did not have to worry about that decision.

Now that she had made all these plans for her death, Audrey turned her thoughts to living! Because she appeared to be in good shape financially, Audrey decided to approach Joanne about spending a long weekend with her at a spa. She thought it would be good for both of them. Joanne was somewhat overweight—she had never really lost the weight she had put on during her pregnancy with Noah. Audrey thought a trip to a spa would help her get started on a weight loss program and would be a good break from her daily routine. Audrey was doing well with her walking regimen and her golf, but the latter was seasonal, and sometimes they used the golf carts instead of walking the course, which she preferred. She thought she might want to buy a treadmill or stationary bike so she could exercise at home in the winter. Spending time at a spa would help her learn more about the various kinds of exercise equipment available to her.

Audrey was going to suggest that perhaps Keith's parents could take care of the children on the two weekdays involved and Keith could manage them on the weekend. If necessary, Audrey would offer to pay for a sitter for the weekdays if Keith's parents were not available.

Elizabeth

Reactions to Developing Her Long-Term Financial Plan

Elizabeth had spoken to Mr. Grossfeldt about the possibility of moving to Florida. He had given her a list of questions to ask the director of Northern Palms, the continuing care retirement community (CCRC) in Florida where Abigail lived. The idea of a CCRC appealed to Elizabeth because it provided both housing and access to health care on three levels:

1. *Independent living,* where she could initially live in an apartment as long as she was physically and mentally able
2. *Assisted living,* when she needed more help with daily activities (dressing, bathing, etc.)
3. *Nursing home care,* available in the same community if she ever needed it

First, Mr. Grossfeldt told her she should ask for an audited financial statement. He said that this statement was important because she needed to be sure that the community would not go bankrupt. If she was intending to live there the rest of her life, this might be 15 or 20 years.

She should also obtain a copy of the contract Northern Palms wanted her to sign that would spell out what she would pay and what she would get in return. Elizabeth needed to know how much the facility would charge as an entrance fee and how much of that fee was refundable if she changed her mind or wanted to will the apartment to someone. She should ask for a written schedule of costs for the independent living apartment she liked but also should ask what the fees would be if she had to move to the assisted living or to the nursing home section of the CCRC. This schedule should spell out what her costs would include (meals, housekeeping, etc.).

Once she had obtained this information from Northern Palms, Elizabeth met with Mrs. Greenfield, her accountant. Together they went over the projected costs to move. She reviewed her current budget and then tried to figure out how these expenses would change if she moved. She also needed to make sure she had sufficient money for moving expenses.

Elizabeth decided she would probably spend more on clothes in Florida—since she and Ben had not socialized much, there had not been much need for new clothes in recent years. She expected the amount she spent on entertainment and travel to increase. She had enjoyed the cruise so much that she wanted to make sure she had sufficient money to travel every year. She probably should budget more for gifts for the wider group of friends she anticipated having than she did in Boston.

On the other hand, she wouldn't spend as much on food because one meal a day would be provided for her at the retirement community. She would have no home maintenance expenses or real estate taxes to pay. After giving Ben's car away, she had spent a fair amount on cabs in Boston, but transportation should not be much of an expense in Florida. Altogether it appeared her annual general living expenses would be reduced to about $14,000. She would join a church there and so would continue donating $1,000 a year.

The director of Northern Palms had told her the apartment she liked would cost $2,000 a month. This fee would include one meal a day, housekeeping, and utilities. When she added these projected expenses, she came up with $39,000, which seemed like a lot of money.

Mrs. Greenfield told Elizabeth there were income tax advantages to her if she moved to Florida because Florida had no state income tax. That was a nice contrast to the high taxes in Massachusetts. Although Florida did tax assets, such as the value of her portfolio, these annual state taxes would be less than they would be if she were a Massachusetts resident. Also, part of her monthly fee would be considered a medical expense and would be deductible on her federal income tax return.

Elizabeth did not need to be concerned about estate taxes in the state of Florida because Florida did not tax estates. She didn't need to worry about federal estate taxes either because her total assets were less than $2 million.[1] Mrs. Greenfield suggested Elizabeth consult with Mr. Grossfeldt for more details about the legal issues of estate planning if she became a Florida resident.

Mrs. Greenfield reviewed the audited financial statements as well as the history of past annual increases in the monthly fees at Northern Palms that Elizabeth had given her. She explained that Elizabeth should expect these fees to go up annually as a result of cost increases, but she wanted to make sure the increases were reasonable and did not go up too rapidly. When Mrs. Greenfield looked up the facility in the *Consumers' Directory of Continuing Care Retirement Communities,* published by the American Association of Homes and Services for the Aging (AAHSA) (800-508-9442) www.aahsa.com, she was pleased to see that this community was accredited. She loaned the book to Elizabeth because it provided the basic description of CCRCs around the country, explained how they work, and suggested what to look for and what to ask before making a final choice.

Elizabeth called Mr. Grossfeldt and told him about her meeting with Mrs. Greenfield. He said if she became a Florida resident, he would make sure that her existing living will and powers of attorney conformed with Florida state law. Because she had put most of her assets in a living trust at the bank, most of her estate would avoid probate fees. He recommended that eventually she should have all her assets in the living trust.

Mr. Grossfeldt asked Elizabeth if she had thought about to whom she wanted to leave her assets when she died if her only heir, Abigail, predeceased her. This was a difficult question. She thought she might like to leave some money to her longtime friend Mabel, who certainly could use it, but she really didn't have any other living relatives or close friends. Mr. Grossfeldt suggested she might

---

1 Two million dollars is the estate tax allowance for 2006 under current law.

consider dividing her assets between two charities: Pastor Appletorn's church and Ben's college. This suggestion of giving all her assets to charity if Abigail died first appealed to Elizabeth because the charities selected represented important aspects of her life with Ben.

Mr. Grossfeldt said she could arrange to have Abigail be the beneficiary of her trust in the event that Elizabeth died before Abigail. This would mean Abigail would receive income from the trust as long as she lived. When Abigail died, the assets in the trust would go to the named charities. If Abigail died first, the assets would go directly to the charities. Mr. Grossfeldt also told Elizabeth that although she named these two charities now, she could add or delete charities later or change the beneficiaries totally if she wished.

Elizabeth really liked these ideas and said she would consider them seriously. In the meantime, her conversations with Mr. Grossfeldt and Mrs. Greenfield were very reassuring. It appeared that the information she had gathered so far seemed to support her decision to move to Florida. She could hardly believe that she was involved in all these financial decisions. She considered herself fortunate to have such informed and empathetic advisors to help her make these monumental decisions. Quite a change from leaving all the financial decisions to Ben, as she had done during their married life! [2]

---

[2] Some of the technical and legal terms we refer to in this chapter will vary from one state to another. In the interests of readability, we use generally accepted terminology.

12
Protecting Your Assets

Woman must not accept; she must challenge.
She must not be awed by that which has been
built up
around her; she must revere that woman in her
which struggles for expression.
—*Margaret Sanger*

AS A WIDOW, having sufficient income and investing wisely are of paramount importance to you. Of equal importance is insurance, which protects the assets you have already acquired. Most people think of life insurance when they hear the word *insurance,* but you should also consider are health, long-term care, disability, car, household, and liability insurance.

LIFE INSURANCE

In the past, life insurance was something men knew a lot more about than women did. This was due to the fact that insurance was sold primarily to men, particularly husbands, as a way to protect their families should something happen to them, the breadwinners. Today, with fewer families having the traditional structure of the nonworking wife and with more women working, the value of insuring the lives of women is more appreciated.

Psychologically, many people resist the idea of buying life insurance because it is connected to the concept of death, and most people do not want to accept this inevitable event. They prefer instead to invest money in assets that provide current income or growth of principal, which they can see and enjoy. The problem is that they may not have enough time to accumulate sufficient money to provide for their dependents or to pay estate taxes should they die before they have amassed sufficient capital.

How Much Life Insurance Do You Need?

The question most often asked is, How much insurance should I carry? You recently completed the exercise of determining if you have sufficient income on which to live. If you are over 65 and your children are relatively self-sufficient, you may feel you don't need any insurance. On the other hand, although you may not need insurance to provide for your children, you may need it to pay estate taxes when you die. As previously noted, under current law, estates worth over $2 million in 2006 will have a federal estate tax liability. You have to decide whether you want to have enough insurance to pay these potential taxes or if you want your heirs to liquidate estate assets to pay them. Unless your estate is very liquid, this may be easier said than done.

If you are a younger widow with dependent children and limited assets, we think you should buy insurance on your life so there will be enough money to take care of your children if you die before they reach adulthood. Actually, in view of their father's untimely death, your children may feel reassured knowing you have life insurance.

There are other dependents to consider besides your children. You may also have siblings who are less economically fortunate than you are or parents who are living in reduced circumstances and need your financial help. To determine how much life insurance you need, review your situation with your financial advisor so that you can determine the amount of coverage to carry.

What Kind of Life Insurance Should You Buy?

Also influencing the decision of how much is enough is the cost factor. When you are younger, insurance is less expensive—logically so, because the chances of your dying at this time in your life are less than when you are older. The cheapest form of insurance is *term insurance.* This type of insurance will cover you for a certain time period—usually a year—and the cost will go up each year. For those of you who will have a need for cash for a limited period of time—such as until your children are through college—term insurance might make the most sense.

One method of payment for term insurance is called level term, where the insurance company calculates what the premiums would be for a longer period—for instance, 10 years. It totals these premiums and divides the total by 10 to determine your annual payment. This means that you will pay the same amount each year for 10 years. Many people prefer level term for budgeting purposes because they like to know what they will pay every year. Be aware that term insurance offers only a death benefit and has no cash value.

For those who want more than a death benefit policy, *whole life insurance, universal life insurance,* and *variable life insurance* are also available. With whole life insurance, you pay a predetermined premium presumably for the rest of your life. Part of the premium pays for the death benefit, and part is invested within the insurance policy. Whole life policies can be structured so that you make payments for a shorter period of time (at least seven years), and then you borrow against the accumulated cash value of the insurance policy to cover future payments. If you build up sufficient cash value, you will be able to borrow against the policy at very competitive interest rates should you need money at a later date.

Universal life insurance is similar to whole life insurance, but, instead of the cash in the policy earning a fixed rate of interest, the rate varies annually according to what interest rates are available in the marketplace. The portion of your annual premium that is greater than the amount necessary to cover your annual insurance cost is invested for you, building up a cash value that is tax sheltered. Universal life is less expensive than whole life, but it is also riskier because the interest rate that the cash value of the policy earns is not as predictable as in whole life and the cost to you to maintain the policy is not fixed.

In a variable life insurance policy, the cash portion is invested in separate accounts, which in turn are invested in stocks and bonds.

Which Insurance Company Should You Use?

If you and your advisor determine you do need life insurance, then you should select what kind of insurance and which insurance company is best for you. Before the 1980s, few people were concerned about the economic viability of insurance companies. However, in the 1980s, in an effort to earn a higher return on their investments, some insurance companies invested in junk bonds (bonds of questionable quality) and risky real estate. This decision came back to haunt them in the early 1990s, when many of the tenants of the real estate properties stopped paying rent and the junk bonds defaulted.

Two primary indicators of a good insurance company are its long-term dividend performance and the strength of its financial ratings. Whether an insurance company is a good one may be determined by comparing the dividends it actually pays to policyholders with the dividends the life insurance agent projected it would pay. The reason this is important is that an insurance agent may give you sheets of paper showing you projections of how fast your cash value is going to increase in your policy. However, these estimates may be based on past interest rates, which may be higher than present ones and difficult to maintain in the future. Always ask to see projections based on an interest rate comparable to what is paid by an A or better-rated corporate bond. For example, if these bonds are currently paying an average of 5 percent, you should not expect more from your insurance company.

Insurance companies are rated by A. M. Best, Standard & Poor's and Moody's. A. M. Best's annual rating guide is available at many libraries or on its Web site www.ambest.com. If you call Standard & Poor's, a representative of the company will give you ratings for five insurers on the phone free of charge (212-438-7280) www.standardpoor.com. Also be aware that rates may vary from company to company, even for term insurance. For instance, a company that wants to build its term insurance business might offer very low rates for these policies but may not be competitive in other kinds of insurance.

Another question to consider is whether you should buy a *waiver of premium.* This term means that if you become disabled and are unable to pay the premium, the insurance company will continue to pay the premium to keep the insurance policy in effect. This adds to the cost of your premium.

These are all issues your financial advisor should check before recommending the best company for your particular situation. As with other investments, a track record and a strong balance sheet are very important.

What Coverage Should You Have?

As a general rule, if you are able to participate as part of a group, the rates are cheaper, the service is better, and you have fewer problems with claims. As far as guidelines go, a comprehensive major medical plan should pay the majority of all medical bills after deductibles. As with other kinds of insurance, the higher the deductible (the amount you will pay out of your pocket), the lower the premiums you will pay. You can save quite a bit if you have a $1,000 deductible versus a $200 deductible.

The lifetime minimum benefit under the policy should be at least $1 million. The policy should be guaranteed renewable and noncancelable. Most insurance is less expensive if premiums are paid annually. Be aware that having dental and psychiatric coverage, while desirable, raises your premiums.

Over the past few years, HMO (*health maintenance organization*) and PPO (*preferred provider organization*) coverage has become more broadly used. HMOs require you to use their doctors and their facilities. PPOs allow you to use either their doctors and facilities or your own doctors and facilities (you pay more for the latter). There are advantages and disadvantages to each kind of plan. Above all, you want to make sure that if you become ill, at least your major costs are covered.

Medicare Insurance

Understanding Medicare is not easy. The subject is covered thoroughly in Medicare brochures available at your local Social Security office or by phone from the Social Security Administration (800-772-1213) www.ssa.gov. You can also obtain the information from Medicare customer service at 1-800-MEDICARE (1-800-633-4227) or from the Medicare Web site www.medicare.gov.

In 2006, Medicare Part A paid all but $952 of hospital costs during the first 60 days. If you need to stay longer than 60 days, your share of the cost will be higher. Medicare Part B pays doctors' bills. You have an annual deductible of $124 (in 2006) and then you pay 20 percent of the remaining fees (more if your doctor does not participate in Medicare).

Even if you plan to keep working, when you turn 65 you should sign up for Medicare Part A since it is free. However, if you continue to work past age 65 and you have adequate health insurance coverage, you may want to wait to enroll in Medicare Part B for two reasons. First, there is no reason to pay for insurance coverage you do not need. Second, there is a six-month period during which you cannot be denied benefits or charged extra by a Medigap insurance provider for preexisting health conditions. The six-month period begins with the month you enroll in Medicare Part B. Therefore, you do not want the six-month period to expire before it is time to apply for Medigap coverage. However, if you do not enroll in Medicare Part B when you first become eligible you may owe a penalty if you enroll later. For this reason, we recommend that you discuss your situation with someone at the Social Security Administration to help you decide when to enroll in Medicare. (Medigap insurance covers what Medicare does not cover. See the discussion below.)

Starting in 2006, Medicare began to offer a third type of

coverage (Part D) which provides prescription drug coverage. There are several Medicare prescription drug plans to choose from, and you will pay a monthly premium to join one of these plans. The plans are provided by private insurance companies who contract with the federal government. All Part D plans must meet a federal standard, but the plans available to you depend on the state in which you live.

The cost of a Part D plan depends on which plan you choose. You can choose a plan with a low premium, but benefits may not be as comprehensive as those in the other plans you could choose. To find the plan that best suits your needs, you will need to compare the total out-of-pocket costs you're likely to incur.

To help you determine which plans may be right for you we suggest you call 1-800-MEDICARE(1-800-633-4227). When you call, have your list of medications, your Medicare card and the names and addresses of your preferred pharmacies in hand. You can also call your State Health Insurance Program for assistance.

At the Medicare website www.medicare.gov you can input your drug information into the "Formulary Finder" to determine which plans cover your medications and whether there are any limitations. Also use Medicare's online "Drug Plan Finder" for the estimated annual out-of-pocket costs for all the plans available to you. Phone numbers for each insurance company are shown so you can call them directly to confirm that you understand the benefits as well as the costs of any plan you're considering.

Enrollment in Part D is optional, but as is the case with Medicare Part B, if you do not enroll when you first become eligible, you may owe a penalty if you enroll later. If you choose not to enroll because your current health insurance plan provides good drug coverage, you should ask you health insurance plan administrator for a written statement saying that your current coverage is at least as good as Medicare's. With this letter you will be able to avoid a late enrollment penalty if you decide to enroll in a Part D plan at a later date. You should enroll in Medicare Part D as soon as you are eligible if you do not have any other prescription drug coverage. If your income is low, you may qualify for extra help in paying for your Medicare drug benefit.

Medigap Insurance

Medigap insurance is supplemental insurance provided by insurance companies to cover what Medicare doesn't cover. You will have a six-month open enrollment period that begins when you apply for Medicare Part B. This is the best time to buy a Medigap policy.

However, if you have good group health insurance through a former employer, then you don't need Medigap insurance.

A variety of Medigap policies are available to you. There are actually 12 standardized model coverages labeled A through L, with A being the most basic and J the most comprehensive. Every insurer must sell the basic A coverage, which picks up most out-of-pocket co-payments for hospital charges and doctor bills. Policies B through J provide increasingly comprehensive coverage. Policies K and L are newer and are designed primarily to cover catastrophic expenses. The premiums for policies K and L may be lower than they are for the other types of Medigap plans, but your out-of-pocket costs will be higher. As you might guess, the price increases as the benefits increase, and the rates vary among insurance companies, so comparison shopping is necessary. (Note: The standard Medigap policies differ for residents of Massachusetts, Minnesota, and Wisconsin.) For more information about insurance to supplement Medicare, you might find helpful a free booklet titled *Choosing A Medigap Policy: A Guide to Health Insurance for People with Medicare,* published by the Centers For Medicare and Medicaid Services.

We recommend comparing the coverage offered by three companies. Once you and your advisor have selected a company and you have paid the initial premium, you have 30 days to receive a full refund. When you apply for Medicare Part B, there is a six-month "window" when Medigap insurers must accept applicants regardless of existing health problems (as long as you have had continuous health insurance coverage for the six months before enrolling), so timely application is important.

DISABILITY INSURANCE

Most people don't realize the frequency or impact of disability. It is the greatest cause of mortgage foreclosures in the United States If you are working, we think disability insurance is as important as health or life insurance. It provides needed income during periods when you are incapacitated because of sickness or injury. This coverage is particularly important if you are a younger working widow with limited resources. Unfortunately, to qualify for disability insurance you have to be employed and earning income. Unemployed individuals cannot be covered.

Most employers provide disability benefits, but they are not generally sufficient to cover all your expenses. What is particularly important is how the insurance company defines *disability*. Would the insurance company refuse to pay if you could do any kind of work (such as sweeping floors)? The desired coverage, which is called *own-occupation coverage,* would pay if at the time of your disability you could not perform the duties of the profession for which you are trained.

You are usually provided with group disability insurance through your place of employment. Initially, this is inexpensive; however, the premium generally increases as you get older. Group coverage has very strict definitions of disability and can be canceled at any time. If you leave your job, it is no longer available to you.

You can buy your own disability coverage that is renewable each year at a cost fixed at the time of purchase. This disability coverage cannot be canceled by anyone other than you. It has a more liberal definition of disability and in most cases will pay benefits even if you are only partially disabled and working on a limited basis. This type of insurance is more expensive than group insurance, but the longer you wait before you receive the benefits (90 days versus 30 days), the lower the premium will be. Coverage, whether group or individual, is usually limited to 60 percent of your current income. The amount of coverage you should purchase depends on your occupation and income level.

When you are reviewing your other insurance needs, make sure you don't overlook disability insurance. It is more difficult to obtain if you are self-employed, but, here again, if you are unable to find individual coverage, some association coverage is usually available. There are insurance companies that specialize in providing disability insurance. Your financial advisor will help you select the right one for your circumstances.

LONG-TERM CARE INSURANCE

One of the major concerns among older people is the possibility that as they grow older, failing health and dependency will require long-term care either at home or in a nursing home. This is also an area of concern for adult children with elderly parents.

According to a 2005 study by the MetLife Mature Market Institute, the average annual cost for a private room in an assisted-living facility was $34,860, compared with $64,240 for a semiprivate room and $74,095 for a private room in a nursing home. Overall prices for a private or semiprivate room in a nursing home increased about 5 percent from 2004 to 2005. The cost of a private room in an assisted living facility, however, increased an astounding 15 percent from 2004 to 2005.

What are the odds you will need this type of insurance? This depends on your sex, health, family history, and family relationships. But the fact is that most people don't want to be dependent on family or charity if they require this type of care.

Many people think Medicare will pay for these costs. Medicare is supposed to pay for 20 days in a skilled nursing home after hospitalization and then a small percentage of the next 80 days. However, it is difficult to meet the many requirements to qualify for this coverage. The balance of payments would be paid by Medicaid, but to qualify for Medicaid you must first have exhausted your personal resources. It is our experience that Medicare and supplementary medical policies provide very little coverage in this area as the care needed is supportive rather than skilled.

Increasingly, individuals are purchasing long-term care insurance before a crisis develops. You hope that you will never need it—but you want to be covered. Unlike medical policies that reimburse you for a portion of a covered medical expense, long-term care insurance pays a daily benefit to help offset costs. You choose the benefit amount you want, the length of time it will be paid, and the time you wait until the payments start. You can also choose inflation protection, which provides an annual increase in the daily benefit.

The long-term care coverage offered today has fewer restrictions and offers more types of care than what was offered a few years ago. Today, the major insurers in this field cover not only nursing home expenses but also home care, adult day care, and assisted living.

To qualify for long-term care insurance, you must be relatively healthy when you apply. As you grow older, the chances increase that you may be rejected for coverage because of a medical condition. Also, like whole life insurance, the younger you are when you buy this coverage, the lower the annual premiums. The coverage you buy should be renewable for life and noncancelable except for nonpayment of premiums. We suggest people start investigating this coverage at age 55 to 60, although those with health concerns may wish to consider it at an earlier age.

Key Decisions to Make When Selecting
Long-Term Care Insurance

Elimination period. This is the length of time you have been in a nursing home or receiving home care before the insurance company starts paying benefits. The choice of waiting periods is usually between 20 and 100 days. The shorter the elimination period, the higher premium you pay. This decision depends on how much of your costs you want to, or are able to, personally pay. We recommend that you select the shortest waiting period (usually 20 days) because we think that the need for short-term convalescent care will increase as hospitals and insurers limit hospital stays.

Daily benefit. The daily cost of staying in a nursing home varies in different parts of the country. Call nursing homes in your area to see what the costs are per day. These costs will vary according to the type of facility and amenities offered. For instance, a private room costs significantly more than a semiprivate room. Decide how much of your own money you are willing to spend. For instance, a room at a really nice nursing home might cost $200 per day, so you may decide to buy coverage of $100 per day and pay the rest from your annual income.

Inflation-adjusted coverage. Nursing home costs are increasing at an annual rate of 4 to 6 percent. Typically, you might sign up for the policy when you are 55 and not need the care until you are 75 or 80. Daily costs could easily triple during that time, so you want to be protected against rising costs. Most policies allow you to buy the option that increases the daily benefit each year in line with a certain inflation rate. We recommend that you take this option. Compound inflation coverage provides more protection than simple inflation coverage.

Length of coverage. Typically, you can select to receive benefits for three years, five years, or unlimited years. Unlimited is the most expensive coverage.

Selection of the insurance company. There are many companies in this field, but only a few are setting the standard for the industry. We think it is crucial to seek the opinion of a financial planner or insurance agent who specializes in understanding this type of coverage. This advisor will be looking at insurance companies that have been working in this market for at least five years. Certain companies are known for paying benefits promptly, while others put the policyholder through a lot of red tape before paying the benefits.

Payment of benefits. The two methods of payment are reimbursement and indemnity. Almost all policies are reimbursement policies, under which the owner incurs an expense, submits the bill, and is reimbursed. In most cases, any unused benefit will be credited to your account. With the indemnity method, you receive the daily benefit even if actual expenses are lower.

It is important to consider the conditions which must occur before the insurance company will approve a claim. These conditions are sometimes called "gatekeepers" and they will be outline in a long-term care policy. For example, benefits may not be payable unless you need help with at least two activities of daily living, which include tasks such as dressing, bathing and eating. The specific words used in the definitions within a policy might narrow your coverage and this will be recognized only by an experienced reviewer. The fewer gatekeepers required by the policy, the sooner the insurance company will start paying your bills.

Type of care to be reimbursed. Assisted-living coverage is important because these facilities are a transitional alternative between your home and a nursing home. This type of care may be sufficient for many elderly who would otherwise be forced into a nursing home. Coverage should also apply at home or in an adult day care center. Coverage for hospice care in a hospice facility or at home can be an added benefit.

Group or individual coverage. As with most kinds of insurance, individual coverage is more expensive than group insurance, but group coverage tends to cover less. Specifically, group insurance tends to include more gatekeepers. It is more stringent about which preexisting conditions it will accept before it will insure you and what it will pay for when you do need assistance.

Qualified policies. Federal legislation effective as of January 1, 1997, established criteria for qualified policies. Ordinarily, the premiums you pay for long-term insurance policies are not tax deductible. In contrast, insurance premiums for qualified policies are tax deductible as medical expenses subject to certain requirements. Benefits up to a certain level will be received tax free. In general, provisions of qualified policies are somewhat more restrictive than those of nonqualified policies. Benefits from the latter type are taxable.

Not everyone needs long-term care insurance coverage. Some experts suggest that anyone with assets between $100,000 and $2,000,000 should consider getting long-term care insurance. If your assets are larger, you may choose to pay these costs yourself. On the other hand, if you wish to preserve your assets for your heirs and not spend them on nursing home costs, you may want to buy at least some long-term care insurance.

In any case, we think it is worthwhile to consider getting this insurance to cover all or part of your potential needs. Insurers are continually upgrading the policies they offer, so we would recommend asking your financial advisor whether this coverage makes sense for you and, if it does, to help you find the best coverage currently available. If you already have coverage, ask your advisor to evaluate it regularly to make sure you have the best coverage available. This may mean changing carriers periodically, assuming you can still meet health requirements.

HOMEOWNERS INSURANCE

We recommend that you review your homeowners insurance annually. It is important that you have your home (the physical structure) insured for 100 percent of the replacement value. If you have lived in your home for many years, your policy limits may no longer cover the actual replacement value. Your insurance agent can help you determine what your coverage should be. It is important to keep this replacement-cost evaluation up-to-date. One way to do this is to add an inflation rider that will increase your coverage annually to keep up with increases in values.

We also recommend personal property replacement-cost coverage. Then, if you have a fire and your sofa is destroyed, you will get enough money to buy a new sofa that is comparable to your original one. A comparatively simple way to keep records is to save receipts for more expensive purchases in a file that is kept off the premises.

Any truly helpful replacement-cost rider requires a household inventory of each item you own, a description of it and its condition, and photographs of each room taken from different angles. If you have a digital camera, you could take the photos and store the memory card off site. Recently the Insurance Information Institute began offering free inventory software to help people document their possessions, room by room, www.knowyourstuff.org You might even want to rent a video camera in order to make an audiovisual record of your home. Keep the inventory in your safe-deposit box or with a friend or relative and hope you never need it.

To cover your valuables, you need an additional policy attachment called a *valuables floater,* which requires an appraisal of your collectible items (art, silver, antiques, stamps, jewelry, and furs). If you do not have this rider and have a loss as a result of fire or theft, you will receive only partial reimbursement of the item's value. Many policies have a maximum reimbursement of $500 or $1,000.

To add insult to injury, if you do not have this coverage and lose a valuable piece of jewelry, not only would you not receive adequate compensation, but it is unlikely that you would be able to deduct the loss on your tax return. Unreimbursed casualty losses must exceed 10 percent of your adjusted gross income to be deductible.

CAR INSURANCE

Your car insurance coverage includes five major areas:

Liability

Liability insurance covers injuries you cause to pedestrians and occupants of other cars as well as damages to someone else's property. We recommend that you have at least $300,000 for bodily injury suffered by one person in each accident, $500,000 for injuries suffered by all persons in the same accident, and $100,000 for damage to property. This may appear on your policy as 300/500/100. Some companies offer a more flexible single-limit policy covering total payments for both property damage and bodily injury that will show one number instead of three.

Medical Payments and Personal Injury Protection (PIP)

This insurance covers medical bills resulting from accidental injury to you or passengers in your car regardless of who caused the accident. It also covers you if you are injured in any motor vehicle accident such as when you are riding in someone else's car or when you are out walking.

If you have no-fault insurance (which some states require) or other medical insurance, you probably do not need this insurance. However, some reasons to consider it are that it may cover your lost wages, funeral expenses, and the medical bills of your passengers who may not have adequate health insurance of their own.

Uninsured Motorists

Accidents involving uninsured motorists are always a potential threat. Uninsured motorist coverage covers losses you incur when involved in an accident with a motorist who is uninsured. We recommend coverage of at least $100,000 per person, $300,000 per accident, and $50,000 property damage (100/300/50). This coverage is inexpensive, worthwhile, and mandatory in many states.

A variation on the same theme, underinsured motorist coverage protects you when you are involved in an accident with a motorist whose limits are too low to compensate you adequately for your damages. It may be part of the uninsured motorist coverage, or it may be offered separately.

Collision Insurance

This covers damage to your car as a result of a collision with another object, such as a tree. You can collect no matter who caused the accident. This coverage usually does not pay more than the current value of the car. A higher deductible will reduce your premium, but the deductible should be set at an amount that you are willing to pay in the event your car is damaged.

Comprehensive

This section of the policy insures you against theft as well as damage to your car from falling objects, vandalism, and so forth. Again, to keep premiums low, set the deductible at the highest level that you would be willing to pay.

Also keep in mind that when you rent a car, a collision damage waiver (CDW) is not necessary if your own car policy covers you. Dull reading as it may be, read your policy carefully or call your agent before you find yourself standing at the rental car counter faced with the expensive CDW option. Many credit card companies also offer collision damage protection with their gold cards.

UMBRELLA OR EXCESS PERSONAL LIABILITY POLICIES

These policies protect you in the event of a claim against you by someone who holds you responsible for an injury. For example, a friend slips on a stair in your home, falls down the full flight of stairs, and breaks both arms and legs. Even a good friend might feel the need to sue you. These policies usually apply to family members and include residence and personal injury liability.

You may have limited personal liability coverage through your existing home or car insurance, but this coverage is usually insufficient. You should have a separate liability policy that provides supplemental coverage. We recommend that you have total liability coverage equal to your net worth to reduce your risk of catastrophic contingencies. As your net worth increases, you should increase the amount of your liability coverage. This coverage is inexpensive and very cost-effective for reducing risk exposure. You can usually obtain it from the carrier of your car or homeowners insurance.

Increasingly, insurance companies are insisting on covering both your car and your home. Using the same company is often more convenient and less expensive; it also prevents duplications in your insurance.

IDENTITY THEFT

Another essential way to protect your assets is to protect your financial identity. Identity theft happens when a criminal uses your personal information to obtain credit or make purchases. In the past, you could protect your identity by keeping an eye on your wallet or purse and by tearing up the carbon copy imprint of your credit card when you bought something on credit at a store. Unfortunately, identity protection takes a lot more work today. Identity theft is not just something that happens to other people

Monitoring all of the activity on your bank statements and credit card statements is the best way to know if there has been any illegal activity, but you want to avoid the problem from occurring in the first place. We suggest you buy a shredder and use it to shred any financial documents you want to throw away. Never give out personal information over the phone unless you are certain you know with whom you are speaking. E-mails are especially tricky, because criminals can design their e-mails to look as if they are coming from a company with whom you normally do business. The safest way to conduct business over the phone or over the Internet is to initiate the contact yourself using the contact information that appears on your monthly statement.

Reviewing your credit report regularly is also important. There are three credit bureaus that keep information about you and your credit accounts in their files: Equifax, Experian, and TransUnion. You should obtain copies of your three credit reports and review them to make sure all of the information is correct and that there are no unauthorized accounts listed. Each agency keeps its own records, so you'll need to review all three reports. All Americans now have the right to receive free credit reports annually. To get your free copy, call toll-free 1-877-322-8228 or visit www.annual.creditreport.com.

A credit score tells lenders how likely you are to repay a loan, so they use it to determine whether you qualify for a loan and what interest rate to charge you. The higher your score, the better your credit rating.

If you think you may be a victim of identity theft, call your bank and credit card companies to notify them of the problem. Place a fraud alert on your credit files by calling one of the credit reporting agencies. Also call the Federal Trade Commission (FTC) Identity Theft Hotline (toll-free) to learn what else you should do 1-877-IDTHEFT (1-877-438-4338) www.consumer.gov/idtheft. Even if you are not a victim, you still may choose to call the FTC and ask them to send you their free booklet that provides guidance on how to best protect yourself. It is also available on the Web site listed earlier.

SUMMARY AND CONCLUSION

As tedious as it is, making sure that you have enough insurance as well as the right kind with the right kind of insurance company is essential to your future financial welfare. We cannot sufficiently emphasize how important it is to make sure your insurance coverage—all of it—is adequate for your personal circumstances should you suffer *any* kind of loss—life, disability, health, home, or car. You need to have appropriate compensation available to you. This is an area where many procrastinate, questioning whether they will really need this coverage. The policies often appear too complex to read, but when disaster strikes, it is too late.

Diane

Reactions to Protecting Her Assets

When Diane met with Dorothy about the implications of her new job, Dorothy suggested that they review her insurance in greater detail. Earlier, Diane had followed Dorothy's recommendation to buy a $1,000,000 life insurance policy on herself. The policy was owned by and payable to an insurance trust set up for the benefit of the children. At the time, Diane had agreed but did not really understand the implications of the trust, so she asked Dorothy to explain the trust to her again.

Dorothy told Diane that when she died, if her estate was valued at less than $2,000,000[1] no estate tax would be due. Currently her estate was worth $1,815,000, so her heirs would not have to worry about paying estate taxes. However, if the $1,000,000 insurance proceeds were added to her estate assets, the estate would be taxed. By having the trust buy the insurance policy and pay the premiums, this would remove the $1,000,000 insurance proceeds from her taxable estate, thus leaving more to her children.

The firm for which Diane was going to work had said it would pay one-half of her medical insurance premiums. This would be particularly helpful when Mark's firm's coverage would no longer be available to them (three years after his death). With Dorothy's help, she had looked into the costs of individual health insurance coverage and found that once she was no longer covered by Mark's plan, the premiums would double from the present levels of $500 to about $1,000 per month. When Diane started working, her premiums would be reduced to $3,000 annually. This meant, in addition to having additional income from her salary, Diane would lower her future expenses by $9,000 a year because the firm would provide her with group health insurance coverage.

Diane also asked Dorothy about her disability insurance. Dorothy told her this insurance would also be available to her when she started working. She said she would be glad to review the coverage to make sure it was adequate for her circumstances.

Dorothy reviewed Diane's household, liability, and car coverage and recommended that she consider using the same company for all three. In this way, she might be able to lower the premiums. Diane reminded Dorothy that Erin was about to turn 16 and would need to be covered by Diane's car policy when she got her driver's license.

---

1. This estate exclusion is $2,000,000 in 2006.

Dorothy told her that the increase in premiums would probably not be that great because Erin was female, a good student, and would not have a car of her own. Diane would have more of a problem when Jeremy required car insurance. Based on accident statistics, insurance companies consider young male drivers to be more of a risk than young females and therefore charge a higher premium for them. Premiums for younger drivers generally decrease once they reach age 25.

Diane was really pleased with her meeting with Dorothy. She felt that she understood her current insurance situation better. What a good feeling that was!

SUSAN

Reactions to Protecting Her Assets

The benefits at Susan's new job were not as good as they were at her old job. Her former employer paid for all of her benefits; the new one paid only part of her benefits. However, she was earning $15,000 more, and if she had to spend part of it for benefits, so be it.

Both associations offered a 401(k) retirement plan. Under current tax law (2006) Susan could contribute as much as $20,000 per year to this retirement plan and receive a tax deduction for the amount she contributed. In addition, the money would accumulate for her, tax deferred. Her previous association contributed to her retirement account, putting in 25 cents for every dollar up to the first $4,000 she invested. Her new association did not match her retirement contributions, but she thought she should take advantage of contributing more to this retirement plan than she had at her last job. She didn't think she could contribute as much as $20,000, but she certainly would do as much as she could to help reduce her tax bill. Also she needed to start being responsible for building her own retirement plan.

At her new job she would have to pay one-half of the medical premiums; however, this was certainly a necessary expense. Susan saw little reason to buy life insurance in addition to the $50,000 coverage provided by the association—the only person she really had to worry about was her mother. If Susan died, she thought her other assets would be sufficient to take care of her mother.

When she called the homeowners insurance agent to ask him to remove the coverage on the cottage, she remembered to ask if her current policy included replacement coverage on the contents of her condominium. After checking, he said it didn't, so she asked him to add that coverage to her existing policy. The agent asked her if she needed a valuable-items rider on her policy, explaining that if she owned any expensive jewelry, rugs, or paintings, they should be separately insured. Susan and Lance had bought some paintings and an Oriental rug when they were married. Lance had also given her a few pieces of fairly valuable jewelry, which she cherished. The agent told her to have these items appraised so he could provide her with appropriate coverage.

He also told her she had no personal liability insurance and recommended that she have about $1,000,000 personal liability coverage, which would be equal to her net worth. He could add this coverage to her existing coverage for about $150 per year. In view of her financial responsibilities, Susan thought this was a good idea.

These were the sort of issues Susan had not been able to face in the early stages of her widowhood. It felt good to be able to focus on these details once again. She no longer was battling against a strong current to merely keep afloat. Finally, she was moving forward.

Audrey

Reactions to Protecting Her Assets

Audrey had been approached by an insurance agent about buying life insurance. The same agent had talked to her about purchasing long-term health-care insurance. She really didn't know this agent, so she decided to call Mr. Silver and ask him what he thought about these ideas. He suggested that she come in with the information the agent had provided her and they could discuss the ideas further.

When they met, Mr. Silver said that her primary reason for purchasing life insurance would be to provide a larger inheritance for the grandchildren. However, at her age—and he struggled to be diplomatic as he discussed this with her—it was expensive to buy life insurance. He thought it would be better to focus on building her current investments.

He suggested instead that Joanne should have some life insurance, which Audrey could fund at least until the grandchildren were through college. If something happened to Joanne, Keith might have a problem financially taking care of the children. Mr. Silver also recommended that, in view of Audrey's concern about Keith's financial stability, it might be a good idea to set up an insurance trust. If Joanne died, then the proceeds of the policy would go into a trust to be managed for the children, as Audrey had provided in her own will. Audrey thought this was a good suggestion and decided to discuss it with Joanne. Knowing how tight their budget was, she would make sure Joanne knew that she would pay the premiums, which Mr. Silver estimated would cost about $462 annually for a 20-year level-term insurance policy for $1,000,000. Should Joanne prematurely die, that would provide support for her children until they had completed college.

Next they discussed the long-term health-care insurance. Audrey had excellent medical coverage through John's company. After hearing some of the horror stories of her other widowed friends, she was exceedingly grateful for this coverage. However, the idea of buying long-term health-care insurance appealed to her because it would prevent her from being a burden to her children if she became unable to care for herself.

Mr. Silver obtained quotes from two different insurance companies. He requested $200-per-day coverage that became effective 90 days after she entered a long-term health-care facility or needed at-home care. The policy had a 5 percent inflation clause and was noncancelable. Mr. Silver obtained two quotes from each company, one that would cover her for three years and the other for lifetime care. The premium for the three years of coverage was $2,600 a year; for lifetime coverage it would cost $5,456 per year.

A friend had told Audrey she could qualify for Medicaid coverage if she needed to go to a long-term health-care facility. Mr. Silver told her that she would have to give away most of her assets to qualify for Medicaid and he didn't think she would want to do that. He was also concerned that Medicaid might not offer the same coverage if and when she had to go to a long-term health care facility some 20 years hence.

Following Mr. Silver's advice, Audrey selected the three years of coverage because she did have other assets as well as the pension and Social Security, which would provide her with income if she needed more care after the three years had elapsed. However, she did want to leave something for her children and grandchildren.

Mr. Silver helped her fill out the application for the coverage. He alerted her to the fact that her premiums might increase in the future, explaining that her premium would not go up unless the company raised the premiums for everyone in her age group.

Audrey felt somewhat badly she had not bought this insurance through the agent who had initially approached her with the idea. On the other hand, Mr. Silver had obtained quotes from several companies before selecting the right one for her situation. The other agent had showed her only one—the one provided by the company for which he worked.

When Audrey had moved into her new townhouse, she had obtained replacement-value insurance on the home and its contents. At the same time, she combined this insurance with her car insurance and bought an umbrella liability policy for $700,000. It looked as if she had protected herself as well as she could with insurance. She was particularly pleased with the decision she had made about the long-term health-care insurance. She was adamant about being able to take care of herself now and in her old age!

Audrey had shared these feelings with Joanne this past week when they were at the spa. Joanne had actually jumped at the chance to go with her mother for the long weekend. She was exhausted from caring for her family and knew she was overweight. Her family hadn't had sufficient funds to take a vacation in years. Her father's death had also taken its toll on her, and she missed him sorely. Earlier in her marriage, before he had become ill, her father had given her a little extra money to purchase something for herself because, as he used to say, she would always be "his little girl." Thinking of those days always brought tears to her eyes.

While they were away, Audrey made sure Joanne understood her feelings about being able to provide for herself. Even though it was a painful subject, she also shared with Joanne her feelings about her own life and why she had requested that Joanne be given her health power of attorney. She told her daughter that she trusted her to make the right decision regarding medical treatment should she be unable to do so. Joanne got all choked up at this thought but understood what her mother was telling her. Mother and daughter hugged each other and wordlessly acknowledged the significance of the moment.

Elizabeth
Reactions to Protecting Her Assets

After reflecting on her conversation with Mr. Grossfeldt, Elizabeth asked him to change the terms of her living trust so that if she predeceased Abigail, Abigail would receive the income from the trust until she died. Given Elizabeth's age, there didn't seem much point in her applying for life insurance. If Elizabeth predeceased Abigail, Abigail would receive a $15,000 annual income from the trust, which should be sufficient for her needs. The charities would receive the trust assets when Abigail died.

Elizabeth had never given much thought to her health-care coverage because she knew she was covered by Medicare. However, she had recently seen a television program in which Medigap insurance was discussed as something you should have to cover what Medicare did not provide. She was totally confused and a little frightened. Perhaps Medicare did not provide her with sufficient medical coverage? As always in these matters, she found herself turning to Sam Weatherly for help.

Sam had already reviewed and selected Medigap insurance coverage for himself and his wife, Sarah. He explained to Elizabeth the purpose and various options of this type of insurance. He then recommended a comprehensive Medigap insurance policy that would provide sufficient coverage for her needs.

Elizabeth also asked Sam about long-term health-care insurance. He pointed out to her that it would be pretty expensive for her to buy at her age. He suggested that she discuss this matter with the staff at Northern Pines and obtain details regarding the costs of nursing-home care should she need to move to that section of the retirement community at a later date. Elizabeth reflected that this was another reason for her to make the move to Northern Palms. Not only would she be near her sister and have better year-round weather, but she could also receive necessary nursing care when and if she needed it.

She had now inquired as to whether or not Northern Palms allowed pets and was pleased to learn that they did. They did not allow large dogs, but that was no problem—Mittens only weighed eight pounds and was a cat! She wondered how he would handle the move. She was quite attached to Mittens now and did not want to leave him in Boston.

13

Understanding Your
Investment Options

You may be disappointed if you fail,
but you are doomed if you don't try.
—*Beverly Sills*

IN CHAPTER 8, you made a list of your assets and liabilities that you provided to your financial advisor. Your advisor will divide the asset list into retirement and nonretirement assets. Next, he will group them under separate asset categories. The basic asset classes are *cash, fixed income, stocks, real estate,* and *other.* Then your advisor will total these assets and tell you the percentage you own in each asset class to give you a picture of your overall investment situation. This list helps you identify the different types of investment assets you own. By this time, your financial advisor will be familiar with your personal circumstances and with this information can recommend any changes that should be made to provide you with sufficient income now and in the future.

Although your primary residence, your cars, and your furnishings are assets, we would not include these under the list of your investments because they do not provide current income and are not easily changed. For instance, even if you sold your home, you are likely to buy another one.

The composite picture would look like this:

Assets	Nonretirement	Retirement	Total
Cash	$_____	$_____	$_____
Fixed income	_____	_____	_____
Stocks	_____	_____	_____
Real estate	_____	_____	_____
Other	_____	_____	_____

This summary can be prepared from the asset list you put together in chapter 8. Here we will discuss each asset class in more detail.

CASH

This category includes any short-term assets that will come due within a year, such as certificates of deposit, U.S. Treasury bills, short-term loans owed to you or the estate, and life insurance proceeds due you. It would also include your checking accounts, savings accounts, and money market accounts.

When listing your assets, you may have found that you had checking and savings accounts in more than one bank. We recommend that you consolidate them into one account as long as the amount in your name in one bank does not exceed $100,000. (In 2006, accounts larger than this amount are not insured by the Federal Deposit Insurance Company.) The fewer accounts you have to keep track of, the simpler life will be.

Typically you would keep about one month's expenses in a checking account. We suggest you keep the balance of your cash in a money market account with check-writing privileges so that you can easily transfer money from this account to your checking account.

These money market accounts pay taxable or nontaxable income. If you are in a higher tax bracket (28 percent or higher), investing your money in the nontaxable account would provide you with a higher after-tax income.

If you establish a money market account, you should still maintain a checking account to handle your smaller expenses. To summarize, consolidate your cash accounts and consider using a money market account for the majority of your cash.

FIXED INCOME

We include in this asset category any investment that pays a fixed rate of income for a year or longer—bonds, preferred stocks, notes receivable, certificates of deposit (CDs), mortgages, insurance policies, guaranteed investment contracts (GICs), and fixed deferred annuities. The following discussion is intended to be an overview of the most commonly held fixed-income investments but is not a comprehensive description. Be sure you understand all the details of the fixed-income investments you hold or before you invest.

Bonds are the most common form of fixed-income investment besides certificates of deposit. Bonds are IOUs from a corporation, the government, or one of the government's agencies. In return for the loan, you receive a specified amount of interest (usually paid in semiannual payments) over a given period of time. You are repaid your principal by a certain specified date (called the maturity date). Some bonds are *callable*, which means the borrowing entity can repay you before the maturity date if it so desires.

There are three basic categories of bonds: government, municipal, and corporate.

U.S. Government Bonds

U.S. government bonds are considered the safest investment you can make because it is generally believed that the U.S. government will continue to pay interest and principal on its obligations. You can buy government bonds through your bank or your broker or directly from the Federal Reserve. This type of investment is usually well suited to a widow's portfolio because it provides a reliable stream of income. The interest from U.S. Treasury bonds is not subject to state taxes, although it is subject to federal taxes. From a tax point of view, owning these bonds is preferable to owning bonds issued by a corporation, where the interest is fully taxable.

U.S. government investments come in various denominations called bills, notes, and bonds. The difference between the three types is in the holding period. Bills come due within one year, notes mature in one to 10 years, and bonds mature in 10 to 30 years.

Savings Bonds

Series E bonds (the so-called war bonds) were issued from May 1941 to June 1980 in amounts ranging from $25 to $10,000.

Series EE bonds have been issued since January 1980 in denominations ranging from $50 to $10,000. Patriot Bonds are a type of Series EE bond that has been issued since December 2001.

Interest on these bonds isn't paid until the bond is redeemed. The interest compounds either monthly or semiannually. You can choose to pay federal tax each year on the interest (the interest paid is free of state and local tax) or wait until you redeem the bond. You must redeem these bonds after 30 or 40 years (depending on your date of purchase), when they stop earning interest. In the past you could avoid paying tax on the accumulated interest if you chose to exchange them for *Series HH bonds,* which pay taxable income semiannually for 20 years. However, in 2004 this option was eliminated.

The interest rate earned on these bonds may have been guaranteed initially, but it will change while you own the bonds. Further, for bonds purchased between May 1995 and April 2005, the guaranteed rate was eliminated. Series EE bonds purchased during this period earn a market-based rate.

Since September 1998 *Series I bonds* have been available. They earn a rate that is tied to an inflation index. The interest accumulates and is paid to you when you redeem the bond. Series I bonds are issued in denominations ranging from $50 to $10,000.

In the past some corporations encouraged their employees to buy savings bonds by deducting a certain amount from each paycheck. Therefore, you may find that you have inherited some U.S. savings bonds. If you do not know what a bond is worth, consult your local bank. They may be able to help you, but they will not be able to tell you the interest rate on your bonds.

For more complete information, contact the Federal Reserve Bank for your region (ask your local bank for its toll-free phone number). Information about savings bonds is also available online from the Bureau of the Public Debt. www.publicdebt.treas.gov/sav/sav.htm. Your financial advisor should also be able to provide you with information about the bonds you own.

If you prefer, there is a service that, for a reasonable fee, will review the bonds you are holding and will send you a report that tells you exactly what your bonds are earning, how much interest has accumulated, and when the bonds will stop earning interest. For further information about this useful service, call the Savings Bond Informer, Inc., at 1-800-927-1901.

Ginnie Maes

Also available are securities that are similar to bonds but invest in federally insured mortgages, where the interest and the principal are backed by the "full faith and credit" of the U.S. government. The most popular of these are issued by the Government National Mortgage Association (GNMA) and are often called *Ginnie Maes*. The yield is usually higher than that paid by U.S. Treasury bonds. Unlike most bonds, which pay interest semiannually and return your principal all at once when they come due, these mortgage certificates pay back a portion of your principal as well as the interest each month so that by the time they come due you have received all the money you are entitled to receive. In other words, you have nothing left. It is similar to your receiving mortgage payments rather than paying them. The minimum purchase is $25,000 and the interest is fully taxable by both the federal government and state governments.

Municipal Bonds

Municipal bonds are IOUs from state, city, or other local government agencies. Income from municipal bonds is exempt from federal income taxes and, if issued by the state in which you pay taxes, is also free from local taxes. Under current law, if you are a resident of Washington, D.C., interest paid by any municipal bond is free of local tax.

There are two types of municipal bonds: *general obligation bonds* and *general revenue bonds*. The difference between the two types depends on whether the income is backed by the credit of the state or city issuing the bond (general obligation) or is backed by the revenue of a particular project, such as a toll bridge (general revenue).

Sometimes the bond is insured, which means that an outside group called the Municipal Bond Insurance Corporation (MBIC) guarantees that both the income and the principal will be paid to you. While the fact that the bond is insured is reassuring, insured bonds usually pay a slightly lower interest rate than noninsured bonds because the insurance feature costs money.

Generally, we recommend buying municipal bonds that are rated A or better by both rating agencies (Standard & Poor's and Moody's). If you are in a higher tax bracket (28 percent or above), municipals may be a better choice for you than U.S. Treasury or corporate bonds because the after-tax return will be higher.

For example, if your $10,000 corporate bond pays 6 percent ($600 per year) and you are in the 30 percent tax bracket, you would have to pay $180 in federal taxes on this income. That would leave you with an after-tax return of $420, or 4.20 percent ($420 divided by $10,000).

If, instead, you invested in a $10,000 municipal bond paying 5 percent, you would receive $500 income and would pay no federal taxes on this income, giving you a higher after-tax return of 5 percent. If the municipal bond was issued by the state in which you live or if you live in Washington, D.C., you would pay no state income tax on this income, which would increase the benefits of investing in the municipal bond.

Corporate Bonds

Corporate bonds are issued by corporations. The interest they pay is taxed as "ordinary income" (at your tax rate). Again, the better the rating (highest is AAA), the less risk you are taking with your principal. However, the higher the rating, the lower the interest rate the bond will pay.

High-Yield Junk Bonds

In the 1980s a new type of bond that gained popularity in some circles was called a *high-yield bond* or, more realistically, a *junk bond.* These bonds had lower ratings (below BBB) or no rating at all. They paid a higher rate of interest to the bondholder than better-rated bonds because the investors were taking greater risks. The companies (or municipalities) that issued these bonds were not as financially sound as higher-rated companies; therefore, investors accepted the risk that the bonds might not be able to pay the income they had promised to pay.

As with any other kind of investment, there are gradations within the category. The lower the rating, the higher the interest rate and the higher the risk the investor takes—and vice versa. Some junk bonds are less risky than others. For instance, there are junk bonds where the issuing company lost money the previous year and therefore the bonds no longer are rated "investment grade." This same company may turn its financial situation around and thus may regain its previous "investment grade" status, which will raise the price of the bond.

Convertible Bonds

There is another kind of corporate bond that is a hybrid—*a convertible bond.* This bond pays a stated rate of interest (just like any other bond), but, if you wish, you can convert it into shares of stock. A convertible bond pays a lower rate of interest than a nonconvertible bond because of this conversion feature. For instance, if the stock price of the issuing company goes up, the price of the bond will go up as well. Thus, a convertible bond gives you more potential for growth of principal than a nonconvertible bond. Investing in these bonds can work out very well but involves more risk than investing in corporate bonds.

Zero-Coupon Bonds

These bonds are issued by the U.S. government, corporations, and municipalities. No coupons are attached, so they are called *zero-coupon bonds.* The term *coupon* derives from the small, detachable segment of a bond certificate, which entitles the holder to the interest due on that date. Although the bond earns a stated interest rate, the interest accumulates in the bond instead of being paid to you, as in a coupon bond.

The drawback to government or corporate zero-coupon bonds is that you are taxed on the income each year, even though you don't receive it. With municipal zero-coupon bonds, you don't receive the income, but you don't have to pay taxes on the income because they pay tax-free income. When the zero-coupon bonds come due, you will receive the principal amount of the bond, which represents your original investment plus the accrued income.

International Bonds

You can also invest in *international government bonds* or *international corporate bonds.* These involve more risk because you are investing in bonds issued by foreign countries and you have no certainty as to the value of the foreign country's currency in relation to U.S. currency over the course of time. This means your bond might go up in value, but, because of the relationship of the U.S. dollar to another country's currency at that time, you might lose money.

How Do You Buy Bonds?

There are three basic ways to buy bonds: individually, in unit trusts, or in mutual funds.

Individual bonds. If you buy an individual bond, you usually invest a minimum of $5,000, and you know exactly which bond you are buying. Although you usually buy bonds through a stockbroker, banker, or financial planner, you can buy U.S. Treasury bonds directly from the Bureau of the Public Debt, Washington, D.C. 20239; (800-722-2678); www.treasurydirect.gov.

Unit trusts. A unit trust invests in a group of bonds at a particular time and then holds them until they come due. This type of investment is not actively managed. Typically these unit trusts sell at a discount from their market value; thus, most people hold unit trusts until all the bonds mature.

Mutual funds. Mutual funds buy a group of different bonds that meet specific criteria as specified in the mutual fund prospectus. In contrast to buying individual bonds or unit trusts, the mutual fund has one or more managers who select and monitor these investments. The manager buys and sells bonds in the portfolio according to a stated investment strategy.

Many different kinds of mutual funds invest in bonds. You can buy a fund that invests in government bonds, investment-grade corporate bonds, municipal bonds, junk bonds, or convertible bonds. You can also buy a fund that invests in bonds with similar maturities. A long-term bond fund would invest in longer-term maturities (20 or 30 years) to obtain the highest yield available. An intermediate-term fund would buy bonds with three-year to 10-year maturities in an effort to protect your principal against rising interest rates. A limited maturity fund invests in bonds with one-year to three-year maturities.

Deferred Annuities

Deferred annuities are contracts issued by insurance companies that pay you income. If you don't currently need the income, then you can let the income accumulate in the annuity, and this income will not be currently taxed. As soon as you start to take the income from the annuity, then all or part of the income will be taxed.

There are two types of annuities: *fixed* and *variable*. Fixed annuities pay a set rate of return for a specified period of time. Variable annuities invest in separate investment accounts. The return on your investment varies according to how well (or poorly) these accounts perform.

You may be the beneficiary of a deferred annuity that your husband had bought. If so, you will be asked if you want to receive regular income from this annuity or if you want to cash it in and make another investment. Should you decide to cash it in, there will be tax consequences.

A fixed annuity can pay you a fixed payment (typically monthly) for the rest of your life. The amount of this payment is based on a number of factors, including the interest rate the insurance company thinks it is going to earn and how long the insurance company thinks you are going to live (based on actuarial tables). The longer or more certain the payment period, the lower the monthly income you will receive. Be aware that the amount an annuity company will pay you may differ from company to company.

In order to receive the highest rate of current income, you would select the *lifetime only* option, which means that the payments stop when you die and the insurance company keeps whatever is left. If you select this option, your heirs are not entitled to receive anything when you die.

To avoid this, you can choose to receive income for your lifetime but stipulate that your heirs will receive payments for a certain period of time after you buy the annuity—such as ten years— even if you die during that time period. If you select this option, your monthly payments will be somewhat lower than if you accepted payments for your lifetime only.

If you do decide to "annuitize" (receive fixed monthly payments for your lifetime), ask your insurance agent how much of this payment will be taxed. Usually, part of your payment will not be taxed because it is considered return of the original investment.

Instead of annuitizing, you could choose instead to withdraw a certain amount of income each month from your annuity. You and your advisor would determine the right amount for you given your circumstances. This is a more flexible arrangement than annuitizing because you can change this amount at any time.

Be aware that typically you are not charged a commission when you purchase an annuity, but there may be a withdrawal charge if you decide to cash in your annuity and receive the money or move to another insurance company's annuity program. The withdrawal penalty varies from company to company. In addition, there can be some adverse insurance consequences. Be sure you thoroughly understand all the implications before you agree to take money out of an annuity.

A Charitable Gift Annuity

A *charitable gift annuity* is a contract between you and a charity. In exchange for your irrevocable gift of cash, securities, or other assets, the charity agrees to pay one or two annuitants, whom you name, a fixed sum each year for life. The older your designated annuitants are at the time of the gift, the greater the fixed income the charity will agree to pay. In most cases, part of each payment is tax free. Payments can be made annually, semiannually, or quarterly. In addition, you will qualify for a federal income tax deduction that will be based on the age of the annuitants and the terms of the contract. If you name another annuitant in addition to yourself, there may be a gift tax involved.

Mortgages and Second Deeds of Trust

If you decide to sell your home, you may be asked to take back a mortgage or a second deed of trust. If you agree to do this, you are assuming the role of the banker and lending the money to the purchaser. The borrower will usually pay you an above-average rate of return for a stated period of time. The risk you take with this type of investment depends on the creditworthiness of the borrower.

You can also invest in mortgages and second deeds of trust through third parties. With these investments, you will not know the identity of the borrower.

STOCKS

Preferred Stocks

Preferred stocks are like bonds because they are issued by a corporation and pay a fixed rate of interest. They are unlike bonds in that they don't have a maturity date—that is, there is no predetermined time when the face value will be repaid. We are not particularly enthusiastic about investing in preferred stocks because they seem to be neither fish nor fowl. It is our opinion that they aren't as safe as corporate bonds, nor do they offer the advantages of common stock. If you want a fixed rate of return, we think you should buy bonds; if you want potential growth of principal and income, then we think you should buy common stocks.

On the other hand, there are convertible preferred stocks available that work very much like bonds. (See convertible bonds section.) These pay a higher rate of interest than the common stocks of the same company. Carefully selected, these stocks might fit into a widow's portfolio.

Common Stocks

Common stocks represent ownership in corporations. In general, stock prices go up and down according to how profitable the company is or what its perceived potential to make money is. Outside factors such as the condition of the general economy, political variables, technological advances, or industry reversals may cause an individual stock to go up or down in price.

For the widow who requires higher current income and doesn't want to be invested all in bonds, stocks that pay a good dividend may be a viable alternative. If you select a stock primarily for income, you should expect less growth of principal from this stock because, by paying out profits to you in dividends, these companies are reinvesting less of their profits back into their own growth.

Many people think that investing in stocks is risky—and it is. But, as we have pointed out previously, every investment involves some degree of risk. We think you can reduce the risk of investing in stocks by buying stocks of good-quality companies, often called "blue chip" stocks. These are stocks offered by large, established companies with well-known brand-name products. A company qualifies as good quality because it has a good credit rating (A or better), which means the company doesn't have too much debt in relation to its total net worth. A good-quality company consistently increases its earnings and dividends annually over a period of years.

International Stocks

Up to now we have been discussing stocks of companies whose corporate headquarters are based in the United States. International stocks are common stocks of companies based outside the United States. As of the end of 2005, approximately 51 percent of the world's stock market capitalization was in non-U.S. companies.(World capitalization is defined as percentage of the MSCI ACWI [All Country World Index])

While we think investing in international securities offers advantages, there are also risks. In addition to the risks taken with any investment, investing outside the United States involves currency fluctuations, political and social instability, differing securities regulations and accounting standards, limited reliable public information, possible changes in taxation, and periods of illiquidity. We think you can reduce these risks somewhat by buying stocks of companies with established earnings records rather than new companies in Third World countries.

If investing internationally appeals to you, we recommend investing in mutual funds rather than in individual stocks. We think investing in a diversified portfolio of stocks as well as taking advantage of the research capabilities of experienced international fund managers could provide you with some protection against these potential risks.

How Do You Buy Stocks?

You can buy individual shares of stock through your stockbroker, financial planner, or banker. You can also buy shares on the Internet.

Shares of well-established companies usually trade on the New York and American Stock Exchanges, as well as on the Nasdaq. You can follow the price of your stock every day in the newspaper or on the Internet.

MUTUAL FUNDS

Advantages of Investing in Mutual Funds

Mutual funds invest in diversified portfolios of stocks, bonds, or both. We think there are several advantages to investing in mutual funds: diversification[1], professional management, and ease of record keeping. By investing in mutual funds, you are able to obtain diversification among various kinds of assets as well as within asset classes. Mutual funds also offer you professional management. Finally, the funds provide flexibility because you can choose one of the following options: to receive the dividends or capital gains (or both) from these funds, reinvest this income into additional shares, or be paid a fixed monthly dollar amount. These income options can be changed at any time.

---

1. **Diversification does not guarantee against loss. It is a method used to manage risk.**

Kinds of Mutual Funds

Mutual funds invest in different geographic locations. *U.S. stock* mutual funds invest only in stocks of companies based in the United States. *International stock* mutual funds invest only in companies based outside the United States. *Global* funds can invest in companies anywhere in the world (including the United States). In addition, there are *emerging markets* international stock funds, which invest in companies based in smaller, less economically stable countries.

Mutual funds have different investment objectives. Mutual funds can be divided into many different groups according to their investment objectives. To keep this initial description relatively simple, we have divided them into five categories:

- *Income funds* (invested primarily in bonds, pay highest income)
- *Balanced funds* (invested in stocks and bonds, pay high income)
- *Growth and income funds* (invested in stocks of established companies, seek to provide growth of income and principal)
- *Growth funds* (invested in stocks with emphasis on growth of principal, pay low income)
- *Aggressive growth funds* (invested in stocks of younger, riskier companies, typically pay no income)

Mutual funds invest in large, small, and middle-sized companies. To add to the confusion, you will also hear the terms *large cap, midcap, and small cap* used to distinguish kinds of companies in which mutual funds invest. *Cap* refers to the size of the company. Large-cap companies are the larger, better-known companies that typically have a market capitalization of $10 billion or more. Midcap companies have a capitalization of $2 billion to $10 billion. Small-cap companies are smaller, lesser-known companies that typically have a market capitalization of less than $2 billion. The smaller the capitalization of the company, the more risk you are taking. Multicap funds can invest in the stocks of companies of all three sizes.

Mutual funds invest in various industries. These so-called *sector funds* invest in companies within a particular industry, such as health care, technology, or energy..

Index Funds

These funds invest in all the stocks included in a given stock market index, such as the Standard & Poor's 500 Composite Index.[2] In other words, an index fund is not a managed fund. It must invest in the stocks in that index in the same percentage that they are represented in the index. Although this index is composed of the stocks of 500 companies, because they are weighted according to the company's capitalization size, there is not an equal weighting for each company in the index.

Exchange-Traded Funds (ETFs)

Exchange-Traded Funds (ETFs) are open-end registered investment companies. Technically, they are not mutual funds, but they offer some of the same advantages. ETFs are made up of baskets of securities combined into one stock and are traded on a national securities exchange. Unlike open-end mutual funds, which are priced at the end of each day, these shares are traded throughout the day just like any other stock. These ETFs usually mirror a stock index, such as the S&P 500 Composite Index, or a particular type of investment, such as energy or precious metals.

Hedge Funds

Hedge Funds also sound like mutual funds but are considerably different. These funds are actually loosely regulated private investment pools designed for wealthy individuals willing to invest larger amounts of money and take above-average risk in hopes of achieving higher-than-average returns. The management fees charged by these hedge funds are tied to the results and are much higher than you pay for a mutual fund. If you inherit a hedge

---

2. The Standard & Poor's 500 Composite Index is an unmanaged index comprised of widely held securities considered to be representative of the stock market in general. Performance of the indexes is not indicative of any particular investment. Individuals cannot invest directly in any index. Past performance is no guarantee of future results.

fund, check with your financial advisor as to the necessary action you should take.

How Mutual Funds Are Valued

Mutual funds can be classified as *open-end* or *closed-end.* These terms refer to how the shares of the funds are priced rather than what kind of investments are held in their portfolios. The prices of open-end funds are based on the total market value of all the assets they hold divided by the number of shares outstanding. (In the newspaper you will see this price called the *net asset value*, or NAV.) In contrast, shares of closed-end funds are priced based on the market's perception of their worth, which may be higher or lower than the net asset value. These shares are traded on a stock exchange.

Investment Styles of Mutual Fund Managers

Mutual funds can also be classified as *growth stock* funds or *value stock* funds. These terms refer to the type of company a fund manager picks to buy for the fund. If a manager invests in growth stocks, he or she selects companies where the earnings have grown at a higher rate than other companies and are expected to continue to grow at an above-average rate.

If a manager buys value stocks, he or she is choosing companies that appear to be selling at a price lower than what they are worth. For example, let us assume a company sold all its assets. If you divided the sales proceeds (the liquidating value) by the number of shares available in the company, you would get $20 per share. If the shares were currently selling at $10 a share in the open market, the value manager would be interested in buying these shares because they are undervalued as compared to the liquidating value of the company.

How Do You Select the Right Fund for You?

Currently, there are approximately 8,000 mutual funds available.   Over half of these funds were started since 1993, according to the *Investment Company Institute 2005 Fact Book.*

Financial advisors approach their mutual fund research in various ways. For instance, we start our selection process by looking at the long-term performance record of the fund (we prefer a fund with a history of ten years or more). Although past performance is no guarantee of future results, we think it is one indicator. A long-term record of good results is reassuring, but it is important for the advisor to ascertain whether the management team that built the record is still in place.

We look for funds that have performed as well or better than the average fund in its category over an extended period of time. For instance, we would compare the record of a small-cap fund with the average performance of other small-cap funds. We think it doesn't make sense to compare the record of a small-cap fund with a large-cap fund because they invest in companies of different sizes. Typically, when small-cap stocks are going up, large-cap stocks aren't, and vice versa. So to get an accurate picture of how a fund is doing, you want to compare apples with apples rather than apples with oranges.

What Does It Cost to Buy a Fund?

We wish there were a simple answer to this question. It used to be that the investor had two basic choices. Either she bought a *"load" fund*, which her full-service stockbroker selected for her, and she paid a commission to buy the shares; or she selected her own *"no-load" fund* and bought the shares directly from the mutual fund management company, usually paying no (or a low) initial commission. In both cases, the mutual fund companies charged annual management fees to manage the fund's assets.

Today, life is not so simple. There are many different ways you can be charged to invest in a fund. What we think is most important is that before you make an investment you understand what it will cost to invest, both initially and on an ongoing basis. You should carefully consider the investment objectives, risks, charges and expenses of mutual funds. This and other important information is contained in the prospectus which you should read carefully before investing. Your financial advisor should provide you with a prospectus for each mutual fund recommended and should fully explain all costs involved.

You may feel confident enough to select and buy your own funds without the assistance of a professional advisor. If you take this approach, you should thoroughly research the mutual funds available that meet your investment objectives, read the prospectuses carefully, make your final selections, and then monitor your own portfolio regularly to make sure the funds you selected are performing competitively.

However, if you prefer to have a professional advisor help you select and supervise your fund portfolio, then you will have to pay the advisor for this help—either on a fee or a commission basis. Your primary objective is to make good investment selections that will help you achieve your long-term financial goals.

REAL ESTATE

Direct Ownership

You can own real estate directly or indirectly. Direct ownership means that you own an individual piece of property as an investment and either manage the property yourself or pay someone else to do so. Real estate you own would include a second home or rental property. You may have been involved in managing such assets when your husband was alive, and it might be a good idea to keep them. However, on objective analysis you may discover that the money tied up in these properties might grow for you more productively elsewhere. Usually you do not have to make these decisions immediately.

Indirect Ownership

Many real estate investments are held indirectly. Typically, they invest in different types of commercial real estate such as shopping centers, office buildings, warehouses, apartments, retirement communities, and hotels. Two common forms of indirect ownership are real estate investment trusts (REITs) and limited partnerships.

Real estate investment trusts (REITs). There are two types of REITs—*publicly traded REITs* and *nontraded REITS. Publicly traded REITs* are common stocks that invest in real estate properties. In order to retain their status as REITs, these companies are required to pay the investor at least 90 percent of the net income they receive from the properties they own. Typically, REIT stocks pay higher income than most other common stocks. Like other stocks, these shares are traded daily on the major stock exchanges, and you can sell these shares at any time. When selecting a REIT stock, we recommend that you invest in one managed by a real estate company with a proven track record in the type of real estate held in the REIT. The income paid from traded REITs is taxed at ordinary income tax rates.

Nontraded REITs are like traded REITs in some ways but not in others. They are similar in that the management company buys and manages commercial real estate properties; they are dissimilar in that the shares are not publicly traded. These REIT companies manage these properties for a certain number of years as stated in the prospectus. At that point the REIT managers expect to sell these properties or convert the units to publicly traded REIT shares. Before then, the only way you can liquidate your investment is by selling your units back to the company. The REIT company may or may not agree to buy your units back, and they may or may not pay you the original amount you invested. These nontraded REITs usually pay a higher rate of interest than do publicly traded REIT stocks. The income is taxed at ordinary income tax rates, but often part of the income you receive is tax deferred because of depreciation taken on the properties.

Limited partnerships. A limited partnership is similar to a nontraded REIT since you invest with others in a particular property or group of properties. A general partner selects and manages the property. You, as a limited partner, put up most of the money to buy the property and leave the selection and management of the property to the general partners.

If you inherit partnership units, the general partners will provide you with an evaluation for estate purposes. This usually is a fairly conservative (low) estimate of the value. The general partners of a limited partnership decide when they will sell the assets in the partnership, so you may find yourself holding this investment for a while. From time to time, a company with which you are unfamiliar may make you an offer to buy your units. Usually, you should not accept this offer because the company is "bottom fishing"—that is, offering you a price below what they perceive to be the true value. It hopes you will sell because you are tired of holding something of unknown value. Your advisor should be able to help you ascertain what you should do with these units.

OTHER ASSETS

This catch-all category includes any investments that don't fall in the asset classes listed above. These other assets would include collectibles, precious metals, commodities, and ownership in privately held businesses. The category also includes limited partnerships that invest in oil and gas production, leasing equipment, and so forth.

Under *collectibles* you would include art, Oriental rugs, antiques, stamp collections, and coins. These items are not easily sold, and although they may provide you with personal enjoyment, you should avoid this kind of investment if you are trying to build an income-producing investment portfolio. (See chapter 14, rule 8.)

In the past, investing in *gold, silver, and other precious metals* as a hedge against inflation was popular, particularly outside the United States. If you want to invest in precious metals, you can do so either directly, by buying coins or bars, or indirectly, by buying shares in gold or silver mining companies. You can also invest in mutual funds or exchange-traded funds (ETFs), which invest in these stocks. Other riskier investments include *commodities, put-and-call options, and penny stocks.*

If your husband owned a *privately held business,* we hope that he had made arrangements as to the disposition of his business on his death. If he had partners, there may be an agreement in place as to how they would buy his shares. If he was the sole owner, you may have to negotiate to sell the business. (In this case you will need a professional advisor to value the business and help you sell it.) We are assuming in both cases you are not in a position or lack the desire to buy the business yourself.

SUMMARY AND CONCLUSION

In this chapter we have tried to give you an overview of the best-known types of investments that you might own or might be suggested to you as potential investments. Obviously, this list is not all-inclusive, nor is it as detailed as it might be. This is a starting point, and if you want to learn more, there are lots of books and courses you can take to expand your knowledge. In the next chapter, we review the basics of investment management—that is, how to put together a portfolio that meets your investment objectives.

Diane

Reactions to Maximizing Her Investment Options

Diane had implemented Dorothy's earlier investment recommendations to invest the $1,000,000 she had into a portfolio of mutual funds, but she had never really understood why these investments had been selected. Dorothy had explained her investment proposal in detail, which involved dividing the money equally among five different funds—a bond fund, a balanced fund, and three different common stock funds. She had given Diane copies of prospectuses and annual reports for each fund, and Diane had even signed a receipt saying she had been provided with this information. Frankly, the information had been overwhelming, and she didn't want to appear any more stupid than she already had by asking Dorothy too many questions. She had asked her father to review Dorothy's written investment proposal, and he had approved it, but Diane now wanted to have a better understanding of what she had done and why.

Dorothy had told her that if she invested all of her money in bonds she could receive annual income of 5 percent ($50,000). However, currently interest rates were rising. When interest rates rise, bonds usually decline in value. Therefore if she invested all of her money in bonds, her principal probably would not increase in value and in fact might lose value. For this reason, Dorothy recommended that Diane invest in a diversified[3] mutual fund portfolio that included both stocks and bonds. Dorothy explained she thought that Diane's portfolio would have a better chance of growing if she was invested in stocks as well as bonds than if she invested only in bonds.

Diane did not understand why it was important for her principal to grow. Dorothy explained that although her mortgage payments would remain constant, her other living costs would increase each year as a result of inflation. In addition Dorothy told Diane that many pundits were predicting that there was a good chance someone her age might live to be 100 or even older. If she wanted her money to last as long as she did, then Dorothy thought she should invest at least part of her portfolio in stocks where there was the possibility that her principal could grow.

Dorothy recommended Diane invest in a portfolio of mutual funds. She explained that mutual funds would provide the diversification as well as professional management of the assets. Dorothy told her she had carefully picked a well-known management group of mutual funds that had been in business for many years.

The first fund Dorothy selected was a fixed-income fund that invested primarily in A or better rated bonds. The second was a balanced fund invested 40 percent in good-quality bonds, 50 percent in U.S. stocks, and 10 percent in international stocks. The third, a growth and income common stock fund, was invested in blue-chip U. S. companies that had increased their dividends and earnings

---

3. Diversification does not guarantee against loss. It is a method used to manage risk.

annually for the past ten years. The fourth fund invested only in stocks of well-established companies based outside the United States, and the fifth fund could invest in large companies throughout the world..

This group of funds paid a combined yield of 3.5 percent. Since this would only provide her with $35,000 in annual income, Dorothy suggested that initially Diane put aside $90,000 of her cash so that she could withdraw from this fund to cover expenses as needed.

Dorothy showed Diane some hypothetical examples of how the funds she had selected had done over the past fifteen years. Although some years were better than others, the amount of money had grown as had the income generated by the investments. Dorothy told Diane that noone could predict what would happen to investments in the future. However since this was a conservative group of funds managed by experienced money managers with a demonstrated track record, she thought the chances were good that her money should grow over an extended period of time

After seeing these examples, Diane began to understand why investing all of her money in either the fixed annuity or bonds would not have been a good solution for her. Even if these funds didn't perform as well over next 15 years as they had in the past, Diane was comfortable with these recommendations. After all, as Dorothy told her, she was not locked into these investments. She could sell them at any time.

Diane's Asset Allocation

Asset Class	Personal Investments	Retirement Investments	Total Investments	Percentage
Cash	$ 80,000*		$ 80,000	6%
Fixed income	280,000		280,000	20%
U.S. stocks	400,000	$300,000	700,000	51%
Int'l stocks	320,000		320,000	23%
Total	$1,080,000	$300,000	$1,380,000	100%

Susan

Reactions to Maximizing Her Investment Options

When Susan reviewed her personal assets, she realized she had more in U.S. stocks than in any other kind of asset. (She did not include the trust assets in this computation because she did not own the assets in the trust.)

Her 401(k) assets at her former association were invested in a fixed-income investment with the insurance company ($25,000). Lance's pension assets were invested 20 percent ($100,000) in fixed-income assets and 80 percent ($400,000) in stocks, reflecting his higher risk tolerance. After paying what was due her stepchildren, she still had $150,000 in Lance's stocks. She had $85,000 in her cash account, which included the net proceeds from the sale of the cottage ($50,000).

Susan's Current Asset Allocation

Asset Class	Personal Investments	Retirement Investments	Total Investments	Percentage
Cash	$85,000*		$ 85,000	11%
Fixed income		$125,000	125,000	16%
U.S. stocks	150,000	400,000	550,000	73%
Total	$235,000	$525,000	$760,000	100%

Susan reviewed her situation with Bob O'Brien, her stockbroker. She explained that she wanted to keep $35,000 as a cash reserve in a money market account paying 3 percent to cover any excess expenses she might have in the coming year. This left $50,000 she could add to her investments.

Bob had reviewed the remaining stocks Susan had inherited from Lance ($150,000). Bob recommended selling the stocks Lance had selected (worth $100,000) because Lance bought stock on "hunches" and unfortunately, his hunches weren't always good ones. He recommended that she keep the remaining U.S. stocks ($50,000) in the portfolio. He followed these companies pretty closely and would advise her whether she should make any changes in the future.

Because all of Lance's stocks were U.S. stocks, Bob recommended that she invest half the proceeds of these sales ($100,000) into an international stock mutual fund and half into a global stock fund.

Susan asked Bob what the difference was between international and global funds. He explained that a global fund could invest anywhere in the world, whereas an international fund could invest only in companies based outside the United States. Thus, global funds offered the manager more choices than a purely international or U.S. stock fund offered.

Susan had heard stories about people losing money by investing overseas and expressed her concern to Bob. He explained that investing in non-U.S. securities offered both advantages and risks. In addition to the risks taken with any investment, investing outside the United States involves currency fluctuations, political and social instability, differing securities regulations and accounting standards, limited reliable public information, possible changes in taxation, and periods of illiquidity.

However, he had tried to reduce these risks as much as he could by recommending that Susan invest in mutual funds with diversified portfolios rather individual international stocks. Bob had selected funds that were not limited to investing in one country or one region, thus giving the manager maximum flexibility. He had also chosen funds where the managers had good long-term records for successful management of international stocks. He thought the managers of these funds had much better access to information about international investments than he had. According to the prospectus of these funds, they were invested in companies with proven earnings records, not start-up ventures.

Bob told her that currently about half the global stock fund he was recommending to Susan was invested in companies based outside the United States and the other half in companies based inside the United States. The net result would be that she would have about $75,000 in U.S. stocks ($50,000 in individual stocks and $25,000 in the global mutual fund) and $75,000 in international stocks. He assured her he would be supervising all of these investments on an ongoing basis.

Next, Bob recommended that Susan invest the money she had left from selling the lake cottage ($50,000, now held in her cash reserve) in a mutual fund that invested in real estate investment trust (REIT) stocks. He selected a fund with a good long-term track record. This way, he pointed out, she could participate in the potential growth of commercial real estate but reduce her risk by having a diversified portfolio of different REIT stocks. At the same time, she would receive a competitive dividend of 4.5 percent.

After Bob had made recommendations for her personal investments, he reviewed her retirement investments. Bob thought she had been too conservative with her 401(k) money at her old place of employment—investing it all in a fixed-income investment. She could roll this money over into a "self directed" IRA account where they could select the investments. He would like this money to be invested in a balanced fund, which he thought should be comparatively safe. This fund would be invested 40 percent in bonds, 50 percent in U.S. stocks, and 10 percent in international stocks.

For her new 401(k) plan, he suggested that she provide him with the list of investment options available at her new place of employment. He would review them for her and help her make an appropriate selection for her current contributions that would fit in with the rest of her investments.

Susan thanked Bob for his advice and went home to review the material he had given her. There was a lot to read, and she wanted to make sure she understood what he was suggesting. In addition to all the information he had given her on specific investments, he had provided her with an asset allocation chart. If she followed all his suggestions for her personal investments as well as the 401(k) money, she would have about 5 percent in cash, 14 percent in bonds, 64 percent in U.S. stocks, 10 percent in international stocks, and 7 percent in real estate.[4] Although Susan was a little concerned about international investing, she realized that only about 10 percent of the total portfolio was invested internationally, which didn't look like taking undue risk.

After reviewing Bob's recommendations, Susan realized that he was suggesting what appeared to be a well-diversified but still relatively conservative portfolio for her.

---

4. The value of your home is excluded from the asset allocation chart as it is not considered an investment for this purpose.

Susan's Recommended Asset Allocation

Asset Class	Personal Investments	Retirement Investments	Total Investments	Percentage
Cash	$ 35,000		$ 35,000	5%
Fixed income		$110,000	110,000	14%
U.S. stocks	75,000	412,500	487,500	64%
Int'l stocks	$75,000	2,500	77,500	10%
Real estate	$50,000	None	50,000	7%
Total	**$235,000**	**$525,000**	**$760,000**	**100%**

Audrey

Reactions to Maximizing Her Investment Options

Audrey realized that her current financial situation was not complex. She had sold her home for $425,000, netting $400,000 after paying Georgia her commission. Her cost basis was $225,000 (half the original cost and half the value at the date of John's death), giving her a profit of $175,000. Because this was lower than the $250,000 profit exclusion she was allowed on her primary residence, she would not have to pay any tax on the gain. Her new townhome cost $325,000, and she had paid cash for it. This left her with $75,000 ($400,000 minus $325,000) net proceeds from the sale of her former home. She spent about $15,000 on curtains, rugs, and new furniture, leaving $60,000 to invest.

Audrey still had about $40,000 in her savings account. Adding the $60,000 from her home sale, she now had $100,000 in savings. Mr. Silver wanted her to keep a cash reserve of $25,000 in her savings account "just in case." This left $75,000 she could invest.

John's company stock was worth $200,000. Mr. Silver reiterated his recommendation that she sell at least some of it in an effort to diversify her holdings. She had been so busy with her family, her volunteer work, and her golf that she hadn't done anything yet. He pointed out that the stock had not increased in value since she inherited it a year and a half ago, and if she were going to successfully combat inflation, she needed to have this investment increase in value. This was cause for concern, particularly as both the Standard & Poor's 500 Index and the Dow Jones Industrial Average had risen considerably during this same period. Further, the company had not raised its dividend over the last three years.

Audrey's Current Asset Allocation

Asset Class	Personal Investments	Percentage
Cash	$100,000	33%
Stocks	200,000	67%
Total	$300,000	100%

Mr. Silver recommended that she sell at least half of John's company stock ($100,000). Her cost basis for these shares was $100,000 (their value on the date John died), and because they were in his name, this became her cost basis. Because the stock had not increased in value since John's death, Audrey would not have to pay any long-term capital gain taxes if she sold the shares. Selling the stock would be a big step for Audrey to take because of their long years with the company, but she could not allow this type of feeling to govern monetary decisions that would impact the quality of her life. She thought that because Mr. Silver had consistently given her good advice in the past, it would be wise to listen to him this time.

Mr. Silver suggested that Audrey invest this money in shares of a balanced mutual fund. The particular fund he recommended was usually invested about 60 percent in stocks and 40 percent in cash and bonds. The fund paid 3.5 percent in dividends and had increased in value, on average, 12 percent a year over the past 10 years. Although he cautioned Audrey that past results are no guarantee of future returns, he was encouraged by the consistency of this fund's results over the years.

Mr. Silver suggested she take the $75,000 excess cash she had left from the sale of the home and invest in a tax-free bond fund. Audrey thought this sounded contrary to his previous advice. If he was seeking diversification, why wasn't he investing in a lot of different bonds? He explained that this was exactly why he was recommending the fund approach. This fund invested in 20 or 30 different tax-free bonds throughout the country. Further, the fund invested in general obligation, revenue, and insured bonds. All the bonds were rated A or better, and their average maturity was eight years. The fund paid 4 percent, which in her tax bracket (25 percent) was equivalent to 5.33 percent taxable income. Audrey was currently receiving a 2 percent taxable return from the stock, so a 4 percent tax-free return sounded pretty attractive to her.

Note: To convert tax-free income to taxable income, take the interest rate of the tax-free bond (4 percent) and divide it by (1 minus your federal tax bracket [25 percent]).

Mr. Silver gave Audrey the prospectus and the most recent quarterly and annual reports on the two funds he had recommended. He also asked her to sign a prospectus receipt form that indicated he had given her this information. He recommended that she read the information and then call him with any questions she had. He explained to her it was his intention to ultimately decrease her stock ownership in John's company to about 10 percent of her total portfolio. Making these investments would be the first step in that direction.

Audrey's Recommended Asset Allocation

Asset Class	Personal Investments	Percentage
Cash	$ 25,000	8%
Fixed income	115,000	38%
Stocks	160,000*	54%
Total	$ 300,000	100%

* Keeping $100,000 in John's company stock

ELIZABETH

Reactions to Maximizing Her Investment Options

Elizabeth continued to consider her potential move to Northern Palms, the retirement community in Florida. She was concerned about how to raise the money to pay the entrance fee for the one-bedroom-plus-den apartment she had selected. She had been given the choice of a standard fee (costing $100,000), a 90 percent refundable fee, or a 100 percent refundable entrance fee. If she selected the standard fee, she would still get part of her fee back (prorated for the amount of time she lived there) over the first 60 months of residence. If she chose the higher costing 90 percent or 100 percent refundable entrance fee, when she died her personal representative could sell the apartment and receive all or part of the sales price. However, because Abigail was really her only heir and it appeared she had already provided for her, the standard entrance fee appeared to be the best choice for her. When she considered the amount of time she had already spent visiting Northern Palms, she couldn't imagine why she wouldn't like living there. After all, Abigail had lived there for several years and was very pleased with it.

Elizabeth had $25,000 in her savings account and really didn't want to disturb her trust assets, so to raise the $100,000 entrance fee it looked like the time had come for her to sell her home. Her friend Lucy had recommended a real estate agent, Mr. Winthrop, to her. He came over to see her home and, after inspecting it, suggested she ask $320,000. In fact, he told her that he knew of several potential buyers for her home.

Although Elizabeth thought she really wanted to move to Florida, when faced with a listing agreement to sign by Mr. Winthrop, she got cold feet. It was a long form full of small print, and she thought she should have her lawyer read it before she signed it. She told Mr. Winthrop she needed some time to think over this idea. After all, this had been her home for most of her adult life! Mr. Winthrop said he understood perfectly. He gave her his card and told her to call him with her decision.

Thinking about selling the home reminded her of the land in Vermont, which she had ignored up until now. If that were sold, she would have those proceeds as well for the entrance fee or to invest. Besides, selling it would simplify her life, and she was interested in doing everything she could to make her life easier. She called the real estate firm in Vermont through whom she and Ben had bought the land. She told the real estate agent who answered the phone she wanted to sell the lot. This was an easy decision for her to make because even if she didn't move, she had no use for the land. The agent she spoke with said she thought she could sell it for $50,000.

As she looked at her assets, Elizabeth seemed to be in pretty good shape. She had $25,000 in her savings account. If she sold the home for $320,000, she would net about $300,000 after paying Mr. Winthrop his 6 percent commission. She could pay the Northern Palms entrance fee of $100,000 from the proceeds. Although she would have a profit when she sold her home, the $250,000 tax exclusion for a single person selling a primary residence meant that she would owe no taxes on the sale, which would leave her with $200,000 to add to her $25,000 savings. When she sold the land, she would have $50,000 more, which would give her a total of $275,000 cash.

Elizabeth's Current Asset Allocation

Asset Class	Personal Investments	Percentage
Cash	$ 25,000	4%
Fixed income (trust)	100,000	35%
Stocks (trust)	300,000	52%
Real estate (lot)	50,000	9%
Total	$575,000	100%

14

Basic Investment Guidelines

If I am not for myself, who is?
—Rabbi Hillel

THERE ARE SEVERAL GOOD BOOKS about investing, some of which we have listed in the financial bibliography. In this chapter we will not try to cover everything you need to know about investment management but rather will try to highlight what we consider to be the basic guidelines to successful investing.

Many of you have never been particularly interested in investments, but now circumstances have forced you to pay more attention to your financial situation. Acquiring knowledge about investments is just like learning in any field. At first you start with a little information. After a while you learn more, and as time goes on your overall knowledge increases. Unfortunately, this is a field that changes constantly. Just when you think you have grasped all you need to know, the tax laws change, a new kind of investment is introduced, or your personal situation changes.

After your husband's death, you may have been overwhelmed by all you needed to know. Initially, you dealt with the basics—making sure you had enough income to cover your expenses and determining your assets and liabilities. Then you identified and prioritized your financial objectives. Hopefully you obtained expert advice as to how to best meet these objectives. In the process, some of you may have decided you enjoyed understanding your investments and actively pursued this new interest. Others of you tolerated it because you knew you needed to know enough to survive. Whichever group you fall into, let us share with you what we think are the some basic guidelines to successful investing. Utilize them as you see fit based on your need, comfort level, and interest.

RULE no. 1: DON'T SPEND PRINCIPAL NOW THAT YOU MAY NEED IN THE FUTURE

When you are first widowed, you should avoid any and all large discretionary expenditures until you and your advisors have looked at your total picture. Initially, your inheritance may seem to be more than you will ever need, so you may be tempted to splurge and spend some of it immediately on various items such as redecorating your home, buying a new car, or taking an expensive vacation. We have seen widows go through substantial sums of money in five or ten years by withdrawing money periodically from their principal.

Fortunately—or unfortunately—all of us are living longer. If inflation continues to average 3 percent a year, as it has over the past 10 years, your expenses will double every 24 years. Thus, if you need $50,000 after taxes to cover your expenses annually now, in 24 years you will need $100,000—just to buy the same things $50,000 covers today.

Although 24 years from now may seem a long way off, the point to keep in mind is that the cost of living is not declining and may in fact increase in the future. You need to make sure that you have enough money to cover your expenses later. Your principal cannot grow nor can your income increase if you are spending your principal as well as income to cover costs. Money may not buy happiness as you grow older, but it certainly can make you a lot more comfortable!

RULE no. 2: TO KEEP PACE WITH RISING COSTS, INVEST FOR TOTAL RETURN AS WELL AS FOR CURRENT INCOME

The difference between these two kinds of returns is often confused in many investors' minds. The terms *total return* and *current return* are often used interchangeably, but they should not be. The current return (or yield) provided by an investment is the annual income you receive each year divided by the current market price of the stock. For instance, a stock that pays an annual dividend of 50 cents and sells for $10 per share yields 5 percent.

Total return represents the change in price of a stock over a stated period of time, as well as any income paid by the stock. For instance, taking the example above, if you paid $10 per share for a stock at the beginning of the year and by the end of the year it was selling for $12 per share, you would have a $2 gain. In addition, during the same year you received the dividend of 50 cents. If you add the gain in value of the asset ($2) plus the dividend paid (50 cents), your total return was $2.50. If you divide this number ($2.50) by the original cost of $10, your total return equals 25 percent.

While it is important for you to receive good income from your investments in the form of interest or dividends, it is also important for your assets to increase in value to keep pace with inflation. Thus, you should focus on the total return of your investments as well as the current return.

RULE no. 3: INVEST IN STOCKS AS WELL AS IN FIXED-INCOME INVESTMENTS

If you need your investments to increase in value over time, then you should invest at least some percentage of your assets in stocks. Some widows want to invest only in fixed-income investments that provide current income, thinking they are avoiding risk. Actually, these widows are taking more risk by confusing certainty with safety. The fact that a U.S. Treasury bond, a certificate of deposit, or an annuity will pay a fixed rate of income for a certain period of time is very appealing. However, as we have previously stated, fixed-income investments historically don't grow in value.

If you had invested $10,000 in six-month U.S. Treasury bills at the beginning of 1975 and reinvested the income, by the end of 2004 you would have had $59,870. If, instead, on January 1, 1975, you had invested $10,000 in the Standard & Poor's 500 Composite Index[1] and reinvested the dividends, by the end of 2004 you would be worth $471,281. Quite a difference!

We have seen some advisors recommend the "Rule of 100" when deciding what percentage of your portfolio should be in stocks and what percentage in bonds. According to this rule, you subtract your age from 100, and the resulting number is the percentage you should hold in stocks. This would mean if you are 70 years old, you should have 30 percent of your assets in stocks and 70 percent in bonds. We think such arbitrary rules don't work. Every person's circumstances are different, and effective asset allocation is more complex than using such a simplistic formula.

---

[1] Standard & Poor's 500 Composite Index is an unmanaged measure of relatively large U.S. stocks. While it is not possible to invest directly in an index, you can invest in an index fund. Figures shown are past results and are not predictive of results in future periods. Investments are not FDIC-insured, nor are they deposits of or guaranteed by a bank or any other entity.

RULE no.4: DON'T PUT ALL
YOUR EGGS IN ONE BASKET—
DIVERSIFICATION REDUCES RISK

Diversification—investing in several different types of assets—reduces risk. For example, let's compare two individuals who invest $100,000. The first person selects an investment that earns 8 percent annually. At the end of 20 years, her investment is worth $466,096. Not a bad record!

The second person divides her $100,000 among five different investments—$20,000 each. After 20 years, the first investment is a total failure, and she loses all her money. The second investment breaks even, and she gets her $20,000 back. The third investment earns 5 percent, the fourth 10 percent, and the fifth 15 percent. Interestingly enough, this person would have $534,947 at the end of 20 years—almost $100,000 more than the first investor! Diversification lowered the second person's overall risk while allowing her to realize an even higher total return than she would have otherwise.[2]

	Initial Investment	Average Annual Return	Value after 20 Years
Investor A	$100,000	8%	$466,000
Investor B	$ 20,000	(total loss)	$ 0
	20,000	0	20,000
	20,000	5	53,066
	20,000	10	134,550
	20,000	15	327,331
Total			$534,947

---

[2] Diversification does not guarantee against loss. It is a method used to manage risk.

RULE no. 5: DIVERSIFY WITHIN ASSET
CLASSES, BUT DON'T OVERDO IT

To reduce your risk further, we think you should diversify not only among different kinds of assets but also *within asset classes.* For instance, in the fixed-income asset category, you might own both government and corporate bonds. If you are in a higher tax bracket (28 percent or higher), you should consider investing in tax-free municipal bonds. With respect to stocks, we think you should own both U.S. and international stocks.

By diversifying your assets among different types of assets as well as within asset types, the likelihood is that you will keep pace with inflation as well as reduce the fluctuations of the overall value of your portfolio. At any given time, one group of assets may do poorly while another does well, so they offset each other. This is why we recommend this approach.

Although diversification among and within asset classes is important, you should not overdiversify. If one-half of a $100,000 portfolio is in two stocks and the other one-half is invested in 23 stocks, the portfolio lacks balance. Let's say 25 percent of your portfolio is in one stock. If it doubles in value, you will be very happy, but if it loses 50 percent of its value, you will be very upset. On the other hand, if one of your smaller positions triples in value, it won't make much difference to your total wealth. Thus, you should have balance among different kinds of assets as well as within asset classes.

RULE no. 6: BUY GOOD-QUALITY
INVESTMENTS

It is difficult to predict exactly when a particular asset class is going to do better than another. Therefore, to reduce risk we recommend that you diversify your investments among different kinds of assets, balance your assets so that no one position dominates your portfolio, and select only good-quality investments in every asset category. In the investment field, *good quality* refers to investments that have a demonstrated record of consistent success over a number of years.

When you are buying bonds (either municipal or corporate), you are safer buying ones with a credit rating of A or better. If you buy less financially sound bonds with lower ratings, you will receive more income than you would from a better-rated company, but you are also taking more risk with your principal.

If you are selecting a good-quality stock, you want to buy a company that has a history of increasing earnings and dividends. You also want a stock with a reasonable price-earnings ratio. (The price-earnings ratio is the current market price of the stock divided by the last 12 months' earnings per share.) As a general rule, the lower the price-earnings ratio, the less risk you are taking. The higher this number, the more risk you are taking.

If you are buying a mutual fund, ask to see its long-term performance record. Look at last year's record, then the average performance over the last five years and over the last ten years. You want to see how the fund has performed in both good and (more important) in bad markets. You also want to make sure that the manager or managers who created the record are still managing the assets at the fund.

Does this mean a fund which was started recently is not a good investment? Not necessarily. It really depends on the previous track record of the manager.

It is also very important to compare apples with apples. In other words, compare a particular fund's record with other funds with similar investment objectives (such as growth or income) or composition (such as international stocks). Performance of funds goes in cycles. One year, smaller-company stocks will not go up; the next year they may go through the roof. One year, large-company U.S. stock funds may do very well and large-company international stock funds do less well; a couple of years later the reverse may be true. You can find this information in financial periodicals or ask your advisor to show you what the recommended fund has done in comparison with the average fund in the same category over various periods.

RULE No. 7: DON'T CHASE PERFORMANCE

You'll usually make more money with a stock that produces consistent modest gains year after year than with one that has big gains most years and big losses occasionally. For example, would you rather invest $10,000 in Stock X, which returned 10 percent annually each year for five years, or the same amount in Stock Y, which gained 20 percent the first year, 15 percent in the second year, and 20 percent in the third year, lost 20 percent the fourth year, and gained 15 percent the fifth year?

Most people would choose Stock Y because Stock Y did better than Stock X every year except the fourth year. However, if you look at the chart below, Stock X would have been the better choice (remember the tortoise and the hare fable!).

With $10,000 invested in Stock X, at the end of the fifth year you would have $16,105. With Stock Y, at the end your $10,000 would have been worth $15,235. In fact, to regain the 20 percent loss in value in Stock Y you took in the fourth year ($3,312), you would need a 25 percent gain in value in the fifth year to get back to the $16,560 you had at the end of year three. In other words, it is more important to seek consistent performance than spectacular gains that entail taking more risk.

	Stock X Value		Stock Y Value	
	Annual Gain	Annual Year-End	Value Gain (Loss)	Year-End
Starting Value		$10,000		$10,000
Year 1	+10%	11,000	+20%	12,000
Year 2	+10%	12,100	+15%	13,800
Year 3	+10%	13,310	+20%	16,560
Year 4	+10%	14,641	–20%	13,248
Year 5	+10%	16,105	+15%	15,235

RULE no. 8: AVOID RISKY INVESTMENTS

We have told you that you can reduce risk by investing for total return, diversifying your investments, and selecting good-quality investments. In addition, you should avoid investments that are generally considered speculative, such as commodities futures, put-and-call options, and penny stocks (previously discussed in chapter 13 under other assets).

What may not be as obvious a risk is investing in collectibles such as art, antiques, jewelry, Oriental rugs, and stamp or coin collections. Collectibles do not pay you current income. They may or may not grow in value, but if you need money, you might have to sell them. Often you will find that you are unable to sell your collectibles for what you paid for them or for what you think they are worth when you need the money. We are not saying you shouldn't buy collectibles for personal enjoyment, but don't confuse buying collectibles with making solid financial investments. Stock and bond certificates may not provide you with pleasure, but, properly selected, stocks and bonds will provide you with the income you need to support a comfortable lifestyle! Buy collectibles with your surplus money.

RULE no. 9: IF SOMETHING SOUNDS TOO GOOD TO BE TRUE, IT IS!

The papers are full of stories of unscrupulous con artists who take advantage of a widow's lack of investment knowledge or loneliness. The problem is that clever salespeople can make a risky investment sound safe.

Keep in mind that any time you are promised a higher return from an investment than is available from a good-quality investment, you are running the risk of losing all or part of your money. For instance, if a 30-year U.S. Treasury bond is paying 5 percent and you are offered an investment that pays 12 percent, this is a red flag. There is a strong possibility that such an investment involves taking unnecessarily high risk.

Our best advice: If someone you don't know and hasn't been personally recommended to you calls you on the telephone to offer a high-return investment, hang up. If you are interested in what the caller has to offer, ask the person to send you the information in writing. Even if you think you understand the material you are sent, show it to a professional financial advisor to review before making a commitment.

The salesperson will most likely use phrases such as "guaranteed" and "can't miss." Don't be taken in by the pitch that this is a "once-in-a-lifetime opportunity" or that you "must make the investment immediately or this special offer will never be repeated."

As we discussed in chapter 5, we strongly suggest that you invest only with someone who has been recommended to you by another knowledgeable person and that you make no investments until you have interviewed at least two different advisors in person at their offices.

One final word of caution: Widows are often lured into investing in lotteries or buying magazines with the hope they will win the big cash prize. Statistically, your chances of winning are very slim. Don't spend your money this way—unless you can afford to lose it!

RULE no. 10: UNDERSTAND THAT THERE IS NO PERFECT TIME TO INVEST

Many investors worry about the market being too high when they invest. They are concerned that once they invest, the market may go down and they will lose money. Unfortunately, whether your investments immediately go up in value after you buy them is really a matter of timing. As you will see in the examples given here, if you are investing for the long term (as you should be), selecting the perfect time to invest really doesn't make that much difference to the ultimate outcome.

For instance, we looked at what would happen if an individual had invested $5,000 a year in the stocks in the Standard & Poor's 500 Composite Index for a 25-year period ending December 31, 2004. Each year, in this scenario, the widow had invested her money on the worst day (when the market was selling at its highest level). Over the period studied, she invested a total of $125,000. At the end of 2004, her investment was worth $707,910, which was an average annual compound rate of 11.77 percent

Next, look at what would have happened if the same widow had made her investment each year on the best day (when the market hit its low point for the year). In this case, after 25 years her account would have been worth $925,205 at the end of 2004, for an average annual compound rate of 13.12 percent. Obviously, she would have been happier with the second result, but certainly she should be pleased with the first.

In summary, there are good times and bad times in the stock market, but, over the long haul, any day is a good day to invest!

RULE no. 11: Don't Try to Time The Market

It is difficult to stay calm when the stock market goes down, but it is important not to panic and get out of the market. Generally speaking, history has demonstrated that the longer you remain invested in stocks, the greater the chance that your investment will grow. (Of course, this assumes you have selected good-quality stocks in the first place!)

The chart given here demonstrates the benefits of buying and holding, assuming you had invested $10,000 in the Standard & Poor 500 Composite Index at the beginning of 1995 and held it for a 10-year period (1995-2004).

If you had held the stocks for:	Your Investment would be worth:
The whole period	$26,388
Missed the 10 best days	$16,451
Missed the 20 best days	$11,335
Missed the 30 best days	$ 8,134
Missed the 40 best days	$ 6,118

None of the market's 10 best days was consecutive, and four of the 10 best days were in one year, while five of the years did not have any of the best days. Amazingly enough, this chart shows that if you had missed the 30 best days, you would have actually lost money!

Although it is sometimes easier said than done, keep in mind that you are investing for the long term, and try not to be concerned about short-term volatility. Remember, investing is a marathon, not a sprint!

RULE no. 12: KNOW WHEN ASSETS SHOULD BE SOLD

Although we are big believers in buying good-quality assets and holding them for the long term, there are times when you should sell investments. When major changes occur within a company or within an industry that negatively impact your investment, you need to consider selling your holdings. For example, a company that once was very good in its field may have new management that is not as strong as previous management. A product that once was dominant in its field may no longer have the same dominance. A manager of a particular mutual fund who did very well might have moved to another fund, or the manager of a smaller fund that did well might not do as well after the fund grew in size.

The best test of whether you should continue to hold an asset is to ask yourself if you would buy it today if you had the cash. If the honest answer is no, then you should sell it. Let's refute some of the various excuses we hear for not selling an investment:

- *Excuse 1: "I can't sell it—my mother gave it to me."* This excuse is based on emotional attachment to a particular investment. It might be stock in the company your father worked for or stock that your mother gave you or stock that did well for you in the past. Recognize that what was good in the past may not still be good in today's rapidly changing environment.

- *Excuse 2: "I don't want to sell it because I will have to pay too much in taxes on the gain."* Although we recognize that people don't like to pay taxes, if you don't follow your advisor's recommendations to sell, you may find that a year from now you no longer have any taxes to pay because the gain has evaporated! (If you are concerned about having money to pay taxes, we recommend that if you make a profit when you sell an asset, put aside enough money from the proceeds to pay capital gains taxes and reinvest the difference.)

- *Excuse 3: "I want to wait for it to go back to the price I paid for it before I sell it."* This third excuse is used by those who don't want to admit they have made a mistake. Actually, your advisor is not happy telling you that you should take a loss on something he or she recommended, but if there is bad news about a stock, such as fraud on the part of the management or a disastrous earnings decline that looks as if it may be sustained, it is time to sell and reinvest in something that looks more promising. Remember, not every one of your stocks or funds will go up (see the example in Rule no. 2); what is important is that the total portfolio increases in value.

- *Excuse 4: "The last time I sold a stock, it went up after I sold it."* It is true that sometimes after you sell a stock it continues to go up despite what appears to be bad economic news. This happens, but what is more important is to review what you did with the proceeds from the sale. If you put it under a mattress, the sales decision was not a good one. On the other hand, if you reinvest this money and your new investment does as well as or better than the asset you sold, then you have made the right decision.

RULE no. 13: DON'T LET SAVING TAXES DICTATE YOUR INVESTMENT DECISIONS

While you should be aware of the tax consequences of investments you make, you shouldn't let saving taxes be your paramount concern. For example, widows who are concerned about receiving as much income as possible might think the best solution is to buy tax-free investments. This inclination is understandable but not advisable. After determining your tax bracket, your advisor will discuss with you whether investing part of your money in tax-free bonds makes sense for you.

Under current income-tax laws, long-term capital gains on assets held longer than a year and qualified stock dividends are taxed at a maximum rate of 15 percent, whereas interest from taxable bonds are taxed at your personal income tax rate, which is usually higher. We think this makes investing in stocks preferable to investing in taxable bonds from both a tax and a growth potential point of view.

Some widows are concerned about the potential estate taxes their children might have to pay on their estate when they die. The obvious solution is to give away your money while you are alive to ensure that the size of the estate at your death will be low enough that no estate taxes will be due. This is an admirable goal, but one that needs to be made based on your total financial situation and estimated personal future needs.

RULE no. 14: EDUCATE YOURSELF

Regardless of your interest in investments, try to become more informed. You don't need to know all the answers, but you should know enough to ask the right questions.

There are various ways to become more knowledgeable. Go to your public library or nearby bookstore to find personal finance books. Given how often the economic climate and tax laws change, be sure the books you select are current (see our financial bibliography at the end of the book). You might want to consider taking adult education courses on financial planning and investments offered by your local community college or university. You also might find it helpful to subscribe to a personal finance magazine such as *Kiplinger's Personal Finance* or *Smart Money*. Read the business section of your newspaper regularly, particularly the Sunday edition.

If you want to learn more about stocks, if only to better understand what your advisors are telling you, consider joining an investment club. These clubs provide a social setting in which you can learn more about the fundamentals of investing. It is a good way to meet other people who are interested in educating themselves. For additional information, contact the National Association of Investment Clubs (NAIC), 711 West 13 Mile Road, Madison Heights, MI 48071; 248-583-6242; www.betterinvesting.org. The association's approach to investing is a disciplined one. If you are not ready for a club, you can join the NAIC as an individual member and receive its monthly magazine, which focuses on stock investing. An informed investor is a better investor.

RULE no. 15: KEEP GOOD RECORDS

Previously we have discussed record keeping in general. Keeping good records of what you paid for your investment is particularly important, both for yourself and your accountant. Record keeping does not have to be too complicated. You can use the loose-leaf notebook method, allocating a page to each investment. We have provided a sample page for mutual fund records (see figure 14.1). You can use a similar format for individual stocks or bonds. In addition, there are several computer programs available that can help you keep these records.

Use whichever method is easiest for you, but keep the records in one place where they are accessible to you and your advisor when needed.

When you make your initial investment, record the date you bought the investment, the type of investment, and the number of shares you bought. If it is a stock or bond, record the price per share you paid and the total amount of your investment. Then as this investment pays income, whether you take it in the form of cash or reinvest it, record this amount and the date paid. If you reinvest the dividend in additional shares, then record how many full or fractional shares you bought each time. If you inherited the investment from your husband, then the value in the estate valuation becomes your cost and the date of acquisition is the date this valuation is made.

FIGURE 14.1 Sample Page of Record Keeping

INVESTMENT:	XYZ STOCK
WHERE HELD:	XYZ COMPANY
	22 MAIN STREET
	KANSAS CITY, MISSOURI
ACCOUNT NUMBER:	#225-352
PHONE NUMBER:	800-222-3333
WEB SITE:	XYZCOMPANY.COM
HOW OFTEN INCOME PAID:	(MONTHLY or QUARTERLY)
REGISTRATION NAME:	JANE B. BROWN, TRUSTEE
	JANE B. BROWN REVOCABLE TRUST
	DATED 1/1/96

DATE	HOW BOUGHT	# SHARES	COST/ SHARE	AMOUNT PAID	TOTAL COST
1/1/00	CHECK	100	$10.32	$1,032	$1,032
3/31/00	DIVIDEND	1	10.00	10	1,042
6/15/00	2 for 1 split	101	0	0	$1,042

When you sell shares, record the transaction on the same sheet. If you sell all your shares, recording it is fairly easy, and you have the information available for your tax preparer. If you sell some of your shares, then life gets more complicated. You can designate the particular shares you sold by date and cost. Then when you sell shares in the same company a year later, you will know the remaining cost. It is complex, but if you have kept careful records, the process is much easier.

RULE no. 16: REVIEW YOUR INVESTMENTS REGULARLY

You may have little interest in your investments other than in the income they generate. If your investments enable you to maintain a comfortable lifestyle, you might be lulled into complacency. However, you must take the time to sit down with your advisor at least once a year to review your investments. Most advisors will provide you with a quarterly or semiannual written report that gives you current market values as well as a commentary on your holdings.

Ignorance is not an excuse. Preservation and growth of your assets is the key to your comfort now and in the future, and you can't afford to ignore them. Learn how to read the statements you receive from your advisor. If you don't understand them, ask your advisor to explain them to you, and if the explanation is not clear, ask again. Don't be embarrassed—the statements are often more complex than they need to be. After all, it is your money, and you need to know what is happening to it.

Economic conditions change, investment options change, and your personal investment objectives may change during the course of a given year. It is important that your portfolio be adjusted accordingly. However, your advisor won't know your situation is different unless you say so. If investments are not your strong suit, bring a more knowledgeable family member or friend with you to meet with your advisor.

On the other hand, don't obsess about your investments. If you want to monitor them regularly, we suggest you update your records on a monthly or, at the most, weekly basis. Keep in mind the big picture. Long-term trends, not short-term fluctuations, are the key to success (see Rule no. 11).

RULE no. 17: GET PROFESSIONAL ADVICE

Although it is important to be a knowledgeable investor, be aware that the field of finance is complex and continually changing. It is not an area for amateurs, particularly when your current and future livelihood depends on your investment results. It is important that the advisor you select to assist you with your investments have experience, expertise, integrity, and empathy.

We think you need a professional financial expert to guide you particularly in the initial stages of widowhood, but it is also important for you to assume the ultimate responsibility for your decisions. Ask your advisor to put all recommendations in writing with supporting documentation. For instance, if your advisor recommends that you invest in a portfolio of stocks, the letter should tell you which stocks are recommended, why these particular stocks were selected, and what income you can expect to receive from them (as well as when and how). The advisor should also put in writing how often you will receive a written review of your investments (usually quarterly or semiannually) and what the charges will be to manage your investments. It is important to understand exactly what you are doing before you do it.

RULE NO. 18: LEARN FROM YOUR MISTAKES

All of us, but particularly widows, are concerned about making mistakes. Even if you follow all these rules, you still may make some decisions that don't turn out as well as you had hoped. Keep in mind you don't always have to be right (see rule no. 4). If you make a decision that later you regret, don't let this prevent you from moving ahead. Instead, identify what was wrong with the decision you made and then move on. Difficult as it is to accept, it is important to realize that making mistakes is part of your learning process.

SUMMARY AND CONCLUSION

We think these 18 guidelines should help you when you are investing. Take the time to reread them periodically because as you gain more experience, they will mean even more to you than they did initially. After a while, you may find you actually enjoy monitoring your investments. It is a great feeling to be in control of your own financial future.

Diane

Reactions to the Basic Rules of Investing

Diane spent a lot of time putting together a workable budget. She had decided what to do about the children's schools and that she needed to go back to work. These were all issues that required immediate action. She had not yet addressed what to do with Mark's pension plan, handled by Scott Truitt, and it was time to do that. She had not liked Scott when she met him and had been intimidated by his glib manner, which led her to postpone dealing with the pension money.

Diane had been receiving monthly statements for the pension fund from Scott. When she last met with Dorothy, Diane had given her a copy of the most recent report. Dorothy asked to see all past copies of these statements so she could determine what progress, if any, had been made over the past year.

When Dorothy looked at the monthly reports, she was concerned about the amount of activity in the account. There had been five or six transactions per month, yet the account today was worth about the same as it was a year ago. This was during a period when the Standard & Poor's 500 Composite Index had gained 10 percent.

Dorothy shared this information with Diane and suggested that she consider transferring the pension plan to an IRA account that Dorothy would manage. Because Diane would not retire until she was at least 62 and would not be receiving current income from this account, Dorothy suggested that she invest more of this portfolio somewhat more aggressively than her personal portfolio. However, she still would invest this money in well-established mutual funds with good long-term records. She pointed out to Diane that although the stock market over the short term is very unpredictable, over longer periods of time it is less so. She showed her a chart of how the S&P 500 Composite Index had fluctuated over time. It indicated that the longer you were able to hold your stock investments intact, the better they were likely to perform (see rule no. 11).

Dorothy suggested they invest the $300,000 of the retirement account in a portfolio of funds—20 percent in bonds and 80 percent in stock funds. In Diane's personal investment account, Dorothy had selected a high-quality corporate bond fund. In this more growth-oriented retirement account, she instead recommended Diane invest 20 percent ($60,000) in a high-yield bond fund.

She would divide the remaining $240,000 between four stock funds—a U.S. stock fund, an international stock fund, and two global stock funds. One of the global stock funds invested in larger companies and the other in smaller companies throughout the world. Diane expressed some concern about investing internationally. Wouldn't that involve more risk than she should take?

Dorothy reminded her of how long this money would be invested before she needed it. She also pointed out that the international companies this fund bought were well-established ones in stable countries. She would not be investing in emerging Third World companies or in new ventures. Further, the managers who were selecting the investments were experienced in investing outside the United States and had several overseas offices.

Although Diane's risk tolerance initially had been very low, now that she had a better understanding of her financial situation and was working full time she thought she was ready to take some risk. The time had come to be more aggressive with her retirement money, as Dorothy had suggested, because she did not expect to need it for many years. Dorothy had not led her astray thus far, and besides, they would review her investments on an annual basis. Dorothy pointed out to her that they could move to more conservative positions at any time if they became concerned about the stock market.

Diane was pleased with this approach and decided to move the pension plan assets to Dorothy. Just a year ago, she realized, not only would she not have understood what Dorothy was talking about but also, as her personality profile at that time had indicated, she would have lacked the courage to make this decision on her own. What a long way she had come!

Diane's Revised Asset Allocation

Asset Class	Personal Investments	Retirement Investments	Total Investments	Percentage
Cash	$ 80,000		$ 80,000	6%
Fixed income	280,000	$ 60,000	340,000	24%
U.S. stocks	400,000	150,000	550,000	40%
Int'l stocks	320,000	90,000	410,000	30%
Totals	$1,080,000	$300,000	$1,380,000	100%

Susan

Reactions to the Basic Rules of Investing

In an effort to become more knowledgeable about investing, Susan had taken the adult education course on investing that Bob O'Brien, her stockbroker, taught at the local community college. She had read some of the investment books from his recommended reading list and had subscribed to a monthly personal finance magazine. As a result, when Susan read the material Bob had given her, she understood it much better and decided to follow his recommendations.

Now that she had taken care of her personal investments and the trust assets, Susan thought it was time to focus on Lance's pension account ($500,000). She had left the pension assets at Lance's firm to be managed because she thought they would be managed well there and she had been overwhelmed by making the other decisions about selling the cottage, investing the trust assets, and dealing with her mother's care.

Susan decided the time had come to discuss this account with Bob in greater detail. She liked the fact that he had been working as a broker with a well-known investment firm for ten years—it gave her a feeling of confidence in his abilities—and she had learned a lot from his investment class. What he said made sense to her.

He suggested she choose among three different approaches for investing this money. The first approach would involve his helping her select an outside money manager who met a certain number of predetermined criteria, which he would discuss with her. To have this manager handle the portfolio, which would be invested in individual securities, would cost her 1.5 percent of the assets a year. Bob was quite open with Susan, telling her that he would receive part of this fee; however, his job would be to monitor the money manager's performance. If, after giving the manager a reasonable amount of time to perform, he thought she should change managers for any reason, he would recommend she make a change.

The second approach would be to have him select mutual funds managed by the same fund company. Because the total amount of money involved was $500,000 and she would be investing with one management company, the initial purchase fee for these "A" shares would be 2 percent of the amount invested. This initial commission would be included in the price of the shares she purchased. After that initial charge, the mutual fund management group would collect an annual average management fee of about 0.75 percent of the assets managed. If she selected this second approach, Bob indicated he would take responsibility for recommending any changes he deemed appropriate among the funds. He pointed out that once investments were made in the mutual funds, there would be no charge to move among funds within the same management group.

The third approach would be for Bob to buy institutional "F" shares of a group of funds managed by different money management companies. When Susan invested in these funds, she would pay no initial commission to buy the shares, but the annual management fee charged by the mutual fund would be slightly higher than with "A" shares. If she chose this approach, Bob would charge her a one percent annual fee of the assets managed to supervise her portfolio of funds.

Although fees were important, how well the investments had performed in the past was even more important. Susan studied the records for the past five years of the proposed outside money manager as well as the two other fund groups Bob had recommended to her. Bob had told her that past records were no guarantee of future results, but you had to start somewhere! She did note that it appeared that the same managers who had created the records at these funds were still managing the same funds.

After considering the three approaches, Susan decided to go with the third one.

The first approach, which looked like it would cost her $7,500 the first year, did not appeal to her. It was not the cost that bothered her, but rather she didn't like the idea of an outside manager buying individual stocks and bonds without her involvement in the decision-making process. She felt she wouldn't learn anything that way.

As for the second approach, Susan didn't mind paying the initial commission of $10,000, but she preferred not to be limited to one fund management group.

She liked the third approach, which would involve her paying Bob's firm $5,000 the first year, because Bob's fee would be based on the value of the account. That way, if the portfolio did well he would share in the profit, and if the account didn't do well he would not. She also liked the fact that he would be free to choose from different fund management groups. This way she would not have all her eggs in one basket. She would be invested in funds that invested in different companies, and then she would be invested with different fund groups. If diversification was a way to reduce risk, she was in good shape!

Susan realized that she could avoid paying any fees to her broker by buying no-load funds directly from the companies, but she didn't feel sufficiently knowledgeable to take this approach. She preferred to have a financial advisor such as Bob select and monitor her funds, and she was willing to pay him to do it. After all, this was his business, and his job was to make sure that the investments continued to achieve competitive returns. (Of course, management fees associated with the mutual fund expenses still apply.)

Susan signed the appropriate papers to transfer the pension account to Bob's firm. The fee she paid would be subtracted from the account on a quarterly basis in arrears. Bob recommended that the asset allocation be 20 percent bonds, 50 percent U.S. stocks, 20 percent international stocks, and 10 percent REIT stocks.

Susan still had the $25,000 in her 401(k) from her previous association, which she was rolling over into a self-directed IRA. She decided to invest this money in the balanced fund that Bob had suggested to her. This fund would be invested 40 percent in bonds ($10,000), 50 percent in U.S. stocks ($12,500), and 10 percent ($2,500) in international stocks.

Bob also reviewed the investment choices for the 401(k) plan at Susan's new association. He recommended that she invest the maximum amount possible and divide it between two stock funds. One would be a U.S. fund, and the other would be an international stock fund. This amount would be deducted from her paycheck on a monthly basis.

Susan's Asset Allocation Chart

Asset Class	Personal Investments	Retirement Investments	Total Investments	Percentage
Cash	$ 35,000		$ 35,000	5%
Fixed income		$110,000	110,000	14%
U.S. stocks	75,000	262,500	337,500	45%
Int'l stocks	75,000	102,500	177,500	23%
Real estate	50,000	50,000	100,000	13%
Totals	$235,000	$525,000	$760,000	100%

Audrey

Reactions to the Basic Rules of Investing

Audrey read the material Mr. Silver gave her. She liked his recommendation of diversifying her investments, and the idea that she would get higher income from the municipal bonds was very attractive.

The idea of the balanced fund that could invest internationally as well as in the United States also appealed to her. John's company stock had not gained in value over the past year and a half. Initially, she had been pleased that at least she hadn't lost any money, but Mr. Silver had corrected that perspective when he pointed out how much the stock market indexes had gone up during the same period. Because the market indexes had gone up and John's company stock had not, she was not satisfied. To add insult to injury, the company hadn't even increased its dividend.

Audrey appreciated Mr. Silver's sensitivity to the fact that she might be emotionally attached to the stock because it was John's company stock. Actually, although John had always done well with the company and they had had a comfortable life as a result, she had always had some issues with the company's corporate decisions. She realized that she personally no longer had a sentimental attachment to the stock. If the stock wasn't doing well, then she thought she should sell it all.

When she called Mr. Silver to tell him her decision, he was surprised but pleased. Indeed, he was trying to move her in this direction but was prepared to do it gradually. His test for whether to continue to hold a stock was whether he would buy it if he had cash. John's stock was not one he would recommend for purchase to anyone.

The next question was what to do with the proceeds of the stock sale ($200,000). Mr. Silver said because she had made this decision, more money was available for investment now. Therefore he would revise his original recommendations. He would still invest the $75,000 in the tax-free bond fund and $100,000 in the balanced fund. With the additional $100,000 now available he would suggest she invest $50,000 each in a U.S. stock fund paying 1.9 percent and in a global stock fund paying 2.5 percent.

Investment	Amount	Estimated Income
Tax-free bond fund	$ 75,000	$ 3,000
Balanced fund	100,000	3,500
U.S. stock fund	50,000	950
Global fund	50,000	1,240
Total	$275,000	$8,690

Altogether Audrey would receive $8,690 per year from these investments, which was more than she had previously been receiving from John's stock and her money market fund. In fact, her after-tax return would be even higher because $3,000 of the income would come from the municipal bond fund, which meant it would be federally tax free.

When Mr. Silver reran her income/expense statement with these new investments, it appeared that she would have more than sufficient income to cover her expenses. He told her that actually if she wanted to give some more money to her children and grandchildren and/or charities, she could do so out of her current income. However, he suggested she wait to make additional gifts until she had a better idea of what her expenses in her new home would be.

Audrey was pleased with this recommended plan. It seemed to offer diversification as well as balance. Mr. Silver assured her that the funds she was buying were good quality and, therefore, he thought they should grow in value over time. This was important to Audrey because she wanted to be in a position to continue contributing to her grandchildren's education as well as give some more to her pet charities without curtailing any of her other expenses. That was a good feeling!

Audrey's Revised Asset Allocation

Asset Class	Personal Investments	Percentage
Cash	$ 25,000	8%
Fixed income	115,000	38%
U.S. stocks	125,000	42%
Int'l stocks	35,000	12%
Total	$300,000	100%

Although Audrey was very pleased with the investment program Mr. Silver had put together for her, she decided she really would like to learn more about investing. One of her friends from the golf club, Janet Pine, told her about an investment club she belonged to and how much she enjoyed participating in the monthly meetings. Apparently, members of the club didn't have to invest that much money—$50 a month. This group of 15 women met on a monthly basis at lunch to discuss their shared portfolio. The club had been in existence for five years and had purposely stayed small, but one of their members was moving to Florida.

Audrey thought she would like to participate in such a group but wondered how the members would feel about having such a novice join them. She decided to ask Janet if they would consider letting her replace the person who was leaving. Janet suggested she attend the next meeting as her guest, which would give her an idea of whether she would like to join.

Audrey attended the next investment club meeting and found she was fascinated. You could not be a passive bystander at this meeting! The money you invested was the smallest part of the commitment. The group started by reviewing the ten stocks they currently owned and discussed whether they should make any changes. Next they reviewed the amount of cash they had and considered what they should buy. They had selected an industry they thought held potential for growth, and five of the members had prepared reports on the primary companies in the industry. After a long debate, they finally picked a stock they liked and decided to buy 100 shares.

Audrey was concerned that she might be overcommitted with her other activities—the symphony, Reading Is Fundamental, and golf—but she knew it was hard to find one of these clubs to join, and she really wanted to learn more about investing. It looked like a fun way to increase her investment knowledge in a non threatening environment. Besides, it seemed like an interesting group of women. She thought about her strong interest in the investment club and realized that she was at a point where she needed to make some decisions about how and where she spent her time.

She reflected back to the weekend she had just spent with Lionel. He had done everything he could to please her. He had bought her a beautiful plant and had complimented her on the way she had decorated the home. They had gone out to dinner alone on Friday evening. On Saturday night, they had joined the Lyons, her oldest and closest coupled friends, for dinner at a restaurant. She could tell they liked Lionel a lot. The evening went very smoothly with no awkward moments. The men split the bill when it came, and it was like old times.

When they got home, Lionel took her in his arms and told her how much he liked her and her friends. She understood by his body language that he wanted to sleep with her. Her instinct was to say no, but another side of her thought she really ought to see how she felt about having sex with a man other than John, and she was attracted to Lionel. She allowed herself to walk upstairs to her bedroom with him, still feeling indecisive but lulled by the wine, the dinner, and the comfort level of the evening. It had been so long since she had been held and kissed by a man. She did miss that type of physical closeness.

Lionel was very considerate of her sexually, which she appreciated. It was easier than she had imagined. However, she slept fitfully and spent a good bit of the night thinking. If she were going to attach to someone, it would be Lionel. By morning, she had reached a conclusion. She knew she had to talk to Lionel and share with him her feelings. She told him he was the first man she had slept with since John's death. Certainly, it wasn't anything Lionel had done, but she didn't feel right about what had transpired the night before and wasn't sure she would feel right about it with anyone. She acknowledged to him her recognition of his need for a permanent relationship with someone and her respect for this need. It was just that at this point in her life she was not interested in a relationship of this sort. Lionel, the charming Southern gentleman that he was, said he was disappointed but assured Audrey that he appreciated her being honest with him.

The remainder of the weekend was very pleasant and smooth except that Lionel slept in the guest bedroom and gave her a warm, friendly kiss on the cheek before retiring for the evening, in contrast with the long, passionate kiss of Saturday night. By the end of the weekend, Audrey was convinced that she valued her current lifestyle and wanted to maintain it rather than become involved with a man, even one as nice as Lionel. She realized that aspect of her life was over, at least for the present. Right now, she wanted to concentrate on her volunteer work, her female friends, her golf, and, above all, her children and grandchildren. She thought that most women would jump at the opportunity for a relationship with someone as considerate and warm as Lionel, but for her it was not right. She had bittersweet feelings, but in her heart of hearts she knew she had made the right decision.

Elizabeth

Reactions to the Basic Rules of Investing

With each person she spoke to, Elizabeth grew closer to making a decision about moving to Florida. Mrs. Greenfield, her accountant, had told her that the retirement community was financially sound and that she had adequate income to cover her expenses. Mr. Grossfeldt, her attorney, had reviewed the legal aspects of the move, and there seemed to be no obstacles there. Sam Weatherly advised her not to buy the long-term care insurance because it would be expensive to buy at her age and it appeared she would be able to afford to pay the expenses of the nursing home facility at Northern Palms if needed. Mr. Winthrop, the real estate agent, had told her she should be able to sell her home for about $300,000. In addition, she would have the $50,000 from the sale of the Vermont property, which has just been sold.

Elizabeth was still reluctant to sever her ties with her church. She thought she should discuss these feelings with Pastor Appletorn. He had always been there for her. When they met, he assured her that, while they would miss her at the church, their loss should not be the primary consideration as to whether or not she should move to Florida. From the information she had given him, it seemed that this move would be good for her. After all, Florida was not so far away that she couldn't come back to visit.

While she was meeting with Pastor Appletorn, Elizabeth asked him about a brochure she received from the church a couple of months ago. It described something called a charitable gift annuity. As she understood it, she could transfer some money to this charity, and in return the charity would pay her income for the rest of her life. She could set it up so that if she predeceased Abigail, Abigail would receive the same amount of income from this annuity for the rest of her life. The brochure she was looking at said the current income from the annuity would be 6.5 percent, payable on a quarterly basis. That sounded attractive to her, particularly when compared with the income she received from other investments.

Pastor Appletorn told Elizabeth that the charitable gift annuity was quite popular with retirees. They liked it because they could have their cake and eat it too—that is, they could receive a competitive level of income for their lifetime and that of a designated beneficiary, and, ultimately, the church would benefit. He emphasized that this was an irrevocable gift. In other words, once Elizabeth invested in the charitable gift annuity, she couldn't change her mind. He explained that approximately 64 percent of this income would be tax free for the first 15 years. Then the income would be totally taxable. In addition to regular monthly income, she would also get an initial charitable tax deduction. Because she and Abigail would receive lifetime income, this deduction would not be as high as it would be if she donated the money outright.

Pastor Appletorn said he would be glad to give her an estimate of how much her deduction would be if Elizabeth wouldn't mind giving him her age and Abigail's. Without hesitation, Elizabeth told him that she was 76 and Abigail was 77. Pastor Appletorn told her if she invested $10,000 in a charitable gift annuity, she would receive a current deduction from her taxable income of $3,783. He further explained that this deduction changed monthly based on IRS rates.

He suggested she review the idea with her accountant and/or her lawyer. He said he'd be glad to answer any questions either of them might have. He also mentioned that her friend Lucy had invested in the charitable gift annuity and, as far as he knew, was pleased with her decision to do so.

Although Pastor Appletorn used an example of a $10,000 contribution, he told Elizabeth that the contribution could be as little as $5,000. Elizabeth thought this information was very helpful. She did not want to tell Pastor Appletorn without first discussing it with Mrs. Greenfield and Mr. Grossfeldt, but she was thinking of investing as much as $50,000 from the proceeds of the home in this charitable gift annuity. Because Elizabeth planned for the church to ultimately inherit part of her estate, she thought why not give it now so she would have the benefit of a tax deduction and greater income? She was about to receive the $50,000 from the Vermont lot sale. Assuming she sold the home soon, she would have another $200,000 even after she paid the Northern Palms entrance fee. It appeared that she would have more than enough cash available to finance her move and anything she wanted to buy for her new apartment.

Elizabeth took these statements to Mr. Grossfeldt and asked him for his opinion about the idea of giving $50,000 to the church in the form of a charitable gift annuity when she sold her home. He liked the idea of the charitable gift annuity but recommended that she move more slowly. He suggested that she give $25,000 to the church now and the other $25,000 after she had settled in her new apartment in Florida. Actually, he thought she should consider giving the second $25,000 to Ben's university. He was sure that the university would be able to offer a similar type of annuity. In this way she wouldn't put all her cash in one charitable basket.

Mr. Grossfeldt reminded Elizabeth that if she predeceased Abigail, Abigail would receive income from the trust as well as from the charitable gift annuity. When Abigail died, the trust assets would be split equally between the church and Ben's college. Because Elizabeth had already planned to split her estate between the two charities, it would be logical that she invest equal amounts in charitable gift annuities with the two charities.

Elizabeth liked Mr. Grossfeldt's approach to the gifting. After all, there was no urgency to do everything at once, and this way she kept her options open. She would talk to the people at Ben's university once she was settled. Actually, she remembered that the nice young man from the university with whom she had spoken had mentioned that he visited Florida regularly to see alumni, so perhaps he could see her there.

Elizabeth's Resulting Asset Allocation

Asset Class	Personal Investments	Percentage
Cash	$ 25,000	4%
Fixed income	250,000*	44%
Trust stock	300,000	52%
Total	$575,000	100%

*Includes $50,000 charitable gift annuity

15

Establishing Your New Identity

Life can only be understood backwards;
but it must be lived forwards.
—Soren Kierkegaard

TYPICALLY, THE NEED TO COPE with the immediate demands of widowhood does not allow time or energy for reflection on where you are on a personal level following this traumatic event in your life. In most cases, such reflection does not occur until several years later. By then, the passage of time has softened the acuteness of the pain you have experienced, and a number of important decisions have been made. You have reached the point where you are beyond simply responding to one demand or another. You have caught your breath and are now able to begin planning for the future.

For some of you, major changes will have taken place, and you will feel you are living a life quite disparate from the one you shared with your husband, whereas for others of you the changes will be much less dramatic and more subtle. You are ready to give some thought to where you are on a personal level today and where you would like to be in the future. What steps need to be taken to enable you to achieve that which you desire to achieve? What, if anything, do you want to change? Are you content with your present lifestyle, or do you feel you have resigned yourself to just existing?

Regardless of your previous behavior patterns, it is likely you have become more self-reliant. Usually with self-reliance comes improved self-confidence and a better self-image. You are undoubtedly familiar with check writing, tax forms, estate matters, and other aspects of life in our changing times. If you had feared making mistakes in the past, you should now be well beyond that stage of your widowhood. We hope that you have mastered the handling of various unfamiliar tasks.

ESTABLISHING PERSONAL GOALS

Widowhood has changed your life in many ways. We hope that by this time you have refocused and are considering your personal goals for the future.

Are there areas of your life you would like to explore that you have never dared to consider? This may sound trite, but it's never too late to try to realize a dream. Obviously, your future plans will be affected by your health, age, financial status, and family situation. However, the time has come to think about yourself and your personal goals.

If you had thought it would be fascinating to explore a certain subject, take a chance and enroll in a class in that subject. Investigate a sport you've always wanted to try. Consider a hobby. Take a trip. Perhaps you had wanted to get involved in some volunteer work but were reluctant to express an interest because you anticipated a negative response from your husband. Now is the hour for you! If you are in a position to focus primarily on yourself, allow yourself to do so—place your own needs above those of others. If you are someone who grew up believing it was your responsibility to always put the needs of others before your own, this may be a foreign and uncomfortable role. Your old beliefs may have worked for you in your married life, but they are not constructive in your present state, which requires you to make and implement decisions for yourself.

All too often, at this point in your life, you will have time to think about the choices you made and possibly the choices you didn't make. Were you an active decision maker, or were the decisions you made in response to what you thought was expected of you or accepted by others as the appropriate path for you?

REMARRIAGE: ISSUES TO CONSIDER

For some of you, embarking on a new path will bring a new relationship. If so, give some thought to the way in which you would like to see this relationship evolve. Would your first choice be marriage? If so, what do you need to consider? It is likely that the man with whom you become involved now has previously been married and that his marriage ended either in divorce or with the death of his former wife. What are his family obligations? Does he have children for whom he is financially responsible? Does he have debts and, if so, to what extent? There are innumerable questions to be asked and answered in order for you to make the best determination for yourself.

If remarriage is your objective, you need to be aware of the following. In general, second marriages are even less likely to survive than first marriages. The probability of separation and divorce in a second marriage varies according to which study you review. In general, the statistics range from 39 to 76 percent depending on the source of the data; the majority seem to cluster around 60 to 67 percent. These statistics do not mean that your particular situation will end in divorce—they are merely something to consider when considering remarriage

If you decide to remarry, you might want to sign a prenuptial (or antenuptial) agreement, which outlines how your existing assets are to be handled after you are married. It should include provisions defining how future income and assets are to be treated and what your financial rights will be once you are married.

If you have established a committed relationship with someone, you will want to evaluate the pros and cons of either maintaining your present single state or remarrying. Before making this decision, you need to weigh a number of factors. Whether or not you ultimately choose to live together, one or both of you may feel it is preferable to maintain your single status for legal or tax reasons. Other considerations include your emotional state, your view of the role of a wife, your religious or spiritual beliefs, your age, your finances, and your health. Also important are your personal or financial responsibilities for a child, children, parents, or another relative.

In today's world, an individual has several choices as to how to establish and maintain a relationship with a new significant other. There are few givens. What is important here is for you to make a decision about what feels right for you at this point in your life. Do not allow yourself to be persuaded that there is only one course of action.

Whatever your decision, examine your motivations. Although there are many factors to consider, we would like you to pay attention to your motivation to reattach—if such is your inclination. Your need might be healthy and appropriate, but some women choose this route out of habit and fear of being alone. If so, reattaching to ease the pain of your loss may only lead to new problems. You may anticipate that by remarrying, you can return to the familiarity and safety of your previous lifestyle. This is not possible. Your new potential mate is undoubtedly an individual in his own right, with his own set of habits, patterns, needs, and expectations. You cannot replace your husband, but you can establish a new, rewarding relationship.

If you are uncertain about your reasons for reattaching or in any way are insecure about your motivations to reattach, seek help from a mental health professional. If you saw a professional at the time of your initial loss, consider some additional sessions with this person to help you clarify and understand what you are now feeling and experiencing. If you did not see anyone then, consider doing so now. Ask a friend or your physician for an appropriate referral.

If you participated in a widow support group and have developed new solid friendships, discuss with these friends your feelings about your new relationship. Sometimes these people have a different perspective of you and can provide you with insights about yourself that may be helpful, given their current impressions of you. Remember: You are not the same person you were when you lost your husband.

Do not hesitate to discuss the decision to marry or live with someone with an appropriate relative, sibling, child (or children), or even a parent. Also, consider discussing this with long-standing close friends. It is hoped that these people will be honest with you and respond with consideration and compassion to your questions and concerns. They will not be able to make the decision for you, but they may share with you some personal experiences and make observations that will help you decide.

Whatever you decide, your choices run the gamut from a valued, platonic friendship with a man to a physical and emotional relationship in which you maintain separate households, share a household, or make the commitment to marry. The key again is to select the best path for you.

WORK: VOLUNTEER OR SALARIED

For those of you whose situation and age preclude the need to find salaried employment, there are a host of worthwhile volunteer activities to which you might like to devote some time. These range from volunteer work at a hospital or other medically related facility to organizations such as the Red Cross and civic and cultural groups. Some communities have foster grandparent programs that many individuals find to be a most gratifying experience.

Some regions have volunteer service bureaus that are usually listed in the phone book under Social Services within the County

Services listing. They can tell you which groups are seeking volunteer assistance and something about each organization. Make an appointment to meet with someone at the volunteer bureau to discuss your interests and availability and to learn more about specific organizations seeking such help. The extensiveness of the list will surprise you.

On the other hand, if you need or want to have a salaried position and have never worked or have not worked in a long time, consider beginning this activity gradually. For some of you, now is the hour to become recertified in the field in which you had been previously employed. If you are able to locate a part-time position in this field, take it and see if it works for you at your present stage of life. The job exposure may allow you to better identify what you might like to do. While working, you may be able to obtain some training that will enable you to get a better job in the same field or in a related field.

At almost any age, you can find entry-level employment in retail sales or as a receptionist. The term *entry-level* means no previous experience is required. Training is usually provided on the job. This type of work appeals to many widows as a means of reentering the job market as well as socialization.

Since this is a time of transition for you. This may present an opportunity to obtain some training in a field in which you are interested and where there is the likelihood for employment at your age. For example, if you had done secretarial work before or earlier in your marriage but have not worked in ten or more years, you would need to brush up on your existing skills and acquire new computer skills to be employable. You can obtain information about training programs in your area from a number of sources such a community college, a university, the Internet, or perhaps in the yellow pages of your phone book.

In many metropolitan areas, certain universities will offer assessment programs for women who are considering a return to the job market but are uncertain as to where to turn. These programs provide a counselor who will meet with you to obtain both your job and experiential history. This latter refers to activities performed while you were married, such as organizational work related to the PTA at your children's school, Girl Scout leadership, or other volunteer work. The counselor may also have you take a number of aptitude and interests tests. At the conclusion of this process, the counselor will help you identify ways to match your aptitudes, interests, personality, and previous life successes to the current job market. In some fields, weekend internships and/or part-time work are available on an initial basis. It is not unusual for this type of work to lead to more full-time employment should you so desire.

If you are not eager or willing to return to the workplace but need some additional income, there are other routes to consider. It might be possible for you to perform a service from your home, such as word processing, general clerical work, child care, pet walking, or home sitting. You might decide to rent out an extra room in your home or garage space. These are some suggestions, but we'll leave to you the task of identifying what might work for you. If you have an idea, ask questions, make calls, follow leads, and see what comes of it! Many widows have found the book *What Color Is Your Parachute?* (see bibliography) helpful in identifying heretofore unrecognized talents and interests that can generate income.

If you are looking to enter or renter the workplace, many resources exist that can be helpful to you in your job search. To identify employment areas that are expected to grow in the future, consult the U.S. Department of Labor's *Occupational Outlook Handbook* at your local library or online at www.dol.gov. Also read books and recent magazine articles on the topic. Another useful resource is Women Work!, a nonprofit organization that works to assist women achieve financial self-sufficiency through job training and employment programs. You can find further information on the programs it offers by calling 800-235-2732 or by visiting its Web site at www.womenwork.org. The Internet also offers a wide range of tools in the area of employment. You can search job listings and post your resume on sites such as www.monster.com or www.careerbuilder.com. With the aging of America, there is an increasing need for individuals who are willing to work with our older population and possess a wide range of skills.

LOCATION AND RELOCATION

At this point, you should reconsider your living space—if you haven't already done so. Some of you have already moved, but for others this is the time when you should review your long-term living situation. Has your home become too difficult for you to handle? Should you move to a smaller place? Do you eventually want to make a move to one of a growing number of retirement facilities? Should you consider moving back to the town or region where you grew up? Should you move closer to your adult child or children? Should you move to a warmer or drier climate? You should consider the advantages and disadvantages of any potential move.

Depending on where you are currently living and what your long-term goals and needs might be in relation to your lifestyle, now is a good time to investigate alternative housing as well as location. For example, if you have friends in Florida and children in St. Louis, you should visit both places to see what is available for you and which location appears to offer the most support. In the final analysis, you might decide to stay where you are.

If you do move and, after a reasonable amount of time, find you are not as happy in your new environment as you thought you would be, do not feel that you have to stay there. Make whatever changes you need to make, including returning to your previous locale.

If you have committed to a new relationship, you and your new mate may want to establish a home in a new location after disposing of your individual homes, condominiums, or apartments. In this manner, you will be creating a new beginning and giving your new relationship its own identity. For others, the preferable decision may be to combine resources and maintain one of the existing households. If you choose this approach, whichever person does not own the home might consider buying part of the home on the basis of a current appraisal. That way you avoid the "my home" conflict!

SUMMARY AND CONCLUSION

Again, depending on where are you are in your life cycle and individual circumstances, allow yourself to identify where you hope to be in the future and how to get there. Whatever you decide, be clear on the degree to which the decision is your own and one that is right for you.

DIANE

Reactions to Establishing a New Identity

As Diane cleared the dishes this Wednesday evening, she realized that in a few days it would be three years since Mark had suddenly died. She couldn't believe how much her life had changed since that fateful day.

She was working full time as a paralegal for a law firm. She viewed her job very differently now than when she had previously been employed, which felt like eons ago. Now, work was important to her, whereas earlier her job had been something to occupy her time before having children and staying at home. She took pride in the skills she had developed in estate planning. This type of work had personal meaning for her. She knew she made a contribution to the clients with whom she met because of her own life experience. The job was not just a way to pay the bills; she felt she was actually helping people.

Diane was also able to acknowledge to herself the assistance she provided to the estate lawyer with whom she worked. He counted on her and often asked for suggestions on ways to approach a particular client given her knowledge and experience. Sometimes he asked her to share with a client the danger of ignoring a particular issue as a result of what she had personally gone through. She felt valued.

She recalled how difficult it had been for her to think about working when Dorothy had finally gotten across to her it was essential for her to be employed. She had reluctantly agreed to take the refresher courses at the University of Maryland. The director of the paralegal program had really been very helpful. When the topic of specializing in some aspect of paralegal work was introduced, she encouraged Diane to consider taking an elective course in estate planning. At first, Diane was hesitant. She thought it would be boring and scary because she didn't like working with numbers. However, the more thought she gave to it, the more she realized it would be right for her.

Diane had dreaded the thought of having to let go of the lifestyle she had enjoyed so much as Mark's wife. Yet here she was three years later, somewhat resentful of the various demands made on her time because of the need to work but feeling good about being productive and appreciated by her employers and her children. She took pride in the way she handled her work and knew she had a reputation as one of the firm's best paralegals. It was not uncommon for her to overhear one of the other lawyers commenting to her boss about how lucky he was to have Diane working for him. The various raises and performance evaluations she had received reflected the firm's recognition of the contribution she made to the firm.

Diane told Alice she would finish the dishes by herself tonight. Alice was delighted, but Diane was not just being considerate of her daughter. She really wanted a few minutes to reflect on her life without interruption. The end of the year seemed to lend itself to this process.

Erin had begun her first year of college this past year. Diane had had to be mindful of costs when going through the college selection process. Together, Diane and Erin had decided that she would attend a state university. Since the costs at this institution were lower than at a private college, they were able to afford tuition as well as room and board. She was enjoying college, had made many new friends with a broad range of economic backgrounds, and was doing well academically. Her strong private-school education had definitely helped her get off to a good academic start at college.

Jeremy was now in eighth grade, in middle school, and Alice was in fifth grade, in elementary school. Both of them attended the neighborhood public schools. They too seemed to be making satisfactory progress academically.

Of the children, Jeremy had had the most difficulty initially dealing with the loss of his dad. Diane had not been surprised by this given that Mark and Jeremy had been very close when Mark was alive. Jeremy particularly valued their time together when they participated in Boy Scout activities. Mark was an Eagle Scout and had encouraged Jeremy to follow in his footsteps. When Mark died, Jeremy dropped out of his troop despite repeated calls from his friends. Finally, the scoutmaster came over and coaxed him back into attending meetings. The scouting activities had been a great help to him as he adjusted to life without his father. The other day Jeremy told Diane that he hoped to become an Eagle Scout. Mark would have been so proud!

Alice seemed to love being in public school. She could walk to school with her friends. She was in the school band and Girl Scouts, both of which took place at school. She was also a crossing guard, a rather prestigious assignment for someone her age and grade.

All in all, Diane was comfortable with the way the children were developing. The most striking difference from the days before Mark died and after Mark died—which was how Diane viewed her life— was the way they functioned as a family. They were now a unit; any important decision was discussed. Diane weighed carefully the children's expressed feelings before arriving at a family decision. She knew with certainty that this aspect of their lives was healthier and the bonds between them were stronger than at any time when Mark was alive. Diane hoped they would carry the present mode of problem solving into their personal relationships in the future.

Tomorrow evening Robyn was coming over to dinner so they could discuss the three-day weekend they were planning together. She made a list of things she needed to buy for dinner on her way home from work tomorrow. As Diane completed her jobs in the kitchen, she realized that the weekend she was about to spend with Robyn would be the first weekend she had spent in her adult life going someplace without her parents, her spouse, or another family. She supposed that now, at the age of 45, she was finally growing up.

She glanced at herself in the hall mirror as she was about to go upstairs to see how Jeremy and Alice were coming along with their homework. She felt pleased with herself for managing to keep the home. She loved it, and its decor represented her major accomplishment in life before Mark's death. She had agonized over every piece of furniture she'd purchased and spent hours debating between this wallpaper pattern or that and whether or not she had selected the perfect fabric. She could hardly relate to the former Diane. She couldn't imagine having the time now to spend in this manner. What a luxury!

She also thought she was in better physical shape now than she had been in those days, thanks to Robyn's insistence on her joining a health club. Robyn practically dragged her there in the beginning, but now it had become a valued part of her week's routine. Diane made a point of going to the health club at least two times a week and often was able to get there three times a week.

She smiled to herself as she walked upstairs, for it was at the health club, about three months ago, that she met Tom. They had gone out several times, mostly informally, and had really gotten along well. She remembered a co-worker telling her, when she had said she worked out at the health club, that health clubs were a great place to meet eligible men. She had laughed at the time and said, "Not if you saw what I look like when I'm working out." Yet here she was dating someone she'd met at the club. She hoped things would continue to go well between them. She and Tom talked so easily. She also found herself very attracted to his quiet strength. She thought in a kind of disbelief that she'd had more significant conversations with Tom in three months than she'd ever had with Mark. She was now a different person. She was at a different place in life. She would always wish the tragedy of suddenly losing her husband and children's father had not occurred, but she was able to readily acknowledge that she liked the Diane of today better than Diane, Mark's wife.

There was no way to compare her present and past levels of understanding regarding financial matters. Before Mark's death, she had comprehended nothing and, in addition, chose to have it that way. This was one area for which she held her parents—or at least her father—responsible. Her parents had indirectly encouraged her to believe such matters were truly best left to men to handle. She now viewed herself as childlike in the way she had asked Mark if she could spend money on this or that, and she didn't like that image at all.

As she had gained financial knowledge, she had been very clear with her dad about his role. She usually had him review Dorothy's recommendations, but she made the final decisions. This was an adjustment for him because, like Mark, he was accustomed to making all the family's financial decisions. But Diane knew her dad had greater respect for her now than he had in the past, and consequently their relationship was stronger. There was no question that she liked herself better for taking charge of her financial life. "Taking charge" was probably not quite accurate. She still relied heavily on Dorothy for guidance, and finances were clearly not her favorite subject, but she no longer abdicated responsibility when it came to decision making.

SUSAN

Reactions to Establishing a New Identity

Susan reflected on how much her life had changed since she had last found herself on a flight winging her way to Minneapolis for an American Society of Association Executives (ASAE) convention. The previous ASAE convention in Minneapolis was the first one she had attended after Lance's death. At that time, she could never have imagined how much her life would change. The self-assured executive of today could not have been glimpsed in the frightened, uncertain, menopausal widow of five years ago.

Today, as the plane carried her toward Minneapolis, she was the director of a relatively small association that had grown under her leadership. The therapy she had undertaken with Dr. Coleman to help her deal with Lance's sudden and untimely death had resulted in her exploring many aspects of her own psyche. She would never have sought therapy for herself because she had no conscious awareness of needing to do so. However, looking at those aspects of her personality had provided her with a much greater understanding of those factors that had impacted the way in which she viewed life, made decisions, and interacted with others.

When Lance died, she suffered a major loss. There would always be an empty place in her heart for him. However, she rarely dwelt on her loss anymore. She was alive and leading an active, productive life. She understood her financial position and was satisfied and comfortable with the accountant, attorney, and investment advisors she had selected. She had renewed her social contacts with some of the friends she had lost touch with when she had been married to Lance. She had formed new friendships that were important to her. Perhaps most significant and gratifying was her relationship with Sean.

About a year ago, at a local ASAE meeting in Seattle, she had met Sean, an attorney who had made a presentation to the group. During the social hour that followed the meeting, Susan found herself talking at length with him about a problem she had at work. She was particularly concerned about the potential legal ramifications. She asked if he would be willing to consult with her further on a professional basis about the matter. He had indicated his willingness to do so, and they had exchanged business cards. Susan's secretary had contacted his office and scheduled a meeting with him for the following week. At the conclusion of their business meeting, Sean had surprised her by asking if she would have time to join him for lunch. She did and proceeded to take the longest lunch hour she had ever taken—three hours.

Sean was an interesting man. Dissimilar to Lance in appearance, he had been a widower for the past three years, attempting to raise his daughter, Melissa, a freshman in college. Although she didn't like to admit it, Susan saw him as more open and somewhat warmer than Lance, particularly when he described his relationship with his daughter. By the time they had finished lunch, it was clear to both of them that there was a degree of attraction between them, and they arranged to go out to dinner the following Saturday. In the course of the evening, Sean was very up-front about his worries about getting into a relationship with a woman because of a bad experience he had had with a woman following his wife's death from cancer. Susan was equally honest with him about her doubts as to whether or not she could ever allow herself to have a relationship with a man who had an adult child. She described the personal pain she had experienced as an outgrowth of the rejection she felt from Lance's children both while he was alive and after his death. Just remembering the way Adam and Leslie had treated her made her shudder. Sean was quick to pick up on her feelings and suggested they allow themselves to continue to date and see what materialized.

In the course of the next month, she saw Sean about twice a week. She was pleased to learn that he, too, was a committed cyclist. He had not taken any long bicycle trips as she and Lance had done, but he was equally enthusiastic. He owned a small motorboat, which he used on a lake not far from where she and Lance had had their cottage.

After seeing each other regularly for about six weeks, Sean asked Susan to have lunch with him and Melissa the following Saturday. Melissa was very interested in contemporary art and had prevailed on him to accompany her to the current exhibit in a particular downtown gallery. He thought it was important for Susan and Melissa to get acquainted. With considerable reluctance and trepidation, Susan agreed. Their relationship was progressing, they were increasingly enjoying the time they spent together, and both knew this was a critical factor in whether they should allow themselves to maintain and pursue their present path.

Susan was amazed at the openness with which she and Sean communicated in view of the limited time they had known each other. When she was being totally honest with herself, she realized she and Sean were better able to share ideas, feelings, and thoughts with each other than she had ever been able to do with Lance. She recognized this sharing was, in part, an outgrowth of her work with Dr. Coleman. Sean, too, had had some psychological counseling and was good at identifying his feelings and expressing them. They had explored so many ideas and feelings in such a short time.

She remembered how she had agonized over her first meeting with Melissa. She couldn't even decide what to wear and must have put on and discarded five different outfits before she settled on a silk blouse, slacks, and a scarf. She expected the worst but hoped they would respond well to each other. Melissa was of medium height with relatively long blonde hair and large deep brown eyes. She had a warm smile and an openness that Susan found very appealing. She could see how fond father and daughter were of each other and how comfortable they were with each other. Susan didn't ever remember the same level of comfort between Lance and Leslie, although perhaps at that point in her life she was less aware of interpersonal relationships.

Lunch was pleasant, and conversation didn't lag. Both women were relieved that they didn't instantly dislike each other. Both were aware of the importance to Sean of their responding positively to one another. Susan was surprised at Melissa's ability to mention her mother in a way that caused no discomfort to any of them. Melissa asked Susan many questions about her work and her background. At this juncture in her life, Melissa was unsure of her own professional goals and had not even selected her undergraduate major. Susan had astonished herself when she suggested to Melissa that perhaps she'd like to spend a day with her at the association getting a firsthand idea of what work of this nature was all about. Melissa was truly pleased by the invitation, and they arranged to do so within the next two weeks. At the conclusion of the lunch, all three of them were aware of just how pleasant everything had been.

Susan smiled to herself as she recalled that it was on the occasion of her next date with Sean following the lunch that she allowed herself to sleep with him. She had been so fearful of this aspect of their relationship not working out and of failing to meet Sean's expectations. She thought she was more nervous about this than her first sexual experience. Perhaps it had something to do with her feeling less feminine because she viewed herself as being in the midst of menopause. She had heard horror stories about women having a variety of difficulties with sex, from a loss of a sense of sexuality to being nonorgasmic. She had been a wreck thinking about introducing this dimension into her budding relationship with Sean and had delayed addressing it with him. She rationalized that she was worried about becoming attached to a man with a child. However, after that critical lunch, she knew she could no longer avoid her own anxieties and would have to address them. When it actually happened, it just felt natural and wonderful.

Sean had taken her to dinner and talked her ear off about how positive Melissa was about her. Susan was very pleased but also felt good about her own positive response to Melissa. All of this was so different from her experience with Lance and his children. Adam and Leslie had never allowed themselves to get to know Susan as a person. They acknowledged her as their father's wife but knew very little of what she did or how she felt about things or what she thought. Melissa probably knew more about her after one lunch than Leslie and Adam had known about her in the 12 years she was married to their father. Maybe it had something to do with their loyalty to their mother.

Later that evening, when Sean took her back to her condominium, he held her in his arms and kissed her gently as he had before. This time Susan allowed herself to respond. She was unprepared for the strength of her body's response to Sean. She didn't know if it was what she had read about menopause, her fears about Sean's daughter, or Lance's memory that had prevented her from allowing herself to respond physically to him before this night. Whatever it was, it melted away as she found herself responding to him. She no longer felt the need to work everything out in advance and was ready to explore this relationship on all levels.

Within the past year their relationship had developed into a very solid one. They had a mutual respect and an acceptance of each other as equals. They shared some common interests and enjoyed participating in them with each other. Above all, they were able to talk to each other in an open and frank manner that was new to Susan. Just this past week they had made the big decision to marry. Susan was so excited she could hardly believe it was real!

She realized the plane had begun its final descent and roused herself from her musings. She wondered if Andrew, her friend from Chicago, would be here. If he was, he'd be surprised to see how much she had changed and grown. She'd have a lot to tell him.

AUDREY

Reactions to Establishing a New Identity

It was well past midnight when the chauffeur-driven car John Jr. had hired pulled up to her front door following the 65th birthday dinner the children had arranged for her. It had been a wonderful evening. She always savored these moments as times to reflect on where she was in life. She seemed to view the present in relation to the past and also the future. She was pleased with her decision not to pursue her relationship with Lionel, even though it would have been so nice to have had him as an escort this evening.

She knew her decision not to move forward with Lionel was right for her, but she did question her motives. Part of it was the geographic distance between them, but it was more than that. Basically, Lionel met all of her requirements: He was charming, in good shape, physically attractive, and financially secure. Yet she had been reluctant to move the relationship forward in the manner he would have liked. Something was missing for her. She continued to feel it was connected somehow to the way she felt about her marriage to John. Was she simply afraid to try marriage again? In her present widowed state, she felt less encumbered than when she was married. It was a feeling she valued. Her experience with married life and that type of commitment now felt like a trap. Many excuses came to mind, but Audrey was honest enough with herself to admit she enjoyed the companionship of men but did not want to remarry and risk falling into old patterns.

She enjoyed all of her present activities and couldn't imagine giving any of them up, although she knew she was losing weight again. She was certain when she saw Dr. PaPadisio next he would scold her about doing too much and not eating properly. She knew she had to pay more attention to her eating patterns. It was just that when she got caught up in an activity, it was not uncommon for her to forget about eating. Audrey was clearly in danger of being overcommitted. Asking herself why she had allowed herself to take on so much was really unnecessary. She knew the answer: It was primarily a reaction to everything she had not been able to do when she was married to John. For the first time she was doing what she wanted to do, not what a good wife was supposed to do to help her husband. There was so much out there to choose from, and she enjoyed so many different things. It wasn't that she hated all of the entertaining she had done for John. It was just that her current endeavors represented her own choices, and that meant so much to her.

Her work with Reading Is Fundamental was particularly gratifying. Audrey found herself giving more and more time to this organization. As she watched her grandchildren develop, she knew how much time Joanne spent reading to them, playing educational games with them to expand their verbal skills, and encouraging them to explore computer games to increase their knowledge. She doubled the hours she gave to her work with Reading Is Fundamental. She felt so badly for those children less fortunate than her grandchildren. She loved seeing the way their faces lit up when the volunteers from Reading is Fundamental came to their school to give them a book of their own to take home!

Sometimes Audrey wondered if she kept herself so busy because she didn't want to think about anything or be alone. This thought didn't seem valid to her. If anything, she spent too much time evaluating what she was doing and the reasons for it. She wouldn't change anything about her relationship with her children and grandchildren. She felt fortunate and thought that few women had the kind of substantive ties she did with her family—ties of mutual respect. All of them felt comfortable living their individual lives, yet there was a richness to the quality of the times they spent together. When possible, they rotated the celebration of major holidays among the three homes. Keith's parents usually joined with her in celebrating the holidays, but her daughter-in-law's family was large and had long-standing holiday traditions of their own, so John Jr. usually alternated spending the holidays between the families, which was fine with all concerned.

Her financial situation was very stable, and Audrey was grateful for that. She met regularly with her advisors and was pleased with the way her money had been invested and managed. She had joined the investment club and remained active in it. In fact, she had been elected secretary this past year. She had learned so many things on a financial level and done so many different things on a volunteer basis she could hardly believe it.

She wondered how John would respond to the Audrey of today. If he were still alive, she knew she wouldn't be the person she was now. Perhaps these were strange thoughts, yet she wondered if he would like her in her present mode. She really believed he would prefer her as she had been and would have something negative to say about women who committed themselves to all these outside activities. All in all, at 65, she was very positive about the quality of her life.

ELIZABETH

Reactions to Establishing a New Identity

Twenty months after Ben had died, Elizabeth found herself ready to make a decision about her living situation. Fall in New England was always beautiful to her, and this morning it seemed exceptionally so. However, with fall came the thought of winter, and Elizabeth didn't know if she was up to facing another winter in Boston on her own.

Last winter there were times when she could not leave her home for days because of snow. The neighborhood was changing, and the young boys she had counted on to mow the lawn and shovel snow were now off at college or launching careers and living on their own. The few homes that had been on the market had been sold to young couples with young children not yet ready to take on these jobs.

She had spoken at great length with Pastor Appletorn, the Weatherlys, Lucy, Mabel, and her other friends about relocating to Florida. Being in the same retirement community with Abigail was really appealing. She had visited Abigail in Florida three times, and each time it seemed more desirable. She had met so many people with whom she enjoyed spending time. There were so many things to do—she was rarely by herself.

Elizabeth also questioned her purpose in life. The majority of her life was behind her. Was she being foolish to look forward to something—sort of a new beginning? Who needed her anyway? Did she have anything to give to anyone, and did it matter? These were grim thoughts that made her feel empty and hopeless. At the same time, she wasn't ready to sit around and wait to die. What would be gained by settling on a retirement community in Boston? The residents of Abigail's retirement community were productive and displayed that productiveness in a number of ways. Some of the residents made craft items, which were offered for sale on special occasions; others volunteered their time to the foster grandparent program at the local elementary school.

On her last trip to Abigail's community, Elizabeth had met two women in their eighties who enthusiastically described their recent trip down the Amazon River. Another woman, who was in her nineties, told her of a recent bridge game she had played on the Internet with partners in Hong Kong, Australia, and Washington, D.C. Still another resident spoke to her of the computer tutor who was helping her learn how to use her home computer. Their enthusiasm for life was contagious. She was eager to get to know these people better. Most important, she thought, was the enthusiasm for life she felt when she visited there. She had no dependents, so it didn't matter where she lived. There was nothing wrong with wanting more out of life at her age. Pastor Appletorn had stressed to her the appropriateness and positive aspects of a productive life. She no longer felt guilty about those feelings or disloyal to Ben for having them.

Elizabeth looked at the kitchen clock. It was already 10:30. Where had the morning gone? She was beginning to get somewhat concerned about her feelings of fatigue. She felt tired a great deal, was sleeping more, and was having a harder time mobilizing. She didn't like feeling this way. If she stayed in Boston, she thought she might become more of a recluse. When she was in Florida, she felt more alive and more willing to participate in the activities available to the residents of the community. From a health standpoint, the move would also be a good idea. She could always come back to Boston in the summer and visit friends.

Her only reluctance about moving to Florida was the finality it represented. It would be closing the door on her life with Ben. Yet Ben was dead now, and she was alive. What did it say about her marriage to be facing a Boston winter and feeling alone and afraid to leave her home with only Mittens to keep her company? Did it make her less of a wife to Ben? She didn't think so. If she moved to Northern Palms at this point in her life, when her health was relatively stable, she would be eligible for their lifetime continuing care program. This would take a great burden off her shoulders. If she became incapacitated, she had no one to care for her the way she had cared for Ben.

As an outgrowth of her visits to Abigail, Elizabeth had developed several new friendships and maintained these contacts through the mail and even by telephone after returning to Boston. Her new friends were trying to persuade her to relocate, citing their own experiences in weighing the pros and cons of the move. None of them seemed to have any regrets, and all encouraged her to move to Florida.

As Elizabeth looked around the familiar kitchen with its somewhat faded wallpaper, she realized that there really was not enough available to her in Boston to warrant staying through the winter. She had basically had a good life with Ben in this home, but it was time to move. Mittens appeared by her side from his favorite corner in the living room as though he knew she needed him to be near her and rubbed against her leg, and she absentmindedly scratched his head. A tear slid down her cheek as she realized she had made the decision to close this chapter of her life. She decided that the Lord would approve and not look at the move as being disloyal to Ben.

Elizabeth felt fortunate knowing she had no financial concerns. She had already spoken with Mr. Samuels, the trust officer at her bank, and learned she could maintain her present trust there or transfer it, should she so desire, after getting settled in Florida. For the present, she would leave the trust in the hands of Mr. Samuels because she felt comfortable with him. Too much change at one time would be unsettling.

Elizabeth couldn't wait to tell Abigail that she had finally made the decision to join her at Northern Palms. Elizabeth knew exactly which apartment unit she preferred. She intended to start the purchase process immediately. She thought she would like to be able to leave Boston no later than December 1. When she reached Abigail on the phone and told her of her decision, she talked so much that Abigail could hardly get a word in edgewise. Abigail was thrilled that at long last her sister was coming south!

Next, Elizabeth called Pastor Appletorn and told him of her decision to move to Florida. She also told him that she had finalized her estate planning with Mr. Grossfeldt, her attorney. She had designated the church as the ultimate beneficiary of half of her trust after she and Abigail died. Meanwhile, she intended to put $25,000 in the charitable gift annuity offered by the church. That way she could ultimately benefit the church but receive more income now. Pastor Appletorn was most appreciative of her generosity and thanked her profusely.

After talking with Pastor Appletorn on the telephone, Elizabeth felt ready to move to Florida. She felt blessed that she was capable of living on her own. Many women her age were not in as good shape physically, financially, or mentally. Although she was somewhat nervous about all of the change she was about to introduce into her life, she found herself looking forward to it.

When she allowed herself to think about it, she realized she acted differently in Florida than she did in Boston. She participated in many more activities there. All of the trips available to the community seemed like fun, and she couldn't wait to have the opportunity to take some of them. She knew she would join both the bridge club and the sewing club as soon as she had her furniture in place. She had attended a few meetings and enjoyed them immensely. The members had all been welcoming and fun. Who knows, perhaps she would try learning how to use a computer. She was tired of hearing about the Internet and not knowing what people were talking about!

Most surprising to her was her present correspondence with Abe, a member of the community she met through Abigail. He was nothing like Ben. He talked a great deal, played a lot of golf, and seemed to love to take trips. Their mutual interest in travel led to their initial conversation. She couldn't believe he had taken the time to write to her, but he had, and he always included the latest community trip information. He told her he was sure these trips would help convince her to make the move.

She felt a little disloyal to Ben for being attracted to this casual, relaxed lifestyle, but what harm was it for someone going on 77? In fact, if anyone had told her she would be excited about embarking on a new phase of life at 77, she would never have believed it.

She would contact Mr. Winthrop in the morning and tell him she was ready to put the home up for sale. Her life and identity as Ben's wife had officially ended. She was ready to be what she now was—a widow by the name of Elizabeth who was ready to start a new life.

Epilogue

There was that law of life, so cruel and so just,
which demanded that one must grow or
else pay more for remaining the same.
—Norman Mailer

UNDOUBTEDLY, YOU HAVE HAD MANY EXPERIENCES since the death of your spouse that have contributed to the person you are today. However, the loss of your spouse was probably the most painful experience of your life to that point. There will be times when you reflect on the range of emotions you experienced during that traumatic time in your life as if it were yesterday—the tangible pain, the agony, the fears about the present and the future, the sense of being bereft of purpose, the vulnerability, the loneliness, and the anger, to name some of the more common feelings. But, most important, you should now have a sense of having experienced on a personal level the rhythm of life: birth, childhood, adulthood, and death—a growth process in which all living things participate. As a widow, you have firsthand knowledge of this life process—its forming, molding, reforming, and remolding.

Few of the widows with whom we have spoken felt they were the same person ten years after the loss of their spouse. Many were more pleased with the person they were today than they were with their former selves. Others acknowledged that they had coped as best they could with their loss but never felt quite the same or as if life held much pleasure for them following this event. You had no choice in determining when your spouse would die, thereby leaving you on your own; however, having by this time coped with the emotional upheaval and the financial responsibilities that accompanied your loss, you have grown. One grows from all of life's experiences. We therefore encourage you to be all that you can be. Following an appropriate recovery period after your loss, move forward. Life progresses for all of us, including you, and you need to allow yourself to drink of its waters.

DIANE

Ten Years Down the Road

Diane, now 52, found herself daydreaming while the family watched with intensity the latest efforts of the Redskins in their bid to play in the Super Bowl. She had been reminiscing about the time five years ago when, after considerable thought, she had decided to accept Tom's proposal of marriage. For several reasons, she had initially found herself ambivalent about his proposal. To her surprise, she had realized she enjoyed being independent and wasn't sure how she felt about giving up this independence. Also, although responsible when it came to most matters, Tom's attitude with regard to money management could best be described as casual. He didn't have nearly as much ambition as Mark had, but he did well and was well thought of by his company. In addition, she wasn't sure how his two grown children would blend with her three children in a combined family unit.

She remembered conspiring with Dorothy about various approaches to involve Tom in the financial planning process. She didn't want to alienate him, overwhelm him, or suggest that she didn't love him, but she knew she would not marry without a premarital agreement. She and Dorothy had finally decided that a straightforward, nonstrategic approach was best. After all, Tom was 55, and it was time for him to pay some attention to retirement planning. As Dorothy had said, they might be retired for 25 or 30 years, and Diane wanted to make sure they had enough money. Even now, five years later, Diane smiled to herself when she recalled that conversation. It certainly had been a reversal of roles. There she was, convincing her fiancé that financial planning was important, when five years earlier she didn't even know what financial planning was.

Tom had agreed to meet with Dorothy because what Diane had said about planning for retirement did make sense. When they met, he liked Dorothy but was a little overwhelmed by everything that was involved in a premarital agreement. However, he knew how important the children were to Diane and realized that both the shock of unexpectedly being widowed and her financial circumstances at the time had made her very much aware of the need for financial planning. As for himself, a recent round of early retirements at his company had made him more conscious of retirement issues. Although his job had not been affected, he had some apprehension about the future he had not had before—since he had worked for the same company for 30 years, he had thought his job was secure. He was no longer confident that was true. He had come to truly appreciate Diane's concerns about their financial future.

She had been musing about the time, following their first meeting with Dorothy, when they had drafted a joint budget as well as an asset statement. There had been surprises for both of them. Diane discovered that Tom had accumulated little in the way of assets other than the equity in his home and his retirement account. On the other hand, Tom was taken aback by Diane's financial situation. Looking at her asset statement, he realized that she had a substantial amount of money for which she was responsible. Dorothy and Diane had done a good job of managing this money for the past ten years. Now he understood why the premarital agreement was important to her.

In putting together the budget, they were able to determine what made the most sense for them as a couple. They had decided it would be best for them to live in Diane's house at least for a while. In this way, Alice could complete high school with no disruption. Tom suggested that he sell his house. Once his house had been sold, then they could come up with a budget that would include his contribution to the household as well as to his retirement account. Planning in this way had been the first step in a truly joint endeavor. It had represented growth to both of them and felt symbolic of their future together.

She roused herself from her musings. It was almost halftime, and Diane was going to put more food out for Tom and the assorted guests, which included Alice's friends as well as a few of Tom's co-workers in the football pool. She could hardly believe Tom was almost 60. She had a hard time accepting that Erin, now 25, had not only graduated from college but also had earned a master's degree. Jeremy, now 21, was in his junior year of college majoring in economics, and Alice was a junior in high school. She didn't feel the way 52 sounded. She certainly felt younger than she had the first year following Mark's death.

Diane valued her marriage to Tom. He treated her as an equal, was loving, and tried to be sensitive to her needs. Their ability to communicate with one another was excellent, and they shared mutual interests. He had no problem with her doing things with her women friends or co-workers. The female friends with whom she was close meant a great deal to her. Before Mark's death, she had not had these types of friendships, and after she remarried, she worked at maintaining them, as did her friends.

Diane thought she was as extroverted as she had previously been, although better organized. Juggling work, her marriage, the children, her parents, and friends was not easy, but being able to handle it all gave her a great deal of satisfaction. She regularly used the stress-reduction techniques she had learned in the special class offered by the health club. The deep breathing and visualization techniques she had learned had been particularly helpful. She tended to practice what she had been taught and found these techniques helped her to solve problems better and, in fact, to function better in all areas. She thought they had also enabled her to gain better control of her emotions. She didn't think she'd ever cry at the drop of a hat the way she once had, nor did she think she "wore her heart on her sleeve" anymore. Sometimes she could hardly recognize the Diane of ten years ago. She was so much more self-sufficient now. She had been through the worst type of personal tragedy she could envision for a woman and had not only survived but had thrived.

SUSAN

Ten Years Down the Road

Susan and Sean were now enjoying their fifth year of married life. They both valued their relationship and felt lucky to have found each other. Neither had expected to find another person who would provide the pleasure and closeness they clearly shared. For both of them, the relationship was different from the one they had with their former spouses. They worked at not making comparisons and were successful at it.

The aspect of her present life that surprised Susan the most was her relationship with Sean's daughter, Melissa. Their initial positive response to each other had expanded. The two women genuinely liked spending time together and had grown to love each other. Susan had never dreamed of being so close to a stepchild and so was unprepared for the rewards of such a relationship. Melissa had graduated from college with a combined graphic arts/business major. While in school, she became involved with a wonderful young man to whom she was now married. She and Susan had planned the wedding, thoroughly enjoying the experience and their collaboration. Melissa had married during her senior year, two years ago, and had just had her first child, a boy. Susan adored her grandson. She proudly showed her grandma's brag-book photo album to all her friends, co-workers, and acquaintances. They all teased her about being a grandmother but tolerated her enthusiasm fairly well. She enjoyed every minute of it.

The deterioration in Susan's mother's Alzheimer's condition had resulted in her needing full-time nursing care. They had moved her to the Alzheimer's wing of the retirement community in which she had been living. Much to Susan's surprise, her brother had married a woman with three children and appeared to have quite a full life. He had maintained his involvement with their mother and over the years had increasingly assumed responsibility for her. He had made small purchases for her and driven her to various doctors' appointments and the hairdresser when he was able to do so. Susan was pleased that her decision to involve Ron had enabled both Ron and her mother to have a closer relationship in her declining years than they had had previously. Susan thought this had been beneficial for both of them. She wondered what would have happened if she had not modified her behavior and encouraged Ron to become more active with their mother. Both of them would have lost something that had become meaningful and special to them.

Susan realized that the Susan of today was a much softer woman than the Susan of ten years ago. Although she continued to be organized, efficient, and dependent on list making to prioritize what she needed to do, she felt she was less rigid and more in touch with her feelings than at any other point in her life. She was also more tolerant and accepting of others, more secure, and less intense. She didn't feel 60, but that was in fact her current age. On rare occasions, she would find herself musing about her life with Lance and the person she was at that point in her life. She wondered if the Susan of today would have been attracted to Lance, and yet she would have described herself as happy with him. It was just that now she realized both she and Lance were uncomfortable with expressing their feelings and thus had never adequately shared them with each other. So much had happened to her in the years since Lance had met his tragic death. If Lance had not died, the Susan of today would not exist. It was a sobering thought to Susan. Without any reservations, she liked herself better today.

On a recreational level, bicycling had been a favorite activity for Susan when she was married to Lance. She had many fond memories of these excursions with Lance and had been very uncertain about how she would feel sharing the same activity with Sean. As with everything else, they talked about it and, for starters, decided to try it out, not revisiting the places she had frequented with

Lance. This worked well, and most recently they had combined a camping-and-bicycling trip in Canada, which both of them had thoroughly enjoyed. Sean had a great deal more experience with camping than Susan had, but she was a willing student and had come to truly enjoy it.

On a professional level, her association had grown under her direction. She had received appropriate recognition for her accomplishments and had even been approached by a larger association to assume the same role with them for more money. She had gone back to Dr. Coleman for a few sessions to discuss the advantages and disadvantages of the new job offer. She had turned the offer down because she felt comfortable managing the various aspects of her current life and at this time was not anxious to take on any more responsibility.

Over the years Susan had increased her investment knowledge. She continued to work with Bob O'Brien, who gave her sound advice. They had built Lance's pension assets to a nice amount. This account, together with her retirement plan from the association and Sean's assets, should provide them with a comfortable income when they retired.

Sean and Susan had been thinking more and more about their retirement. They had even considered moving to a warmer climate, but because they really liked the Seattle area they had decided not to move. They felt the apartment where they lived was ideal for the present as well as the future. Susan and Sean had even attended a retirement lecture Bob O'Brien had given and had started to complete the worksheets he provided. They weren't ready to retire yet but wanted to be prepared when the time came.

It was hard to believe how content Susan was only ten short years after Lance's death. Back then she had trouble envisioning life without him. Now here she was with a better job, physically active, financially secure, and emotionally content. She was truly a fortunate person.

AUDREY

Ten Years Down the Road

Audrey took a long, luxurious bath before dressing for the Reading Is Fundamental gala scheduled for this evening. She was one of the honorees in recognition of her contributions to the organization over the past nine years. She had done such an excellent job of chairing her chapter's fund-raising luncheons in the past three years that it had raised more money than at any time in its history. She didn't feel that she had done anything extraordinary, but the numbers spoke for themselves. Everybody with whom she worked was impressed.

She was glad her children and grandchildren would be present. J. T., now 24, was in graduate school working toward a master's degree in business administration, and Casey, age 22, was in a combined master's and doctoral program in environmental sciences. Both had told her they would make every effort to attend this event in honor of their very special "Gran Gran." Of course, it was no problem for Joanne's children to attend because they were all still living at home.

Audrey looked in the mirror and thought she looked pretty good for a 72-year-old woman. She was slim and paid meticulous attention to her appearance. It was now ten years since John had died, and she had a hard time remembering how it felt when she was married to him. She had done so much in the past ten years. She also felt lucky to be alive.

Almost four years earlier, during her routine physical, Dr. PaPadisio had identified what he thought was a small lump in her left breast. The mammogram she had the next day confirmed his fears. She had a biopsy shortly thereafter, and Dr. PaPadisio had told her that it confirmed a malignancy. However, he was quick to assure her that the type of cell identified was a slow-growing type and not at all comparable to John's situation. She really didn't believe him about the prognosis but was determined to go along with the recommendations of the surgeon to whom he referred her. The surgeon recommended that Audrey undergo a mastectomy and breast reconstruction immediately thereafter. Audrey reviewed all of this with John Jr., who agreed with the treatment plan after looking at the X-rays and lab reports and talking to both of her doctors. Everyone had been very supportive. She had had the surgery, and things went well.

Audrey was fortunate because her recuperation was smooth. She had heard nightmare stories from her friends about their experiences with breast reconstruction. In fact, for whatever reason, her weight stabilized following her surgery; even Dr. PaPadisio had commented on it. She had not had any health problems since that time, and she had regular six-month checkups.

She was totally committed to her walking routine. Achilles had died of old age, and she had debated for some time about replacing him. She didn't know if she wanted the responsibility of a new dog but missed the companionship of Achilles. Finally, she broke down and bought an irresistible German shepherd puppy that she called Zeus. She had decided she was more likely to maintain her walking routine if she had a dog to walk. Zeus was a handful, but she really got a kick out of him; he was just adorable. Joanne's children also loved to have him around.

After her initial visit with Joanne to the spa so many years ago, Audrey had purchased a stationery bicycle for use at home. She used it regularly and thought the combination of the bike and her walking kept her in good physical shape. She had actually enjoyed the spa so much she made it a practice to go every year with her daughter. Both mother and daughter valued these trips. She sometimes wondered why she hadn't done anything like that before John's death. It was just one of many things she had never thought about doing when John was alive.

Going to the golf clinic with her married friends had also become an annual event. Only now she was not the only widow in the group since another woman had lost her husband. Actually, she had run into Lionel again at one of these clinics. He had remarried and told her that he was happy with his new wife. He went on to say she would always be very special to him and he held her in the highest regard. Their brief relationship was a good experience for both of them. Both knew what might have been, yet both were satisfied with their present lifestyles. Audrey was so glad their paths had crossed again. It confirmed for her the correctness of her decision to remain unattached, yet it reaffirmed her fondness for him.

She had also taken trips with various groups. She was still active in the investment club and had attended a couple of their international meetings. She had gone to London with Heather and had also taken some trips with her friends sponsored by the symphony. Her horizons had widened considerably. Audrey had her annual visit with Mr. Silver last week and was very pleased with the current status of her portfolio. Just as Mr. Silver had originally predicted, the municipals had not grown much in value, but they had provided a steady stream of tax-free income. Her two mutual funds had more than doubled in value over the past ten years. She had finally sold the rest of John's company stock and invested in a couple of stocks she had researched in her investment club. They had done quite well.

Although she certainly maintained an active lifestyle, Audrey had not had any difficulty keeping within her budget. She had been able to maintain her gifting program with John and Joanne and felt it had helped stabilize Joanne's marital situation. Keith had finally found a job he liked and had been working for the same company for five years. Now that the children were in school full time, Joanne had gone back to college to get her degree and was teaching in a local elementary school.

As she put the final touches on her makeup this evening, Audrey thought she was fortunate to have had a husband who provided her with the financial resources to develop a life of her own after his death. He could not have related to the Audrey of today, yet he had contributed to her creation.

ELIZABETH

Ten Years Down the Road

Elizabeth smiled as she opened her mail. There was the familiar anniversary card sent to all the members of the retirement community to recognize the number of years they had been in residence. My, my, eight years! It didn't seem that long, and yet it seemed even longer. This certainly was not a new feeling; so many things seemed both forever and yet fleeting. If she had been in the retirement community for eight years, that meant it had been ten years since Ben passed away. She didn't think about him that much these days, although she did have fond memories of her married life. It was a different time and place, and she was different.

Mittens brushed against her leg en route to sitting in his favorite spot of sun in the morning. My goodness, if Ben had been dead 10 years, that made Mittens about 13 now. One would never know it. He was still very peppy and loved to sit in her lap, purring away, when she was settled in for the evening. She always thought of him as a little piece of Boston that had moved with her. She was glad she had decided to take him in, although she didn't rely on him for companionship the way she had in Boston.

She often thought about her present life at Northern Palms in contrast to her life with Ben. She could accept that her present life was now a much fuller one. She continued to be an active participant in both the sewing and bridge clubs she joined on moving to Florida. Fortunately for her, she had experienced very little memory loss and didn't have a hard time keeping track of the cards at bridge games—except when her mind wandered and she allowed herself to daydream, usually about an upcoming trip. Elizabeth was continually surprised at how important travel had become to her. She never thought she would be so interested in going to different places. She always took at least one trip a year, and she especially enjoyed the cruises. She guessed this wanderlust was an aspect of her personality that lay dormant throughout her marriage to Ben because he had no interest in travel.

She had better stop daydreaming and get moving. She had to attend a meeting of the welcome committee, of which she was the past president. Over the years the committee had incorporated some of her suggestions into the standard welcoming package presented to all new residents. She was pleased with her contribution and derived considerable satisfaction from it.

She also wanted to stop and spend some time with Abigail before the meeting. Abigail had suffered a mild-to-moderate stroke several years ago and had limited mobility. She had residual partial paralysis of the right side, which particularly affected her right leg. She was therefore somewhat of an invalid and could really get about only in a wheelchair. Elizabeth was pleased that she could be with her now. She knew it meant as much to Abigail as it did to herself.

While getting dressed to see Abigail, Elizabeth listened to the morning news. According to the weatherman, Boston had just gotten six inches of snow. She certainly didn't miss those winters. The warm Florida weather really agreed with her. Initially, she had been concerned about the humidity, but it had not turned out to be a problem. Last summer, when she had visited Boston to attend Pastor Appletorn's retirement dinner, some of the parishioners told her she looked younger and was more animated than when she left Boston eight years earlier. She never got tired of hearing, "My, that Florida life certainly agrees with you. I've never known you to be this talkative."

It had been good to see so many of the church members. Unfortunately, Mabel and some of her other acquaintances had died. She missed them, but she enjoyed reminiscing about them with mutual friends. On behalf of the congregation, Pastor Appletorn expressed appreciation for her generosity to the church. She was able to stand and smile when she was asked to do so in recognition of her contribution. Ten years ago, she would have wanted to hide under a table if so recognized, but now, although she was somewhat embarrassed, it posed no problem.

She had affiliated with a church near Northern Palms. She enjoyed it and the people, but this affiliation didn't feel quite as rewarding to her as that with her church in Boston. Perhaps this was the result of all the support she had always felt was available to her there. In fact, the only void in her life as a result of the move was the loss of Pastor Appletorn and other church members, such as the Weatherlys. In the overall scheme of things, she thought this was a relatively small price to pay for her otherwise presently happy life.

Thanks to Ben, she had no financial worries. Elizabeth was pleased with herself for having made the time to see Mr. Samuels at the bank in Boston and tell him how much she appreciated how well he had managed her account. About four years ago, after talking to several friends in her new location and listening to a lecture by a trust officer from a local bank, she had decided to transfer her trust account to Florida. It seemed to be the right thing to do given her current residency. As always, Mr. Samuels had been very helpful and reassuring to her regarding the advisability of this decision. She was especially thankful to him for never making her feel stupid or unimportant. She wanted to express her gratitude in person.

In her new setting, she had developed many rewarding friendships. She thought it was the first time in her life people related to her for herself. She had a hard time expressing this feeling to anybody, including Abigail, but she thought it was true. Abe, the man with whom she had corresponded eight years ago before deciding to relocate, had become a valued, special friend. They really enjoyed each other's company. They both loved to travel and always took the same trips offered by the retirement community. They had structured their lives so they could spend time together every day. Neither she nor Abe ever openly discussed it, but what they shared was comparable to married life. At the end of the community activities each evening, they would retire to her apartment, she would prepare something to drink, such as iced tea, and they would have a snack. They would watch TV and talk. She thought he seemed to have more respect for what she thought than Ben ever did, but she didn't allow herself to dwell on such thoughts. Abe was also very complimentary, always remarking on a new outfit or her hair or something. Back in

Boston with Ben, she had sometimes felt she was invisible or a piece of furniture.

As she thought about her new life in Florida (now not so new) and the agony she went through in making the decision to relocate, Elizabeth wondered what her problem had been. The move to Florida had been very positive. It had been a wonderful idea, and she was so pleased she had acted on it. She had no regrets. She was more self-confident and more outgoing than she had ever been in her life. She had discovered things about herself she had never imagined were there. She discovered that she truly enjoyed people and was more adventurous than she had realized. She had a hard time fathoming that now, in her eighties, she was still discovering facets of her personality that had been dormant all of her adult life. But such was the case. There was no question in her mind: Her present life was fuller and more rewarding than most of her previous existence.

Psychological Bibliography

AARP has several useful publications available free of cost
(see Resources for website and telephone number)

Beattie, Melody. *Journey to the Heart.* San Francisco: HarperCollins 1996.

Bolles, Richard Nelson. *What Color Is Your Parachute?* Berkeley, Calif.: Ten Speed Press, 1999.

Brabant, Sarah. *Mending the Torn Fabric: For Those Who Grieve and Those Who Want to Help Them,* Amityville, NY:Baywood Publishing C. 1996

Brothers, Dr. Joyce. *Widowed.* New York: Ballatine Books, 1992.

Caine, Lynn. *Being a Widow.* New York: Penguin Books, 1990.

Caplan, Sandi, and Gordon Lang. *Grief's Courageous Journey: A Workbook.* Oakland, Calif.: New Harbinger Publications, 1995.

Curry, Cathleen. *When Your Spouse Dies.* Notre Dame, Ind.: Ave Maria Press, 1997.

Colgrove, Melba. *How to Survive the Loss of a Love.* Los Angeles, CA:Prelude Press, 1993

Feinberg, Linda Sones. *I'm Grieving As Fast As I Can: How Young Widows & Widowers Can Cope & Heal.* Far Hills, N.J.: New Horizon Press, 1994.

Felber, Marta. *Finding Your Way After Your Spouse Dies.* 2000

Felton-Collins, Victoria. *Couples & Money.* New York: Gabriel Books, 1990.

Fitzgerald, Helen. *The Mourning Handbook.* New York: Simon and Schuster, 1995.

Fontana, Marian. *A Widow's Walk: A Memoir of 9/11.* 2005

Gates, Philomene. *Suddenly Alone.* New York: Gridiron Publishers, 1990.

Ginsburg, Genevieve Davis *Widow to Widow – Thoughtful, Practical Ideas for Rebuilding Your Life.* 2004

Grollman, Earl A. *Living When a Loved One Has Died.* Boston: Beacon Press, 1997.

James, John W. *The Grief Recovery Handbook: A Step-by-Step Program for Moving Beyond Loss.* New York, NY: Harper Collins, 1998.

Kubler-Ross, Elizabeth. *On Death and Dying.* New York: Simon and Schuster, 1997.

Kushner, Harold S. *When Bad Things Happen to Good People.* New York: Avon, 1994.

Lewis, C. S. *A Grief Observed.* San Francisco, CA: Harper, 1994.

Lord, Janet Harris. *No time for Goodbyes:Coping with Sorrow, Anger & Injustice After a Tragic Death.* Ventura, CA:Pathfinder Publishing, 1999.

Mellon, Olivia, and Sherry Christie. *Money Shy to Money Sure: A Woman's Road Map to Financial Well-being.* 2001

Neeld, Elizabeth Harper, Ph.D. *Seven Choices.* New York: Centerpoint Press, 1997.

Parkes, Colin Murray, and Robert S. Weiss. *Recovery from Bereavement.* Northvale, N.J.: Jason Aronson, 1995.

Plate, Shannon. *Degunking Your Personal Finances.* Scottsdale, AZ: Paraglyph Press, 2005.

Prend, Ashley Davis. *Transcending Loss.* New York: Berkley Books, 1997.

Rando, Therese A. *Grieving: How to Go On Living When Someone You Love Dies.* Lexington, Mass.: Bantam Books, 1991.

Sheehy, Gail. *The Silent Passage: Menopause.* New York: Pocket Books, 1998.

———. *New Passages: Mapping Your Life Across Time.* New York: Ballatine Books, 1996.

Staudacher, Carol. *Beyond Grief: A Guide for Recovering from the Death of a Loved One.* Oakland, Calif.: New Harbinger Publications, 1987.

Tatelbaum, Judy. *The Courage to Grieve.* New York: HarperCollins, 1984.

Temes, Roberta. *Living with an Empty Chair.* Far Hills, N.J.: New Horizon Press, 1992.

Viorst, Judith. *Necessary Losses.* New York: Fawcett Fireside, 1998.

Worden, J. William. *Grief Counseling and Grief Therapy.* New York: Springer, 1991.

Zonnebelt-Smeege, Susan J. *Getting to the Other Side of Grief: Overcoming the Loss of a Spouse.* Grand Rapids, MI: Baker Books, 1998.

Financial Bibliography

Bach, David, *Smart Women Finish Rich.* New York: Broadway Books: Second Edition 2002.

——. *Fraud! How to Protect Yourself from Schemes, Scams & Swindles.* New York: MA Publications, 2000.

Bodnar, Janet, *Think $ingle!* Chicago, IL: Dearborn Trade Publishing 2003

Judith Briles. *10 Smart Money Moves for Women: How to Conquer Your Money Fears.* Lincolnwood, Ill. Contemporary Books, 1999.

Chilton, David. *The Wealthy Barber.* Updated Third Edition. Rocklin, Calif.: Prima Publishing, 1998.

Clason, George S. *The Richest Man in Babylon.* New York: Penguin Books, 1955.

Drenth, Tere. The Everything Budgeting Book. Adams Media Corporation: 2003

Eisenberg, Lee. The Number: A Completely Different Way to Thank About the Rest of Your Life. New York: Free Press, 2006

Frankel, Lois. *Nice Girls Don't Get Rich.* New York: Warner Business Books, 2005.

Hannon, Kerry. *Suddenly Single: Money Skills for Divorcees & Widows.* New York: John Wiley & Sons, 1998.

Hemphill, Barbara. *Kiplinger's Taming the Paper Tiger at Home.* Washington, D.C.: Kiplinger Books, 1998.

Hicks, Zoe M., Esquire. *The Women's Estate Planning Guide.* Chicago: NTC Contemporary Publishing, 1998.

Kiyosaki, Kim. Rich Woman: A book on investing for Women. Rich Press, 2006.

Levin, Norma Jean. *How to Care for Your Parents: A Handbook for Adult Children:* Friday Harbor, WA: Storm King Press, 1993.

Lloyd, Nancy. *Simple Money Solutions: 10 Ways You Can Stop Feeling Overwhelmed by Money and Start Making It Work for You.* New York: Random House, 2000.

Mellan, Olivia. *Overcoming Overspending: A Winning Plan for Spenders and Their Partners.* New York: Walker & Co., 1995.

Morris, Kenneth M., & Virginia B. Morris. *The Wall Street Journal Guide to Understanding Money & Investing.* New York: Lightbulb Press, 1999.

Rottenberg, Dan. *The Inheritors Handbook.* New York: Bloomberg Press, 1999.

Savage, Terry. *The Savage Truth on Money.* New York: John Wiley & Sons, 1999.

Savage, Terry. *The Savage Number.* Hoboken, N.J.: John Wiley & Sons, 2005.

Steen, Joanne M. & M. Regina Asaro, *Military Widow: A Survival Guide.* 2006

Warren, Elizabeth & Amelia Warren Tyagi. *The Ultimate Lifetime Money Plan.* New York: Free Press, 2005.

Resources

PSYCHOLOGICAL RESOURCES

American Association of Retired Persons
Grief and Loss Program
601 E Street, NW
Washington, DC 20049
888-687-2277
www.aarp.org/families/grief_loss
Email: griefandloss@aarp.org

American Counseling Association
5999 Stevenson Avenue
Alexandria, Virginia 22304
703-823-9800
Toll Free: 800 347-6647
www.couseling.org

American Psychiatric Association
1000 Wilson Boulevard, Suite 1825
Arlington, VA 22209
703-907-7300
www.psych.org

American Psychological Association
750 First Street, NE
Washington, DC 20002
202-336-5500
www.apa.org

Elderhostel
11 Avenue de Lafayette
Boston, MA 02111-1746
Phone: 877-426-8156
www.elderhostel.org

National Association of Social Workers
750 First Street, NE, Suite 700
Washington, DC 20002
800-638-8799
www.socialworkers.org

Bereavement and Loss Center of New York
170 East 83rd Street
Suite 4P
New York, NY 10028
212-879-5655
(no Web site)

National Self-Help Clearinghouse
Graduate School and University Center
City University of New York
365 5th Avenue, Suite 3300
New York, NY 10016
212-817-1822

National Hospice and Palliative Care Organization
700 Diagonal Road, Suite 625
Alexandria, VA 22314
800-989-9455
www.caringinfo.org

Women Work!
1625 K Street NW #300
Washington DC 20006
Phone: 202-467-6346
www.womenwork.org

FINANCIAL RESOURCES

Social Security Administration
800-772-1213
www.ssa.gov

American College of Trust and Estate Counsel (ACTEC)
3415 South Sepulveda Blvd.
Suite 330
Los Angeles, CA 90034
310-398-1888
www.actec.org

The American Association of Daily Money Managers
P.O. Box 6998
Woodbridge, VA 22195
703-492-2913
www.aadmm.com

Alliance of Claims Assistance Professionals (ACAP)
843 Brentwood Drive
West Chicago, IL 60185
www.claims.org

The National Association of Professional Geriatric Care Managers
1604 North Country Club Road
Tucson, AZ 85716-3102
520-881-8008
www.caremanager.org

Consumers' Directory of Continuing Care Retirement Communities,
    published by the
**American Association of Homes and Services for the Aging
(AAHSA)**
2519 Connecticut Ave, NW
Washington, DC 20008
800-508-9442
www.aahsa.org

A. M. Best's Annual Rating Guide
(available at many libraries)
www.ambest.com

Standard & Poor's
212-438-7280
www.standardpoor.com

The Savings Bond Informer, Inc.
P.O. Box 9249
Detroit, MI 48209
800-927-1901
www.bondhelp.com

U.S. Treasury Bonds
The Bureau of the Public Debt
P.O. Box 9150
Minneapolis, MN 55480-9150
800-722-2678
www.savingsbonds.gov

National Association of Investment Clubs (NAIC)
711 West 13 Mile Road
Madison Heights, MI 48071
248-583-6242
www.better-investing.org

American Institute of Certified Public Accountants
1211 Avenue of the Americas
New York, NY 10036-8775
212-596-6200 or 888-777-7077
www.aicpa.org

National Association of Enrolled Agents
1120 Connecticut Avenue, NW
Suite 460
Washington, DC 20036
202-822-6232
www.naea.org

The Financial Planning Association
4100 East Mississippi Avenue
Suite 400
Denver, CO 80246
800-322-4237
www.fpanet.org

Society of Financial Service Professionals
17 Campus Boulevard
Suite 201
Newtown Square, PA 19073
610-526-2500
www.financialpro.org

AICPA Personal Financial Planning Specialists
Harborside Financial Center
201 Plaza Three
Jersey City, NJ 07311-3881
888-777-7077 option #4 or
   201-938-3099
www.aicpa.org

Financial Web Sites

The Women's Institute for Financial Education
www.wife.org

WomensWallStreet
www.womenswallstreet.com

Index

Order a copy of
On Your Own
for a friend or loved
one

Contact the office of Alexandra
Armstrong CFP®
www.afmfa.com
202-887-8135

Printed in the United States
72026LV00003B/40-42